ATLA Monograph Series
edited by Dr. Kenneth E. Rowe

1. Ronald L. Grimes. *The Divine Imagination: William Blake's Major Prophetic Visions.* 1972.
2. George D. Kelsey. *Social Ethics among Southern Baptists, 1917-1969.* 1973.
3. Hilda Adam Kring. *The Harmonists: A Folk-Cultural Approach.* 1973.
4. J. Steven O'Malley. *Pilgrimage of Faith: The Legacy of the Otterbeins.* 1973.
5. Charles Edwin Jones. *Perfectionist Persuasion: The Holiness Movement and American Methodism, 1867-1936.* 1974.
6. Donald E. Byrne, Jr. *No Foot of Land: Folklore of American Methodist Itinerants.* 1975.
7. Milton C. Sernett. *Black Religion and American Evangelicalism: White Protestants, Plantation Missions, and the Flowering of Negro Christianity, 1787-1865.* 1975.
8. Eva Fleischner. *Judaism in German Christian Theology Since 1945: Christianity and Israel Considered in Terms of Mission.* 1975.
9. Walter James Lowe. *Mystery & The Unconscious: A Study in the Thought of Paul Ricoeur.* 1977.
10. Norris Magnuson. *Salvation in the Slums: Evangelical Social Work, 1865-1920.* 1977.
11. William Sherman Minor. *Creativity in Henry Nelson Wieman.* 1977.
12. Thomas Virgil Peterson. *Ham and Japheth: The Mythic World of Whites in the Antebellum South.* 1978.
13. Randall K. Burkett. *Garveyism as a Religious Movement: The Institutionalization of a Black Civil Religion.* 1978.
14. Roger G. Betsworth. *The Radical Movement of the 1960's.* 1980.
15. Alice Cowan Cochran. *Miners, Merchants, and Missionaries: The Roles of Missionaries and Pioneer Churches in the Colorado Gold Rush and Its Aftermath, 1858-1870.* 1980.
16. Irene Lawrence. *Linguistics and Theology: The Significance of Noam Chomsky for Theological Construction.* 1980.
17. Richard E. Williams. *Called and Chosen: The Story of Mother Rebecca Jackson and the Philadelphia Shakers.* 1981.
18. Arthur C. Repp, Sr. *Luther's Catechism Comes to America: Theological Effects on the Issues of the Small Catechism Prepared in or for America Prior to 1850.* 1982.
19. Lewis V. Baldwin. *"Invisible" Strands in African Methodism.* 1983.
20. David W. Gill. *The Word of God in the Ethics of Jacques Ellul.* 1984.
21. Robert Booth Fowler. *Religion and Politics in America.* 1985.

22. Page Putnam Miller. *A Claim to New Roles.* 1985.
23. C. Howard Smith. *Scandinavian Hymnody from the Reformation to the Present.* 1987.
24. Bernard T. Adeney. *Just War, Political Realism, and Faith.* 1988.
25. Paul Wesley Chilcote. *John Wesley and the Women Preachers of Early Methodism. 1991.*
26. Samuel J. Rogal. *A General Introduction of Hymnody and Congregatio* Song. 1991.
27. Howard A. Barnes. *Horace Bushnell and the Virtuous Republic.* 1991.
28. Sondra A. O'Neale. *Jupiter Hammon and the Biblical Beginnings of African-American Literature.* 1993.
29. Kathleen P. Deignan. *Christ Spirit: The Eschatology of Shaker Christianity.* 1992.
30. D. Elwood Dunn. *A History of the Episcopal Church in Liberia, 1821-1980.* 1992.
31. Terrance L. Tiessen. *Irenaeus on the Salvation of the Unevangelized.* 1993.
32. James E. McGoldrick. *Baptist Successionism: A Crucial Question in Baptist History.* 1994.
33. Murray A. Rubinstein. *The Origins of the Anglo-American Missionary Enterprise in China, 1807-1840.* 1995.
34. Thomas M. Tanner. *What Ministers Know: A Qualitative Study of Pastors as Information Professionals.* 1994.
35. Jack A. Johnson-Hill. *I-Sight: The World of Rastafari: An Interpretive Sociological Account of Rastafarian Ethics.* 1995.
36. Richard James Severson. *Time, Death, and Eternity: Reflections on Augustine's "Confessions" in Light of Heidegger's "Being and Time."* 1995.
37. Robert F. Scholz. *Press toward the Mark: History of the United Luthera* Synod of New York and New England, 1830-1930. 1995.
38. Sam Hamstra, Jr. and Arie J. Griffioen. *Reformed Confessionalism in Nineteenth-Century America: Essays on the Thought of John Williamso* Nevin. 1996.
39. Robert A. Hecht. *An Unordinary Man: A Life of Father John LaFarge, 1996.*
40. Moses Moore. *Orishatukeh Faduma: Liberal Theology and Evangelical* Pan-Africanism, 1857-1946. 1996.
41. William Lawrence. *Sundays in New York: Pulpit Theology at the Crest* the Protestant Mainstream. 1996.

Sundays in New York
Pulpit Theology
at the Crest of the
Protestant Mainstream
1930–1955

by
William B. Lawrence

ATLA Monograph Series, No. 41

The American Theological
Library Association
and
The Scarecrow Press, Inc.
Lanham, Md., and London

SCARECROW PRESS, INC.

Published in the United States of America
by Scarecrow Press, Inc.
4720 Boston Way
Lanham, Maryland 20706

4 Pleydell Gardens, Folkestone
Kent CT20 2DN, England

British Cataloguing-in-Publication Information Available

Library of Congress Cataloging-in-Publication Data

Lawrence, William Benjamin.
Sundays in New York : pulpit theology at the crest of the Protestant
mainstream, 1930–1955 / by William B. Lawrence.
p. cm. — (ATLA monograph series ; no. 41)
Originally presented as the author's thesis (Ph. D. — Drew
University, 1984).
Includes bibliographical references and index.
1. Preaching—New York (N.Y.)—History—20th century.
2. Liberalism (Religion)—New York (N.Y.)—History—20th century.
3. Liberalism (Religion)—Protestant churches—History—20th century.
4. New York (N.Y.)—Church history—20th century.
I. Title. II. Series.
BV4208.U6L38   1996   251'.009747'10904—dc20   95-41484

ISBN 0-8108-3079-5 (cloth : alk. paper)

Printed in the United States of America

☉™ The paper used in this publication meets the minimum requirements of
American National Standard for Information Sciences—Permanence of
Paper for Printed Library Materials, ANSI Z39.48–1984.

CONTENTS

EDITOR'S FOREWORD

Since 1972 the American Theological Library Association has undertaken responsibility for a modest monograph series in the field of religious studies. Our aim in this series is to publish two quality studies each year. Titles are selected from studies in a wide range of religious and theological disciplines. We are pleased to publish *Sundays in New York* by William B. Lawrence in the ATLA Monograph Series.

William B. Lawrence is a Phi Beta Kappa graduate of Duke University and earned the Master of Divinity degree cum laude at Union Theological Seminary (NY). His doctorate in Historical Theology and Homiletics was conferred "with distinction" at Drew University. Following several United Methodist pastorates in New York and Pennsylvania and a term as district superintendent in the Wyoming Conference, Lawrence was appointed Professor of the Practice of Christian Ministry and Associate Director of the J. M. Ormond Center for Research, Planning and Development at Duke University Divinity School. Author of several articles and reviews, this is his first book.

Kenneth E. Rowe
Series Editor

Drew University Library
Madison, NJ 07940
USA

PREFACE

For about twenty years, I lived not far from the banks of the Susquehanna River, which drains a watershed that reaches the Adirondacks to the north, the Appalachians to the west, and the rolling landscape nearby in central New York and northeastern Pennsylvania. On several occasions during those years, the melting snows in springtime or the torrential rains of summer would feed countless creeks that in turn feed the mainstream, causing the Susquehanna to rise against its levees. Local authorities would monitor the rising stream, giving hourly readings on the height of the water and waiting for the river to begin receding. When the level started to fall, they would report that the river had "crested" and the valley would sigh with relief. One only knows that the crest has occurred after it has passed.

Among the terms useful for describing the Protestant establishment in America has been "mainstream denominations." At the beginning of the twentieth century, their level of cultural influence and ecclesiastical domination was rising. At the end of the twentieth century, they are receding. Somewhere during these hundred years, the mainstream denominations crested.

One of the most characteristic activities of that establishment has been preaching. Four of the most celebrated figures who rode the crest are the preachers examined here. On Sundays in New York, they delivered sermons to the congregations gathered before them and beyond their sanctuary walls. By the time their ministries ended, the crest of mainstream Protestantism had occurred, but it was not obvious at the time.

Ralph Sockman, Paul Scherer, Harry Emerson Fosdick, and George Buttrick are the preachers who can best be used to measure the crest. The standard of measurement here is theological. By examining their sermons from the perspective of historical theology, it may be possible to discover in some degree why the crest passed.

As the table of contents will make clear, this book contains five major sections. Part One identifies the contexts that provide definition for the period, the preachers, and the theological propositions to be addressed. In two chapters, with several sub-divisions, these contextual matters are covered. By the end of this first part, it should be clear that specific theological issues have emerged and that dramatic social, cultural, political, and economic factors offered discrete historical boundaries in which those theological issues were addressed by America's leading preachers. Parts Two, Three and Four examine their sermons in theological detail during the thirties, the war years, and the decade following World War II. Each of these parts includes chapters, one for every preacher under review. And each chapter has sections for discussing specific doctrines. Part Five offers a concluding assessment. Interludes provide transitions between the major parts. Finally, Part Five offers a concluding assessment of Sockman, Scherer, Fosdick, and Buttrick as pulpit theologians in the Protestant tradition.

These preachers labored in the relatively recent past. Yet they are strangely distant from us now. Nearly twice as many years separate us from Fosdick's death in 1969 as separated his birth from the end of the Civil War. All four of them used the King James Version of the Bible. All of them know only one pronoun form—masculine singular—to refer to God and used the terms "man" or "men" generically when referring to humanity. They spoke in the language of their day, to the issues of their day.

Beneath such idiosyncrasies lie deeper issues. When the crest passes, the stream is not only at its greatest height, after all; it is also at its greatest depth. My hope is that an exploration of their pulpit theology will probe the depths.

ACKNOWLEDGMENTS

Within these pages lie the results of a study that draws together a number of disciplines. It is an exercise in historical theology that gives serious attention to the pulpit as an arena for theological discourse. It recognizes the social and cultural context as the defining environment for preaching. And it reflects historically upon the powerful presence of a few key personalities in a turbulent age.

But there is an aspect to this study that is personal, also.

My maternal grandfather spent his entire career working in and around the hard coal mines of northeastern Pennsylvania. His formal education was meager, but by self-discipline and apprenticeship he mastered the skills to be an electrician. It was his job to maintain the generators and the motors that kept apparatus functioning so that some measure of safety for the miners might be maintained. During all the years that I knew him, he was on call twenty-four hours a day. On any day, he might be summoned before dawn to repair an exhaust fan in order that the miners would face no danger from methane gas. Generally, he worked six days a week. One Saturday in his seventy-eighth year, he came home from work at the usual hour of three o'clock, sat down in his favorite chair, and died.

Back in the 1930s and 1940s, this undereducated, black-collar man maintained a Sunday routine. He attended the Men's Bible Class at the Methodist Church, worshiped with his family at the service that followed Sunday School, went home to a big dinner prepared by my grandmother, and then turned on the radio to hear a sermon by Harry Emerson Fosdick. It is part of the mystery of preaching that the urbane, well-educated, upper-class, liberal, big-city ministry of people like Fosdick meant so much to the coal miners and farmers as well as the intellectuals who filled the pews of Christian churches on Sundays in America. My concern is not to dissect that mystery, but rather to show my respect for it by examining it theologically and historically.

I hope that the ensuing pages will clarify why this period (1930 to 1955) and why these preachers (Sockman, Scherer, Fosdick, and Buttrick) were selected. What may not be clear is the significant role that others have played in making this work possible.

First, I must acknowledge with deep appreciation Seth Kasten at the Burke Library at Union Theological Seminary in New York, Eleanor Gallagher and the staff of the George Arents Memorial Library at Syracuse University, and Harley P. Holden, Curator of Archives at

Harvard University. The notes at the end of this volume identify specific citations for the manuscript collections that I was allowed to see. In particular, Dr. David Buttrick assisted me in gaining access to his father's sermon manuscripts at Harvard, and I remain grateful for his interest and for his permission to quote from his father's sermons, which I read in their unpublished form courtesy of the Harvard University Archives.

Second, I deeply appreciate the technical wizardry and professional support of Paige Ann Scarlett and Cynthia T. LaMaster at the J. M. Ormond Center of Duke Divinity School. Any credit for the quality of appearance in the final manuscript belongs to them. They and I benefited from valuable assistance provided by John Abbott Reeves.

Third, I acknowledge the many teachers who have encouraged my work. Charles Rice has been a generous friend and gracious host as well as an able teacher and inspiring preacher. Russell Richey has been my teacher, and is now my colleague, but remains valued above all as a friend. Kenneth Rowe has demonstrated the sheer delight of scholarship, and helped immensely in enabling this publication to appear. But more than anyone else, it is the late Bard Thompson whom I wish to acknowledge. As Dean of the Graduate School at Drew and chair of my dissertation committee, he was the very model of administrative leadership, scholarly dedication, and teaching excellence. His untimely death deprived his family, the church, the community of scholars, and his university of a unique voice.

Finally, I thank my wife Naomi for all that we have shared in our twenty-six years of marriage and for all that she has endured while I have pursued the ministries to which God has called me. With her, and our sons Jonathan and Todd, I continue to enjoy the discoveries of love.

William B. Lawrence
Duke University
Advent, 1995

PART ONE

PULPIT CONTEXTS

CHAPTER I
THE OPENING OF AN ERA

On a cool autumn Sunday in New York, nearly six thousand people gathered to wait for the doors of a building to open.[1] It was October 5, 1930, and at eleven o'clock in the morning on Riverside Drive between 120th and 122nd Streets, the Riverside Church was to become a house of worship for the first time. No one was to be admitted until an hour before the start of the prelude, but by nine o'clock there were already more would-be worshippers on line than even this great nave could accommodate. Besides that, most of the 2400 spaces in the black oak pews would be claimed by persons with tickets—members of the congregation, representatives of the contracting firms, and artisans of the stone and stained glass.[2]

Perhaps those without tickets decided it was worth waiting in the cold wind anyway, on the chance that they might somehow gain admittance and experience first-hand what it means to praise God in a four million dollar church.[3] Perhaps they hoped to enjoy the pleasure of having John D. Rockefeller, Jr., Riverside's chief benefactor, take up the collection at their pew.[4] Perhaps they simply wanted to record in their scrapbooks that they had heard the first sermon delivered by the nation's foremost preacher [5] at the opening of the nation's largest church.[6]

In any case, barely half of the gathered throng gained admittance that day. And, of those who did, about eight hundred had to listen in an overflow room to the amplified voice of Harry Emerson Fosdick, preaching on "What Matters in Religion."[7] The others would simply have to go home content that they had been there for the grand opening, and had stood beneath the country's tallest steeple which housed the world's largest carillon.[8]

Riverside had overcome both controversy about its construction[9] and a costly fire during the building process.[10] But at last it was "open for business."

A. The Heritage of Wealth

The "business" imagery is intended to be substantive as well as figurative, for Riverside's opening was in many respects the culmination of an alliance—spectacular evidence of what American Christianity and American business at their best could accomplish together. Riverside offered the supreme example of the "gospel of wealth"[11] at its noblest: people of immense property exercising faithful stewardship of their resources and doing good with their wealth.

A long tradition undergirded that "gospel," stretching back to those Protestants who saw wealth or prosperity as a token of divine favor.[12] Americans, in their typical nineteenth-century style,[13] saw the practical side of the "gospel of wealth" principle and turned it into a mission program. So Horace Bushnell could be remembered saying that when the power of money is consecrated to God, the final revival will come, and the Kingdom of God will arrive in a day.[14] Riverside did not exalt that "gospel." But it did enjoy the benefits of it.

In the early thirties, though Walter Lippmann commented that Americans held their financial and industrial leaders in low esteem,[15] American cynicism about big business and skepticism about the claims of Christianity had not yet taken hold of the nation's soul. Indeed, the best-seller lists still included Bruce Barton's 1925 volume, *The Man Nobody Knows*, which claimed that if Jesus were alive in the modern world He would be an account executive for an advertising agency.[16] Furthermore, in the days preceding Riverside's formal dedication on February 8, 1931, there was front page evidence that corporate and ecclesiastical organizations took care of their own—even in a depression. The Standard Oil Company of New York, which was the Rockefeller firm, was establishing a pension plan for its employees' retirement. And the Episcopal Diocese of Long Island was adding a clergy life insurance program to its ministerial pension benefits. The pension fund had been established fourteen years earlier by the denomination at the urging of its Massachusetts Bishop, William Lawrence.[17]   Bishop Lawrence had declared in 1900 that "Godliness is in league with riches. . . . Material prosperity is helping to make the national character sweeter, more joyous, more unselfish, more Christlike."[18]

But in so saying, the Bishop was merely putting into sensible language the doctrine of property and stewardship made popular by a famous Baptist preacher from Philadelphia, Russell H. Conwell, in his "Acres of Diamonds" lecture. "Money is power," Conwell said. "Every good man and woman ought to strive for power, to do good with it when obtained."[19]

John Davison Rockefeller, Jr., was a devout Baptist. He was also a man who possessed enormous property and who was possessed by a profound sense of personal stewardship. He had found a career for himself as a professional example of the gospel of wealth: giving away money was a serious vocation and a full-time business for him. Inheriting the resources of his father's petroleum empire, he devoted his energies to the Rockefeller philanthropies. And richly benefiting from his largesse was his Church—over the years he donated more than $21 million to its ministries.[20] In addition, he directed the building committee for the construction of Riverside, taught the Men's Bible Class, and became an advocate for programs adopted by the Church even when he did not personally favor them.[21] He was deeply committed to the interdenominational spirit which was among the driving forces behind the establishment of Riverside. And he personally negotiated with Fosdick to become pastor of the congregation whose new cathedral would be dedicated "for the facing of this hour" and "for the living of these days."[22]

Those negotiations involved Fosdick's refusal to be the minister of "a small group of financially privileged people" who worshipped in a building "situated in one of the swankiest residential areas of the city."[23] That issue led to the decision to undertake the new construction on Morningside Heights, near Columbia University. Among the other issues[24] were Fosdick's theological objection to the policy of Park Avenue Baptist Church, which limited full membership to those who had been immersed, and Fosdick's disinclination to be "the pastor of the richest man in the country," as he told Rockefeller.

"Do you think," the philanthropist replied, "that more people will criticize you on account of my wealth than will criticize me on account of your theology?"[25]

B. The Notoriety of the Preacher

Certainly Fosdick's theology had become well known. He was fifty-two years old and at the peak of his powers when Riverside opened.

He had already published eleven books, including four widely circulated devotional guides, and a score of articles. For twenty-two years he had been teaching a generation of aspiring ministers at Union Theological Seminary. Professors of divinity, parish ministers, and the general public all recognized his name.

His views were notorious. In his 1923 Beecher Lectures, published as *The Modern Use of the Bible*, he had boldly declared that he believed neither in the resurrection of the flesh[26] nor in the second coming of Christ.[27] "I have never subscribed to [the creeds] nor repeated them," he wrote.[28] In the early 1920s Fosdick had been the lightning rod for a spectacular controversy between Fundamentalists and Liberals (or Modernists, as he preferred to say) on matters of biblical interpretation. Two General Assemblies of the Presbyterian Church had focused on his views and eventually forced him to leave the pulpit of the First Presbyterian Church,[29] where he had been preaching while serving on the Union faculty. Since about 1922, he had been developing a radio following, with sermons that reached the city, then the nation, and eventually around the world.[30] On that scale, radio was a rather new medium, and Fosdick was one of the first to become alert to its potential. Along with some others of his time who took to the air—Jack Benny, Father Charles E. Coughlin, Franklin Delano Roosevelt—Fosdick was helping to define the character of broadcasting.[31]

That contribution to radio came in the form of a particular kind of sermon, which he had been delivering since his days in the First Presbyterian Church pulpit. On one Sunday morning, he had offered to give some of his time for pastoral (that is, personal) counseling. He found himself swamped with requests.[32] Out of that experience (and certainly out of the sensitivity established by his having endured a personal emotional trauma that included a near suicide), Fosdick developed a new idiom for sermons. He focused not on the exposition of biblical texts, nor on the explanation of random subjects, but on the personal needs of people and on the attainment of an object[33]—namely bridging the gap between those personal needs and the unsearchable riches of Christ; then allowing those riches to cross that bridge and meet those needs.[34]

So the six thousand who stood on the sidewalk under a cloudy October sky on that Sunday in New York did not come to hear a reed shaking in the wind. Harry Emerson Fosdick was a formidable force with a national reputation when he stepped into the Riverside pulpit for the first time.

C. The Centrality of the City

But if his fame spanned the continent, his platform was uniquely New York. In those days, Manhattan was for all practical purposes the nation's capital. The business of America was still business, and the corporate power of the country was in New York: "directors meetings were more important than presidential cabinet meetings," wrote Joseph D. Ban.[35] The burgeoning radio industry was centered in New York. Journalistic standards were set by the newspapers in New York, notably by the *Herald Tribune* and *The New York Times*.

> Most big national problems were decided in New York, where the money was; when federal action was required, Manhattan's big corporation lawyers Charles Evans Hughes, Henry L. Stimson, and Elihu Root came down to guide their Republican proteges.[36]

The city itself was building up and out. Its frontier had been moving steadily northward; now it was moving westward and skyward as well. In 1931, the year of Riverside's dedication, the Empire State Building was opened and ruled the world's skylines. That same year saw the opening of the Waldorf Astoria, touted in one ad as the "Citadel of the gracious art of modern living."[37] Rockefeller Center was under construction, with the seventy-story RCA tower to be opened in 1933.[38] Access to the city's glories was improving: with the completion of both the George Washington Bridge and the Bayonne Bridge in that same year, 1931, doorways into the city had been made available for the private automobiles of New Jersey. Years later such routes would become pathways *out of* the city for suburban commuters seeking to flee the teeming urban streets. But in the early thirties, city life was still the dominant cultural motif, since it was in the city that most people still lived. "Suburban areas had begun to form, but only nineteen percent of the population lived there. It was still feasible for a man and his family to live decently within walking distance of his office."[39]

So the middle class considered New York their home, their place of work, and their place of worship.

The mighty did, too. Charles Evans Hughes, that corporate lawyer who exercised so much influence in New York and Washington, who had been Secretary of State under Warren G. Harding, who had lost a narrow electoral college decision to Woodrow Wilson in the 1916 Presidential race, and who would arouse President Roosevelt's wrath while serving as Chief Justice of the Supreme Court, happened also to have been a member of Riverside, a teacher for its Men's Bible Class, and the first elected president of the Northern Baptist Convention.[40]

Thus, it was more than a house of worship that drew six thousand people to Riverside Drive on that October Sunday in New York. It was a way of life that Riverside Church symbolized—that unique combination of the dominant preacher, in the dominant religious ethos, of the dominant economic ideology, in the dominant city in the land.

D. The Way of Life and the Churches

But Riverside symbolized more than the reigning social cultural, religious, and political mores. It symbolized also a commitment to new patterns of church and community life. The building itself, according to Fosdick, inaugurated a new era in church construction, whereby a congregation was committed to, and had the physical resources for, a program of services to the community seven days a week.[41] Its gymnasia, bowling alleys, and twelve kitchens were an integral part of Riverside's whole ministry.

Moreover, Riverside was a monument to the rejection of divisive denominationalism. Its interracial, interdenominational polity was an affirmation of congregational independence (a hallmark of the Baptist tradition, of course) and also of community-based (rather than dogmatically-based, ethnically-based or economically-based) social inclusiveness. It enjoyed the benefits of the gospel of wealth, but forsook the swanky neighborhoods for the pluralism of the university neighborhood and the poverty of Manhattanville and Harlem next door. It took to heart Fosdick's declaration at the climax of the controversy with the Presbyterians in 1924 that "creedal subscription to ancient confessions of faith is a practice dangerous to the welfare of the church and to the integrity of the individual conscience."[42] To become a member of Riverside, one needed only to affirm faith in Jesus, with no further specification of the content of that faith.[43] New York had seen that before, when Henry Ward Beecher declared the independence of his Brooklyn congregation.[44]

Not every congregation subscribed to this new brand of ecclesiasticism, of course. After all, there were Presbyterians who were willing to pay one and one-half million dollars for the right to worship in a "little cathedral" in a swanky neighborhood.

And just a few blocks south of the former Park Avenue Baptist Church, a Methodist congregation was about to construct its own edifice of Byzantine elegance at Park Avenue and Sixtieth Street. Formed by the merger of the Madison Avenue and East Sixty-First Street Methodist Episcopal Churches,[45] this new congregation was led by Ralph Washington Sockman, a Columbia Ph.D. who had studied preaching under Fosdick[46] and who had been pastor of the Madison Avenue M. E. congregation for over a decade by the time of the decisions to merge and build. Construction started on its three million dollar facility in 1931 (the year of Riverside's dedication) and the new building was put to use two years later.[47]

It, too, was caught up in the new ecclesiastical self-image celebrated by Riverside. At the very least, its name was a devaluation of denominationalism: the new congregation called itself "Christ Church, Methodist"; by separating the denominational label from its proper name it became known simply as "Christ Church."[48]

Nor did its architectural design give any clue to its denominational heritage. Ralph Adams Cram, the foremost ecclesiastical builder of the age and the recognized authority on Gothic style, decided that the Gothic emphasis on verticality was lost amid the city's corporate towers. Instead, he conceived Christ Church as a "small precious jewel" set amid the "prongs" of the city's skyscrapers.[49] Benefactors enabled the builder to use gilded mosaics and imported marble in a design that no visitor would ever surmise had come from the Methodist tradition.

Sockman, meanwhile, like his mentor at Union Seminary, began to develop a wide personal following. He started his radio preaching in 1932 as a summer replacement for a Brooklyn Congregationalist named S. Parkes Cadman. And when Cadman relinquished his microphone in 1936, Sockman became a national radio voice every week. At least three of his books and a dozen or so articles were in circulation by 1931.[50] Thus the combination of Sockman's personal appeal and the attraction of a marvelous building soon helped to make Christ Church the largest Methodist congregation in the city.

The largest Presbyterian congregation in New York was neither the one that had reluctantly yielded up Fosdick in 1924 nor the one that had purchased his forsaken "little cathedral" on Park Avenue, but rather the Madison Avenue Presbyterian Church at Seventy-third Street. In 1927 its pastor, Henry Sloane Coffin, had moved on to become the president of Union Theological Seminary. His successor was thirty-four year old George Arthur Buttrick, who had come from a pastorate in

Buffalo where he reclaimed the First Presbyterian Church there from utter disrepair and remodeled it in Byzantine style.[51] Buffalo had been Buttrick's first Presbyterian assignment. He was raised in England's Primitive Methodist Church, where his father was a minister, and then he chose the Congregational Church for his own worship and theological education in Britain. Following graduation from the Lancaster Independent Theological Seminary, he came to the United States, served two early pastorates in Vermont and Illinois, and then went to Buffalo.

Coffin, long before Riverside's example, had led the Madison Avenue Church to a sense of inclusiveness in the community. Like many fashionable East Side congregations, it had a social program designed to reach poor, immigrant families in the geographical parish. But the program was considered a mission, with a separate minister and social work staff. A child who lived on Fifth Avenue would be enrolled in the Madison Avenue Sunday School, for instance, while a child who lived in the tenements east of Third Avenue would be assigned to the mission Sunday School. Coffin found this division intolerable, and he worked to incorporate the people and the program of the East Side mission into the parent Church.[52]

So Buttrick stepped into the pulpit of an influential congregation which had an ambitious social vision. Such well-known personalities as Thomas Watson of IBM and Henry Luce of Time were among his parishioners. New construction came to his mind here, too, with plans for a new chancel, a larger seating capacity, and a remodeled parish house.[53] And he had a perspective of the congregation's life without denominational limits.[54]

Buttrick, however, cultivated a less "popular" image than his colleagues. He did not develop a radio ministry, perhaps because of a self-conscious dislike for his own voice and perhaps because of an expressed preference for face-to-face preaching.[55] Yet, by 1931, one could find two books from his pen, among them his highly acclaimed Beecher lectures at Yale.[56] He declined to publish his sermons, however—at least in book form—until well after his departure from Madison Avenue.[57] But his printed sermons were a monthly feature of the parish newsletter, to which hundreds of ministers subscribed.[58]

So it was on Manhattan's East Side that New York's pre-eminent Methodist and Presbyterian churches were located. And it was from Baptist roots there that Riverside Church was sprung. Along the way, before the Park Avenue Baptists had sold their "little cathedral" to Central Presbyterian Church, another group of Protestants had shown interest in the building. The Evangelical Lutheran Church of the Holy Trinity, situated on Central Park West at Sixty-fifth Street had studied the possibility of a move to Park Avenue.[59] The East Side, some thought, might offer the congregation a changed fortune. Its membership had slumped in the first two decades of the twentieth-century and had managed only to stabilize itself after the arrival of a new pastor, Paul Ehrmann Scherer, in 1920.[60] He had been raised in a succession of Lutheran parsonages, mostly in the South, during his father's ministerial career. Now the senior Scherer was a denominational executive, the author of a book on Christian unity,[61] and a member of the Holy Trinity congregation.

Eventually the decision was made to stay on the West Side of Manhattan. Among the factors influencing that choice was the presence of a similarly-sized Lutheran Church across town already, at St. Peter's. Despite the reality that only three percent of the population in its neighborhood claimed to be Protestant, the beauties of Central Park were just across the street from Holy Trinity's front doors, and the troubled environment of the old Hell's Kitchen was safely distant—a dozen or more blocks to the rear of the church building, in the west and south.[62]

So, in 1931, when Riverside Church was dedicated and Christ Church was begun, when the city was setting new standards for bridges, office towers, and luxury hotels, George Buttrick could tell his Yale audience that preachers had to be ready with an "approach to a new age."[63] And Paul Scherer could tell the Holy Trinity congregation in his first sermon for the new year

> We have come to the point of thinking of ourselves fairly well established. As we look back over the sixty-seven years of our history, covering the period of New York's great expansion, we are conscious of the difficulties we have overcome. A generation ago it was thought that the best answer to the changing conditions of lower Manhattan was to move northward with the drifting population. . . . Today the future of this church is humanly more secure than it has ever been. . . . We have forgotten the psychology of defeat. We are face to face now with the equally dangerous psychology of success.[64]

E. A Double Inheritance

It is curious that churches were spending, or were committed to spend, or were willing to consider spending millions of dollars on new construction or relocation when the depression had just begun. It is an anomaly that a preacher could alert his parishioners to the threat of success hanging over them, while the nation's greatest economic failure was occurring. The ambiguity of the situation became apparent to the churches themselves before long.[65]

But the fact is that the four prominent churches heretofore identified were among those ecclesiastical bodies that possessed a double inheritance in their liberal denominational traditions. If certain leaders, such as Bishop Lawrence, had provided their Protestant heirs with the insights of the "gospel of wealth," other leaders of the same era had been advocates of a "social gospel." In the Hell's Kitchen neighborhood near Holy Trinity Lutheran, Walter Rauschenbusch had labored a generation earlier for the physical as well as the spiritual salvation of the people. Sockman frequently admonished his listeners to see the social as well as personal dimensions of sin, once pointing out that it does little good for a businessman to be smug in his having kept the seventh commandment, if he pays his secretary a wage so low that she has to break the commandment in order to have enough money to survive.[66] At the Madison Avenue Presbyterian Church poor children were now attending Sunday School with the elite. And Riverside Church was busy serving people's physical and spiritual needs seven days a week,[67] with Fosdick appealing to what was essentially the motivation behind the gospel of wealth for the support of those ministries.[68]

Trying to combine the gospel of wealth and the social gospel was a matter of delicate balance.[69] A theological rationale which embraced care for the poor by good stewardship of wealth seemed most elusive, given the fact that the social gospel had arisen in critical reaction to the gospel of wealth.[70] The popular mind would have to synthesize two best sellers from opposite perspectives: Bruce Barton's *The Man Nobody Knows*, which identified Jesus with the promoters of prosperity; and Charles M. Sheldon's *In His Steps*, which advocated social responsibility in the form of self-sacrifice that imitates Christ. So Christians had to decide whether their religion was calling them to accumulate wealth or to deny themselves of it: the choice seemed to lie between self-promotion and self-sacrifice. Those who already had wealth should be giving it away for good. But to those who did not yet have it, or once had it and lost it in the crash, or might never get it—to them the religious question was whether Christians should acquire wealth first and then be benevolent, or engage in self-denial from the start in a faithful life that seeks to do what Jesus would do.

Congregations like Riverside, Madison Avenue Presbyterian, Holy Trinity Lutheran, and Christ Church stood as heirs to both gospels in many ways. From their pulpits would have to come the formative theology to effect the synthesis and to forge doctrine for the thirties and beyond.

CHAPTER II
PULPIT THEOLOGY

It is not customary to think of the pulpit as the arena for theological work to be done.[1] Typically, doctrinal reflection is a task reserved to the academic theologians, whose minds are presumed to be inherently sharper and outwardly not dulled by the clutter of diverse responsibilities laid upon parish ministers.[2] A preacher is normally that person who prepares for ministry in a congregation by studying under the real theologians and then engages in an active ministry while attempting to do enough personal study to maintain contact with current trends in theology. Rarely, if ever, is a systematic theologian also a full-time working pastor. Seldom are doctrinal explorations affected by the pulpit.[3]

Yet week after week, in pulpit after pulpit, theological arguments are being made and doctrinal presuppositions are being laid upon the listeners. It may not be the case that quantum advances in theological technique are being accomplished in pulpits. But the impact of even subtle shifts can be extremely significant, simply in terms of the number of lives potentially affected. What's more, poor theology from an academic theologian can be critically reviewed by a colleague and then consigned to gather dust on a shelf somewhere—unread, except for the unlikely possibility that an unsuspecting undergraduate might stumble upon it and be impaired. Poor theology from the pulpit, on the other hand, does not die so mercifully, but lives in dinner-table conversations and mid-week circle meetings of the parish. Sunday after Sunday, it is reinforced.

> Part of the much discussed problem of American preaching lies in homiletics' having too long shirked its responsibility to do serious theological thinking on its task of preaching in relationship to the corrective insights of systematic theology and systematics having too long shunned its responsibility to relate itself seriously to preaching.[4]

The academic theologian, it is worth noting, has certain advantages over the homiletical theologian. The professor submits papers, delivers lectures, and writes books to a relatively controlled audience: the content is shared in a professional jargon which is common currency among them; the words written and said by the academic theologian never purport to be more than his or her own words about a given doctrine or set of doctrines; at the end, the doctrinal argument can reply to a negative critic that the respondent has failed in some way to understand the originally stated position.

The pastor, however, engages in public discourse with an audience where there is never an assurance of common coin in language or experience. The careful preacher struggles constantly with the need to find a word or phrase or image that fits both the doctrine being proclaimed and the audience whose ears can hear. Moreover, the preacher (at least in the traditional Protestant view of the sermon's purpose) is bringing the Word of God to the people, not just the words of an interpreter of the Word. Symbolically and practically, the preacher's words are in some sense given over to the Spirit of God. They are never strictly the preacher's own. The words become vehicles of the listeners faith—words which therefore cannot be called back by the preacher who claims to be misunderstood. The words become public domain, blown where the Spirit wills.

A. The Dominant Pulpiteers

And although there were many pulpits to which one might turn for some representative sample of the pulpit theology being forged at the dawn of the thirties, there is good reason to focus on the four preachers already cited. To be sure, there were eminent Protestant pulpiteers in cities all over the country: Edwin McNeill Poteat in Raleigh, Henry Hitt Crane in Scranton and Detroit, Ernest Fremont Tittle in Chicago. Even within New York City alone, several prominent figures held forth besides those four already mentioned: Walter Russell Bowie of Grace Episcopal Church and Allen Knight Chalmers of Broadway Tabernacle, for instance. Yet, the reasons are compelling to pay particular attention to Buttrick, Fosdick, Scherer, and Sockman.

First, they were all well-established in their Manhattan pulpits by the time the new challenges of the thirties arose, and they served for a substantial period into the succeeding decades.

Fosdick, for instance, had been elected to the pastorate of the Park Avenue Baptist Church in 1925. But he had been preaching in the First Presbyterian Church for six years prior to that. Indeed, he had risen to a level of prominence in the city before the twenties, and his acquaintance with its streets had begun in the early years of the century when his seminary student work took him to the Bowery and to the Madison Avenue Baptist Church, where he served as an assistant and where he was ordained. His only pastorate outside New York City was in Montclair, New Jersey, still within the sphere of influence of Manhattan. Besides these pastoral positions, Fosdick had been teaching at New York's Union Theological Seminary since 1908: until 1915 as a part-time instructor; thereafter as the full-time Jessup Professor of Practical Theology.[5] Thus, since the day he arrived as a student transfer from the unfulfilling environment of Colgate Theological Seminary, Fosdick took New York City as his home.

Ralph Sockman had come to New York as a young man from Ohio, to do graduate studies at Columbia, pointing toward an academic career teaching history on the college level. To help underwrite the costs of his graduate work, he became the intercollegiate secretary of the YMCA and he handled other chores in the building where he resided with other students. Some of them were medical students who, in 1911, invited Sockman to accompany them to Sunday morning worship. Together they attended services at the Madison Avenue Methodist Episcopal Church. In 1913, Sockman became a member of the congregation. Shortly after that he began theological studies at Union, and he was added to the staff of the Madison Avenue Church as a part-time assistant. Graduating with his divinity degree in 1916, he moved to full-time status as a minister at the Church. And when the senior minister left in 1917, the year Sockman received his Ph.D. at Columbia, he moved up to lead the congregation's ministry. It was a position he never left, until his retirement in 1961.

So, by 1931, when plans were established for the construction of Christ Church, Sockman was already an unusual Methodist in that he had held one pulpit for fourteen years.

Three years after Sockman assumed the ministerial leadership of his East Side congregation, Paul Scherer was called to the Evangelical Lutheran Church of the Holy Trinity on Central Park West at Sixty-fifth Street. Raised in the home of a Lutheran pastor and a literature-loving mother,[6] Scherer had been an uncertain recruit to the ministry for some time. He had taught English and rhetoric in college, had served as an assistant principal in a public school, and had considered careers in medicine, teaching, and law—but not ministry, in part because he

considered himself an agnostic, if not an atheist, while in college.[7]
Eventually he did study at Mt. Airy Seminary and intermittently taught
there while serving as an assistant minister in Buffalo. In 1920 he came
to New York, to lead the congregation where his parents were members.

It took ten years, by Scherer's own accounting, before positive
signs of growth began to appear in the parish.[8] But, by 1931, his work
was well-established.

Seven years after Scherer moved from Buffalo to Manhattan,
George Arthur Buttrick made the same journey. Called from the First
Presbyterian Church there in 1927, Buttrick seemed quite young at
thirty-four to step into the pulpit previously occupied by the illustrious
Henry Sloane Coffin. But in the year of Riverside's dedication, he
delivered the prestigious Lyman Beecher Lectures on Preaching at Yale.
Thus, the pastor of New York's largest Presbyterian congregation made
his presence felt rather quickly. By 1931 it was clear that he would
secure his own eminent place. As the thirties opened, all four were firmly
established in their respective ministries in New York.

Second, their influence extended well beyond the congregations
and the city in which they served. Of the four, only Buttrick did not
develop a national radio following: Fosdick, of course had taken to the
air in the twenties; Scherer and Sockman were to command the
microphone in the thirties. All four wrote and published widely: two
volumes each from Scherer and Buttrick, five from Sockman, and six
from Fosdick appeared in the thirties alone; articles in a variety of
publications, directed to different types of readers, flowed from them.
All four spoke to audiences besides their own on Sundays in New York.

Moreover, all four of them were teachers of preachers—at one
time or another, all of them taught at Union Seminary. Fosdick held his
professorship there throughout his Riverside years. Buttrick taught one
afternoon a week at Union during his twenty-seven years at Madison
Avenue Presbyterian. Sockman taught there periodically during his
ministry at Christ Church, and periodically at Yale. Scherer left Holy
Trinity in 1945 to accept the Brown Professorship of Homiletics at
Union. Like Sockman, the others taught elsewhere, too, at institutions
both prestigious and humble. That they all taught at Union, however, is
significant on several levels. The Seminary was known internationally,
strictly for its theological stature, and not in terms of its place at a great
university, nor by its ties to a denomination. When Emil Brunner and
Dietrich Bonhoeffer [9] came to America for theological study, they came
to Union. The school was, in addition, recognized as an uncompromised

champion among seminaries: it had been founded in 1836 as an institution free from denominational restrictions;[10] early in the twentieth-century, the Presbyterians looked askance at any candidate for ministry with credentials from Union; in 1928 the Seminary invited Reinhold Niebuhr, then in his socialist period, to join the faculty; in 1934, an unorthodox philosopher named Paul Tillich would arrive.[11] It was a stimulating community for teachers of preachers to hone their theological skills for the pulpit.

As colleagues, Buttrick, Fosdick, Scherer, and Sockman respected and appreciated one another's work. When Buttrick was editing the twelve-volume *Interpreter's Bible*, he included his active Manhattan colleagues among the contributors.[12] On one of his favorite topics, prayer, Buttrick quoted Fosdick's *The Meaning of Prayer* approvingly.[13] When Scherer, in his Beecher lectures, recommended preachers whose sermons might be valuable to any aspiring pulpiteer, he listed Buttrick, Fosdick, and Sockman among the top five.[14] Fosdick considered Sockman's student sermons equivalent to those of a seasoned master.[15] Sockman admired Fosdick as the ideal among preachers.[16]

Beyond the esteem in which these four held each other, their colleagues evaluated them as the best among homileticians. In the mid-fifties, William McLeister surveyed more than a hundred theological schools in America, asking the chairmen of the homiletics departments whom they considered the best preachers: the names Fosdick, Sockman, Buttrick, and Scherer topped the list.[17]

In 1945, after twenty-five years at Holy Trinity, Scherer left the pastorate to teach full-time. In 1946, at the age of sixty-eight, Fosdick retired from Riverside and from the Union faculty. Both continued to preach: Scherer at James Chapel in the Seminary and elsewhere, including an infrequent return to Holy Trinity; Fosdick from time to time at Riverside and elsewhere.

Buttrick remained at Madison Avenue until 1954, after which he went to Harvard as Preacher to the University and Plummer Professor of Christian Morals. Sockman remained at Christ Church until his retirement.

If their careers took them to comparable levels of eminence, their early lives also bore some interesting similarities.

They all came from non-urban backgrounds: Buttrick, born in an English seacoast village, was the offspring of the small-town parsonage; Fosdick, a native of upstate New York, spent most of his young life in rural settings outside of Buffalo; Sockman was an Ohio farm boy; Scherer followed the trail of his father's pastorates in the South. They were raised in regions where the dominant institutions were school and Church: where the term religion was almost synonymous with "Christian," even with "Protestant"; where poverty was a personal family problem, or at most a neighborhood concern, not a pervasive pressure crushing thousands of lives concentrated in crowded tenements.

The city, especially New York at the start of the depression, presented a ferocious challenge to their own experience. The English seacoast or the farms of rural America might have imposed a certain discipline, but urban life discarded all such natural discipline. Residents of the city were not limited to the Church's opinion for moral guidance, since urban life could offer alternate counsel through art, theater, film, and other media. Whereas the Church in some regions might provide a believer with security and confidence, the city's pluralistic intellectual climate treated Christian faith with skepticism, if not contempt.[18] In the week after Riverside opened, the *Christian Century* warned that "multitudes" suspected

> the church, and its message, are extraneous to the affairs of modern life, and have quietly withdrawn from fellowship with it. Particularly in our cities has this process of seepage gained distressing proportions.[19]

Theologically, one reaction to the encroachments of urbanization was to yearn for simpler, pre-urban values, while holding stubbornly to secure beliefs. In fact, it has been argued that the real strongholds of fundamentalism were in America's big cities—Boston, Philadelphia, Pittsburgh, and Minneapolis as well as New York.[20]

Buttrick, Fosdick, Scherer, and Sockman certainly had the conservative personal religious backgrounds to tempt such yearnings. Buttrick's father was a Primitive Methodist minister and an advocate of biblical fundamentalism.[21] Scherer came from a long line of preachers of Lutheran orthodoxy, magnified through the lens of some stringent indoctrination under Henry Eyster Jacobs at Mt. Airy Seminary.[22] Sockman was raised in the atmosphere of revivalism.[23] Fosdick was tutored under the grim judgments of *Line Upon Line*, *Precept Upon Precept*, and *The Peep of Day*.[24]

But all four of them rebelled against their early training and took refuge in more liberal views. Buttrick, for example, told his Madison Avenue congregation that if they wanted to read something that was to be

taken as literally true, they should read the telephone directory![25] He saw
the Christian faith to be in no jeopardy if God's story written in the
Scriptures said the world was created in six days, while God's story
written in the rocks said the world was created in billions of years.[26]
Fosdick left no doubt that liberal theology had saved him from
abandoning all faith.[27] He is remembered for having said that the
achievement of liberal theology was that it enabled a person "to be both
an intelligent modern and a serious Christian."[28] Like Buttrick and
Fosdick, Scherer and Sockman also accepted the discoveries (if not all of
the premises) of modern science, and they explored new ways to
articulate the faith in the light of modern knowledge.

And yet, to say that they held liberal views is not necessarily to
say that they endorsed liberal theology. Buttrick spoke of the
"discredited liberalism" of his day.[29] And Fosdick, according to Jaroslav
Pelikan, was one of those who most clearly understood liberalism's
flaws.[30] For liberal theology involved more than avoiding stodginess or
stubbornness about doctrine.

According to Kenneth Cauthen's careful study, American religious
liberalism stressed three principles: the *continuity* of human history as an
evolving process on the one hand and of humanity's relationship with
God on the other, neither of which disintegrates through human failure or
divine revelation; the *autonomy* of human reason and experience, without
needing to appeal to external authorities; and the *dynamism* which
supplants the perception that truth is embodied in static dogmatisms with
the proposition that truth is found in the evolving historical experience
and social progress.[31] Cauthen wrote that these three principles—
continuity, autonomy, and dynamism—"are seen most clearly in the
emphasis on the immanence of God, on the centrality of religious
experience, and on the evolution of nature and history."[32]

At some point in the early 1930s, these principles were
victimized by a formidable critique. The naive, sentimental hopes which
they fostered were insufficient to face the challenges of a new era.[33]
"Recoil from liberalism is the most important feature of the present
situation in theology," wrote Henry Pitney Van Dusen at the time.[34] But,
with the necessary correctives, Fosdick (for one) believed that the future
of the Church lay in the liberals' hands.[35]

B. The Horizons of an Era

Historical eras seldom correspond exactly to the chronological periods from which they take their names. The nineteenth-century, for instance, did not really end until it was blown away by the guns of August, 1914. The fifties, which popular culture tends to romanticize as "happy days" in America, probably existed (if at all) for a few years in the mid-decade bounded by the end of the Korean Conflict and the Army-McCarthy hearings on the one side and ascent of Sputnik on the other.

Similarly, one could say, the "thirties" began before the decade arrived on the calendar.

On Thursday, October 29, 1929, the stock market crashed. On the same day, John Roach Straton succumbed to the consequences of a stroke.[36] Straton, pastor of New York City's Calvary Baptist Church, had been for years the arch-foe of everything that Fosdick and Riverside Church came to represent. It was Straton who had accused Fosdick of forsaking his Baptist ministry to assume the pulpit of the First Presbyterian Church because the Presbyterians had the money: he labeled Fosdick "a Baptist bootlegger," "a Presbyterian outlaw," and "the Jesse James of the theological world."[37] When negotiations between Rockefeller and Fosdick resulted in the noted preacher's call to the Park Avenue Baptist Church, Straton said the call showed "the deteriorating influence of great wealth on religion."[38] When plans were announced for the construction of the as-yet-unnamed new building on Riverside Drive, Straton proposed that a large electric sign atop the building identify it as "The Socony Church," since its captivity to the gospel of wealth would make it not the servant of God but of Rockefeller's Standard Oil Company of New York. The Church needed by twentieth-century America, Straton declared, would not be built Fosdick's way but only "upon the foundation of the Bible as God's Word" and upon "the other great truths of revealed religion."[39]

The gospel of wealth, the social gospel, and the liberal interpretation of Scripture were all anathema to Straton. But on that October day in 1929, the prosperity of the roaring decade and the asperity of the Fundamentalist-Modernist debate were silenced.

Straton's successor at Calvary Baptist, William Ward Ayer, continued to deplore the Rockefeller influence and the reigning liberalism.[40] Fosdick saw such complaints as confined to the "backwaters."[41] From such back waters, of course, fundamentalism would flow with new force in years to come. But, for the moment, Fosdick—like Buttrick, Scherer, and Sockman—turned his attention to other agenda in the new era.

The economic collapse offered the most compelling challenge of the thirties. Between 1929 and 1932, the total national income fell by more than one half, from $83 billion to $40 billion.[42] In December 1932, one fourth of New York City's work force was unemployed. Death by starvation and suicide reached record numbers in the city.[43]

At the same time, an intellectual crisis boiled. Heretofore, the prevailing American thought had generally played variations on a theme which left intact some sensitivity to religious assumptions. Now Theodore Dreiser's novels found a wide audience for the message that human life is at the mercy of forces—and not benevolent forces—beyond our control. Walter Lippman wrote *A Preface to Morals* without the premise of God. The preachers of New York City no longer had the luxury of carrying on strictly intramural debates within the family of believers. Unbelief was a legitimate, even fashionable, perspective. "For the first time in history," George Buttrick wrote, "belief seems the exception and unbelief the rule."[44]

There was a doctrinal crisis as well. John Bennett, himself identified with the liberal school, mourned "the disintegration of liberalism."[45] In Europe the reaction to the failures of liberalism had become known as "crisis theology." The American most easily identified with such critical neo-orthodox trends was Reinhold Niebuhr, whose *Moral Man and Immoral Society* appeared as the thirties began. At the time, Paul Scherer used the slang of the day to deride it as "a blue book, a very blue book indeed."[46] Later, he developed a better appreciation for Niebuhr's critical perspective. So did Buttrick, who confessed that Niebuhr "stamped out in me the last remaining elements of a discredited liberalism."[47]

Thus, with economic gloom hovering everywhere, preaching in New York during the thirties had to cope with rigorous intellectual and doctrinal challenges, too.[48] There apparently were some measurable institutional consequences of those challenges. In a lecture at the end of the thirties, Sockman rehearsed some statistics he had picked up at a National Stewardship Conference in Chicago.

> For the years 1932 to 1937 we Americans increased our expenditures for jewelry twenty-four percent, for automobiles one hundred and eighty-eight percent, for whiskey one hundred percent,

> for radio sets two hundred and twenty percent, and for beer over six hundred percent. During the same period we decreased our giving to churches nineteen percent, to church benevolences twenty-eight percent, to community chests including hospitals, twenty-two percent.[49]

Those numbers represented the national picture. But the local situation in New York was not much different. At Riverside Church in 1932 all staff members took salary cuts, including the paid Sunday School teachers, even though there was a waiting list of students seeking to enroll in classes.[50] At the Madison Avenue Presbyterian Church, the budget for 1935 was about thirty-four percent smaller than the 1930 budget, with benevolences cut by more than half.[51] And its Sunday School experienced a steady decline through the decade, from a high of 1500 in the early thirties to a low of 1100 in 1938.[52] The Sunday school at Madison Avenue did recover to about 1200 students by the end of the thirties, but net losses like that were indicative of a general problem existing in New York City—declining population. Manhattan lost a quarter-million residents during the thirties.[53]

Despite the grim circumstances, the number of persons who listened week after week to the sermons of Buttrick, Fosdick, Scherer, and Sockman remained high—and even grew. The public media continued to chronicle their efforts. *The New York Times* and, to a lesser extent, the *Herald Tribune*, provided regular coverage of sermons each week. On Sundays in New York, preachers would proclaim theology from their pulpits. On Mondays, *The New York Times* would fill a page with reports headlined "What Was Said in New York's Pulpits Yesterday."

Under the guidance of Rachel McDowell,[54] the paper's religion editor, summaries and extensive quotations of a dozen or more sermons would appear each week. There is evidence that this was a service valued by readers,[55] and one that the executives of *The New York Times* were reluctant to change when Miss McDowell retired.[56] Moreover, it was a field actively cultivated by many clergy—some of whom submitted sermon scripts, or portions thereof, in advance of the delivery on the ensuing Sunday.[57] Thus they could try to control which of their words would actually appear in print on Monday. Meanwhile the paper used its sermon coverage as a way to field-test and groom young reporters. "If a young man could not reliably cover a church sermon," wrote Gay Talese, "he could probably not reliably cover anything."[58] Fosdick and Sockman received extensive coverage of their sermons; Scherer and Buttrick were less frequently cited.[59] And Buttrick on at least one occasion found it necessary to tell his congregation that *The New York Times* had misrepresented him in the report of his previous Sunday's sermon.[60] Perhaps because of the fear of being reported inaccurately, Buttrick specifically invited the paper not to cover his sermons.[61] It continued to do so nevertheless.

In 1940, *The New York Times* began devoting less space to the coverage of sermons. By 1946, George Dugan had taken Miss McDowell's place as religion editor. For reasons of journalistic and religious principle, he felt that less attention should be paid to sermons and more to ecclesiastical matters such as the development of the World Council of Churches and meetings of denominational bodies like Methodist General Conferences, Presbyterian General Assemblies, Lutheran Synods, and Baptist Conventions. He also felt that less space should be reserved to the type of sermon coverage provided by a "church page" and more should be commanded by religious institutions and issues competing for space in general with other news reports.[62] Gradually, these changes took effect. By the mid-fifties, the sermon reports that were printed had to share columns with engagement notices,[63] crossword puzzles,[64] stock summaries,[65] new hairdos,[66] and the Italian soccer scores.[67] After 1956, *The New York Times Index* did not even bother to list "Sermons" as a categorical heading.[68]

If, however, journalists in the mid-fifties considered Sunday worship to be less appealing, the general public did not. Crowds of church-goers were filling the Church's pews and swelling the membership rolls. Scarcely six percent of the American people in 1954 dared to say they did not believe in God.[69] The Methodist Council of Bishops that same year reported a "great upsurge in church life."[70] In 1956, Bishop Lawrence's dictum that "Godliness is in league with riches" became official national policy: the slogan, "In God We Trust," which had been on United States coins since just after the Civil War, became the legal motto of the country.[71]

In 1955, John D. Rockefeller, Jr., donated an additional six million dollars to Riverside Church "for the construction of a new wing which architecturally will balance the nave and Gothic tower."[72] It was the culmination of his support for a building that symbolized a way of faith and life—a way he described in the year of Riverside's dedication as follows.

> There are many apparent differences between the beliefs of various bodies of Christians . . . but if I should say that by Christianity I

> mean sympathy, sacrifice, service, and love, there will be something
> upon which I believe we all can agree. . . . Probably all of the
> religion of mankind will ultimately unite in recognizing this spirit. . .
> Religion . . . is as fundamental as life itself, as enduring as the
> human race.[73]

By the year of his gift, American society seemed to have agreed.
Religion had broad social appeal and was being widely practiced and
enjoyed. America's Sunday Schools "taught that God was really just a
pal; that religion was fun, like the movie nuns who played softball and
rode around in helicopters."[74] To Will Herberg, however, such signs
merely served as evidence that American religion actually had "lost much
of its authentic Christian (or Jewish) content."[75]

So in many ways the middle 1950s became a crucial sifting time
for religion in America: never more popular with ordinary citizens, its
stock was declining with influential journals; blessed with social respect,
it was condemned by social critics; materially prosperous to the eyes of
most, it was theologically bankrupt in the eyes of some. Edward L. R.
Elson, however, argued that theology professors in their "splendid
academic aloofness" did not understand the needs of "the ordinary seeker
of religious reality." He cautioned Christians to recognize that while
"correct doctrine is important in the church . . . men are not saved by
theology."[76] But Frederick Schroeder saw the other side, and complained
that the pulpit had actually abandoned its theological responsibility:
"American preaching," he wrote, "may well have obscured and
obstructed the word of God, rather than conveyed it."[77]

So just as the opening of Riverside Church symbolized the dawn
of a new age for Christianity in America, the religious situation in 1955
was itself visible evidence that a new parting of the ways had come. It
was a dramatic quarter-century. And given the preachers, the churches,
and the powerful events of those twenty-five years, it was a watershed for
the Church. In particular, it was a watershed for Protestantism. Did the
religious situation in the middle fifties mean that Protestant hegemony, so
obvious at the time Riverside opened, had merged with the culture? Or
did it mean that Protestantism had used the period from 1930 to 1955 to
forsake its theological responsibility? What theology was being
proclaimed from the dominant pulpits in the land during those
two-and-a-half decades? What was the pulpit theology of those four
leading preachers? How Protestant were they?

C. The Fundamentals of Protestant Theology

Before any Protestant preacher had to warn a congregation about the perils of success, as Paul Scherer did in 1931; before anyone felt the impulse to stand in the cold wind waiting for a Protestant preacher to declare "What Matters in Religion," as six thousand people did in 1930; before multimillion dollar commitments could be made to build a Protestant house of worship for a congregation that would de-emphasize its denominational Protestant label; before Protestants were denominated as Lutherans or Presbyterians or Methodists or Baptists; before Protestants were encamped as Liberals or Modernists or Fundamentalists or revivalists; before Protestant preachers spoke of a "gospel of wealth" or a "social gospel"—they spoke of a Gospel. Beneath the various manifestations of Church life and belief that have marched under the banner of Protestantism lay a few irrepressible theological convictions about that Gospel.

Protestants acquired their identity hurling infamous invectives at the papacy in the sixteenth-century. But beneath all the lurid talk was the basic issue, that the Pope sat atop a sacramental system which offered men and women hope, that if they would do certain things or conduct themselves in certain ways, then all that is wrong would be right in their relationship with God and in their hope for salvation. The Reformers called that process "justification by works" and found it to be incompatible with the Gospel which proclaims "justification by faith":[78] namely, the gift of a relationship of trust in God, who has done all that need be done to bring about hope for our salvation and who has made right all that is wrong. By faith alone can one have a right relationship with God, said the Reformers; by faith alone can one receive that grace which is God's good will toward humanity; by faith alone can humanity find freedom.[79]

The effect of this Protestant doctrine was to foment institutional rebellion. But the fundamental issue was neither the rebellion against the sacramental system nor the understandable attempts by the papal establishment to suppress it. Rather the fundamental problem focused on the authority by which any Reformer dared develop such teaching. The papal Church, after all, could point to its tradition, which was traceable back to the Scripture, and which bestowed upon the Church the authority to determine doctrinal truth; otherwise each believer becomes his or her own priest, his or her own arbiter of saving power.

Precisely, said the Reformers, but only because the authority is neither the individual's experience (or belief) nor the authority of ecclesiastical tradition, but rather that of Scripture alone.[80] To be sure, various Protestant camps viewed this principle of biblical authority from different angles: some felt that what the Bible specifically enjoined was to be practiced; others felt that only those things the Bible specifically prohibited were to be rejected, while in other matters Christians were at liberty.[81] Yet, no matter *how* the authority was construed, the Reformers agreed that *the* authority was Scripture alone. By this authority, *sola scriptura*,[82] all theology that claims to fall heir to the Protestant Reformation must be judged.[83]

There is one more fundamental issue for Protestants. It exploded in the debate between Luther and Erasmus on the "freedom of the will."[84] If through faith alone one receives the grace that bestows freedom, and if through Scripture alone one finds the authority for this claim about faith, what choices must one make in order to find faith? The Protestant answer was that no human initiative or choice makes the grace of God operative. Medieval theologians, for instance, had taught the principle of *facere quod in se est*—to wit, that one could activate the grace of God by doing the best that one can.[85] But to the Reformers, such a principle involved the failure to perceive the truth about human nature—enslaved to sin, without the capacity to make justifying choices or accomplish justifying deeds—and a failure to perceive the truth about the nature of God, who is revealed fundamentally in terms of grace which has already chosen to save humanity. This is not to say that humans are without freedom of choice. It is to say that humans need not be burdened by the dilemma of choosing among alternative behaviors that might bring about their salvation.

That this principle was most often articulated by the unpopular (and thoroughly medieval) doctrine of predestination may be true, but it is beside the point. "The authentic view of the Lutheran Reformation is that human persons are neither free nor equal by nature, but only by destiny," writes Wolfhart Pannenberg.[86] So, "There is no true freedom except by faith in Christ."[87]

A concept of the freedom of the will implies "the capacity for the eternal, for God."[88] But the authentic position of Protestant theology is not that free humanity has a capacity for God; rather, God's grace is a gift which includes the capacity for freedom given to humanity. In other words, Protestants affirm not that humanity has a capacity for God but that God has a capacity for humanity.

So whatever else may be said about Protestantism, it is at bottom a theological movement and needs to be evaluated fundamentally as a theological movement.[89] That is what this study proposes to examine in a focus on the Protestant pulpit in twentieth-century America.

D. A Quarter-Century of Pulpit Theology

What follows, therefore, is an exercise in historical theology. Under consideration will be that twenty-five year era from the founding of Riverside Church in 1930 to the crucial and confusing situation in American Protestantism in 1955. Riverside stands as the symbol for all that liberal Protestantism had come to represent ecclesiastically; its opening signified the pinnacle of Protestant success in America. By 1955, that "success" had come seriously into dispute.

So the questions come. What was happening theologically in the pulpits occupied by Buttrick, Fosdick, Scherer, and Sockman during the quarter-century from 1930 to 1955? How did they stand in the Protestant tradition of preaching on the fundamental doctrines: justification by grace through faith alone; the authority of Scripture; the "freedom" of the will? Since Protestantism has been fundamentally a theological movement, how Protestant were they?

The resources for responding to such questions are, fortunately, quite extensive. Published sermons range from voluminous for Fosdick to rather limited for Buttrick, but collections of the unpublished manuscript sermons by all four are accessible and have been consulted. There is, therefore, a substantial quantity of data to show what these preachers said.

Furthermore, preaching involves not only what is said but also what is heard. And there are published records of what some listeners heard. *The New York Times'* reports about what was said in the city's pulpits on Sundays in New York help reveal the auditors' perceptions of the doctrines proclaimed by Buttrick, Fosdick, Scherer, and Sockman. Such information makes it possible to note the distinctively public character of pulpit theology, over against the purely academic variety.

Of course, all of this is to be examined in the context of the public crises during this quarter-century. The depression of the thirties determined the national mood until the onset of the war; chapter three will introduce the period and chapters four through seven will assess each preacher's pulpit theology during the depression.   World War II consumed the attention and the resources of the nation in the early forties; chapter eight will set the context of the war years, and chapters nine through twelve will focus upon war-time sermons and doctrine. Prosperity, materialism, cold war, and the arrival of religion at the core of the American way of life filled a decade after the war; chapter thirteen will survey the situation from 1945 through 1955, while chapters fourteen and fifteen will examine the pulpit theology of the two who continued as pastors in New York. Through sermons and the newspaper accounts of those sermons, a picture will emerge of what these preachers said and how they spoke theologically to the great transitions in society during the period of their homiletical dominance.

    The four preachers under consideration were keenly aware of the doctrinal issues being scrutinized here. "Truth blazed out at the Reformation," Scherer wrote,[90] and his annual celebration of Reformation Sunday at Holy Trinity Church included a sermon on one of the key doctrines at the basis of Protestantism.[91]   Sockman proposed in his Beecher lectures a revival of doctrinal preaching.[92] Fosdick published volumes which traced the roots of Reformation doctrine back to Wycliffe and Huss, and which told the story of Luther to young readers.[93] Buttrick knew the Reformers' work intimately and cited its importance throughout his career.[94]

    Paul Scherer, near the end of his career, restated in *The Word God Sent*[95] a point he had made in a lecture at Southern Baptist Theological Seminary in March, 1956—that the Christian pulpits in America have been "reducing the cost both of the Christian faith and of the Christian life."[96] It remains to be seen whether this indictment aptly suited the state of preaching in the mid-fifties, or the quarter-century preceding his remarks. It remains to be seen whether the objects of his concern were the preachers of the mid-fifties (many of whom he and his colleagues had taught) or the preachers of the era then drawing to a close—namely those who had dominated the homiletical field for the previous twenty-five years, Buttrick, Fosdick, Sockman, and himself.

PART TWO

THE THIRTIES

CHAPTER III
PREACHING GOOD NEWS TO THE POOR

Within a year after Riverside Church was dedicated, something new was being constructed along Riverside Drive just three blocks north of the church: a shantytown. It was one of many so-called "Hoovervilles" to be seen around the country, hovels made of tin, cardboard, burlap, and other scraps.[1] For the prey of the depression who had been evicted from their homes, this was the shelter of last resort.

The magnificent shadow of Riverside fell not only on the homeless, but on the hungry as well. Two blocks from the church, someone found a family with two starving children.[2] At least they were found in time to be helped. In 1931, four of New York City's hospitals attributed the cause of ninety-five patients' deaths to starvation.[3]

New York's great Protestant congregations were hardly indifferent to the agonies of the city. Perhaps they offered nothing quite like Father Divine's feasts,[4] but they did in varying degrees attempt to help the hurting and the hungry. Paul Scherer, who was no fan of the social gospel,[5] proposed that Holy Trinity Church establish a dental clinic for the neighborhood.[6] George Buttrick insisted that Christ was to be found among the poor.[7] His Madison Avenue Presbyterian Church provided one of the most comprehensive programs of social service available anywhere in the city: there was a sewing project, in which women came to the church and used sewing machines provided by the congregation to make articles of clothing, and besides being compensated for their work they were permitted to take the finished goods home for their families or leave them at the church for distribution to other victims of the depression; children were sent to summer camp at no cost to their families; beds in a nearby hospital were reserved and then filled (on a first-come, first-served basis) with patients who had no other way to pay for their own medical care; and loans for parishioners who were facing bankruptcy were undersigned by the church.[8] Buttrick himself had plans for an East Side housing project on his desk.[9]

Ralph Sockman was convinced that the only way a church in the 1930s could lay claim to any authority was to master human welfare.[10] And Fosdick, who had envisioned Riverside as a "seven-day-a-week" proposition right from the start, said that only "stupidity" prevented churches from developing a ministry for the whole week.[11] He claimed that the virtue of Riverside's ministry lay more in the $225,000 worth of jobs the church found for unemployed persons during the first three years of the depression[12] than in the crowds that overflowed Riverside's nave on Sunday mornings.[13]

Yet Fosdick and his three most prominent Manhattan colleagues were known precisely because of their preaching. Sunday worship was built by theme and liturgical structure around the sermon. Fosdick preached for upwards of thirty-five minutes each week, his sermon manuscripts (typed and double-spaced) running to twelve or thirteen pages. Sockman's sermons dominated the order of worship and defined his ministry at Christ Church. Scherer began his work at Holy Trinity by claiming that a recovery of preaching was needed to revitalize the church.[14] Buttrick and his staff at Madison Avenue Presbyterian led four services every Sunday—a youth service at 9:25, and preaching services at eleven, four, and eight o'clock—in addition to a mid-week service on Wednesday.[15]

So they did not, even amid the horrors of hunger and homelessness, see a diminished importance for preaching. But they did want some changes to be made.[16] Fosdick told a Yale audience in 1924 that preaching had to become biblical again, and he proposed a new model for doing that, based on the premise that the Bible reveals the unchanging verities of human experience in changing categories of thought.[17] The sermon, he said, should inspire people to "reproduce a life."[18] By focusing on life situations and human problems, he wrote in an influential 1929 article, the preacher can best relate the word of biblical experience to his listeners' experiences and be sure he is "bowling down their alley."[19]

Ralph Sockman took that principle and turned it into a proverb—a preacher's authority, he said, lies not in claiming to come from God but in giving evidence that he gets to people.[20] If that sounds as if sermons were to be hammered out on the anvil of popular appeal, not even Buttrick was distressed: in our age, preaching should exalt a man's individual worth,[21] Buttrick's Beecher lectures assert. He saw more than that in preaching,[22] but he agreed there was at least that to be stressed.

Such concerns became vital homiletical issues with the enormous social and economic pressures of the thirties. All four of these pulpiteers agreed that they were preaching in a new age. Sockman suggested that Manhattan's new skyline was the symbol of the change. "Metropolitan society has become an aggregation of towering financial successes rising to a height never dreamed of by our fathers, but the little folk alongside seem to serve only as areaways for the favored few."[23] That Fosdick took such symbolism seriously also shows in the opening lines of his first sermon at Riverside. "Amid the impressiveness and beauty of this sanctuary, it behooves us all to remember that Christianity began in a carpenter shop. The natural affiliations of the gospel of Jesus are with lowly places and humble men."[24] And the message of the Church in that context, he said, is that "nothing matters . . . except the things that lead men to abundant life."[25]

In any age, the reality of the city forces a confrontation between the loftiest and the lowliest:[26] there the homeless must huddle in the shadow of a Christian congregation's magnificent new home; there the Church must confront the obvious disparity between the reactions of the rich and the poor to the biblical promise of "abundant" life; there the Church must identify with greatest clarity those "things" which lead to abundance. From Paul Scherer, the message was clear:

> It never has been and never will be the place of the organized church
> as such to drive out slavery or war or poverty or industrial injustice.
> That's the job of Christians; and when the church presumes to take it
> over she adulterates and complicates her own timeless message.[27]

That was two weeks after Riverside opened.

On the Sunday before Riverside's first service, George Buttrick had warned the congregation at the Madison Avenue Presbyterian Church that some things may appear to signify abundant life and yet in fact may be cruel deceptions. "A church whose eyes are set upon buildings or prestige or any form of earthly power will have no eyes for God. An industrial order that . . . seeks gold and oppresses the poor is not likely to see God as He goes quietly to His new cross."[28] In succeeding weeks, Buttrick declared that "the real redemption is the redemption that will save the whole self." He insisted that better transit, old age pensions, and similar social needs had to be connected to the saving truth of the Gospel. To attend to "social schemes" without the saving Word would be "like swallowing a pill to escape an earthquake."[29] Yet "in a time of suffering and crisis, two prime duties are laid on the Church. One duty is to quicken compassion so that suffering may be cancelled; the other is to strengthen the reserves of faith lest crisis should breed despair."[30]

There was not much doubt that faith was fighting despair. Within a year of the stock market crash there were already 300,000 New Yorkers out of work.[31]

CHAPTER IV
A CRISIS OF CONFIDENCE

Of the four most prominent pulpiteers to be heard on Sundays in New York, Ralph Sockman was surely the most optimistic about prospects that the crisis could be weathered and despair be defeated. "Jesus would not have been content to save souls and leave cities rotten," he said.[1] He was less timid than Scherer about embracing promising "social schemes" and less timid than Buttrick to trust human resources to carry the day. When President Hoover met with leading bankers in the first week of October, 1930 to enlist their support for his economic program, Sockman found the appeal to be "born not merely of engineering insight but of fundamental religious faith." In a time of social crisis, Sockman said, religion serves two valuable purposes—it helps "to stabilize our citizenry" and "to reawaken the spirit of enterprise and investment."[2]

The truth is that Sockman saw the early depression period as a crisis not of economics but of confidence. On October 19, 1930, according to *The New York Times*, he told his congregation that the "world wide business depression is basically a thing of the mind's creation. . . . The trouble with our world is not that it has lost money, but that it has lost confidence. . . . Religious forces will have to give the answer."[3] He blamed the relative lack of "patience and fortitude" for public complaints in the 1930s and said that similar conditions would have occasioned far less lament "in the days of our fathers."[4] He hinted that if conventional churches could not find ways to restore the people's confidence, alternate religious agencies would be devised to do so.[5] He saw no point in a church's appeal to "superhuman forces." Instead, his prescription for the mainline church was to "demonstrate its divine authority by showing its mastery of human welfare," to forego its posture as "a divinely appointed executive" and seek status as "a democratically recognized expert in things moral and religious." More to the point, Sockman said that each church "must set out to discover its duties rather

than to defend its doctrines."[6] Generally speaking, he found most "doctrines" out-dated and indefensible.   "Even if we could restore the
old-fashioned beliefs in divine authorities, we could not guarantee
obedience in our democratic age."[7] So the ministry of the Church, from
Sockman's perspective in the early thirties, must be practical and utilitarian.   Theology has to have a "useful purpose" he told his
congregation.[8] And the people need less criticism of their moral efforts
and more encouragement—perhaps "some old-fashioned doses of hero
worship" and sincere romanticism would "revive their spirits."[9] He had
written in 1924 that Christians needed a better composite of faith and
human effort; they could look to Jesus, he said, as the "perfect balance"
of the two.[10] His sermons in the early thirties suggested the directions in
which the Christ-like example might be followed: take inventory of our
material wealth; see it as evidence of our power; rise courageously to the
challenges that have shaken our confidence.[11] In the autumn of 1930 and
into the spring of 1931, he was convinced that those human efforts would
succeed.

A. Justification by Faith

By the fall of 1931, the bloom of Sockman's optimism had
faded. He felt a new burden of responsibility upon his preaching—the
heaviest burden in his fourteen years at the church, he said—not so much
to "thunder against the ways of men" but rather to bring "pulpit light on
the ways of God."[12] And yet the character of his preaching did not
change; it still appealed to human effort as the way to carry this heavier
burden of human despair. In his final sermon for 1931, Sockman said the
Church has "to create a demand for Christ-like honesty and Christ-like
idealism."[13] The following Christmas he reminded his parishioners that
Christ remained their example: "He was master of himself in every
situation" and he can "impart" that self-mastery to others by his
example.[14] In no situation did Jesus admit defeat, nor should we.[15] If
anything, Sockman said, hard times may help us cultivate "larger and
better human resources" and may prod us to renew "our spiritual
resourcefulness."[16]

He admitted in the spring of 1932 that the optimism of
Pollyanna would not be enough to endure the depression,[17] and he
complained that the Church could achieve more if women played less
bridge and men less golf.[18] But he realized that not even the noblest
human efforts, not even the most rugged individualism, could promise to

break the grip of the depression, for the spectre of unemployment was haunting society's best.

It is one thing for a nation to have "a few million ignorant idle; it is quite another thing to have several million educated idle."[19] He knew that there were limits to human nature's ability to tolerate the mood of the depression and, if only by wishful thinking, he offered his city a straw in the wind: "the rebound toward hope and cheer is upon us."[20]

By the spring of 1933, his optimism was buoyed again. His earlier laments about the lack of fortitude and patience were set aside, and he applauded the people for having manifested "a magnificent morale through these years of depression."[21] Much of his renewed confidence can be attributed to his enthusiasm for the early efforts of the recently inaugurated president, Franklin Delano Roosevelt.

> In two dramatic weeks we Americans seem to have rediscovered ourselves. . . . The church should rise to the occasion and show a magnanimity to match the mood of the hour. . . . We have begotten a war-time spirit of cooperation without a wartime spirit of hatred.[22]

In short, Sockman's refreshed hope was the result of human accomplishments in the political structures of American democracy. To those who feared that the new president's emergency policies were an imposition of dictatorial rule and a subversion of democracy, Sockman suggested that common sense be used: the national emergency required more efficiency than the traditional constitutional checks and balances allowed; the gospels reveal Jesus to be a man of "healthy, rugged common sense"; and His example could serve Americans well. "Never more than now do we need the good old-fashioned grace of common sense to serve us."[23]

All of which points toward a general suspicion about Sockman's preaching during the early thirties: namely, that human attitudes and human efforts are the forces that foster a personal sense of well-being in the world; for they are the forces which sustain the assurance that one has found a proper place for oneself. "We must demonstrate our divine claims," he said, "not by the apostolic hands laid on us but by our ability to lay helping hands on the world's burdens."[24]

Doctrinally, it amounted to a version of justification by works, more akin to sixteenth-century humanism than to sixteenth-century Reformation theology. Jesus was redeemer by example, and salvation was defined as a recovery of the resources of hope and enthusiasm which are endemic to the human spirit and are energized by human achievement. "Salvation comes to us only through trying to save others," he said at Christ Church in 1935.[25] Jesus' way was to overcome evil with good, Sockman held, and by His example Christians must do the same.[26] "The forces of good must seek to surpass, and not merely to supress [sic] the forces of evil. . . . Unless Christianity can generate more zeal than communism or naziism or militarism, it will retreat before these rivals."[27]

When the world finds itself in the grip of fear, the Church must "counterattack this contagion of fear by a contagion of courage."[28] When man's powers are "untamed" we must find ways to control them.[29] Then will persons be in a just, righteous relationship with themselves, with others, and with God.

Though sorely tested in the depths of the depression, Sockman's confidence in the power of human effort remained strong. And by the mid-thirties he apparently felt that his optimism had been vindicated. According to *The New York Times*, his Christmas sermon for 1935 "declared that in America this would 'be the gayest holiday season'" in six years, and he spoke of the Church's new duty to lead people toward deeper forms of joy in the "post-depression world."[30] The nation and the world had survived economic calamity, and the human spirit in which he never completely lost hope had endured.

> The raw material of human life, I believe, is just as sound and healthy as it was before this depression. . . . With the proper kind of leadership, with local laboratories for the proper guidance of our ideals, with faith again that man is master of his destiny in large part, I am sure that we can make the manpower of tomorrow a fit match for the horsepower of our machines.[31]

Just as the hardships of the depression carried spiritual as well as financial portents, so the recoveries of the post-depression period offered spiritual as well as financial promise. Sockman did not shrink from the prospect of seeing "spiritual rewards" manifest themselves in the "material realm."[32] In fact, he found theological merit in such a notion; for, he said, Jesus had "so merged the kingdom of heaven with earthly experiences that the boundaries became blurred."[33]

But favorable economic prospects were hardly the only signs of promise to be found. The reins of New York City government were in different, more honest, hands; a stronger sense of social justice and ethical practice prevailed among business leaders; women were making positive contributions in the business world. In short, Sockman felt that a Manhattan preacher had many reasons to be optimistic. Elsewhere, he could point to the displays of human courage in "the brave resistance of those German pastors who have defied the un-Christian demands of the Nazi regime."[34] Altogether, there were more than enough signs for

Sockman to praise "the inherent soundness of common people" and to reassure his listeners that "the world must get better, for evil will eventually defeat itself."[35]

Therefore, well into the late thirties, Sockman continued to preach a doctrine of justification by works which incorporated optimism about human progress, confidence in the power of such human qualities as courage, and the conviction that heaven and earth constituted one realm of experience and promise.

But during the late thirties came a discernible shift in his views, as his preaching began to suggest that perhaps the lines between heaven and earth were not so blurred after all. In the spring of 1934 he had spoken of religion as an essential component of culture, to the extent that one cannot be integrated into modern society if one remains aloof from religion: "to live without prayer is to be as far behind the times as to live without electricity."[36] By the spring of 1936 he had begun to fret about this intimacy between Christ and culture. "The Church is too much the echo of the crowd and too little of the voice of God. We must guard against the trend toward class consciousness in religion."[37] The Church was losing not its popularity but its authority: those outside it were indifferent rather than hostile; those inside were mostly "faint unbelievers" who recite "casual creeds."[38]

Sockman even claimed to have detected a doctrinal flaw in much preaching of his day, and he laid the blame for the Church's troubles there. Pulpits, he said, "have largely replaced theology with such modern subjects as sociology and psychology"; those pursuits are "a vital part of religion," he agreed, "but they are not the heart of the gospel" or "the center of its power."[39]

> In this so-called land of the free, the pulpit is not always the home of the brave. Too often our utterances only confirm the prejudices and pet ideas of our pew-holders. We ministers, in our efforts to say the timely and popular thing, are prone to veer with the changing winds of current opinion. The true prophet is not a weather-vane of worldliness but a guidepost toward godliness. If the church would regain its popular prestige, it must show that it can bring a higher power to bear on our human problems.[40]

Whereas Sockman had earlier thought it enough to justify a claim of divine authority by demonstrating effective human service, he began to see the need for churches to "recover their divine standing in order to keep from being swept off their feet by the various secular interests which seek to use them."[41] This recovery of a "sense of divine authority," he said, is the Church's "most difficult task," for it must undertake the recovery in an age when the claims of scientists are treated with the deference reserved for "experts" but the claims of religion are relegated to a realm where "one guess is as good as another."[42]

His solution to the dilemma was to reawaken our "'need of divine redemption'" by making "moral duties desirable."[43] But a gospel of "airy ideals" would not make that happen[44]; rather, he said, we need "a renewed study of . . . vows and fixed rules . . . a strengthening of standards"[45] and "strict disciplines."[46] To drive home his point, Sockman resorted to what had to be in those pre-war days the ultimate illustration: Hitler demands everything from his people and gets it; the Church demands nothing of its people, and gets it.[47]

From a doctrinal perspective, what Sockman did in this shift of emphasis was not to abandon his theological reliance on a version of justification by works. That remained essentially in place. His switch was to turn away from proclaiming a gospel of idealism and romantic hope to preaching the law without an apparent context of grace—it was still justification by works, simply under a revised rubric. "You never do your best work unless you do it with a sense that you're failing to do something better. The best work is always done in the shadow of an eluding ideal. . . . The Church . . . exists to tell us to seek something impossible."[48]

In effect, then, Sockman's turn in the late thirties to proclaiming the law fit very well with his earlier sense of optimism about human works. He did not counsel Christian perfection, but rather granted that "as long as you are pulling up to [Christ], I think you can keep the title Christian."[49] He saw a mutual link between our work on behalf of Christ and His on behalf of us: we are called both to be "followers" and "forerunners" of Christ, Sockman said, for Christ will follow after our efforts.[50] Our "fortitude, fidelity, and patience" will find a way through and as long as we "hold faithfully to the landmarks of decency" we will have our trust in God's guidance restored.[51] In the meantime, the Church must lift up "the high moral absolutes until men work out ways of attaining them."[52] Stern—but not hard—rules[53] which embody the Christian principles of brotherly love "form the basic solution of the problems of the world."[54] The living of those principles may impose tremendous burdens on Christ's followers: indeed, some have died that we might be free; but "the privilege of being a Christian was bought with a price . . . and [there is] the price we have to pay to keep it."[55]

Though he understood that the human search for God and the human effort to perform the works of God's law lay at the base of the Christian religion, Sockman did assert that our "search for God is called out by some reality. . . . God is the hunger as well as the food."[56] It is still our human responsibility "to get close enough to Jesus [to] feel the magnetic pull of the man."[57] But at the very least, "we have been cured of our overweening confidence in our ability to save ourselves by cleverness and secular science."[58] Some revival of "the basic doctrine of divine sovereignty" is a necessity, Sockman said at the end of 1940.[59]

And yet if the theology from Sockman's pulpit was not Pelagianism, it was not neo-orthodoxy either. He rejected with disdain what he called in a March 1941 sermon "a German brand of theology 'which makes God a dictator with man helpless in His hand.'" Sockman was willing to accept the "corrective" touch of an "emphasis on the sovereignty of God" but in the long run he considered such teaching to be a threat to democracy because it discounted human reason and freedom.[60]

Sockman's willingness to tolerate such doctrinal "correctives" is manifest throughout his sermons. Ultimately, he admitted, our only hope to solve the human dilemma or to stay out of war is to rely on God's "infinite grace and mercy."[61] Yet these adjustments to the prevailing doctrinal pattern of his sermons do not alter the general course of the theology from his pulpit; basically, he preached a version of justification by works, rather than by faith, through the decade.

This reliance on human works and human effort seems to have victimized him: especially in periods of mounting economic challenge and international political crises, his views were subject to uncertainty and inconsistency. In September of 1931 he expressed the hope that hard times might lead people to cultivate "larger and better human resources" and "spiritual resourcefulness."[62] But six months later he recognized that financial pressures had not brought families together but rather had been destructive to family life.[63] In the fall of 1939 he admitted

> Some things I believed even five weeks ago I no longer can hold. I had come to the belief that the church of Christ had now reached such strength and conviction on war that it could prevent a large-scale conflict again. . . . I had reached the belief that the German leaders were conscientious in their objections to communism and that they were holding their people in subjection because of the fear of the communist alternative. . . . Yes my faith has been bombed at some high points. . . . But . . . the foundations still hold. I still believe in a sovereign God who reigns by justice.[64]

Even that profession of faith in divine sovereignty, however, remained ill-defined and relatively weak amid his broader reliance on the human responsibility to work out the terms of justice.

Sockman's link between his doctrine of works and his political optimism was apparent both in its dreams and in its disappointments. He saw evidence of human progress in Japan's willingness "to justify her Manchurian policy before the bar of world opinion" in 1932.[65] He remained confident in 1937 that twenty more years of "peace education" would build a "real and lasting peace" on earth.[66] He expressed hope that Chamberlain's visit to Munich would "reverse the landslide [of war] to the way of peace."[67] But in his final sermon for 1940, he admitted that appeasement did not work.[68]

In March, 1938, he told the Christ Church congregation that no government could defy the people if Protestant and Roman Catholic Christians would join hands in a "'determined stand for peace.'"[69] Early in 1939, he said a call for peace had to be issued by persons "powerful enough now to be above suspicion of fear" and he named the president of the United States and the pope as the "only two such personalities" available.[70] Interestingly enough in late 1939 President Roosevelt did convene a national panel of Roman Catholic, Jewish, and Protestant leaders[71] to seek a way to peace. But on the first Sunday in January, 1940, Sockman spoke gloomily of the prospects for such a panel's success. "The God in whom we of the Hebrew-Christian tradition believe is not the God recognized in Tokyo, Moscow, or the Berlin Chancellory. Consequently religious sanctions of morality do not reach across war frontiers. There is no common ground for moral appeal."[72] A year later, in January of 1941, the former appeal returned: he told his congregation that "representative leaders of all religious faiths" should be convened to develop a policy for the peace that will follow the war.[73]

Sometimes Sockman drew unclear distinctions, as when he declared that "Christ Himself was the supreme example of moderation" and urged his listeners to follow Him; and in the same sermon he warned of the dangers of lukewarmness.[74] Sometimes he flatly contradicted himself, as he did when he followed a sermon late in 1938, in which he advised his parishioners that we have to compromise some of Christ's principles in order to live in the real world,[75] with a sermon in late 1940, in which he declared "We are lost when the church begins to temporize with expediency."[76]

One way to comprehend Sockman's confusions, apart from the shifts in perspective that come to all persons with time and changing experience, is to attribute them to work habits in sermon preparation. He travelled and preached widely, and his sermon manuscripts reveal that he worked on the run. One could almost chronicle his journeys by following the trail of hotel stationery on which he made his sermon notes.[77] Typically he would transform his notes into a full manuscript on Saturdays, writing well into the night before retiring around 2:00 a.m. Sunday. Once a manuscript was written, it was rarely revised.[78]

He was not unaware of the problems that such work habits could create. "Preaching often spreads itself too thin. By hasty, ill-considered utterances, based perhaps on insufficient data, the pulpit often forfeits the respect of careful thinkers."[79] Perhaps his warning was, in part, self-directed.

But another way to account for the inconsistencies, the fluctuations of hope and despair, the shift from idealism to legalism in his sermons during the thirties, is to recognize that there was a fundamental doctrinal problem in the theology from his pulpit on Sundays in New York. The insight of Reformation theology to see faith as a gift is almost totally absent from Sockman's message. God's grace is an "extra goodness which God puts into every situation above what man can expect or imagine"—in other words grace is a codicil rather than the covenant, it is an amendment rather than a new constitution. The entrance to salvation is not by the offer of divine grace but by "earthly discipline." The gospels portray earth as a classroom where those disciplines are learned to prepare us "for heavenly living."[80] Even when the human relationship to God is spoken of as "trust," the trusting seems to connote human endeavor rather than a response to divine grace: the very existence of Christ, he was heard to say at the Christmas service for 1940, is dependent on the individual's willingness to believe;[81] only those are dependent on Christ, he wrote in 1936, who allow themselves to be served by Him and who admit they cannot get along without Him.[82]

There was one important moment in the mid-thirties when Sockman did lead his congregation back to the piety of the sixteenth-century. It was on November 22, 1936, the third anniversary service of Christ Church, when a Russian reredos was dedicated in the sanctuary. The elegant altar screen, originally fashioned in the 1500s and recently brought to New York from the Church of the Czar in old St. Petersburg, was a fitting symbol of the breach that had opened between the doctrinal principles of the Reformation and one popular Protestant preacher's practice. In his dedicatory sermon for the occasion, Sockman was reported to have said "I should like to see the church of today put less emphasis on preaching and more on religion. In the early church one sat in the presence of symbols till one felt oneself attuned to the truth."[83] So he yearned for a doctrine both older and more authoritative than what lay in the classical Protestant standards.

B. The Authority of Scripture

His church and his ministry both seem to have been built on a foundation of theological tradition that differed markedly from Reformation formulae. A glance at his sermon manuscripts, nevertheless, suggests that his preaching was built upon some commitment to the authority of Scripture. Every long-hand pulpit composition starts with a biblical text. And there is no reason to doubt that Sockman saw himself as a biblical preacher. Robert Bruce Hibbard, author of the only doctoral dissertation so far on Sockman's work, sees him in those terms. "Dr. Sockman is a biblical preacher . . . Through preaching he attempts to encourage his listeners to turn to the Bible and familiarize themselves with its adaptability for today's needs."[84]

Certainly Sockman would not yield the territory called "biblical preaching" exclusively to fundamentalists. But he was reluctant to debate the matter. Back in the early twenties, while Fosdick was still at New York's First Presbyterian Church and was embroiled in the Fundamentalists' struggle within the Presbyterian denomination, Sockman found himself drawn into the debate. On May 6, 1923, he delivered a sermon at Madison Avenue Methodist Episcopal Church, using Matthew 1:21 as his text. The following day, an account of the sermon—"a rather sensational account" in Sockman's view—appeared in the *New York Tribune*.[85] The newspaper reported that Sockman had repudiated the doctrines of the Virgin Birth and the verbal inspiration of Scripture, but Sockman's own interpretation both of his words and their intent found no such repudiations at all. Rather, he believed that such doctrines were not "the real fundamentals of Christianity" at all; the fundamentals of any religion he said, involve neither its sources nor its ideals but "the means which it provides for obtaining the aims of that ideal."

The episode suggests that the authority of Scripture for Sockman, at least in the twenties, was functional in character—limited to its usefulness in helping promote the cause of Christian ideals. He sent the same message to a wider audience in *The Suburbs of Christianity*, which was published the following year. "The Bible is an authority, but it does not ask us to take its word on the divinity of Christ. It simply invites us to use its method in the laboratory of experience and find out the truth for ourselves."[86] That point of view persisted into the thirties— neither "logical demonstration" nor "external authority" offers a true test of the reliability of Scripture, he wrote in 1931; the only valid measure of the authority of the Bible comes in "the response it stirs in human experience."[87] True moral authority, he declared on the first Sunday of 1931, is demonstrated not by some claim of "divine dictation but by the record of human service which is established.[88] And the authority of Christ becomes recognizable when we see how clearly He conforms to our experience of ourselves. For example, a man of common sense could discover in the gospels that Jesus was a man of "healthy, rugged common sense," too.[89] In such ways, Sockman felt the Bible could be made amenable to the twentieth-century.[90]

That there were dangers in such trends of thought was not lost on him. Late in 1934 he expressed concern that Christians had drifted away from their biblical base.

> While our forefathers may have made a fetish of the Bible by considering it too sacred to study intelligently, so many of their sons are making nothing of the Bible at all. . . . Many preachers, especially the younger, seem to steer away from scriptural preaching and give topical sermons on all sorts of secular subjects . . . but very little of the Bible.[91]

In such a situation, the Church becomes more "the echo of the crowd" than "the voice of God," Sockman feared.[92] But, he insisted, there is a remedy: return to Bible study; "get back to it and it will cast its own spell."[93] Then reason will prevail in religion, opposing points of view will be tolerated, and still the confidence of religious truth will not be impaired—as long as in trying to see all sides of a question, Christians do not neglect to decide upon one course of action[94] and as long as the contradictions within biblical details about Jesus' birth and resurrection do not deter us from the truly important contributions of Scripture "for the Christian values Jesus gave to the world are important and factual details are not."[95]

This reinforces the judgment that Sockman's view of biblical authority in the early twenties was fundamentally unchanged in the mid-thirties: namely that Scripture is useful in promoting Christian values and ideals, and that its authority is a function of its success in this moral promotion.

As he continued to fret over the decline in the Church's authority, Sockman perceived a direct connection with the decline in biblical authority in churches and in homes.[96] Citing Paul's advice to Timothy, Sockman said we need "a good spiritual foundation" on which to build the future.[97] So, for countless decades, our ancestors started each day with a passage of Scripture, meditating on their own sins and recognizing the Bible's authority over our lives in its ability to probe into our faults with forgiveness. Nowadays, Sockman said, we begin each morning with the radio news or the morning paper, which prods us to ruminate on others' sins and thereby lose the biblical touch upon our lives at home. Moreover, unless we imitate the churchly habits of our forebears, we will lose the biblical touch in our worship life also. For twenty centuries, Sockman argued, the pulpit has stood on the authority of the Bible—and that remains an honorable position to occupy.[98] "The preacher who stands with the church behind him and his ear to the Bible . . . is getting something from God."[99] After all, the Bible is "a record of man's search for God."[100] What spawned Hitler, Sockman declared in the fall of 1941, was "the failure to believe in the Bible and the authority of God."[101] So he urged the Church to focus less of its attention on peripheral developments in current thought and more on the center of the gospel—which is salvation.[102] He recommended a recovery of biblical preaching, the pattern for which he found in Fosdick's approach: direct sermons toward objects, rather than using them to discuss subjects; start sermons with life situations and then guide the congregation to biblical sources for solutions to those life-situations.[103] Then, he said, the Bible becomes the Word of God for us at the depths of our being[104] and not just as some imposition of absolute rules about moral behavior or about the end of the world.[105]

That raises an interesting point. In the late thirties and early forties, during the months of deepening European war, Sockman was exhorting the Church to return to some basic standards and fixed rules. Yet his brand of legalism seems to have been more fundamentally moral than biblical.

> The gospels unite in presenting Christ's claim to a totalitarian authority. . . . Yet Christ did not rest his claims to authority on himself. . . . He had so completely surrendered himself to God that he felt the divine spirit had surrendered to him. . . divine authority, a way was open. It was the road of mora. To those who sincerely and earnestly sought the certainty of Jesus' obedience.[106]

The authority of Christ, in other words, is to be found in the law rather than in the gospel.

But it is the law which is determined in our own experience to be authoritative—that is the law we follow. So biblical authority is subordinate to and an instrument of human experience, in Sockman's view. The laws to be followed, apparently, are those that comport favorably with one's experience. To the degree that Scripture promotes moral values and inspires obedience, it acquires authority. But only to that degree.

Therefore, in Sockman's approach, the Bible is a secondary authority with derivative strength at best. Despite his longing for a return to biblical preaching, Sockman in the thirties did not endorse the Protestant premise called *sola scriptura*.

C. The "Freedom" of the Will

There is not much doubt that Ralph Sockman found himself theologically least compatible with the tenets of traditional Calvinism. He considered the coordinate doctrines of total depravity and predestination to be vestiges of "the dark medieval era."[107] It was no recommendation, as far as he was concerned, that some twentieth-century Calvinists had retained them; for to Sockman that theological package was a form of determinism, and he rejected every form of determinism on the ground that the worth and dignity of the individual must be protected.[108] The supernatural, divine determinism of medieval theology and the naturalistic, atheistic determinism of intellectual thought in the 1920s and 1930s, he believed, were akin in their violation of human integrity: modern scientific determinism treats human existence as the mere chance development of the collision of atoms, the plaything of "impersonal forces"; medieval theological determinism imprisons and oppresses humanity in a divine autocracy.[109]

Either way, human freedom is demeaned.

And for Sockman, the crucial theological issue was human freedom. No fixed destiny or oppressive heavenly decree determines our situation or our service, he believed. Only in freedom do creative and redemptive powers operate. Thus, Sockman affirmed that "we can make ourselves love,"[110] we can create brotherly love "by an act of will,"[111] and we enter eternal life "by way of earthly discipline rather than heavenly fiat."[112] What we freely and obediently will to do, in other words, creates our eternal destiny.

Yet, before the thirties had dawned, Sockman was careful to say that human freedom is not absolute. He agreed with the critique of late nineteenth- and early twentieth-century theological liberalism—that it had gone too far in relying on human initiative and had "distracted the minds of men from seeking the 'mysteries of God.'"[113]   Salvation, Sockman wrote, cannot be "simplified into a combination of intelligence, effort, and adjustment."[114]   Something more than free will is involved, something conveyed by firmer theological categories, something that cannot be set aside just because we find it too heavy.[115]   The ambiguities of human freedom must be faced, he confessed. The mysterious ways of God offer to guide us to our redemption: we are free to follow or forsake those ways; were we to follow and obey this divine authority, we could find salvation.   On the one hand, obedience cannot be guaranteed, let alone compelled;[116] on the other hand, "authority" and "obedience" are not merely the "words" we use to label the burden of human responsibility "by which we can work our way out of the moral and religious chaos of modernity."[117] Therefore, without freedom of the will we cannot be free; so the Calvinists are wrong. But freedom alone does not make us free; so liberalism is wrong. New formulae are needed to join human freedom and the mystery of divine guidance, Sockman said. "The time has come for the verbal coins of the older theological preaching to be restamped in the mint of modern experience."[118]

Toward that end, Sockman offered his own contribution. He began to place his own stamp on the doctrine of the "freedom" of the will—that is, the relative capacity of the human will to initiate, or have an effective impact upon, human reconciliation with God, redemption, salvation, deliverance, freedom.

Sockman understood the human psyche in terms of two categories: the imagination and the will. The "practices in action," which are the efforts of the will, are shaped by the "pictures in the mind," which are the province of the imagination.[119] The imagination is stronger than the will,[120] and therefore Jesus came to convert not only the will but also the imagination.[121] This conversion occurs, says Sockman, with an act of human will which allows Christ to take over our imaginations.

> We must start as did Peter by surrendering our wills to him. . . . As
> we try to imitate Christ's goodness, we come to marvel at his
> amazing power . . . his unruffled calm and poise . . . his intimacy
> with his heavenly Father . . . his authority. There is no realm of
> human experience where he is not master.[122]

In this way Sockman put some distance between his own position and that of "many easy-going good persons" who declare that the answer to all of our social problems is to follow the Golden Rule.[123] Such a prescription, he said, overlooks the fact that it takes a certain amount of imagination to know what persons would wish to have done toward themselves "if they were in the other fellow's place."[124]

He was convinced that the free human will in itself could not bring about deliverance. "Evil habits are not best overcome by frontal attacks of the will. The more one sets his teeth and focuses his mind upon them, the more entrenched they become in his thought and desire."[125] In order to act with "Christ-like courage" in the service of public rather than selfish interests,[126] individuals and groups need more than will power: they need the "moral power" which only religion supplies.[127]

But the will must take the initiative, invoke its "strong ally," and use what the imagination "pictures" to envision the practical actions that imitate Christ. Thus does the circularity of Sockman's argument finally depend on an act of the human will after all: only when the imagination quickens the will can one absorb the practical directions of imitating Christ; only when Christ quickens the imagination does the will receive power to follow His way; but only when the will invites Christ to come into the imagination does His power quicken the imagination.

Such serendipitous patterns of thought about the relationship between the human will and the saving power of God in Christ represented for Sockman a real departure from the heady days of the previous decade when bold human initiative was deemed able to master every kind of adversity: in the twenties, he said, "confident man was crying for mastery"; in the thirties, "subdued man is crying for a master."[128] Sockman preferred that people be mastered by some legitimate heroes to whom they might romantically turn.[129] He hoped they might find a model for good will in "the enduring attitude of the Divine Creator to his creatures"[130] and try to organize their own good will rather than dissipate it in bursts of spasmodic sentiment. Yet he knew that other masters were clamoring for the commitment of people. And he knew that Fascists were finding a responsive chord among those who were "looking for leadership rather than personal freedom."[131] In his Palm Sunday sermon for 1933, Sockman denounced Hitler's effort to nationalize the German Church, and appealed for a commitment of free human wills to a nobler Master. "No man ever became a poorer father to his family by putting the principles of Jesus first in his life. No citizen ever became a poorer patriot through his conscientious adherence to Christ."[132]

What becomes clear—from the optimistic twenties, through the depressed early thirties, and well into the political tensions of mid-decade—is that shifts of theological emphasis may be adduced by external circumstances, but the fundamental doctrinal orientation remains the same for Sockman. It is still the free human will that chooses by whom it will be mastered, to whom it will listen, and in whose paths it will follow.

This is not to say that the human will can prevail against every tide. Willful dictators, for instance, will ultimately fall because they cannot reverse the evolution of civilization toward greater freedom.[133] Human beings have a destiny, and our freedom is to cooperate with that destiny:[134] to derive zest from its limitations, to challenge the frustrations those limits impose, and if necessary to accept those limitations as an encouragement to do other things better.[135]

It was this side of Sockman's position that received heavier emphasis as the decade lengthened. He began to recognize more significant constraints on the freedom of the will, allowing for example that while we cannot blame our troubles on the devil we can look for the successors of Satan in scientific laboratories and economic forces.[136] The prospect of freedom, he declared in a March 1940 sermon, is found not within ourselves but in a loyalty higher than ourselves. And the threat to freedom lies in surrendering to "loyalties which bring out the baser elements of our natures," which in turn may make groups more immoral than the individuals who constitute them.[137] Theology can protect against the threat and promote true freedom, he said at the end of 1940, by reviving the concept of divine sovereignty[138] which includes the recognition that "even governments must submit" their allegiance to God.[139]

However, that nuance did not displace from Sockman's preaching his prior concerns to safeguard the freedom of the will. The first step to deliverance, he said in his New Year's Eve 1939 sermon, is to "open your will to the Lord's voice."[140] He cautioned against the rising "spirit of fatalism" which is bred by stresses like those of the late thirties and early forties.[141] And he warned that any renewed concept of divine sovereignty should not discount "man's reason and freedom" or endanger democracy.[142]

Sockman does seem to have been bent on saying that a basic structure of destiny exists in the universe, one that can withstand our loss of confidence in humanity and even a loss of faith in God. So, in the spring of 1941: "There is a run on the bank of God. . . . God gives us freedom, and some men [using] their freedom can burn up a great deal, but the framework of the universe is fireproof."[143] The initiator in the process of salvation remains the human will. But people "exist in a frame of reference which is more than human and are governed by a reality that transcends themselves and are supported by an administration which guarantees the triumphs of personal and spiritual values."[144] The will can be enslaved, even be in bondage, but this is an inner captivity to habit: a declaration of the independence of the will can be accomplished by "patient endurance and discipline."[145] For Sockman, an apt illustration of the relationship between the freedom of the will and the structure of human destiny can be found in one's attempt to master the piano. "I may own the piano . . . but I am not free in the sense that I can make the piano do my bidding . . . unless I by patient discipline master the finger exercises."[146] So the structure of the universe cannot be rebuilt by the force of the human will, but the will can set itself free from enslaving inner forces and master the harmony by which the universe endures.

Sockman preached with that kind of confidence on Sundays in New York as 1941 drew toward a close. He had come through the decade to see a balance between the freedom of the will and the providence of God. The sovereignty of God and the sanctity of the individual man, he said in November of 1941, are twin pillars that must ever be preserved. The former relegates rival deities like the state to a subordinate position while the latter "guarantees the treatment of man as ends in themselves and not as pawns in the political game of government or as the tools of tyrants."[147]

In the early thirties, Sockman might have been more concerned that the Calvinists' God was the noisome tyrant. In the late thirties and early forties, tyrants were more obviously human—and a sovereign God had become doctrinally more desirable after all. Still, the human will was free to choose its preferred master, free to serve the lord of its choice, free to pursue false messiahs, free to obey the disciplines of truth.

CHAPTER V
THE DANGERS OF FALSE HOPE
AND FALSE DESPAIR

Early in 1940, a group of students from Union Theological Seminary became regular worshippers at the Evangelical Lutheran Church of the Holy Trinity, and regular listeners of the sermons preached by Paul Scherer. After a service one Sunday in New York, a member of the student group commented to Scherer, "You are neo-orthodox." Scherer replied, "Before neo-orthodoxy was, I am."[1]

It may have been his way of suggesting that he was so thoroughly schooled in the old orthodoxy that he needed no new version of it to lead him back. He had been taught systematic theology by Henry Eyster Jacobs, editor of *The Book of Concord* and stalwart expositor of Lutheran dogma.[2] And he was the fourth generation Lutheran preacher in the Scherer family line. For 136 consecutive years, orthodox Lutheran dogma had been preached by his father and grandfather, and great-grandfather before he came to Holy Trinity.[3]

It may also have been his way of suggesting that he was not a follower of theological or ecclesiastical fashion, and that his ministry did not fit the interpretive models one might use for other preachers and theologians. He did not trouble to identify himself with a contemporary theological camp, nor did he seek to dissociate himself from the traditions in which he was raised and trained. The kinds of controversies that draw popular attention to preachers never seemed to attach themselves to Scherer; the platforms that seemed to suit some of his colleagues never readily accommodated him.

Scherer hardly labored in obscurity. He certainly had a following beyond his own parish—due in part to the availability of his published works and in part to his radio ministry. Yet he never enjoyed the fame accorded Sockman, Buttrick, or Fosdick. He and Sockman were the supply preachers on Cadman's National Radio Pulpit; but Sockman was eventually offered the microphone alone, first as the regular summer replacement and then as the permanent preacher in 1936.

For thirteen years, from 1932 to 1945, Scherer was Fosdick's replacement during July and August on the live broadcasts of Sunday Vespers, while Fosdick relaxed in the cool comforts of the Maine coast.[4] Fosdick, Buttrick, and Sockman had all added their names to the roster of Lyman Beecher lecturers before Scherer was invited to New Haven: Buttrick, in fact, had already been there twice; and Fosdick had begged off repeated invitations to return.

So one might say that Scherer experienced the type of limited celebrity status which is granted to those whose names never rise on the marquee above second billing.

Meanwhile, his pastoral accomplishments were not without note. The Holy Trinity congregation grew quite remarkably during the thirties, largely (in Scherer's opinion) because of a program of home meetings and visitation which he helped to institute. From an attendance that averaged around 160 at the start of the thirties, Scherer was preaching to a congregation of nearly one thousand by the middle of the next decade.[5] That, apparently, was satisfaction enough for him: only rarely did he hint that he envied the more popular acclaim which his Manhattan comrades enjoyed.[6]

In any case, there was a different kind of distance—a quality, rather than the quantity of fame—that separated him from his more celebrated fellow-preachers. The double inheritance that fell to almost all of (non-Fundamentalist) Protestantism in the thirties probably had less impact on Scherer than it did on any of the others. That Scherer was not enamored with the social gospel is rather well-documented. Readers of his *Facts that Undergird Life* knew that in the mid-thirties he had deplored sermons which sought to put their first emphasis on social reform. "That kind of loose talk is a sharp blade which cuts humanity's throat. The hope of this world lies in the mind of Christ which only the redeemed can ever have."[7] In 1931, he was heard to say that redemption "is a matter of pedigree" rather than environment, and that changing a person's social or physical surroundings "does not change his spirit."[8] He did agonize over the plight of those whom the depression treated most severely: "God pity us . . . with the winter ahead," he said in the fall of 1931.[9] But it was prayerful rather than partisan compassion. In 1932 he expressed his pleasure with the shift in popular religion away from the premise that education and a sermon or two could produce the Kingdom of God,[10] and he expressed disdain for those who still felt that salvation is really a matter of being "dazzled by the beauty of a radiant ideal" for which Jesus is merely teacher and example.[11] In 1934, he sharpened the point.

> There is something inside the individual that has to happen first. I have no enthusiasm for any attempt to clean up 65th Street by hanging pictures on the walls of every apartment and repairing the wash-basins; I am saving my enthusiasm for the attempt to go straight at the heart of things and change men and women—after which presumably both the art and the plumbing will come in for some improvements.[12]

Not that many of his church members were desperate for material improvements, however. And that suggests there was something curious about his lack of enthusiasm for the gospel of wealth. The senior members of Holy Trinity were the upper-class, old money aristocracy,[13] and from his pulpit in the spring of 1930 Scherer held up a mirror before the congregation: "we're so comfortable. We are gasoline-propelled and fur-coated; steam-heated and electric-lighted; cunningly-upholstered and warm-bathed."[14] And in the winter of 1931, though some of his parishioners were unemployed, many enjoyed circumstances that were substantially unchanged by the economy's troubles.[15] Fifteen months later, the depression was at its lowest point, but Scherer doubted that his own church members were suffering very much.

> I am amused at *our* hardships which we set up before us and gaze at with such owl-like solemnity! . . . The mighty problem which confronts us, heroes that we are, is how to keep from being depressed on reduced incomes. Shame on us![16]

He was not unaware of the changes brought on by the surrounding economic calamity. From the twenties to the thirties, he observed, "our roseate vision of endless prosperity had turned a sickly grey."[17] He served among those who were protected from the depression's agonies by their wealth: yet that did not translate for him into the gospel of wealth. Six weeks after the dedication of Riverside Church, Scherer complained that Christianity too frequently joins hands with business "in a subtle alliance."[18] The threat, he said, comes from the willingness of religious forces to adopt the laws and practices of business as the tenets of faith. The evidence convinced him that "business has become a religion" with skyscrapers as its modern cathedrals:[19] those towers, he argued, soar to the sky as if to overcompensate for what humanity sees as its own "pygmy stature."[20] Contrary to Sockman, he could admit no connection between faith in God and material rewards on earth.[21] Two years later, the issue still troubled him: a concern for business is "childish," he said, when it is compared to the true message of salvation.[22]

Thus, impressed as Scherer was by the material promise of secular business or the social promise of reform-minded churchmen, he cast a jaundiced eye on claims of Christ-like power for the things of the earth.   Efforts to get clergy cooperation for a page of religious advertising, sponsored by willing patrons, appalled him.[23] He launched into enough jeremiads to be told that he was "too grim" in the pulpit at the same time as Ralph Sockman was earning his reputation as an insufferable optimist.[24] Such grimness seems to be a strange attitude for a man who once expressed his desire to edit a newspaper with all the news that is "true and honest and just and pure . . . lovely and of good of report."[25]

Ten years of economic worry and the crescendo of war managed to sour many, of course, and it would be wrong to attribute none of the ambiguities in Scherer's thought to social forces.   But beneath his pulpit attitudes lay doctrinal concerns: he wanted to keep his distance not only from the social gospel and gospel of wealth, but also from any theological scheme that tended to dissolve the gospel in some earth-bound brew.   There is no happiness, he said, apart from the Christ-like life. "It's a queer philosophy," he confessed. "But the one that went to pieces in 1929 is queerer still."[26] He wanted his listeners on Sundays in New York to see the dangers of false happiness and false despair. "The world can look as black as it likes; but God isn't dead. He didn't close heaven and pull down the shades in 1929."[27]

So Scherer was not turning his back on the world. In the fall of 1931, when it was clear (even to Sockman) that the depression was no mere lack of confidence, Scherer asked the Christians of New York City to "put aside their passive attitude toward the economic depression and actively participate in the alleviation of the suffering, starvation, and destitution."[28] Exactly what he meant, however, by the expression of hope that Christians would "actively participate" in the relief effort appears to have been built upon an unshakable conviction: "I haven't seen the mess yet," he told his congregation in the spring on 1933, "that a little decent faith wouldn't have cleared up."[29]

That phrase, "a little decent faith," did not imply for Scherer some blend of human endeavor and heavenly hope, nor did it suggest some strategy by which the kingdom of the earth could stretch itself out to become the kingdom of our God and of the Christ. Scherer, the proper Lutheran, was reluctant to blur any of the distinctions between the realm of the spirit and the realm of the flesh. By the summer of 1940 he was willing to affirm that democracy is "the only adequate expression . . . of a full-grown spiritual stature,"[30] and that the Protestant tradition is indissolubly linked with democratic government.[31] But through the early thirties, at least, he was less inclined to let the two—heaven and earth, spirit and flesh—be seen as one.

The pitfalls of that approach became obvious in the spring of 1933. On April 9 of that year, Ralph Sockman and Harry Emerson Fosdick were among the preachers whose sermons excoriated Hitler's move to nationalize the German Church. Scherer demurred. After the service on that morning at Holy Trinity, a reporter asked for his comment about the situation. He began by assuring his questioner that no actions taken in Germany would affect the American Lutheran Church. Then, he continued: "In my opinion, too much stress has been given the changes that may take place in the Lutheran Church in Germany. I believe that the subject has been exaggerated out of its true importance."[32]

Had the reporter pressed Scherer for some hint about the strategy he would recommend in any such tense situation, the Holy Trinity pastor would probably have answered with the kind of counsel that he gave in an August sermon that same year: the woes of the world can only be removed by faith in Christ; faith will not come by short-cut or miracle; we have to make Christians out of people.[33] Domestic social problems, too, would yield only to the same evangelical method: plans for unemployment relief and social security will only stir the hostility of privileged classes, without positive benefits, unless we become "truly Christian" under "the great perspective of eternity."[34]

Those comments were made in 1936. Five years earlier he identified how that eternal perspective could be rediscovered and retained even against the dangers of the modern age. The trends of the contemporary experience in themselves, he said, are not the culprits—any form of Christianity that cowers before the pressures of the present is "already dying or dead."

> The danger point is being reached when folks like us begin to show more concern about the stock market than we do about religion, when not getting to the office is a tragedy, and not getting to church means no more than a Sunday at home; when newspapers take the place of Bibles and prayer becomes a tradition . . . and being a Christian means doing the best you can under the circumstances.[35]

One can draw the inference that Scherer saw conventional remedies as still being tenable: go to Church, read the Bible, pray, trust

in God. In the fall of 1934, one of his sermons validated that inference:
"Attendance at church," he said, "restores what ideals we may have lost
temporarily."[36] The following spring, he pressed the matter further.

> In the process of building up its defenses, the Christian religion
> undertook to desert a score of its ancient strong-holds. Going
> intellectual itself, it moved so far away from God into philosophy,
> and so far from the Bible into human tradition, and so far away from
> divine sanctions into experimental laboratories, that there was
> astonishingly little left to defend.[37]

Those were all human efforts to work out salvation. Paul Scherer
believed that a more appropriate strategy was to develop no strategy at
all; instead, he preferred to trust a sacramental kind of preaching in which
God is proclaimed rather than defended,[38] in which humanity is not just a
poor beggar but the beneficiary of a king's ransom by divine grace,[39] and
in which the Christian by God's grace is "one other chance God has for
his world."[40]

A. Justification by Faith

It is in this broader theological context that Scherer's handling,
during the thirties, of the doctrine of justification by grace through faith
can best be understood. With variations through the decade, Scherer
preached the character of faith as "gift." When his choice of words
referred to the "pedigree"[41] or "character"[42] of a person, it is clear that he
meant to focus on the quality of that person's life as transformed by
divine grace: faith is not a belief or set of beliefs which one strains to
hold, nor is it properly described as a human trust which lays itself upon
some hope for divine care. Before it involves any of these elements,
according to Paul Scherer, faith is a gift of God's grace which makes a
person a new creation.

> God never intended anything that could be better to be as it is.
> That's why he gave us faith.[43] . . . Faith is very largely a matter of
> character. You must be a certain sort before you can believe a
> certain kind of thing.[44]

The "sort" of person one has to be in order to believe is not
decided by human qualities, human works, or human initiative, in
Scherer's view. Christ does not let His followers seek Him.

> He takes the initiative and goes out to seek them. . . . They have not
> found Him; He has found *them*. They haven't built up the faith that
> holds them; He has built it up *in* them.[45]

Scherer linked this understanding of the work of divine grace to the
Reformation, and he found dilemmas in contemporary theology that were
analogous to those confronted by Luther. What troubled Luther was that

too much reliance on the organized Church had sapped the vitality of religion, Scherer declared, and contemporary theology had enervated its vitality with too much reliance on human works.[46] The Reformers had brought forward a doctrine of "justification by faith." In the Protestant tradition, he said, faith

> doesn't mean assenting to something with your intelligence; it doesn't mean simply trusting God for the ultimate solution of your own soul after you've done what you pleased with your life: that's rubbish. It means thrusting out, in the spirit of a pioneer, on these great promises of God. It's a moral adventure today and tomorrow.[47]

It should be clear from this that Scherer did not want his reliance on Reformation doctrine about faith to degenerate into a kind of antinomian freedom: faith is not just an adventure, but a moral adventure; Christians are pioneers claimed by a promise, not vagabonds liberated to abuse their freedom. Besides, faith is not a human possession—it is a divine gift, bestowed by grace, which means "mercy and truth . . . divine favor . . . the power of God."[48] "There is no Truth that we have arrived at: it's a truth that was arrived at for us! We didn't discover it, it was given us."[49]

The themes that Scherer presses remain rather steady through the decade, so that doctrine is handled in similar ways, whether in the depths of the depression or under the darkest threats of war. A sermon delivered in 1932, and repeated in 1934, makes the point that the Christian faith cannot be learned but must be experienced through the grace of Christ.[50] Nor can faith be limited to one's "fall-back" position of security; instead, faith is a courageous forward leap "with your eyes open."[51] Faith is an experience of vitality, it is a brave activity, but it is all of that because it is primarily not a human responsibility but a divine blessing. It is, from start to finish, a gift. "God's final word to your life and mine has not to do with everlasting demands: it has to do with everlasting arms."[52]

Scherer's listeners could, nonetheless, hear the "demand" emphasis. Happiness and security will only come when we follow in Jesus' way, he was heard to say in February of 1940: "to reach the Kingdom of God man must begin to travel on the road that Jesus pointed out."[53] There is even the message that Christianity bears the burden of redeeming western civilization; but it is one thing to lay a demanding challenge upon Christians and another to make clear the given power with which they can begin to meet the challenge.

> Our lives must be Christ-centered, not on His character or
> teachings—they are only attributes—but on the Godhead in His
> person. . . . Build a religion around Jesus as an ordinary man if you
> want to, but don't call it Christianity.[54]

If there was a detectable shift in Scherer's handling of the doctrine of justification by grace through faith during the thirties, it may have been in his increasing awareness of the connection between the Christian faith and the Christian life. On October 5, 1941, he told his congregation that Christians have been "puttering around in the sphere of a very private salvation long enough."[55] Europeans had already been choking on the clouds of war for nearly three years. Asians had been in battle for longer than that. Americans' debates over entering foreign conflicts were about to become moot. And Scherer called for Christian soldiers to form ranks.

> It's a total warfare that we of the Christian Church have to wage.
> The choice lies all around us: and it's a choice between doing good
> and by the refusal to do good doing evil.[56]

Back in 1932, he had feared that the nation was facing not only financial but also moral bankruptcy. And he suggested that "a thorough-going revival of genuine religion" was the only way to reverse the slide into ruin.[57] By 1938, he had come to the conclusion that the world did not need a revival of religion any less than it needed a revival of morals.[58] "Our moral confusion is as much a cause of our defection from the faith as it is the result of it."[59]

Even in the early thirties such issues were not totally ignored: he was capable of laying before his parishioners an ardent challenge, complaining about how "soft" and "safe" and "mediocre" their Christianity had become, perhaps suggesting that their social status was the source of the trouble.

> We who are up and in have a way of thinking that a few doctrines,
> plus a few ritualistic observances, plus a few prescribed and
> so-called Christian virtues equal religion. Especially the virtues.
> We do the best we can under the circumstances and think it's a
> special crusade. There has come to be a certain formal, accepted,
> and—yes, mediocre—way of life that bears the high name of Jesus
> Christ and dishonors Him![60]

Imbedded in such complaints were his concern that a few human "virtues" and formalities had been substituted for a true faith in God. Christians saw themselves as being justified not by their faith but by their efforts to attain mediocrity. "There is work to do," Scherer insisted,[61] but it is only by the true faith—not by some charade—that the work can be done.

That faith is "in the unassailable good will of our God which He has made manifest nowhere else as in Christ Jesus"; it is the "strong confidence that He's in control."[62] It is not confined to the boundaries of the mind or the limits of the intellect: "nobody believes in God with his mind only."[63] Nor is it so formless as to do away with thought entirely. In a sermon on the Sunday in New York just one week before Riverside's dedication, he made clear his distaste for Riverside's institutionalized anti-creedalism: "how futile it is to talk of dispensing with creeds . . . . To dispense with creeds is to dispense with thought."[64]

The point for Scherer is that Christianity is not built upon some human standard of respectability—aesthetic or cultural, moral or intellectual. Rather, Christianity is built—as the leaders of the Protestant Reformation recognized in a "cleansing discovery"—upon "the eternal needs of a human soul and God's eternal answer."[65] Human thought, taste, and moral efforts may be the manifest and measurable components of the power of that faith. But no human righteousness, he said, can substitute "for the righteousness which is by faith in Christ."[66] And that justification by faith has to be experienced within the individual,[67] in a person's relationship with God, not with the dictates of a social custom or ecclesiastical rule. There are no human works that can bring one to the truth of justifying faith.

B. The Authority of Scripture

If Paul Scherer differed from Ralph Sockman in such matters as the approach to justification by faith and the appreciation for the gospel of wealth, the two did at least share one homiletical principle: almost without exception, every sermon began with a biblical text. Yet they used the Bible differently. The manuscripts of Scherer's early sermons at Holy Trinity suggest that his preaching started with a text, developed that text, and ended with the text: on Sundays in New York during the twenties, his pulpit efforts were typically Lutheran in their straightforward expositional approach. They had a timeless quality: life-less enough to inform, and to bore, congregations with equal effect in almost any age.

It is impossible to say whether Scherer changed his style on his own, or was led to change by the influence of another.[68] Regardless, his sermons in the late twenties and early thirties began to acquire a more lively character, less confined to exposition, more expressive of real human situations, and much more fully illustrated. Even with this change, however, his sermons did not lose their biblical basis, nor did he conclude that an individual's life situation could determine the applicability of the Bible to that person.

> The suggestion I'm trying to make is that you don't have to wait
> until you suffer a nervous breakdown to begin to indulge in the right
> sort of relaxation, nor put off your discovery of the Book until you
> "face defeat."[69]

An individual's experience does not affect the authority of Scripture; the authority of Scripture surpasses that experience. The Scriptures are "living records of actual experience."[70] Stark human realism fills the Bible, together with faith and hope and love.[71] Scriptures know all the patterns explored by human lives, but they are also "the very fabric of life."[72] For the Bible contains the words of Jesus, and "every word that He uttered stands forever,"[73] because Christ's words are God's words.[74] God had made His purposes known to us in history and in Scripture, even though we "insist on acting like strangers to every purpose He had written in the years and in a book."[75]

For Paul Scherer, the Book is the key—no one can get rid of the Bible.[76] Of all that our faith is built upon, it is built first upon a Book, the Word of God.[77]

Not that the Book is to be worshipped. "We adore, not the Book, but the God it progressively unveils, and the Savior at last Who revealed Him utterly. He is the ultimate authority, not in the Bible but through the Bible. . . ."[78] Scherer no more wanted to assent to the Fundamentalists' lordship of the Book than to the Modernists' exaltation of reason.[79] However, he did see the Bible as the unique point of contact between humanity and God: "the Bible is a place of meeting."[80] It is insufficient to say that the Bible contains the word of God, as some critics tried loosely to define the matter: "the Bible is demonstrably more reliable than the people who try to discredit it."[81] It is also insufficient to say flatly that the Bible is the Word of God, as if to make some objective verbal criterion the litmus test for its authority.[82] Instead, the Bible both records the experience of God meeting humanity and also creates that meeting.[83] "God Himself speaks through the words of the Bible. . . . This is revelation: the moving in of God upon human life to bestow Himself relationally in the person of Jesus Christ."[84]

As far as Scherer was concerned, this view of the authority of Scripture was an insight of Reformation theology. He considered the Reformation a "providential event,"[85] whose achievements and discoveries are too often neglected by contemporary Christians. The "open Bible" which is essential to the Protestant heritage has, like some traveler on the Jericho road, fallen among thieves and now is passed by most church members.[86]   Most people, said Scherer, regard the contributions of the Reformation to have lain in such principles as the "freedom of thought and conscience,"[87] which we have used as our justification for aligning the Gospel with democracy. Actually, he said in 1938, the Reformation upheld two principles far more fundamental: one was "the intrinsic worth of personality"[88] and the other was the Word of God.[89] The temptation in any age, including the decade of the thirties with all of its troublesome challenges, is to find a way to make the Scriptures fit the exigencies of the time, Scherer believed.   And Christians should not yield to the temptation. "It is not our job to adapt the Word of God: it's our job to wield it . . . to confront those moods [of our time] with the challenge of Another Mind."[90]

Should anyone clamor for some authoritative reason for accepting the Christian faith, Scherer would have them turn to "this body of revelation which we call the Bible" as the instrument more worthy than all human endeavors, even in art or music or science, of "humanity's profoundest devotion."[91]

C. The "Freedom" of the Will

Despite the accusation that Scherer became a rather "grim" preacher during the decade, it was his contention that grimness was characteristic of the larger culture and not of the gospel.[92]   Modern writers like Theodore Dreiser and Sinclair Lewis were the heralds of pessimism, Scherer said, not the ancients who wrote Scripture.[93]   Of course, the theological question is whether Scherer saw the path of human hope through reliance upon an inviolable will of God[94] or through a human choice to see life as hopeful and promising.[95]

Among the scholars who have studied his work, there is disagreement about his theological "liberalism" on the role of the human will, especially in his preaching during the twenties.   Willis Stanley Gertner says "There is some evidence that liberalism's optimistic view of human nature found expression in Scherer's earlier sermons."[96]   Indeed evidence does abound that there was a liberal cast to his theology, even in publications late in the thirties. Scherer advised, for instance, that if one's face were set "not toward the good one *could* do" but rather "toward the good one can do" then "the answer to it all" would be found.[97]   He offered practical counsel to strain not for perfection but for the possible, and he said it is within the freedom of the human will to choose to do that.

> The first solution of the problem of evil in a world of God lies in an act of the human will. . . . Then, and only then, when our Spirits leap free against the world, do we discover that God is standing by, not as one who looks on and does nothing but as one who is ready to run up at a gesture and throw down all he has.[98]

So is God less the Revealer of the Divine Self than the Responder to ourselves? Is it the divine will or the human will that initiates the work of salvation?

In the late twenties, Scherer had told his congregation that all good human effort "is nothing in the world but a search after God in Christ."[99] And he urged his parishioners to go out and make such efforts, assured that they can "expect a living companionship" in their good works.[100] God changes human "conduct . . . desires . . . affections . . . by His influence."[101] Christ and His way of life will grow on you if you give Him and it a chance."[102] Does that make God less the conqueror on a Cross than the stimulant which lobbies for human good?

When expressions of doubt arose about the prospects for human good, Scherer protested. Not long after the appearance of Reinhold Niebuhr's *Moral Man and Immoral Society*, Scherer stood before the Holy Trinity congregation and characterized Niebuhr's work as "a blue book . . . a *very* blue book, in which he tries so hard to avoid even the appearance of sentimental optimism that he leans over backward in the arms of despair."[103] Scherer believed that Niebuhr had condemned religion to failure in any effort to improve humanity, and he insisted that the Christian faith should give us zest, not bewilder us with anxiety.[104]

Linn James Creighton discounts such data, however, and insists that Scherer was never a "liberal." He dismisses the evidence adduced by Gertner as unconvincing, though he offers little or no reason to support his own opinion.[105]

The dispute is not easily resolved. Perhaps one has to recognize that, when it comes to an analysis of preaching, the truth is in the ear of the beholder. *The New York Times*, for instance, reported that one of Scherer's sermons had declared "Human nature is essentially good, but knowledge is needed to combat the evils of everyday life."[106] However, the manuscript of a sermon for a Sunday in New York less than eight months later shows his conviction that to describe human nature as essentially good "isn't realism; it's nonsense."[107]

In their own ways, both Gertner and Creighton may be right—and wrong. Scherer was more attuned to liberal theology than Creighton wishes to allow, but he was comfortably enough ensconced in orthodoxy to see in the neo-orthodox reaction a legitimate challenge to liberalism. His initial reaction to Niebuhr notwithstanding, he told a Good Friday congregation fourteen months after the "blue book" condemnation that a nation does usually act "on a moral level lower than that of its individual citizens."[108] He declared in 1925 and repeated in 1931, that he could not accept a predestinarian perspective which eliminated the significance of free choice,[109] any more than he could accept some modern mechanistic scheme of reductionism and evolution which made no room for freedom of choice.[110]

The vestiges of liberalism, moreover, did not disappear after the twenties. In April, 1938, he declared that Jesus never lost his faith in humanity.[111]

But in the same period he was telling his parishioners that the human will does not hold the possibilities for bringing about deliverance. "There is an inviolable will of God about our days, and it isn't subject to revision."[112] And when Europe was committed to war, Scherer rebuked the hand-wringing that accompanied the cries of those who had lost faith in humanity.

> That's because we've been far too busy pinning our foolish faith to humanity, and making light of sin in the process, relegating God to the limbo of kindly old gentlemen who are "nice" but they really don't matter any more![113]

As early as 1931, he was saying that religion had lost its vitality for us because we had been relying too much on ourselves.[114] The depression, he believed, had at least one positive aspect, and that was to help us "quit forever depending so thoroughly on ourselves to get us through."[115] But he feared that as soon as the clouds of economic gloom parted, "our old self-esteem" would return.[116]

What Scherer did recognize about human existence was a deep-seated flaw in the human personality, which wants to celebrate the power of a free will but traps itself in falsehood and impotence by doing so. It is not our free will but our "eternal uneasiness" that is the source of "the only dignity we have under the sun."[117] That makes human beings misfits in the world, he said—we are never at home here. "Whatever else you say about the world you've got to say that it's wrong. . . . You may not like the doctrine of a Fall, but you've got to face the facts of it."[118]

So Scherer was unhappy, even in the early thirties, with a theological perspective that relies too much on the human will. At the same time he was unhappy with a view of predestination that left no room for the human will. Relying on an interesting exegesis of the Scriptures, he used the author of Romans to oppose predestinarian views. Paul "requires that man himself become a new creature in Christ Jesus"[119] but predestination leaves no room for the "freedom of choice" to do that: "the only hope of redemption lies in being born well. . . . You see what havoc that works with religion."[120]

Scherer resolved the dilemma with a reliance neither on freedom of the will nor on predestination but on an incarnational theology which stresses the divinity over against the humanity of Christ. A religion may be built upon Jesus "as an ordinary man," an example for us all, a source of encouragement to us, a goal for our free wills; but such a religion is not Christianity, according to Scherer.[121] Instead, Christianity is built upon God, incarnate in Christ.

> If he was a man I can no more be like him than I can be like Julius Caesar. . . . If he was the very incarnation of God Himself then he brought into life something that guarantees my triumph. . . . The gulf was crossed and God was in the midst of the world.[122]

Furthermore, Scherer said repeatedly that the Christian religion must never be construed as the human effort to do the best one can.[123] On one occasion, he castigated such doctrine as "stupid rigamarole"[124] and on another he considered it a sign that Christianity was in mortal danger.[125]

He did admit that Christianity involves a commitment of one's will: one has to make a deliberate choice to yield one's own will to God's will;[126] even when one loses faith it can be retrieved "by committing oneself to [God's] gracious will."[127] The choice, of course, involves "leaving these wills of ours out of the picture" by submitting to God's will for our lives and hope;[128] therefore the saving power lies in the divine rather than in the human will, for Scherer. Yet he understands that a free human choice is necessary before God's will can become a saving power in a person's life. In effect, an act of human will gives God's redeeming work a chance. "I am not particularly thrilled by the chances God gives me: I am thrilled in every nook and chimney side of my soul by the chances I may manage some day to give Him."[129]

So the freedom of the will, for Paul Scherer, exists as the free human choice to bring into play the saving power of God. It does not mean human control[130] but rather it means exercising a choice within certain limited conditions. "God imposes those conditions on Himself.

The very nature of life imposes them on us."[131] Ultimately, therefore, even the freedom of the will as Scherer construes it is a freedom limited by "the inviolable will of God" and that divine will is not "subject to revision."[132] Nor is it fully known to us: we operate "under sealed orders" which God gives to us; they run only so far, and after that new orders will be issued.[133] That is both the promise and risk of prayer.

> When we pray we risk having God's will done through our lives
> instead of our own, and then we will drop our racial prejudices and
> pride, for God's will is economic justice and righteousness and
> letting the other fellow have a right to live.[134]

In summary, Scherer says we are creatures endowed with freedom to bring into effect the purposes of the divine will. But we are not pawns of an arbitrary will.

He won't force His bounty on us whether "we want it or not. . . . We can twist ourselves resentfully out of His hands and squander the whole precious gift of life."[135] We are so free as to be able to waste life, but not free enough to destroy it; we are free enough to enjoy and share life, free enough to open ourselves to the power of its Creator, but not so free as to redeem squandered life. There is, therefore, a structural "hopelessness" about human life. "We just weren't intended to be equal to Life. . . . Our helplessness, if you please, is part of the plan!"[136] To recognize that is to stand at the limit of human power and to step forward into the power of God.[137]

Scherer's position here seems a bit confused, on the one hand leaning toward a Lutheran distinction between necessity and compulsion, on the other embracing a Melancthonian notion of the concurrent causes of salvation. But neither is terribly refined in his work, leading to the charge that his views are "theologically superficial and biblically shallow."[138] Willis Stanley Gertner, for instance, contrasts the shallowness of Scherer's sermons at Holy Trinity with the depth of his thought in his later career, when he had turned to full-time teaching.

Yet there is another consideration, one that involves the uniqueness of pulpit theology as distinguished from academic theology. Theology from the pulpit is "occasional" theology, which proclaims doctrine in a very narrowly defined set of circumstances that may provoke the shading of an observation in some way not consistent with an earlier word. Week after week it is proclaimed in an environment whose local coloration provides the tone for a nuanced phrase or a neglected emphasis. With Paul Scherer's preaching, as with that of others, certain broad patterns seem to emerge with relative clarity across a given historical period. On a specific Sunday in New York the theme was treated in its context: it is inevitable that contemporary preaching must in some sense be temporary.

Of course, Scherer was consciously preaching in a larger context, too. He felt himself very much an heir and transmitter of the theology of the Reformation. The "sole meaning of the Reformation," he said, is that "in every individual life God can come first." And it takes a personal choice to effect that relationship.[139] He was sensitive to the issues which the Reformers raised, even if not so profoundly sensitive that he could articulate classic Reformation doctrine in terms which could clearly transcend the irreconcilable differences between an old orthodoxy and a weakened liberalism. Still, as a pulpit theologian, he was very much a part of the doctrinal turbulence of the thirties. The theological debate of the decade was not an academic affair alone. Paul Scherer helped make it a homiletical concern, too.[140]

CHAPTER VI
APOLOGIST FOR A PERSONAL LIFE

In 1929, Harry Emerson Fosdick wrote that "religion at its fountainhead is an individual, psychological experience."[1] He said truth is lost when religious institutions drown themselves in debates about dogma. "Religion," Fosdick believed, "is essentially the release of life through its committal to the highest that we know."[2] But ecclesiastical forces tend to constrict life by their petty, bothersome definitions of sacraments. What people are longing for, said Fosdick, is "intellectual justification for a sustaining faith."[3]

In a positive sense, Fosdick's identification of—and attempt to respond to—the desire for this intellectual justification for faith is a mark of his pastoral awareness. On Morningside Heights, in the intellectual milieu of Columbia University, Fosdick saw himself as an apologist in search of credible Christianity. In fact, among all the labels attached to his work, he felt most comfortable being identified as a Christian apologist.[4]

However, the turn of phrase which stresses a justification *for* faith is almost certainly not a casual one, but a significant clue to Fosdick's own views about the history of doctrine—specifically Protestant doctrine. "Will you say now that Protestantism redeemed the Christian movement? Does it look that way? Let us cease our foolish idealization of Protestantism. . . . The Protestant Reformation was a half-way affair. It left dogmatism almost more accentuated than it was before."[5]

Fosdick's complaint was that sixteenth-century doctrine, no matter how compelling, can never obviate the need for theology which takes the *weltanschauung* of one's own age seriously. Even classic teaching on justification by grace through faith alone needs an intellectual justification for faith in the first place. Immense intellectual changes have overtaken humanity since the Reformers, and yet Fosdick saw Protestant Orthodoxy locked into rigid forms that pre-date the advances of modern science.

The Protestant Reformation was a valiant stroke for liberty, but it occurred before the most characteristic ideas of our modern age had arrived. The Augsburg Confession is a memorable document, but the Lutherans who framed it did not even know that they were living on a moving planet, and Martin Luther himself called Copernicus a new astrologer. The Westminster Confession is a notable achievement in the development of Christian thought, but it was written forty years before Newton published his work on the law of gravitation. Protestantism, that is, was formulated in prescientific days. Not one of its historic statements of faith takes into account any of the masterful ideas which constitute the framework of modern thinking—the inductive method, the new astronomy, natural law, evolution. All these have come since Protestantism arrived. Protestantism stiffened into its classic forms under intellectual influences long antedating our modern world, and the chaos and turmoil in Christian thought today are the consequences.[6]

In other words, classic Protestant theology is not part of the solution for the twentieth-century Church, it is part of the problem.

The solution, for Fosdick, lay in the coming of modernism which adapted, adjusted, and accommodated Christian faith to contemporary scientific ways of thinking.[7] One key test involved evolution, and Fosdick's work through the thirties showed that biblical scholarship and the tenets of the Christian faith could be understood with the application of evolutionary principles.[8] The forward march of human progress was a clear sign of the coming Kingdom of God: "The doctrine of Jesus is in conformity with the progress of our time."[9] Reformation thought was not wholly irrelevant to modern times: Luther, for instance, had a marvelous notion about freedom, Fosdick believed; generally, though, Luther's approach was no different from that of the fourth-century creeds.[10]

And those creeds fail to offer the modern Christian very much. "When God wished to reveal to us the truth to live by, he put it not into a creed, not into a book, but into a life."[11] That was Fosdick's theological formula for setting aside the creeds, as he expressed it in his Christmas sermon for 1932, a formula made necessary by his personal confession in that same sermon that "I cannot believe all these complicated creeds."[12] As Fosdick had said in the first sermon ever delivered from the Riverside pulpit, "Nothing matters in Christianity, not even things with long traditions and accumulated sanctity—not creedal forms nor ritual observances nor institutional regularities—nothing matters except those things that bring abundant life to personality."[13]

So no creeds were recited at Riverside Church,[14] both because they lack intellectual credibility for the twentieth-century and because they are a positive hindrance to any insight into the truth about Christ. Dogma, in Fosdick's view, is a way to disguise Christ and to foster vain adoration of Him.[15] In any case, Christianity is simply not something to be affirmed; it is something to be done.[16] To be a Christian is to become a disciple of an exemplary Christ: "Vital Christianity is nothing in the world except a game of follow the leader."[17] Without that commitment to follow, with no more than a "merely theological faith," the content of faith could just as effectively be "in one God" or "in the rings of Saturn" for all of the impact it would have on human "character."[18]

Fosdick's bold abandonment of creeds and traditional doctrine invited criticism, during his career and afterward, that he was "not theological enough."[19] Joseph Calvin Hall spoke for more scholars than himself when he found "little real doctrinal basis" in Fosdick's sermons.[20] A. B. McDiarmid suggested that the reason for this deficiency may have been psychological rather than theological. Fosdick, he says,

> seems to be dominated by the feeling that theology in some way has been blocking him, and that the birth of his real ministry coincides with his emancipation from it. Something seems to have developed in him an almost compulsive dislike for theology, and it could well be his childhood experiences with hellfire preaching. . . . Fosdick does not intend to take theology lightly, but he does intend to reinterpret it in terms of current psychology, and this led to an over-emphasis on one aspect, namely man, to a distortion of other aspects.[21]

McDiarmid may have a point, though he seems content to offer a psychological analysis of the psychological sources of doctrinal flaws. Sometimes theological reflection alone can find theological flaws, without having to resort to another form of logic. Fosdick was not intimidated by doctrine. He wanted to adjust it for better synchronization with the rhythms of modern times: "In every realm," he said "doctrine . . . is basic"; however, doctrines cannot "win their way" unless they are adorned "by attractive lives."[22] So, in strictly theological terms, the critical concern is his handling of the relationship between those "basic" doctrines and the "lives" that adorn them.

On November 3, 1935, Fosdick delivered a sermon which has suggested to many[23] that he was going into a wary retreat from an approach that put too much stress on the adornment and too little on basic doctrine. Titled "The Church Must Go Beyond Modernism," the sermon came not long after a forced absence of several months from the Riverside pulpit.[24] In that sermon he defended modernism as a necessary adjustment and "a desperately needed way of thinking"[25] which has "already largely won the battle" that it set out to win.[26] However, like all remedies with undesirable side affects, these intellectual adjustments caused the elimination of standards for moral judgment.[27] And Fosdick was eager for an antidote, if not a new remedy. His suggestion was to rediscover the merits in some of the old, abandoned prescriptions. "Underline this: Sin is real. Personal and social sin is as terribly real as our forefathers said it was."[28] There are some things, he seems to be saying, that no adornments can mask.

But it would be wrong to suggest that Fosdick came to this conclusion in the mid-thirties under the aegis of some ascendant neo-orthodoxy. This celebrated[29] sermon signified no sudden shift in his thought, yet it was symptomatic (if not symbolic) of a trend in his thought that had been developing for years. In October, 1933, he had admitted that the liberal view of inevitable progress had forgotten much about life that his father's generation had known "with terrific clarity and announced with compelling power"—life is not a smooth and gradual process but a movement around corners from crisis to crisis, from birth to death.[30] On Sunday, January 17, 1932, he delivered "A Fundamentalist Sermon by a Modernist Preacher," in which similar concessions were made: "Old-fashioned Christianity," he said, "did have in it something deep and powerful which we modernists often miss."[31] Near the conclusion of the sermon, he suggested why that profound and potent "something" was missing in the thirties.

> You see, we modernists have often gotten at our faith by a negative process. We do not believe this. We do not believe that. We have given up this incredible idea or that absolute doctrine. So we pare down and dim out our faith by negative abstractions until we have left only the ghostly reminder of what was once a great religion.[32]

Not that "great religion" can be recovered by a reapplication of layers of doctrine which, over the years, have been peeled away. Fosdick was not about to concede the premise upon which he had built his own theological position. Traditional teachings and ancient creeds were still largely irrelevant to the issues of modern science, he felt, for science had made too much obsolete.

> We could not go back to [Martin Luther's] theology even if we wanted to . . . he thought that the earth was stationary . . . that demons caused thunderstorms. . . . Yet once Martin Luther stood in the presence of the Emperor saying "Here stand I." . . . What a religion! It produced something that our modernism often does not produce, the unconsenting individual conscience. If there is one thing that society has a right to expect from religion it is that.[33]

Likewise Augustine's theology "would be impossible for us" and should be forsaken by us even though it provided him with "power over tumultuous passions within and desperate circumstances without."[34]

Still, our own experience shows that the old theology was not totally wrong. For instance, Fosdick could not believe in predestination, yet he found it obvious that some children are born imbeciles and thus are "damned" while others are born with all sorts of advantages and thus seem "chosen."[35] It was to experience, therefore, that Fosdick made his ultimate theological appeal: the experience of observations made in the real world; and the experience of inner receptivity to the power and presence of God. "Modernism has stressed activity. . . . Admirable as that is, our forefathers understood that religion is not simply activity but receptivity. . . . We Protestant modernists have sometimes been so anxious to be liberal that we have forgotten to be religious."[36] But not just any experience would do. He lamented the version of Christianity that was "emotionally sentimental and morally easy-going," calling it "superficial modernism."[37] At the other end of the decade of the thirties he expressed a similar concern. "I do not believe the old theology. . . . But how can one be content with this soft, sentimental, complacent type of liberalism that thinks comfortably of human nature?"[38]

Meanwhile, experience had brought him a new insight. Through the mid-thirties and beyond, Fosdick recognized that the forces which were ascendant both in the United States and abroad were doctrinal forces—science, communism, and fascism were all notable patterns of doctrine; and in October 1934, he described doctrine as "one of the most exciting things in the modern world."[39] Two years later he went beyond a general affirmation of doctrine to a specific theological dimension of it. "We will never recover a powerful religion until we get back to doctrine; that is to say, to teaching, the sharing of information about what is true."[40] He knew that liberals would hardly feel attracted to such a notion, since they preferred to understand Christianity as "a way of life" and to "let sleeping dogmas lie."[41] But Christianity faces competition from alternate doctrines such as those offered by Stalin, Mussolini, and Hitler. "Our great enemy . . . is that strong capacity in man to forget himself in something other than himself, to give himself to a dictator, to a national state, to something less than God."[42] Liberals, he said, had wrongly supposed doctrine to be unpopular; the thirties showed that the world was prepared to go to war over doctrine.[43] And in a conflict, no assortment of "kindly feelings" could defeat "well-argued doctrines."[44]

Back in the 1920s, Fosdick had been aware of modernism's limitations, but he suffered no loss of confidence in the liberal churches. Create more of them, he had said, and "the day is won."[45]   Even Fosdick's bitterest theological opponents at the time feared that he was right. William Ward Ayer, successor to John Roach Straton as pastor of Calvary Baptist Church, deplored the state of "evangelical" Protestantism as disorganized and defenseless while the liberal churches had the machinery of the Federal Council of Churches with which to work and the backing of the Rockefeller millions to keep the machine fueled.[46] There were corrections to be made in modernism's course, Fosdick consented, but the future of the Church lay in liberal hands.[47]

Which is to suggest that Fosdick's appeals for a return to doctrine were not intended to encourage any drift away from liberal principles. But what kind of doctrine did he want?

There is one sermon that seems to have spanned the decade of the thirties; it was preached in 1933 and again in 1939, and it was published in 1934.[48]   Titled "The Towering Question: Is Christianity Possible?" it begins with an admittedly blunt thesis.

> Christianity is primarily something to be *done*. It is not first of all a finished set of propositions to be accepted; it is first of all an unfinished task to be completed. It is a way of thinking about life and living life to be wrought out personally and socially on earth. The question to be asked about it is not simply, "Is it true?" but, "Can we ever in this world make it come true?" not simply "Is it credible?" but "Is it possible?"[49]

The doctrine which Fosdick would have reinforced, it appears, is a reliance on the continuity between the things of heaven and the things of earth, a reliance on what is possible through human resources and effort: in short, a doctrine of works. Defining religion as "zeal" and "emotional driving power," Fosdick said in a February 1931 sermon that religion and intelligence together form an irresistible force. "What a step forward mankind does take when high religion and high intelligence are blended! Nothing on earth can withstand that combination."[50]   In the gathering gloom of the depression, he expressed confidence that the nation's business brains could solve unemployment if they would turn from their own self-interests to the larger social problem, for the benefits of "social engineering" could surpass any salutary effects that "individual goodness" might have.[51]   At the same time, he was aware that modern beliefs in "progress" and "strenuous effort" were hardly the holy ground upon which to build a life of positive moral consequence.[52]   Nevertheless, he saw religion, like science, as having utilitarian value in the world: "a means to overcoming it, and instrument of the good life." And when *The New York Times* reported on the sermon in which Fosdick expressed this view, the column headline read "Dr. Fosdick Denies Faith Explains All."[53] The lasting qualities of religion lie in self-assurance and benevolence, not dogma. "I am not sure that all my theological opinions will stand remembering. I am sure, however, that charity and tolerance and magnanimity will. I am sure that confidence in God behind all our partial ideas of God will."[54] Deeper than doctrine can probe, he said,[55] the Christian religion is a way of seeing life which enables the Christian to share in Christ's "way of seeing."[56] Jesus needed faith to produce courage, said Fosdick, and so do we.[57] Humanity needs the "self-esteem" to believe in "human possibilities" and the Christian faith contributes that.[58]

So any attempt to evaluate the importance of religion in general or the Christian religion in particular must be done not in terms of denomination but discipleship, not in terms of doctrine but deed. Fosdick declared that the crucial issue is not whether one is a modernist or a Methodist, a conservative or a Congregationalist, but whether one cares about "international peace, economic justice, civic righteousness, and, at the heart of all, high-minded character."[59] And to that end, the preacher's task is "to inspire the building of a better society."[60]

This is not to say that Fosdick reduced faith to noble moral effort. Quite the contrary, he believed that the economic crisis of the early thirties proved that religion will not "work" if it is merely "a few ethical principles."[61] Instead, religion is the "zeal"[62] and "enthusiasm"[63] that gets the effort started; religion inspires the patience and endurance which will be needed to finish.[64] What he had written in the twenties, he still believed in the thirties to be true.

"The whole mental process by which we build a unified, orderly, and reasonable world is saturated with faith. . . . By faith, therefore, man builds the world in which he lives."[65]

So faith is not simply human effort, nor is it separable in thought or practice from human effort. And that is because of the incarnational character of Christianity, in Fosdick's view. Christianity is neither a theology nor an organization, he said: it is primarily "a personal life."[66] Its source is a mystery, but a rather generalized mystery: human personalities, powerful ideas, and material creations from subways to skyscrapers arise from the same mystery.[67] Which is to say that the source of religion, however mysterious, is still a human mystery in the sense that it is imbedded deeply in some ineradicable human desires.

Those desires include a longing for faith in back of life, "the lure of a worthwhile adventure ahead," and awareness that one can be of useful practical service in life.[68]

Faith, therefore, has human roots. It is the function of human desire and, perhaps also, of human achievement.

A. Justification by Faith

During one pre-Christmas sermon in 1934, Fosdick spoke to the point quite clearly. "All great faith in God springs out of moral character and moral effort," he said, adding "All great faith in God springs out of moral devotion."[69] To be sure, religion offers an initial enthusiasm, but human effort requires more than the initial zealous burst to endure the long trials of life. So religion feeds on and arises from the continuing work that one does. "Our faith is not Christian unless it thus springs from and reacts upon the way we live. . . . Not only does a great faith in God spring out of moral character and effort, but it produces them."[70] That this has metaphysical implications, Fosdick understood: "this universe does respond to man's moral life."[71] "The social gospel," Fosdick said, "is at the very center of the New Testament."[72] Personal and social salvation, he would say in the early weeks of 1941, require that the Christian ethic be recaptured and put into practice.[73]

There seems little doubt, therefore, that faith for Fosdick is a thoroughly human capacity. In the estimation of Charles Earl Leininger, Fosdick's position grants anyone the freedom to dispose of particular ideas about God, but "there is no escape psychologically from faith—from that inward vertical relationship with some ideal or with the mystery of life, from that ineradicable necessity in man to believe in something, to give himself to something, to belong to something."[74] Such a position certainly offers breadth enough to accommodate faith as a human experience, which is in no way contingent upon a divine presence or a divine action. "The faith Fosdick promotes as the core of his preaching and counseling," wrote A. B. McDiarmid, "is, therefore, not specifically Christian."[75]

In one of his exceedingly popular devotional hooks, Fosdick had described faith as "a necessary faculty of the soul, . . . the power by which we commit ourselves to any object that wins our devotion and commands our allegiance."[76] His sermons during the thirties maintained that theme: faith is a practical, human power that can be used or misused, but it cannot be set aside.

The right use of faith involves recognizing it as "our capacity, standing on a frontier, to hazard our lives on something as we move out into the unforeseen."[77] The particular "something" for which the risk is taken is neutral. It lays no claim upon the one who runs the risk of faith and confers no status upon the one who does the trusting. "It is not alone the just who live by faith; lacking it, there is no real life anywhere."[78] So what classical Protestant doctrine meant by the phrase "justification by grace through faith"[79] is far removed from Fosdick's own interpretation of faith. Faith, to Fosdick, implies no necessary justifying relationship between God and the Christian: it is the exercise of a human capacity, not the joy of a divine gift.

Of course, one could say that Fosdick apologetically set aside the peculiarly Christian doctrinal content of justification by faith and pushed the believer's relationship to God back to Creation. Expressed in a few of his characteristic formulae, Fosdick's position is that we cannot get rid of God because there is a "flame" within us that "will not go out"[80] and because "the best in us is God in us."[81] But the mystical "divine spark" in his approach has more to do with human experience than with the ultimate divine origins of human experience, and less to do with the work of a redeeming savior than with the work of one who follows Jesus' way.

During the thirties, Fosdick emerged as a responsible critic of the more naive dimensions of theological liberalism.[82] As early as February, 1932, he was telling his parishioners that "spiritual power" comes from being receptive and responsive, not from "blowing on your hands" and putting forth "strenuous effort."[83] Mainly, however, it was in the mid to late thirties that a positive critique of liberalism effectively found its place in his pulpit. On Palm Sunday in 1939, he said that liberal Christians have often watered down their faith, "thinned it out, accommodated it to prevalent ideas," and turned it into the lowest common denominator of human acceptability.[84] Later that same year, he was more explicit.

> We take it for granted that we here are liberals in religion. We have broken away from authoritative creeds, and, requiring no theological subscription in this church, we are at liberty to formulate our own Christian experience in contemporary terms. . . . As I review some of the sermons I have preached here . . . I am impressed with the vagueness that enshrouds much of our liberal Christianity.[85]

He went on in that sermon to suggest that the liberal virtues of broad-mindedness, inclusiveness, and tolerance needed to be set over against definiteness, clear-headedness, and certainty "about what Christ wants of life and could do with us if he could."[86]

One specific mid-course adjustment in his pulpit theology re-defined faith as being sought by God, not just searching for God. A truly distinctive religious experience, Fosdick said in a 1936 sermon, goes beyond a person's feeling of belief in God to the feeling that one is being "pursued by God . . . and laid hold on by God."[87] True security, he said in the following year, "is not so much what we have . . . as what has us."[88] And true freedom, he said in his first sermon for 1940, means belonging "to someone who sets him free."[89] Thus the character of his approach did shift in mid-decade and afterward: the person of faith came to be understood as the recipient of what faith could grasp; and faith itself was understood not as a human quality to be capitalized upon but as a power to be received.

One consequence of this change in Fosdick's emphasis was his increased awareness of the declarative theological mood. There had always been the element of "demand" in his proclamation.

> Faith in God, when a man takes it seriously, lays heavy claims on his life. It says to him that what ought to be can be, so that even in days like these, when catastrophe makes multitudes despair, a man with faith in God must still go on believing in moral causes and investing himself in them.[90]

Yet that was tempered with the assurance that "the primary element in the Christian's morals is not an ideal concerning what we ought to be, but a message concerning that we are."[91] As he gradually shifted in the mid-thirties and beyond toward a positive critique of liberalism, he also shifted the mood of his theological grammar from the imperative to the indicative.

> Especially in liberal circles, religion is conceived as presenting to us ideas of . . . what should be, could be, might be, ought to be. Today, I venture to protest against that. We will never have a powerful religion that talks all the time in the subjunctive and imperative moods. Powerful religion starts in the indicative mood . . . it begins by believing profoundly that something *is* true.[92]

He stressed the basic truth that Christianity began not as a call to moral action but as a declaration of good news, proclaiming what is everlastingly true.

That was in the mid-thirties. In the closing years of the decade, Fosdick's views had reached what for him was an acceptable balance between the works-righteousness of naive liberalism and the faith that is dead for lack of works.

> Christianity . . . is something that one believes and it is something that one ideally tries to be and do. It is a faith one assents to; it is an

> ideal one endeavors to follow. While the complete Christian
> experience includes both of these, it is not at its creative source
> either the one or the other.[93]

In fact, his views began to tilt more heavily toward the reliance on faith
alone—in short, toward the substance of classic Protestant doctrine.
Certainly he was increasingly sensitive to sinful humanity's inability to
save itself.[94] And he had come to see clearly that human confidence in
inevitable progress was folly.[95] Fosdick implored his congregations—at
Riverside and on radio—at Christmas, 1939, to see that Jesus was not a
popular idealist but rather the "supreme realist" who "spoke to man's
actual condition."[96]

Nevertheless, the saving power of Christ lay in the area of
works more than faith. For even as the decade was drawing to a close
amid the flames of European war, Fosdick held to the conviction that
"nothing can ultimately save mankind except Christ's way of life."[97]
Deliverance, it seems, must still come by the moral effort of a disciple:
the Word and the faith given by a Savior are not, for Fosdick, the ultimate
power to save sinful humanity; that power abides in the kind of (human)
life He lived, and in struggling humanity's adoption of His example as
the pattern for its own earthly journey.

It is not raw "confidence in man" that Fosdick retains in the later
thirties; that, he said, had been replaced by the knowledge of man's
desperate need for salvation.[98] The "deeply founded confidence" of faith
arises from the assurance that one has the "backing" of God, he declared
late in 1941.[99] Yet it is a rather formless confidence—a bold human
daring that may make a great leap forward on flimsy authority.

> Faith is believing in the positive evidence of a single footprint,
> against all the negative evidence that would deny the possibility . . .
> believing, on the basis of a few lovely homes against the mass of
> negative evidence . . . believing, on the basis of some victorious
> spirit, that a man can by God's grace rise triumphant over adverse
> circumstances and carry off an inner victory, against the vast mass of
> negative evidence.[100]

It is a will to believe that seems to lie at the bottom of Fosdick's
confidence in faith. What one associates with classic Protestant doctrine
he appears to set aside, replacing it with a broader conception. Gone are
the creeds: either discarded altogether, or collated into some general
synergy of belief. "This is the creed of creeds, the final deposit and
distillation of all man's important faiths—that he should be able to
believe in life."[101]

Charles Earl Leininger has suggested that, although Fosdick
does not use the phrase "justification by faith" or employ the term

"justification" to describe his system of faithfulness, nevertheless Fosdick "does lean toward a dynamic view of what theology means by the term."[102] What Leininger seems to have in mind is the problem of how one knows where to place one's faith. How does one decide what can be believed? Fosdick's answer, according to Leininger, is that one knows by "the authority of experience."[103] "Fosdick's epistemology moves from experience to faith (man's response to experience) to reason (man's attempt to make his faith acceptable to his intelligence) to knowledge."[104]

In the early thirties, Fosdick tended to build his position about faith on the foundation of reason: a modern scientific world had to have some reasonable justification for faith. Into the middle of the decade, in fact, he preached as if he were continuing the effort he announced in 1929 to provide the intellectual rationale for religion.[105] His language at times echoes the ontological argument for the existence of God—the One than whom nothing greater can be conceived. In such fashion Fosdick addressed the problem of Christology.

> Christians have called Jesus God. In some meanings I cannot consent to that. I do not think that Jesus was omnipotence, omniscience, omnipresence masquerading in a human body. That would make of him a monstrous unreal being, impossible to imitate. But if . . . we think of God in terms of our real loyalties . . . I cannot imagine a higher object of devotion than Christ presents.[106]

Later in the decade, "reason" as a pole of authority subsided and a kind of mysticism crept into greater prominence. Though he admitted, in a 1938 sermon, that theology, ecclesiastical institutions, and liturgical traditions were "important," he said that Christianity is mainly "the dropping of a new personal influence into the chemical composition of men's lives until their formulas have changed."[107] In the same year, he defined religion almost wholly in experiential terms. "A supremely religious man or woman is one who believes deeply and consistently in the veracity of his highest experiences."[108] And early in the following year, he declared candidly that only some kind of faith experience can bring about the needed salvation. Faith cannot be transmitted from person to person by reason or by tradition.

> If we are to make a real return to vital Christian faith and practice, it must be an inner personal matter, a rediscovery of the living God, each man for himself. . . . No man ever can inherit religion. He must get at it for himself as an inner, personal, noninheritable experience.[109]

Fosdick's transition to the authority of experience coincided with his concern for a revival of doctrine,[110] but the connection may have been more than coincidental. Vital Christian experience had been forsaken by a liberalism that encouraged neglect of the rituals which fostered Christian experience. In other words, it was a vicious cycle. Liberal Protestantism, said Fosdick, "has been more and more throwing away the techniques, methods, and observances by which spiritual life is nurtured and disciplined. . . . We have the faith, but we have thrown away the methods by which faith becomes real in life."[111] Moral effort as a source for faith was a diminishing emphasis in Fosdick's preaching as the thirties lengthened. The zeal, ,or enthusiasm, which religion initially affords became a more important value. "Great Christianity starts with something profoundly reinforcing, regenerating, reassuring within, from which, as an inevitable consequence, comes an immense release of energy."[112]

Yet even such firm reliance on faith as experience did not take Fosdick to the position where faith is a "justifying" experience. Religious faith is still neutral. "In its effect religion is as ambiguous as fire," he was quoted as having said in a spring, 1941, sermon; "it can warm and serve and enlighten, or it can destroy."[113]

Which comes down to the conclusion that despite his shifting theological emphases through the thirties, Fosdick never preached a doctrine of justification by grace through faith alone. The so-called "dynamic" view of justification was really a doctrine of works-righteousness, even in its most experiential terms, for the religious experience itself remained ambiguous until an individual worked out its details in creative or destructive forms.

That message of justification by works came through in his preaching at various levels and under several forms. Sometimes there was the undisguised demand for a conversion to take place: an almost graceless appeal for people to take themselves to God, with the implication that the prospect for any revival of faith was a strictly human affair. "I want some personal conversions here this morning," he said on more than one occasion.[114] Sometimes salvation was more explicitly laid as a burden upon human shoulders, as in sermons at the beginning and near the end of 1941. With tensions continuing to build around the world in January of that year Fosdick appealed to his congregation at Riverside and on radio. "If you have any contribution you can make to build here a juster, kindlier world, you had better make it now."[115] Scarcely a month later, he linked the American way of life and the Christian way of life into one package, suggesting that the effort to achieve one was the same sort of effort needed to maintain the other. "The American way of life ultimately rests upon the kind of people that Christ and his church came to produce."[116] Then, within just a few weeks before America was to be drawn fully into war, Fosdick declared that "the crucial question for all of us" is "how to pull ourselves together."[117]

Salvation seemed to be a humanly achievable personal wholeness, for Fosdick. And faith remained something that Christians have to justify, not something through which they are justified by the grace of God.

B. The Authority of Scripture

On September 30, 1915, Fosdick was inaugurated as the first Morris K. Jessup Professor of Practical Theology at Union Seminary. In his charge to the new professor, the Reverend Dr. Henry M. Saunders spoke of the climate of biblical criticism at the time.

> We believe that as a result of this critical study we have a Bible
> more intelligible, more credible, more authoritative than ever before.
> It would seem, therefore, that the time has come when religious
> teachers may well put emphasis on the constructive rather than on
> the critical aspects of their work. . . . Criticism has its rightful place,
> doubtless. . . . But it involves peril—the old reverence may be lost
> while new knowledge is being acquired. . . . The very process of
> taking a flower to pieces, botanically, destroys its fragrance; the art
> of dissecting the bird, in the interests of ornithology, kills the
> song.[118]

Fosdick's own inaugural address that day focused on what he considered the "constructive" outcome of critical biblical scholarship.   The old models of Scripture as oracle, allegory, or proof-text were obsolete, he said, but critical efforts had regained for Christians "a real religious history, a record of God's actual dealings with men, infinitely more impressive and more preachable than all the allegories that the ingenuity of Philo or Augustine ever could devise."[119]

Fosdick's revisionist view of biblical authority, however, was not enough to satisfy his detractors. He found himself at the center of heated controversies over the matter; and, because of that, his views on Scripture have been more aggressively criticized than any of his other theological positions.   "The fundamentalists," he wrote in his autobiography, "have hated me plentifully."[120]

Criticisms of his work, though, were not uniformly visceral. Eugene May wrote in 1950 that Fosdick preached a happy "blend" of "the authority of the Bible and the authority of experience to evaluate and direct life."[121] Within that "blend," for Fosdick, the Bible was a "unique instrument . . . the greatest instrument for influencing people in a helpful way."[122] Yet, for all that, biblical authority *per se* did not find its way into his sermons. May studied about 250 of Fosdick's messages and found nary a hint of the authority of Scripture.[123] H. Gordon Clinard in a study of pulpit approaches to the problem of suffering found that Fosdick's preaching "lacks the authority of true biblical content."[124] Robert McElroy Shelton concluded that Fosdick had an inadequate view of biblical authority.[125] And Samuel Weaver attributed Fosdick's theological deficiencies to his "failure to recognize the Bible as the Word of God."[126]

Those opinions of scholars who later examined Fosdick's work were scarcely a surprise to the man himself. He had heard—and even made—similar criticisms decades earlier. As far as he was concerned in 1928, the preacher's knowledge of Scripture and the importance of biblical authority for preaching were too obvious to require mentioning. The homiletical crisis, which was generally believed to exist at the time, could be resolved by preachers' bringing the Bible "within reaching distance" of people.[127] He knew the perils of the loss of biblical preaching, and he warned his Yale audience during his 1924 Beecher Lectures that theological drift and doctrinal destruction were the rewards for abandoning the life-shaping perspective of Scripture.[128]

It was in those lectures that Fosdick first explored fully his own concept of biblical authority. He rejected the fundamentalists' premise that the Bible must be swallowed whole, like Jonah, with its original mental framework intact. "What is permanent in Christianity," he said, "is not mental frameworks but abiding experiences."[129] "The first essential of intelligent biblical preaching in our day: a man must be able to recognize the abiding messages of the Book, and sometimes he must recognize them in a transient setting."[130] Fosdick's critics rightly saw that the authority of human experience rather than the authority of scriptural words lay at the base of his theological approach. He believed that the human intellect used changing categories to describe experiences, but that the kernel of human experience transcended temporary categories.

To those who felt that this point of view pushed the Bible away from the center of Fosdick's interpretation of experience, he had a ready reply.

> This does not mean that the Bible's importance in preaching diminished. Upon the contrary, I had been suckled on the Bible, knew it and loved it, and I could not deal with any crucial problem in thought and life without seeing text after text lift up its hands, begging to be used.[131]

But the critics were not dissuaded. Joseph Calvin Hall found the locus of authority for Fosdick to be Christocentric rather than Bibliocentric,[132] but it was the Christ of experience rather than the Christ of Scripture or tradition to whom Fosdick turned. He saw the Bible not as the Word of God but as a manual of repeatable experience; and he made experience too much the determining characteristic of his theology, according to Samuel Robert Weaver.[133]

Even those assessments, however, do not fully describe the directions of Fosdick's pulpit theology during the thirties. In his autobiography, Fosdick wrote about his basic "conviction that theologies are psychologically and sociologically conditioned."[134] Presumably that applied to his own theology as well, for (as with his colleagues Sockman and Scherer) a discernible shift in emphasis marked his homiletical doctrine from the early thirties to the later part of the decade. As the dominant factor of external history, World War II supplanted the depression. And Fosdick's internal history, under the impact both of his liberal academic training and his own tormented psychological development, saw the power of the human personality as the organizing center of life. Experience is authoritative because the personality integrates it.

So in accordance with Fosdick's own conviction about the sociological and psychological conditioning of theology, he can be said to subsume biblical authority under the rubric of the human personality and its experiences. The New Testament, he said in a 1931 sermon, believes "in the moral competence of the empowered personality to master life."[135] That "moral competence" in turn became the hermeneutical principle for interpreting Scripture: thus, he saw the concept of "vicarious sacrifice" as the "organizing center of the gospel."[136]

In the early thirties, at least, this moral mastery that Fosdick celebrated was an intellectual endeavor. He had described religious modernism in the late twenties as an effort to "rationalize religion": he agreed that reason alone cannot reach the depths of religion; but he also agreed that reason "has the right of veto" on other human faculties.[137] In 1931 he declared that the authority of Scripture extended to what the intellect would grant to it. "If you cannot understand all the Bible, make something worth while out of that much of it you can understand."[138] His 1917 devotional guide, *The Meaning of Faith*, had counseled that faith must be founded on real experience and reasonable thought.[139] And somewhat later he renewed the point that the Bible is best understood as a set of reflections upon experience. "The great texts of Scripture are the classic formulations of abiding human experience. They come out of experience, reflect experience, and are valuable only because they express an experimental fact of abiding poignancy and significance."[140]

Of course, there are many sources that stand as legitimate, authoritative reflections upon human experience. And some of them claim to be "sacred scripture" to their readers. "Acceptance of an inspired book is no peculiarity of Christians," Fosdick wrote.[141] Also, in the Christian milieu, the Bible scarcely stands alone as an arbiter of right conduct: common sense, sportsmanship, and whether an action would meet with the approval of the person whom one most admires, are other reasonably authoritative standards.[142]

When Fosdick did identify Scripture as authority, it was generally after he had already demonstrated intellectually that an idea or course of action was right. Even in his sermon preparation, the purpose of a sermon had already been determined before Scripture was consulted. "Every sermon's central motive should be some definite objective to be achieved. . . . Having chosen an object, I look for the relevant truth, and at that point the Bible invariably steps in."[143] The Bible, therefore, supported the point of the sermon more than the sermon declared the good news of the Bible. Scripture reinforced what Fosdick had previously decided to say in the pulpit.

That technique was apparent in a sermon on "The Peril of Privilege," in which he defined the Pharisees' problem as their attitude toward their own privileged status. Having thus articulated the issue, he then invoked scriptural support. "What I am saying today is biblical, so biblical that, were we to take this message out of the two Testaments, what would be left would be like a forest after a fire has swept through it."[144]

Those words came in the winter of 1937. His technique had remained the same as in the early thirties, but something else was different.

In the spring of 1935, Fosdick underwent surgery for the removal of a bladder tumor. He did not return to the Riverside pulpit until September of that year. It is not possible to state with any conviction that the surgery or the forced absence from preaching was causally related to subsequent theological shifts. After all, academic theology itself was shifting and Fosdick's pulpit theology was part of the flow: "we did hold romantic, unrealistic faiths about human affairs, from which we have lamentably fallen," he said,[145] admitting that the liberal optimisms of the past were gone. Neo-orthodoxy—whose adherents included, not least, Fosdick's colleague on the Union faculty, Reinhold Niebhur—offered a view of sin-wracked humanity that surely had some influence upon Fosdick's thought about the nature of human existence.[146]

But specifically on the matter of the authority of Scripture, he began to see in the late thirties that one could not discard those portions of the Bible which seemed intellectually unacceptable. Rather, the Bible had to be seen "as a whole, [for] its unity, its spiritual supremacy, its amazing timelessness, its unique revelation of man to men and of God to his children."[147] In contrast to the days when Fosdick might have seen the Bible as a source of individual encouragement which was "subjectively stimulating" whether or not it was true, he declared in a sermon first preached in March, 1938, that the New Testament proclaims both what is "objectively true" and what arouses confident faith.[148] Furthermore, in contrast to his formerly understood scriptural warrant for a confident human faith,[149] Fosdick asserted that the Bible paints a portrait of humanity needing God's redemption. "This is what the New Testament is all about, trying to get man to take a serious view of himself and then seriously seek a cure for his malady."[150] And he went so far as to say that the "basic principle of the New Testament" involves humanity's need to learn that this redemptive power is not our own.[151]

However, it is misleading to isolate that statement. For "the basic principle" of the Scriptures or "the center" of the Gospel is variously identified throughout the corpus of his sermons. Depending on the "object" to be attained or the "relevant truth" to be cited, Fosdick might say that the concept of vicarious sacrifice is at the center of the Gospel,[152] or that the Social Gospel is at the center of the New Testament,[153] or that good will is at the center of the Christian faith,[154] or that the "first" message of the Gospel is not what ought to be but what is.[155]

Fosdick's was a moving, shifting theology during the thirties. And the authority of Scripture, to the degree Fosdick cited it at all, was adduced to meet the changing categories of his thought. In his more rationalist period, he could summon scripture as an adjunct authority for those points of view which reason would allow, and he could rely on reason rather than the Bible as his authoritative standard for prophetic judgement.[156] Later in the thirties, as he moved toward a kind of practical mysticism which longed for more absolute standards, he could find in the Bible objective truth.[157] Then the imagination to apply biblical truth became the focus of his concern.[158] And the application was a matter of the human will.[159]

C. The "Freedom" of the Will

In his final Sunday sermon for 1940, Fosdick told the Riverside Church that there are two philosophies of life—determinism and free will. "Either one by itself is false," he said. "Those two partial insights must be added together to get the truth."[160] It was a conclusion toward which he had been moving through the thirties, since the days when a free human will had seemed resource enough to achieve salvation, and since the days when science had suggested that all human actions are determined by heredity and environment rather than the free exercise of the human will.[161]

The notion that either was "false" did represent a change of perspective for Fosdick. Never a bald determinist and rarely a proponent of absolute free will, he denied in a sermon used at least twice at Riverside that he was a "fatalist" while insisting that "there is no such thing as free will."[162] Yet it was clear that the emphasis given in his earlier work had placed great confidence in the powers of the human will.

In one of his early devotional guides, he had ascribed to the human will a nearly absolute freedom to deploy faith in anyone or anything. "Since I must and do use faith on something, I will choose the highest. It is with such a rational and worthy choice that the Christian turns to Jesus."[163] In another, he narrowed the range of free human choice somewhat, saying, for instance, that God does not have a will in general but a will in particular for individual lives.[164] Yet each person remains free to avoid or embrace what God would have anyone's life become. And Fosdick left no doubt about the place of free human choice in the Christian scheme of hope.

> You cannot choose to be Christlike and attain your choice by trying;
> but you can choose Christ for your Friend, his Kingdom for your
> Cause, the Bible for your Book, the Church for your Brotherhood,
> and these consciously chosen influences will unconsciously
> transform your life.[165]

He did not agree that this amounted to a "moral influence" theory of atonement.[166] But in a 1932 sermon at Riverside, he implied that the influence of Jesus is all the world needs. "So long as Jesus has influence in his church, there is only one place where the gospel can end—with the kingdom of God on earth, which is a better social order."[167] And that aspect of his thought never really disappeared from his sermons during the thirties. In 1936, he did not proclaim Jesus as the only Lord and Savior, but instead called Jesus' way of life "the best I know."[168] Two years later he remained sure that Christianity was essentially "the dropping of a new personal influence" into human life: "Christ came in," he said.[169]

With no more than such "influence" at stake, any claims that Christ made a unique contribution to humanity are hard to make. But Fosdick did not try to make them. Jesus was a man: different from the rest of humanity in His capacity for God, but not in substance or quality.[170] Jesus differed in degree, but not in kind, from the rest of humanity. Fosdick could imagine no higher object of devotion than Jesus, but he could not consent to the usual Christian affirmation that Jesus is one of the Trinity. "I do not think that Jesus was omnipotence, omniscience, omnipresence masquerading in a human body."[171] Perhaps Jesus is the personification of great religion, Fosdick said, but He is not God.[172] It is just that He "knew God so well that he could trust him anywhere."[173]

So no divine compulsion reaches out from Jesus to touch the rest of humanity. The human will is free to choose how and by whom it will let itself be influenced. Fosdick knew that the pulpit runs dry when it offers a perpetual stress on the will, and that a deeper fellowship than human will can supply is necessary for spiritual strength:[174] "reformers who have nothing in their goodness except militant will" are "like clanging cymbals," he said.[175] But human choice is still at the base of those fellowships by which one allows oneself to be inspired. When human effort is righteously put forth, the universe responds "to man's moral life";[176] when diligent moral labor is put forth, "great faith" arises.[177]

Against this evidence that Fosdick's pulpit theology was built upon the work of the free will is his sensitivity to the ways in which doctrine is shaped by the varieties of human experience which impinge upon voluntary choice. For instance, he concluded during a trip to the holy land that the desert is the best place to be a Calvinist, or some other kind of determinist: Islam, he said, is a term which means "submission"; what more fatalistic religion is there, he wondered rhetorically, than the religion which Mohammed propagated across the world's great deserts?[178]

One could extrapolate Fosdick's argument, then, to explain why determinism would not prosper in the intellectual freedom of the American democracy and in the sophisticated pluralism of New York

City. Fosdick was convinced that the "will of God" is not something to which God's people submit, but something which they work out.[179] He felt that neither fascism nor communism was compatible with Christianity (though in 1936 he feared fascism more), and yet the incompatibility was psychological rather than theological.[180] We decide our destiny. There are choices to be made, choices which only a free human will can determine.[181] And in his view the church was only true to the Gospel when it encouraged freedom. "There are two kinds of religion. Never mix them up. . . . One of them, ecclesiasticism, has always sinned against freedom and oppressed conscience . . . [with] external regimentation . . . . [whereas Jesus] tried to release people from within."[182]

Fosdick's pulpit theology, in turn, stressed how free Christians were, and what they were free to do. During the opening weeks of 1932, he reminded the Riverside congregation of the great power represented among them—"intellectual, professional, political, financial" power.[183] It was a specification for his own people that fit very nicely with a general principle he had articulated eleven months earlier—that business and political leaders can use their management skills to engineer a solution for every national dilemma. "Unemployment will not be solved . . . by individual goodness alone. That is going to take brains of the kind that business has so magnificently used for its own purposes, turned now to the solution of a social problem."[184] He recognized that being unemployed was irritating in life, but counseled his listeners to follow the example of the oyster and turn life's irritations "'into pearls of patience and love.'"[187] He applauded human achievements, like New York City's political success in ridding itself of "a worse than useless mayor"[188] as evidence of what people can do. And he credited the Christian faith with responsibility for confidence in humanity. "Christian faith has made an incalculable contribution to humanity's self-esteem by its belief in human possibilities."[189]

Those possibilities are fulfilled, or are left unfulfilled, according to the choices of the human will, not fate or destiny, in Fosdick's view. Indeed, he resented any dogmatic or literary portrayal of a person as "a helpless victim of fate," insisting that the church "should assert its message concerning `the moral competence of the empowered personality to handle life.'"[190] And he saw no one who lacked "the capacity to become in some fine degree an empowered personality."[191] One need only choose to embrace the power.

Nor were Fosdick's convictions about human possibilities eroded away as the depression years continued. In the fall of 1935, he assured his congregation that people remain responsible for their own spiritual welfare in any crisis: the outcome "of any situation, however difficult, lies within ourselves."[192] Three months later, he interpreted Christmas as the inspiration for people to go forward "not the whipped victims of circumstance but the creators of change in the world."[193] His outlook fundamentally seemed no different from what it was nearly five years earlier, when he allowed that "Certain old formulations of free will have been exploded by the new psychology, but freedom has not been exploded. . . . In every situation, something more is present than the facts; namely, the possibilities. . . . God gives us possibilities."[194]

Thus, the possibilities that exist in every situation are God-given, not of our own making: "Nothing comes merely by trying";[195] yet, the effort of will is "indispensable."[196] As Fosdick says in one of his most often-repeated phrases, we cannot assume that troubles will be overcome just by "blowing on one's hands" and going to work.[197] But even in an unyielding depression, the power of human initiative must not be diminished. In 1934, he said that people often reacted to the dilemma of determinism versus free will by claiming freedom for themselves in good or prosperous times while blaming fate or the will of God for their hardships in difficult times. "At no time in a man's life, however, does he so deeply need to believe that he is a free, creative person as when he is in trouble."[198] So the depression scarcely softened Fosdick's position with regard to the saving impact of the free human will, which chooses "to take in your strong hands the love ethic . . . until we make it victorious in the institutions of mankind."[199] All that Christians need to be free from "moral bondage" and to be released "into moral victory" is the will to find deliverance—if "we really want it."

Fosdick's rather exuberant confidence in the freedom of the human will doubtless had some affect upon his judgment when he looked askance at some proposals for deliverance from the depression. In the mid-thirties, for example, he opposed the Townsend plan[200] on the grounds that it would foster too much dependency on the federal government while at the same time undercutting the virtues of self-reliance and personal character.[201] As profound as the nation's problems might be, and as deeply as Fosdick's sensitivities ran, he still found that political freedom surpassed governmental mandates—in the same way that theological freedom surpassed heavenly mandates—as the reservoir of deliverance. What the will cannot perceive on its own can be

rediscovered in a renewal of "faith and devotional practice," he said.[202]
Whatever causes or loyalties gain mastery of a person must be the causes
and loyalties by which one chooses to be mastered. Whether to have
Christ as one's leader is a person's own choice, Fosdick noted.[203] True
freedom awaits the individual who makes the choice and volunteers to
have Christ as one's object of loyalty.[204] We decide which ideas will use
us.[205] Again it could be said that his perspective had not substantially
changed in the mid-thirties from what he had declared at Riverside in
October, 1930, when he advised his parishioners to follow "the way of
moral independence, to get your own high and interior standard of what
is good, to judge of yourself and for yourself what is right."[206]

To Fosdick, at least through the mid-thirties, there was no
impediment in the will to prevent its making the noblest and most salvific
choices. Any errors that were made, he believed, were the fault of human
"stupidity"—a correctable fault at that. In 1929, having successfully
argued for Riverside to be a seven-day-a-week church, Fosdick wrote that
only "stupidity" prevented all churches from offering services seven days
a week.[207] In April, 1933, when Hitler was moving under the Rosenburg
plan to seize control of the German church, Fosdick called it a "stupid"
move: unenlightened, perhaps, but not fatally or irreparably flawed.
"The Athenians who put Socrates to death were not wicked but
stupid. . . . The torturers of Galileo were not iniquitous but ignorant."[208]
The same deficiency killed Christ: "He was nailed on that cross by
human stupidity."[209] And it threatened the United States as well:
"Nothing can destroy our American democracy except our own
stupidity—but that can."[210] Through the early thirties at least, Fosdick
remained convinced that humanity could will its way into deliverance
from such threats, could choose not to remain ignorant, could save a
nation. And even when he admitted that there were certain limits to the
power of a free will, his admission did not exceed the realm of the
obvious.

> Our possibilities of choice are not limitless . . . rather our lives are
> set within boundaries predetermined by heredity and environment
> and, furthermore, we are in an economic and social system which
> keeps many from getting out of themselves all that is there. . . . In a
> nursery group I know, there is now a little boy whose major problem
> is to decide whether when he grows up he will be a man or a
> woman. Some day he will discover that his possibilities are not so
> extensive as he had supposed, that there is some truth in
> predestination and that there are limits to free will.[211]

In any case, an intense effort of human will was the *sine qua
non* of Fosdick's argument. He knew that "our capacity to be inspired"

and "changed" by companionship with God was essential to what the will might achieve: "reformers who have nothing in their goodness except militant will" are like clanging cymbals."[212]   But the bottom line of his theological accounting was the role of the will.

> I do not see how we are going to rid ourselves of the worst aspects of an economic system that issues in unemployment and the tragedy of men unemployable at forty-five without putting our wills into it. We cannot be rid of war . . . without putting our wills into it. We cannot get rid of high tariffs that raise the price of living for everybody, raise wages for almost nobody, and raise profits for a few, without putting our wills into it. We have to have militant will in the struggle for social righteousness.[213]

Perhaps the most significant test of this theological commitment to the power of the free will developed for Fosdick during the thirties with regard to his pacifism.   In his moving 1933 Armistice Day apostrophe to "The Unknown Soldier," he described war as "the prostitution of the noblest powers of the human soul to the most dastardly deeds."[214]   Then he went on to make this unqualified declaration: "We can have this monstrous thing or we can have Christ, but we cannot have both."[215]

> I renounce war. I renounce war because of what it does to our own men. . . . I renounce war because of what it compels us to do to our enemies. . . . I renounce war for its consequence. . . . I renounce war and never again, directly or indirectly, will support or sanction another.[216]

Three years later, in his first sermon for 1937, Fosdick expressed confidence that war will go the way of torture chambers and slavery, and that the renouncers of war—who were dismissed as sentimental optimists—will prove in the long run to have been the true realists.[217]   In the fall of 1938 he again hailed with confidence those who willed and worked for peace, identifying in particular Neville Chamberlain, who had gone to Munich to meet with Hitler. "As an American Christian, I salute with admiration and gratitude the British Prime Minister. . . . I suspect that history will justify him."[218]   Within weeks, of course, events conspired to discredit Chamberlain's effort and Fosdick's prediction. And Fosdick turned from an enthusiastic apologist for the will to pacify the world and became a melancholy voice prophesying in the wilderness of a burgeoning world war. A year after applauding Chamberlain, he pleaded for the United States to stay out of the war and to build an international organization that would keep the peace.[219] Two weeks after that, he said that if America entered the war "I should have to be a conscientious objector."[220] On May 5, 1940,[221] May 19, 1940,[222] May 26, 1940,[223] March 2, 1941,[224] and April 27, 1941,[225]

Fosdick repeatedly proclaimed the folly of American involvement in the war.

> The question which America faces today is no longer whether in any military sense we shall get into this war. No competent person I know of, pacifist or non-pacifist, supposes that we could get into this war with any good effect even if we wanted to. . . . This immediate war will be settled in Europe and beyond the weapons we are already sending there is little more that even the most militaristic among us could effectively do about that. . . . [We're going to need millions of people with] an unshakeable faith in God, in the moral order of the world, in the victory of righteousness, and in the possibilities of human life.[226]

So some of the rhetoric about human possibilities remained into the forties, yet it was tempered a bit: "A silly optimism is one of our worst enemies," he cautioned.[227]

His stand on the war seems to have lost its footing in any assurance about what the free human will could do to stop it. That insight had occurred to him before, as he reflected on the meaning of the First World War and the depression.

> When my generation was young, we were optimistic. . . . The catastrophe of the war broke through the thin veneer of our civilization and revealed the savagery beneath, and the succeeding economic disaster has deepened the pessimistic mood. . . . We have a chance now to be more soundly realistic than we used to be.[228]

But a more significant *theological* transition occurred when Fosdick allowed not merely that the will has its limits, but also that there exists the structural possibility of a flaw in the will, a basic "impotence."[229] Early in the thirties, he hesitated to use the word "sin." "What would you call pride, for example? A sin? Let us rather say that a conceited man has a sick mind."[230] He then went on to identify Jesus as the physician who came to heal the sick "by the presence of a radiant personality" which affords people "a healthy way out" of their guilt through their "penitence, confession, restitution, forgiveness, a new start, and new nerves of strength."[231] The prescription for recovery was thoroughly human—and the prognosis was promising.[232] By the end of the thirties, however, he was prepared to acknowledge a different aspect of his religious tradition. "Christian faith at its deepest has always held that man is a desperate sinner. . . . There is a Power not ourselves that makes for righteousness."[233] And in the fall of 1940, at the age of 62, he discovered a new topic on which he could preach.

> Never before in my ministry have I preached upon the familiar biblical figure of speech to which I ask your thought this morning— cleansing. . . . This is a dirty world. . . . If in any real sense we are to be unspotted from the world, it will be because we have resources

for cleansing, inner experiences of the soul that bathe us from the sullying dirt of life.[234]

Lest anyone think that the dirtiness is an external quality which a free human will could rinse away, Fosdick made it clear that neither the corruption nor the cleanliness was a matter of choice. "Commonly we think of sin as something we choose, a deliberate and wrong decision of our wills. Yet how much of our moral evil is not that at all! We do not choose it. We unconsciously accumulate it."[235] Acts of will neither cause our sinfulness nor cure it, he seemed to say: for it is in what human choice does not affect that one is soiled by sin; and it is without the achievements of one's ambitious free will that one can be set free from sin. Fosdick said that the experience came for him one day in the Connecticut hills, "when I saw a scarlet tanager playing in a full-blown dogwood tree what had thus, without my volition, sullied my life, was, without my volition, washed away."[236]

Yet it is not easy to date this experience or to be certain that it refers to a unique moment of cleansing for him personally. What seems clear is that at some point prior to autumn 1940, Fosdick surrendered a good bit of his confidence in the freedom of the will. In the spring of that year, he had admitted to the fact of sin as something more than an individual's lusts or outbursts of bad temper: "My sin is my share in the corporate evil that . . . brings down its tragic consequences upon the innocent."[237] In that same sermon, he affirmed that there is no salvation from such consequences by the acts of the sinner's free will, but only when "some one, who does not need to do it, voluntarily takes the burden on himself as Christ did on Calvary" and thus forgets oneself and gives oneself for the sake of others.[238] Free will, therefore, seems capable only of vicarious victories.

This was part of his pulpit theology as early as the first Sunday in December, 1937. "Our generation has obviously shifted from an enthusiastic faith in man as a savior to a fearful recognition of the fact that man desperately needs to be saved."[239] On the following Sunday in New York, he explained that the "reason we are so sunk now in disappointment is that we did hold romantic, unrealistic faiths about human affairs."[240] Those "faiths," he confessed, were gone.

As might be expected, Fosdick's developing deference to the relative impotence of the human will went hand in hand with his developing discovery of the reality of sin—a shifting nuance in his pulpit theology whose roots are also hard to locate. Charles Earl Leininger, aware that "a deepening conception of sin" appears through the years, cautions that the influence of neo-orthodox theology should not be considered "solely responsible for this development."[241]   Katherine Bonney put the matter directly to Fosdick himself in an interview, and he traced his rediscovery of the depth of sin to the First World War, not to the impact of neo-orthodoxy;[242] yet she still found a more realistic sense of sin in his later sermons.

Certainly, a re-examination of Fosdick's preaching supports her impression. Only in the late thirties did he seriously address himself to the implications of intractable evil and an impotent will.   In late September, 1938, he advised liberals to "respect" sin, and he exalted the "need of the gift which a high religion can bestow."[243]   Just a week before Christmas that same year, he opened up the matter of "The Modern World's Rediscovery of Sin," in which he confessed: "There is something wrong in human nature itself."[244]   Five years earlier, he had blithely proclaimed that "everything that Jesus taught is livable,"[245] whereas in the closing years of the decade he said that the Gospel "came to save men from that inner wrongness that curses human life."[246]   To speak of a free human will was no longer, for Fosdick, a declaration of unqualified optimism.

> Liberal Christianity . . . has on the whole been complacent about human nature. . . . Now, however, we face a difficult era with such cruel and depraved things afoot in the world as some of us have never seen before. . . . Human nature presents us with something new and different—freedom, that high and terrible gift of freedom that can take the holiest and make the worst out of it, and an inner wrongness that, so misusing freedom, brings to futility and grief the fairest hopes of men.[247]

And nothing exposes this perversity so vividly in human life as does war.[248]   The free human will seems incapable of choosing to renounce war.

And yet, for all that, Fosdick never completely forsook his trust in the freedom of the will to find and explore human possibilities. He was certainly suspicious of those "weary liberals who turn back now to authoritarian creeds"[249] when the old maxims about freedom seem to have been rendered ineffectual. If it could no longer be said that an individual could find deliverance by a free will potent enough to locate the formula for salvation, it remained true that persons could still release one another from bondage through the spirit and the action of self–sacrifice: "Self-sacrifice . . . is the most powerful, moral, lifting force in the world."[250]   According to Fosdick in the fall of 1941, the crucial question remained "how to pull ourselves together, how to become well-organized, consistent persons, how to get the whole of us on the side of the best of us."[251]   And the "ultimate answer" lay in "the positive attitude of aroused and sacrificial dedication by which "we can tap" God's power.[252]

It is instructive that a sermon which Fosdick delivered in the spring of 1930, even before the opening of Riverside, was still preachable in the summer of 1941, with its message extolling the freedom of humanity to "make the best of a bed mess." His premise was the difference between existence and life: "Existence is what you *find*; life is what you create."[253]

What had happened to Fosdick's views on the freedom of the will during the thirties, it seems, was that he combined two nearly irreconcilable perspectives.   Given his unwillingness to relinquish his basic commitment to human liberty, and given his growing awareness that human capacities were too impaired by involuntary sin to will (let alone do) the work of salvation, Fosdick juxtaposed both principles. And, on a Sunday in New York in 1938, he packaged them rather neatly.

> Two methods are indispensable for living. The first is trying hard, putting will into effort, being aggressive, making the direct attack on life. But the second is something else altogether—being inspired, falling under the spell of life's regenerative forces until stimulus and strength come up into one as from a great deep. . . . Volitional attack on life—that is one. Releasing power from beyond ourselves—that is the other.[254]

And the organizing center, for both receiving the inspiration and launching the attack, is the human personality: it embraces what God gives, and it goes to work on what an individual can achieve. "Personality is partly a gift and partly an achievement. . . . Personality is thus the profoundest and most potential factor in the universe, and each of us had been trusted with it. This is the central fact of life."[255]

Clearly, in Fosdick's view, the will remained free enough to fulfill the dimensions of the human personality. The will could impinge upon the power of "life's regenerative forces" and attack life directly with that power.   And no impairment of the will could prevent it from discovering and obeying the Creator's laws.[256]

At least one of Fosdick's colleagues in New York had substantial doubts about that. For just three weeks earlier, George Arthur Buttrick had said

> God does not ask obedience: He asks only love. . . . And there's the paradox! Life is a discipline, but the discipline is congruous with our deepest nature; and therefore not a discipline. Life is an obedience, but it is obedience to a Fatherly Spirit like unto Christ; and therefore not obedience, but filial joy.[257]

CHAPTER VII
MEDIATING A PRESENCE

That Buttrick's pulpit theology differed from Fosdick's is sometimes apparent in bold relief, sometimes in subtle shades and nuances. For example, across town and fifty blocks to the south from where Fosdick's anti-creedalism was so elegantly housed, George Buttrick, too, had some words about creeds. From his pulpit at Madison Avenue and Seventy-third Street, Buttrick declared early in 1934 that "following Jesus does not mean signing your name to a long creed."[1]

> It is the wisdom of Christianity that it builds not on creeds (which sometimes offend, and which for any Thomas are hard to accept), nor on an ethic (which is finer than other ethics only in degree) but on the one Soul compact of courage, faith, and love; and on our own soul which at its deepest movements inevitably goes out to Him.[2]

One could conclude that, in having jettisoned the authority of the creeds, Buttrick had turned to the human personality as the locus of authority for Christian preaching. At least he inferred that Jeremiah intended to say as much when the prophet argued that the ark of the covenant would be relocated in the human heart.[3]

> Jeremiah did not say that all authority had gone. The Ark was now in man's own soul. . . . Man is the true dwelling place of God. . . If personality is God's best temple, we must reverence personality. . . .The new ark of the covenant is personality.[4]

Yet, for all of the allowable similarities, Buttrick's pulpit theology begs to be understood in categories other than those which may be applied to Fosdick, Scherer, and Sockman. A key illustration of that involves his—as distinguished from their—approach to the language, the words, of a creed. Others address themselves to the creed as moderns trying to explain (or explain away) what is confessed in the creed. The words of an affirmation of faith constitute, for them, a set of propositions: the Virgin Birth, the Resurrection, the Trinity. The credible words are to be interpreted for human understanding and the incredible concepts are to be interpreted so as to constitute no barrier to human understanding.

Scherer, in particular, was a careful steward of words. At the age of four, he could deliver speeches from Shakespeare, which his

mother had taught him to memorize.[5] As a college student under the
Jesuit classicist Thomas della Torre, Scherer's classroom recitations
included oral readings of Greek texts followed immediately by his own
oral translations of each passage into Latin.[6] He wrote a Master's thesis
on "The Use of the Infinitive in Horace."[7] So Scherer "loved words,"
including the words of the creed. Fosdick and Sockman, feeling much
less bound to the creedal language, handled the traditional confessions of
faith as propositions which required interpretation in twentieth-century
terms, and required disavowal if those fourth-century propositions
seemed incompatible with the experience and philosophical perspective
of the modern world.

Buttrick, however, did not see a creed as propositional, but
rather as poetic. Like Scherer, he cherished the words but for their
metaphorical and mythical qualities as well as their grammar and
dogmatic content. Like Fosdick and Sockman, he knew that the world's
mindset at ancient Nicaea was incongruent with the mindset of his own
New York. But he declared that Nicaea had plenty to do with New York
because of the way its creed "breaks into poetry about Christ." Art,
rather than philosophy, was at issue for Buttrick. "A creed should be
more akin to poetry than logic—a banner to be unfurled or a glad Te
Deum, rather than a set of propositions to be debated."[8] Or, as he put it in
a sermon during the winter of 1931: "A poet will always say it better
than a theologian. We shall never treat our creeds aright until we chant
them instead of arguing about them."[9]

Given that, Buttrick devised a simile of his own to describe the
non-creedal character of the parish he served: "it holds creeds as a crab
holds its shell—as something to be outgrown and sloughed off that a
larger shell may appear."[10]

A. Justification by Faith

Sitting loosely to the propositions of Christian dogma was only
one way in which Buttrick's views appeared to have kinship with those
of his leading New York colleagues. In the same sermon where he
described his congregation as "not creedal," Buttrick also spoke of
Madison Avenue Presbyterian as "not denominational" and "not a class
church." He said "Its tests are religious rather than theological."[11] And
he seemed to have a rather broad understanding of the term "religious."
He spoke of humanity's "hunger for the Eternal" as the "deepest common
denominator" shared by the race.[12] The basis of religion is faith in God,

he said,[13] and faith is something that every person has: "we all have faith (at least in certain radiant moments) and we all have doubt."[14] In the late twenties, Buttrick had described faith as a person's "birth-right,"[15] as "courage,"[16] and as "the bedrock of human nature" which Jesus "illumines" and "gathers . . . into the clarity of flesh and blood."[17]

Thus, faith seems to have been a very human commodity which rallies "to some ideal (as, for example, the ideal of Christ)"[18] as an "affirmation of our best hopes."[19] One might even conclude from Buttrick that faith is not much more than "a certain outgoing of the soul" which is as common to human beings as is their doubt; and the choice between the two, whether to live in faith or in doubt, is an option selected by free human decision.[20]

Yet his sermon corpus, even in the early thirties, offers another dimension of preaching which separates his proclamations about faith from those of his contemporaries who understood faith essentially in anthropological terms. The "outgoing of the soul" from the human side of the relationship was, in Buttrick's perception, encountered by a similar striving from the other side of the relationship. So faith was not a subjective effort but an objective engagement: "*Grace* means the outgoing favor of God who seeks us"; and the faith that we do have is built upon the evidence of that grace in the records of Jesus' deeds and words and of the disciples' response to Him.[21] Furthermore, there was nothing naturally human about the encounter. "There was in the disciples no natural tendency to such a faith. There was, we might say, a natural antipathy to such a faith."[22] Therefore, what was accomplished by grace through faith involved, in Buttrick's view, not the fulfillment of a natural human striving but the overcoming of a naturally human resistance to any such relationship.

That, in turn, gives preaching a new purpose. Some of the goals which Buttrick had for the pulpit were not unconventional: sermons should show compassion, exalt individual human worth, declare the duties of private morality and public responsibility, lift the people to the promise of redemption. But there was one thing more—"*the mediation of a Presence*," which Buttrick labeled the preacher's consummate responsibility.[23] "To mediate that Presence—that is at once the preacher's burden, his sovereign gift, his sufficient credential, his enduring joy."[24]

In short, both a classic view of justification by grace through faith and an exalted view of the preacher's task operate in Buttrick's pulpit theology. One is redeemed by the power of divine grace seeking humanity and encountering persons through faith; and preaching is what makes the encounter possible. But it happens only insofar as the preacher declares the priority of divine grace in the encounter: for, in the human dimension, faith exists only as response to the "friendship" which God offers through Christ.[25] Yet even that response is not simply a function of some human decision. "A genuine faith is not something to be chosen like a new necktie or a new hat: it is written on the fleshly tablets of the heart."[26] So Buttrick's pulpit theology effectively excluded from the matter of salvation any question of human achievement or striving or merit. The encounter with Christ—the relationship with divine grace which brings freedom from sin and death—demands no human prerequisite. "People say they are not good enough to come to Christ. Nobody comes because he is good enough: he comes because he isn't good enough, and to be made good."[27] In fact, the saving encounter with Christ does not require that God's ways be made intellectually compelling or comprehensible: "'If we understand Him we could not worship Him.'"[28]

Buttrick thereby avoids the theological trend (manifest in Fosdick and Sockman, at least) toward a doctrine of justification by works. Thus, it was on theological grounds that Buttrick kept his pulpit at a distance from the debate about repeal of the Eighteenth Amendment to the Constitution: sainthood is not accomplished by the passage or repeal of a law, nor is it fostered by pulpit propaganda on behalf of some legislative act.[29]

However, that is not to say Buttrick kept his homiletical distance from the social application of the gospel. He believed that an indivisible bond linked faith to social service,[30] and he found it irreconcilable with Christianity that ten percent of the American people owned ninety-five percent of the nation's wealth in 1932.[31] Human effort had to correct injustice.

And sometimes it was risky business. Buttrick often spoke of faith as a venture, suggesting for instance that the authority of Christ is often demonstrated in His power to take the "little enigmas" we bring to Him and release their grip on us as we "forget them in the vaster challenges which He returns on us."[32] This is the "adventure" He has left us,[33] one which lets us prove our faith only "at dangerous risk."[34] Not that faith can be acquired by throwing oneself into some abyss, but rather that Christians celebrate the certitude[35] of faith "when they dare a hope . . . and when they pray into a silence. Then confidence comes, and a Beckoning."[36]

Again, this theological argument had an implication for preaching, and Buttrick was explicit that this adventure into faith's certitude had some very special leaders.

> Not the comfortable preachers in fat pulpits who have carefully diluted their word, but the real preachers ordained and unordained, who at risk and at cost have espoused causes of justice and charity years before other men have been willing even to follow.[37]

Buttrick understood personally that preachers could be jeopardized by their principles.[38] After all, pastors and parishioners had to live in the real world.

> A true man hates the compromise in which he is inevitably involved in our civilization. . . . But however much we wish to escape from this world, we cannot. We should be convicted of cowardice if we tried; and that conviction would be worse than the turmoil and bruising of everyday.[39]

Yet he knew that the world could never be "our home,"[40] and he deplored those who tried to make it so.

> We in our time have made of Christianity a pleasant custom, eminently respectable and socially advantageous. We have filed smooth the eagle's beak, and drawn his talons, and blinded him and made him a household pet. But Christianity is not what we have made it. . . . A Christian is known by his enemies as well as by his friends.[41]

Buttrick yearned for the kind of faith that was free to break stride and run against the tide of social custom.

> I wish Christianity were not so respectable. . . . I wish its enthusiasms had not been disinfected and sterilized and institutionalized. I wish there were more Christians to do crazy things—like Mary breaking a box of precious ointment!—like Christ dying on a cross. I wish faith could be dramatized.[42]

The point of the Christian life, then, is to cherish the gift of grace that God gives through faith and to run the risk that will demonstrate the power of the gift.

> Here among the factories and bakeshops of earth we must keep alive the poet in us and the prophecy of a city that is to be. By prayer, by a stirring up of the gift that is in us, by being willing to be reckoned as fools or bedlams or outlandish men, we must be pilgrims.[43]

Such courageous efforts for Buttrick are the works that a justifying faith does, never the works that justify nor the labors that amount to a justification. After all, God's does not depend on the diligence of our service,[44] any more than God deals with us according to our sins.[45] Indeed, there is an inevitability about God's sovereignty which no human failure or triumph can alter: "Nothing can separate us from His purpose," Buttrick declared in the spring of 1932. "Nothing can thwart His plan of love."[46]

As the decade rolled along, from the depth of the depression through the New Deal, from the rising of tyranny in Europe and Asia to the clashing of swords, Buttrick's pulpit theology retained a remarkable consistency. Changes of emphasis were far less noticeable than in the sermons of his Manhattan colleagues, and adjustments of doctrine were rarely to be found.[47] The elements of faith remained invisible surmise and courage.[48] In late 1937, he spoke on a Sunday in New York of grace as the "free favor" of God[49]—the very same phrase he had used at the start of the decade at Yale.[50] In the same year, he declared "that God Himself inspires our search for the meaning of Reality," adding that "if God provokes the search man must respond."[51]

Again, throughout the decade, Buttrick saw the gift of faith and the receiver's response as inseparable. His was no antinomian view: salvation, he said, "is not merely rescue" and "not cowardice or slothful ease"; rather, it means "to be saved from cowardice and selfishness."[52] "Courageous trust" is the characteristic of faith, but not the cause of faith.[53] The Christian works with confidence and courage for righteousness. But not with self-righteousness: "How can a man be inflexibly right," Buttrick asked, "except by God's pardon and sustaining grace?"[54]

Here, too, Buttrick's approach to homiletics is a deliberate consequence of his pulpit theology. The preacher, he said, is not engaged in an argument or debate, but rather is making a confession of faith and a plea.[55] The standards of righteousness and propriety to which a preacher is to be held accountable are not those of the contemporary age but rather those of the future and of God.[56] So preaching is not captive to the shifting sands of the landscape, nor is it vulnerable to the changing moods of an era; rather, the faith which the preacher confesses remains secure, and the word which the preacher delivers endures forever.

Thus, in the theology from Buttrick's pulpit, one finds a rather clear description of what Christianity is, and is not.

> Christianity is neither a blind credulity (saying that every syllable in the Bible is true), nor a vague altruism, nor any particular economic pattern (since economic patterns must forever change). Christianity is a being laid-hold-on by Jesus, and an answering avowal that He is what God means, and what life with its joys and sorrows would have us become, and what the whole universe must finally honor. Christianity is neither a dogmatism nor a sentimentalism: it is the leap into light of those who, seeing Jesus, exclaim . . . He is mine and I am His.[57]

The Christian faith is built not upon some spark of hope or generosity that is endemic to human life, but rather it lives because faith is "the gift of God" and "the shadow of His life in us." "Faith obeys. . . . Faith endures. . . . Faith labors—in love. . . . Faith ventures. . . . But all that it does, it does in prayer."[58] Faith is the yoke given to us—the yoke which at the same time as it binds us to our work brings us our salvation.[59]

It is a hard, objective yoke, too. For, as Buttrick expressed himself across the decade, faith is the gift to humanity which God made possible by an event of holy sacrifice and suffering.[60] In Buttrick's pulpit, the theology of the cross is no mere illustration of the moral significance of vicarious sacrifice; instead the cross was that historical event which transcended history in a way that only myth and metaphor can declare. The cross, Buttrick said in March of 1938, is "the nailing down of our lower nature" and "the liberation of the higher self."[61] The cross is at once our stumbling block and our salvation. "Going from faith to skepticism, the cross is a barrier. Going from skepticism to faith, it is a door."[62] Buttrick was willing to admit that at times skepticism seems to prevail and that the cross then becomes an insurmountable barrier for many people. There are always those who prefer the tangible realities of their own making as the place to lay their ultimate confidence. But the ultimate victory belongs elsewhere. "Skepticism has an hour: faith can afford to wait. Faith has the eternities."[63] And the proof of that is God's response to our strenuous efforts to build security and strength for ourselves. The city's magnificent towers, he said in 1939, testify after all not to our might but to our impotence: the Empire State Building stands half-empty, towering over the East Side slums; Rockefeller Center stands in the midst of urban congestion, another contribution to the already overstocked real estate market, the cause of fictitious rises in rentals, an additional chance for the city to be imprisoned and poisoned by gasoline fumes.[64] While skeptics and doubters churn in their chairs about human attempts to escape from these forms of suffering, even questioning claims of divine benevolence in view of human achievements which create injustice and oppression, God could gleefully and derisively laugh at us. But instead of laughter at our futile efforts to create our own security or to build our way to divinity, God went to a cross for us.[65]

So faith, first and forever, is a gift[66] which is attached to Christ[67] by the pull of the cross. In another of Buttrick's metaphors, grace is a ladder (Jacob's ladder) which God builds and by which God "draws near to men in redemption."[68] To the offer of redemption comes the Christian response in which faith is an adventure[69] and an assertion of meaning which is imprinted upon life.[70] But all our "journeys lead back to the cross."[71]

For Buttrick, this kind of pulpit theology is a conscious effort to reclaim the doctrines of the Protestant Reformation for the challenges of the twentieth-century. As he had written earlier, Christianity needed "an ampler doctrine of 'grace' instead of the dreary rubric of works!"[72]

One could find justification only by grace through faith. That tenet remained true for the Christian faith in the twentieth-century as it had been in the sixteenth because of the inescapable and compelling fact of sin. If there is an important movement to be found in the nuances of Buttrick's pulpit theology during the thirties, it may lie in the relatively larger expression which he gives to the sinful human condition in the latter years of the decade. But, if so, it needs to be added that this adjustment represents a quantitative change in the number of times he discusses the nature of sin not a qualitative change in the presumption of human sin. There is that about our life, Buttrick notes, which we cannot change:[73] "Sin has become our prison."[74] The anomaly is, as he was heard to say in autumn, 1939, that we want to stay incarcerated even though an escape route is available to us: "Secretly we plan to go on sinning. . . . Secretly we know the way out."[75]

It is as if some cosmic conflict is being waged in our souls. He called it a "civil war" in human nature whereby "we suffer the torment of a divided soul."[76] From this war between heaven and earth raging within us,[77] we can be—indeed we are—saved only "by a Man . . . by a Cosmic Mercy."[78]

> Our only salvation is to cast ourselves on the mystery of God and His mercy. He only can rekindle our jaded heart. . . . We come, thus, our life open to a Divine faith and fire. . . . We come with altar flame almost dead. . . . We are waiting now for an unseen Hand to kindle again the vital warmth of life.[79]

Those words were preached and printed in grim days. By the spring of 1941, one large industrial component of the economic recovery was the growth in American military hardware manufacturing. The pain of the depression was being eased by the pain of war. That made "the presence of God" seem a fatuous notion. Yet even a hidden God, in Buttrick's pulpit theology, is a gracious God. "His apparent absence is not cruelty, but grace," for in the dim and lowly places He lurks and in whispers He speaks to us still. "But we must follow His whisper . . . then we shall find ourselves—and Him."[80]

The problem is that while the world prepares for, and goes to, war, the war within keeps raging. Buttrick declared, "The times are dark but morning will come,"[81] yet he recognized that "light is uncomfortable to waking eyes."[82] Therefore, faith remains an adventure that must be risked: "We must walk by faith rather than by sight, by the soul's surmise rather than by the mind's logic."[83]

And faith remains a gift: "too daring and too profound ever to have come of man" and "too splendid . . . ever to be untrue."[84] Buttrick knew that in the agonies of the earth, at the close of the thirties, it was not easy to proclaim or receive the word that faith abides. Yet the preacher must proclaim the truth of faith while the nails are being driven again and again into a cross. For the cross abides. In the spring of 1938, that meant that Niemoller was infinitely stronger than Hitler, Buttrick said.[85] And as the winter of 1941 approached, it meant that God's "redeeming love can turn the worst into the coming of God in the earth."[86]

B. The Authority of Scripture

In the mid-thirties, Buttrick published a complaint about one of his colleagues, "a well-known preacher" who proclaimed that immortality must be true because the human race needs it to be true, and because life would be meaningless without it.[87] Buttrick's protest was against all vain efforts to build a theology out of human reason or even human need: the issue is not whether pulpit theories are helpful, but whether they are true. Humanism builds upon the practical conviction that "there is no God."[88] That theory may or may not foster social chaos, but that is hardly the point as far as Buttrick is concerned. The issue rests, rather, on how well the theory rests upon fact.[89] And, as in geometry, the basic facts are those not susceptible to rational demonstration or proof, but those that are accepted as axiomatic. "God is perchance the main axiom which we accept before we can begin to live. . . . God perchance is the assumption that makes life possible."[90]

Again, as in geometry, there are certain postulates which are inescapable and yet undemonstrable. Such postulates generally go by the name of doctrinal standards. And Buttrick assailed the conventional wisdom about such standards. "We say that loss of standards comes from lack of faith, but it is more often true that lack of faith comes from denial of standards."[91] One such standard for him was the authority of Scripture.

Yet his intolerance for a theology that merely recycled human experience (building a doctrine of immortality on the human need of it, for instance) did not mean that he considered the Bible to be a hard, impenetrable rock against which human experiences and hopes are forever to be dashed. Instead, he believed that it was within human experience that the truth declared by Christianity was most clearly manifest: "New Testament theology was an interpretation of experience," he wrote.[92]

> A man's compass points to magnetic north . . . it is naturally drawn to a magnetic something out there in space. There is a magnetism in us. Call it conscience—hint of an Eternal Rectitude. Call it compassion—type of an Eternal Love. Call it truth—foregleam of an Eternal Verity. Call it hope—prophecy of an Eternal Day. Call it what we may: it is but a mysterious magnetism of human souls pointing like the mariner's little compass to a vast Magnetism out of sight. How shall we know that Christ is God's word? How but by the swing of the magnetic needle in us toward Him?[93]

Half a decade later, Buttrick said to his congregation, "The Bible is a transcript of man's deepest experience."[94]

Of course, there was an obvious dilemma which modern human experience posed for the standard of scriptural authority: namely, the advances of science. For instance, there are always those who want the case for or against the authority of Scripture to rest on the outcome of the battle between creationists and evolutionists. Buttrick preferred to change the structure of the debate. He focused on the error of post-Reformation theology which, having deposed the authority of "an allegedly infallible Church" and then finding itself still "craving external supports," elevated "an infallible Book to the vacant throne."[95] The authors of Scripture were far less troubled by the convictions of contemporary scientists than are moderns. They "accepted the science of the day which ever changes," and uttered the word of a "Presence which in all change is ever the same": the Lord is still my shepherd, "whether the earth is flat or round."[96]

Believing that "the Bible can take care of itself,"[97] Buttrick said that the validity or authority of Scripture is to be tested not in some contest against science but by the way it mediates God to human experience. To be what it claims to be, the Bible must enable humanity's "noblest seeking," which is "man's quest for God," and "God's quest for man in its most gracious finding" to encounter each other. "The Bible as inspired writing stands or falls by that test—and indubitably it stands!"[98] The Bible is, therefore, neither a textbook for science nor a rulebook for human conduct but "a jet of light" that shows us the way to our meeting place with God.[99]

Samples of Buttrick's preaching and published writing through the thirties show the consistency of his concern. While others may have chosen to look beyond a supposedly completed debate between

Fundamentalists and Modernists, Buttrick perceived that the controversy was by no means frozen, and he recognized that a struggle remained for some proper understanding of biblical authority. He admitted that the doctrine of verbal inspiration or "literal infallibility . . . was vital at the core" for it amounted to a "confession that in and through the Book God has spoken."[100]   However, inerrancy was in itself no principle of redemption. As Buttrick had declared back in 1928,

> a telephone directory is literally true, and the parable of the Prodigal Son is not; but the telephone book is not salvation, whereas that story of human folly and divine mercy is like a daybreak on our darkness.[101]

Religion should never have gone into battle with science, he said: "We have fought where we should have worshipped."[102]   And the fighting has produced only confusion. Buttrick addressed that problem in two sermons preached in the early months of 1934 and again five years later. "If Genesis says the world was made in six days and God's other book of rocks and ocean say it was made in millennia of years, the mind in is conflict."[103]

> The Book of Beginning says, or seems to say, that God made the world in six days, by arbitrary decree, a few thousand years ago. The Book of Rocks and stars, in whose pages we live, says that our planet alone is a billion years old; that creation moves by evolution. . . . Which book shall we believe?[104]

Christianity is, after all, not a "blind credulity" which lurches at every scriptural syllable.[105]   It is not an obsession with dogma that uses the Bible merely as a text book of theological theory.[106]   It is an encounter with the living, life-shaping Presence of Christ.[107]   And the Bible mediates that encounter: it is "not a book of definitions" but of "faces . . . and stories";[108] its writers were not "dictaphones"[109] but individuals whose personal points of view and measures of understanding made a difference in the transmission of the truth; its forms of inspiration are not a "level tableland"[110] but a mixture of hills and valleys, wild primitive lands and placid green pastures.

> The Bible is a book written and translated by men, whatever be its divine origin or provocation. Here set in the realm of the human it cannot be shielded from man's questing mind, which also is given of God. The Book itself under reverent scrutiny must attest our theory of inspiration: otherwise it is not "a lamp unto our feet," but only a puzzle and self-contradiction.[111]

If Buttrick's view of biblical authority, then, requires an answer to the question he posed—whether the Book of Genesis[112] or the Book of Rocks is to be believed—the answer lies in the reverent scrutiny of the reverent story-telling that constitutes the biblical "myth."   Once we understand what myths are, and how ours differ from others, "we shall have found peace for this war-scarred cathedral of Genesis" and we will see that the Scriptures manifest a transcendent truth which is available to us nowhere else. "Men did not find God by logic: He found them by inborn reverence and by the very terms of life. . . . The knowledge of God is primal—like human freedom."[113]

So God is the axiom of life. And the Bible is the declaration of what is axiomatic.

All of which has a direct impact upon preaching. To begin, Buttrick often expressed the view that we do not read the Bible; rather, the Bible reads us.[114] That is to say, the person who picks up the Bible to study it, or the preacher who lifts up a text to preach upon it, is not reading the Bible so much as being read by it—even "staggered" by it.[115] He felt that his own generation of church-goers was less literate biblically than preachers of previous eras had enjoyed. "The preacher of yesteryear could count on some knowledge of Scripture on the part of the congregation: the measure of that knowledge today is not great."[116] It is not surprising, therefore, that "life situation preaching" should find such a wide following among the clergy.

For his part, Buttrick almost invariably began his sermons with, and crafted his sermons out of, a biblical text. However, his perspective on biblical authority entertained a remarkably comprehensive view of the relationship between Scripture and the situations in life to which Scripture speaks.

> Beginning with the Bible, true expository preaching will carry it to life. But if we begin with life, we shall end with the Bible, for the Bible is omnific. . . . A preacher need not be limited to the Bible for his texts. But if he stays within the Bible, he will still not be limited, for the Bible has no limits.[117]

The one thing life situation preaching could not do, of course, was to mitigate the effect of biblical illiteracy in the Church. Buttrick regretted that his own parishioner, Bruce Barton, could legitimately describe the Bible as *The Book Nobody Knows*, when it "ought to be the Book every[one] learns and loves."[118] Even more did he regret that the general ignorance about the Bible may be the fault of the Church, which so often misused God's word as a bludgeon in matters of controversy or ecclesiastical discipline.

> The Bible is ignored or renounced—not (be it noted) for what it says in itself (for few people read the Bible for what it says in itself) but because of what the Church, now disavowed, has said of it.[119]

Buttrick's careful structuring of his sermons recognized both the limitations which ignorance of the Bible imposed on the pulpit and also the legitimate authority of Scripture for preaching. He envisioned the sermon as the product of a ladder and a set of stairs.[120]

Text-Topic (Heaven)

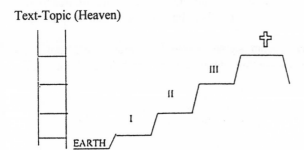

As Buttrick explored it in one of his lectures,

> The text will be taken and brought down to earth; then step by step the sermon will take the participant up to the various levels, taking time to rest there, until he has lifted the text back to its level before the Cross. Thus the ground of life on which "Bill Smith" was living is lifted to the level of the text . . . and then falls away in a plea for a verdict.[121]

Thus it seems clear that Buttrick's pulpit theology affirmed a classic Protestant view of the authority of Scripture, while distancing himself from that Fundamentalist version of Protestant Orthodoxy which sought to encapsulate biblical authority in a doctrine of inerrancy. His sermons, in structure as well as doctrinal content, were rooted in the authority of Scripture—not at the expense of speaking to the real dilemmas of human life, but that the redemptive work of God might be mediated to human life in an encounter of deliverance and hope.

In Buttrick's view, such an encounter was a *sine qua non*. As he surveyed the unhappy situation facing humanity in late autumn 1941, he found an array of unpleasant political choices—all of which "spring from man's wrong-doing."[122] To understand that life situation, Buttrick believed, one had to trust the authority of Scripture for an explanation and an encounter with a sign of hope. "The Bible says that we cannot solve our dilemma, that we cannot heal the cleft in our nature; but that God can do what man cannot do."[123]

C. The "Freedom of the Will"

In his first contribution to the Beecher lecture series at Yale, Buttrick offered an illustration (which he frequently found useful) to demonstrate the degree to which humanity is free: "We are free to jump from the top of a fifty-story building, but not free in that jump to cancel gravitation."[124]

Human freedom is given within the bounds of strict limits. For instance, we do not choose our parents or our individual aptitudes of mind and body.[125]

> Physical freedom is always within limits. . . . Mental freedom is always within limits; a proposition cannot at once be true and untrue. Moral freedom is always within limits; there is a moral law.[126]

Thus, the notion that a person can live by "self will" in "unfettered freedom" is "the primeval lie."[127] In this sense, freedom is one of the gifts of creation and as such is subject to the limits of the cosmos, such as gravity or ancestry.

At the same time, as a gift of creation, freedom is essential to humanity; and for Buttrick that means that freedom persists beyond this world and into the next, "for when freedom ends, essential humanity ends."[128] In every person, he said, "there remains some inviolable inner realm of freedom,"[129] which is "axiomatic in our consciousness."[130] That, in turn, has implications for the issue of salvation, for what is essential to humanity (namely freedom) must be part of the process of redemption, or humanity is not saved. Therefore, in his sermon on the Sunday before Christmas, 1931, Buttrick declared that "A forced salvation is no salvation; and not even God can save us without our free consent."[131]   And he held to that premise throughout the thirties, as indicated in a sermon preached late in January, 1938. "What God wishes to do for us He cannot do without our help—for that would rob us of our freedom."[132]

So, in a rather delightful paradox, human freedom is safeguarded by divine authority.[133] Human freedom is protected by the conviction that God cannot be other than God. "God is not free to be capricious," because "He is bound by the holy love which is His nature."[134]   God gives us our freedom, and God cannot violate our freedom: and precisely because of that, we can only have our freedom when we are free unto God.[135] Perfect freedom, Buttrick wrote, lies in being bound to the Holy Spirit.[136] We are free, in short, by the destiny in which God holds us.

What Buttrick strenuously resisted is the notion that this "destiny" has to mean some cavalier predestiny. He rejected a rigid doctrine of election that said God "chooses a few for His elect and condemns the rest (babes included) to the unending torment of fire."[137] The trouble with most iron-clad dogmas of predestination, he said in the late twenties, was that the "adherents" of the scheme were "always among the elect."[138]

Yet Buttrick knew that such doctrines of election were the logical outcome of convictions like his own that the destiny of the individual is to be found in God. In a sermon on a spring Sunday in New York in 1931, he pronounced the matter a conundrum.

> How human freedom and God's governance are to be reconciled, I do not know. Nobody knows. One generation will emphasize the sovereignty of God—Calvin's generation, and ours (though we call that sovereignty "natural law"); other generations emphasize the freedom of man . . . . No one has solved the riddle.[139]

He was persuaded that human freedom included human responsibility and would not allow doctrinal logic to overrule the point that to be human is to be free. Like a parent eagle forcing young eaglets to fly, he said, "God nurtures us—but the day comes when God breaks the nest" and confronts us with the necessity of our own freedom.[140] "It is hard for Him—for He loves us. But it is essential for us."[141] And, as Buttrick put it in the spring of the depression's worst year, "Nothing can thwart His plan of love."[142]

If anything, the depression was a test of the doctrinal jousting over predestination and freedom that was part of the pulpit theology in the thirties. Buttrick had made his position clear, that free human beings "can stubbornly resist God's love, and by resistance they are hardened in spirit."[143] At the end of 1931, he faced the question bluntly. "Did God send depression? He gave us a measure of freedom and set us in this kind of world where, if we abuse our freedom, depressions are almost bound to occur."[144] In effect, we are victims of our own freedom, since "we can and do, by our own folly, sometimes induce our own blight."[145] Economically and politically we are free to undo ourselves, to cause ourselves harm or pain.[146]

Consistently, Buttrick held to the proposition that human choice must be a real choice between good and evil in order for it to be a free choice, and in order for goodness to be good: late in 1929, Buttrick declared as much;[147] in February of 1937 he said that a person "cannot be free without the power of wrong choice and its accompanying pain";[148] in the following month, his language was, if anything, clearer. "Some pain comes of our abuse of the necessary freedom of the will. We say "necessary" for if a man is to be genuinely good, he must choose goodness."[149]

So human decisions turn the things of the earth, including our own flesh, to evil. The things of the earth "are not secular" but "sacramental"; it is we who "make them evil."[150] By our human judgments, we err. Jesus takes our human judgment and redeems it.[151] The key doctrinal questions plead for an answer—By what process does His redemption work? Can the erring judgment, the human will, choose to be redeemed from error, or is redemption the destiny chosen for the individual's will? The answer, as directly as Buttrick gives it, is that we are called to choose because we have already been chosen: not that we *can* choose, but that we *must*. "Daily we must choose . . . And daily the best—and is not Christ the best—lays hands upon us. . . . Joy comes as our choices meet."[152]

There are times in Buttrick's preaching when he seems to have given priority to the human act of choosing. In a sermon from March, 1932, when he focused on the role of the will in the process of salvation, Buttrick stated his obvious assumption that "our will is not completely free" and then went on to list the steps by which the will might be "revitalized and made victorious": first, focus one's attention on Christ; second, He becomes one's "example"; third, He becomes one's desire; then He becomes our strength; then He becomes one's salvation as the self is cast upon God.[153] To which Buttrick added that a bad will cannot be repressed but "a new course of movement in the mind" can be substituted for it, carving "its own channel" and establishing "its own beneficent habit."[154] Even with the caveat that he presumed the will not to be free, there scarcely seem to be any limitations on the will's power.

But then there are times when Buttrick seems to have found the will in utter bondage, or at least to be afflicted with impotence. In the fall of the same year that brought forth his list of steps in the process of salvation, Buttrick told his congregation that neither the world's chaos nor a world of brotherhood has been willed by humanity. Moreover, he suggested, the will had no such power. For such things come about only because there is "a Will which strangely works through the blind will of men."[155] Three years later he made a similar point: "We cannot live as we choose . . . we are under a Will far stronger than our own."[156]

Perhaps the presence of these contradictory themes in Buttrick's preaching during the thirties is no more than an indication of what can be found once one isolates individual elements of a sermon from its entire text, or separates the doctrinal content of one sermon from the pulpit theology of a preacher's full work. Yet there may also lie here evidence of a continuing struggle within Buttrick the preacher to resolve the conundrum of God's governance vis-a-vis humanity's freedom. Such a resolution required a Christological focus.

> If God should yearn to make Himself known to us, yet without any violation of our freedom or compulsion of our will, what better way than through a man living our life and dying for our sins and abiding with us a comradely Presence. What better way? In nature God seems a tantalizing Other-than-earth. In conscience God seems the righteous ground of life, but in Christ God is Mother and Father and Friend. The door swings wide in Him and we see the Eternal Love.[157]

Even then, the Incarnation had to integrate divine authority and human freedom.

> What God wishes to do for the world He chooses to do through human agency. . . . What God wishes to do for us He cannot do without our help—for that would rob us of our freedom. We are His workmanship, and what we can do is little; but that little is essential. . . . His little is apparently as essential as God's much.[158]

After all, God cannot act according to human wishes and remain Godlike,[159] nor can human freedom be compromised.[160] In sermons at the close of 1938 and the dawn of 1939, Buttrick affirmed both premises.

However, also by the late thirties, a new accent was finding its way into Buttrick's preaching. Never absent from his pulpit, the expression of the "bondage" of the will came more frequently: "There is some perversity in us" was the way he phrased it in March, 1938.[161] Later, the point was more forcibly made. "All men are sick. . . . We are sick because there is a defect of the will. Man has made of Himself a God."[162] The outbreak of war in Europe made the issue a compelling reality, not just an abstract debate, for this "ingrained perversity of human nature cannot be trusted" with concentrations of power in the world.[163]

But persuaded as he was that "we cannot heal the cleft in our nature,"[164] Buttrick would not subscribe to a doctrine of salvation that made persons less than free agents in the redemptive process. In the early thirties, he had said that life is not a series of helpless moves on a chessboard, nor are people the pawns.[165] In 1940 he remained convinced that God "cannot rob us of our freedom without destroying our manhood, and He cannot coerce us without Himself becoming a dictator."[166] Even when we deny freedom, he said, we assume that the denial is free.[167] God does not coerce, but rather beckons, us; sometimes more. "He does more than beckon: He hides behind a closed door. Then? Then we must knock—sometimes with bruised knuckles in the dark."[168]

INTERLUDE: The Threshold of War

By the end of the thirties, the darkness was palpable, and more than knuckles had been bruised by the hard knocks of the decade. It is worth noting that one of the most durable cultural contributions of the era was Margaret Mitchell's story called *Gone with the Wind*.[1] In the novel and on film, its extraordinary popularity had at least something to do with the responsive chord it struck in its audience, who could with sympathy observe the ways of the old south disintegrate; for their own world had been markedly altered by years of sorrow and change.

Surely the Church was different, too. Having entered the thirties with a double inheritance of the social gospel and the gospel of wealth, the prevailing Protestant way suffered losses in both estates. The depression had spawned an unprecedented level of hunger, homelessness, and social need. And, as Fosdick noted at mid-decade, after 1929 benevolence giving declined sixty percent.[2] So at the very time when the social gospel was most profoundly needed, the Church was increasingly less able to deliver it. As for the gospel of wealth, it was diminished also. Those great stewards of worldly resources, whom Andrew Carnegie had modeled as the benefactors of society, were being taxed massively—not at their death, as Carnegie had suggested the least generous of them should be, but in every year of their lifetimes. Some members of Riverside Church, according to its pastor, turned over eighty-seven percent of their incomes to the tax collectors.

> There is nothing in history to compare with the munificence poured out from vast accumulations of wealth upon the universities, the philanthropies, and the churches of this nation. But, my friends, we are at the end of that era. Make no mistake about it, that epoch draws to its close.[3]

If the ethical and economic patterns of church life had been markedly affected during the decade, doctrinal patterns were hardly left unchanged either. In academic circles, liberal presuppositions had been challenged and to some degree supplanted by neo-orthodox trends. A Pauline sense of justification by grace through faith alone, a recognition of the authority of scripture over human experience and reason, and an acceptance of an irremediable defect in the human will all were factored into the discussion.

But such Reformation tenets did not claim all of the prominent pulpit theologians on Sundays in New York during the thirties. In various ways, a doctrine of justification by works, a relativized authority of scripture, and a reliance on the free human will to effect deliverance continued to prevail in the leading American pulpits. Paul Scherer and, with greater consistency and clarity, George Buttrick tended to uphold the classic principles of Protestant doctrine. Fosdick, his views tempered by the stormy decade, seemed to acknowledge a greater place for Reformation teaching at the end of the decade than he had earlier. Sockman remained the least Protestant of them all.

The distance afforded by sixty years allows us to see more sharply the theological presuppositions which they employed in their preaching. But they were not without sensitivity to the ears of a later generation. Buttrick, at least, openly affirmed the right of future Christians to judge his generation.

> Fifty years from now those reading the records of this church, and stumbling by some misfortune on a printed sermon, may say:
> "There were men called Black and Jones and Buttrick in this church fifty years ago". . . . With all respect and a most genuine affection, we preachers are not responsible to you; but to the congregation that shall sit in these pews fifty years from now; and to that God.[4]

Buttrick spoke those words in a sermon that addressed the question of whether a better way than war can be found to resolve the differences between nations. As the thirties waned, Europe and Asia were engulfed in flames. Then, on a Sunday in New York, Sockman and Scherer and Fosdick and Buttrick, like all other Americans, received word that the United States was aflame also. With the smoke and the fire following dawn's early light over the Pacific, America left behind the world of the thirties; and her preachers searched homiletically for ways to bring good news in the wake of the bad news from Pearl Harbor. Some preachers would turn to the resources of Reformation theology to find the Word. Others would cling to their old optimisms and confidences, thereby missing the irony of Scarlett O'Hara's denouement. "With the spirit of her people who would not know defeat, even when it stared them in the face, she raised her chin."[5] They would appeal with greater determination to human wisdom and the human will.

PART THREE

THE WAR YEARS

CHAPTER VIII
BEATITUDE AND BLITZKRIEG

One Sunday in New York just a few weeks before Christmas, Paul Scherer stood in his pulpit at Holy Trinity Lutheran Church. The previous week he had told his congregation that the world in which they lived was "half wild" and "half saved."[1] On this day, he told them how hard it is to know which half is which. Preaching from Romans 15:12, where Paul echoed Isaiah's word about God's gift of hope for those outside the chosen circle, Scherer began his sermon with the words: "There was God again, off the fairway, out of bounds, over in the rough, among the *Gentiles*."[2] God has a habit, he said, of "taking up with the Gentiles—Wops and Dagos and Chinks would be the language of the twentieth-century."[3] And he warned his listeners about the fragility of some assumptions.

> You can't go on assuming that you know how He works and understand Him thoroughly; that He's all for democracy and the United States, and couldn't possibly be bothering with the Axis or Japan. . . . You can't even be certain that He's on the side of the Church as we know it, or of Christianity with what we've made of it, where everybody recites the right doctrines and we all catch on easily to His ways.[4]

That same day, however, Harry Emerson Fosdick seemed ready to have his congregation at Riverside Church make the assumptions of which Scherer was wary. "Christianity and democracy preach the same gospel," he said, in that both are "founded on voluntary loyalty to the common good."[5] Beneath his words lay certain convictions: the historic Protestant premise of the Church as a gathered body of persons who choose to associate in the name of Jesus; and the civic premise of a democratic nation whose existence depended upon the willingness of people to uphold the general welfare of all. Both Christianity and democracy celebrated freedom of choice to substitute "inner voluntary loyalty for outward constraint."[6] So Christians could find no better home than in a democracy.

George Buttrick told the Madison Avenue Presbyterian Church that same day about the "homelessness" of the age. "The tragedy of our time," he said, "is the homesickness of the soul."[7] We are lost in the vastness of the universe, lost in the expanse of time beyond our few years, and lost "among the ruthless forces of our age."[8] And Buttrick appealed to his parishioners to "come home" to God through prayer.[9]

About a mile away, at Christ Church, Methodist, Ralph Sockman seemed to concur with Buttrick's diagnosis of the human ailment, though he described it psychologically rather than theologically as "anxiety." Together with sin and death, Sockman said, anxiety is one of the enemies threatening us. Nevertheless, he pointed to a channel of assurance by which God could disarm all our enemies. "If we could commit our causes to God knowing that if they are just he will not let them fail . . . think how many of our anxieties could not get at us."[10] In Sockman's understanding, God redeems us from the enemies who hate us for our badness and God makes us immune to the enemies who hate us for our goodness. Either way, we are safe. At least it seemed so to him that Sunday morning in New York.

By afternoon, of course, things had changed. New Yorkers and other Americans learned that their "safety" had been shattered. Listeners who tuned their radios at 4:00 p.m. for Fosdick's radio sermon never heard him finish. In the midst of his broadcast, he was interrupted with the news that would take precedence over his preaching:[11] an enemy had arrived with the Pacific dawn and ended America's serenity in an attack on Pearl Harbor.

Chaotic days followed. Scherer called it "a wave of hysteria."[12] During the week, a meeting of New York clergy was held to discuss the crisis and the pastoral response to it.[13] Back in 1935, two hundred ministers had met at Riverside and joined in a covenant of peace, vowing to renounce war.[14] Now some of them wondered if they should resign.[15] Some of Scherer's radio listeners wondered if he would change his pacifist views.[16] He would not. "For years I have been a convinced pacifist. To me that was light. I walk by it still."[17] In the fall of 1943, reflecting on the questions of those who thought he might sing a different tune, Scherer bristled. "It's one of the most completely disintegrating tendencies in modern life: to say this while it pays, and that when it doesn't."[18] Nor did he want Americans to respond to Pearl Harbor with a thirst for more blood. If our reaction is solely to be better prepared and better defended the next time, he said, and now fight to crush the enemy for a hundred years, then we will have learned nothing.[19]

Sockman, of whom it has been said that he was a pacifist until war came and then he became a patriot,[20] tried to address the crisis with a calming perspective. He said that the force which America was now committed to using should be seen as a police effort to put down lawlessness, not as a venture in hate and revenge. There are Americans of German, Italian, and Japanese ancestry, he noted. "In winning the war, let us not lose the ideals which have inspired the American way of life," he said.[21]

Fosdick returned to his Riverside and radio pulpits on December 14 with a word about building peace at the beginning of war. He warned against racial animosity toward Japanese.[22] And he offered churches a challenge to minister to spiritual needs, to sustain a living fellowship, and to "keep alive . . . the qualities of spirit that will make a just and constructive peace possible."[23] Otherwise, Fosdick said, the costs of war will be wasted.[24]

George Buttrick agreed that the Church had to build the peace, but he made the point more crisply.[25] Buttrick was among those whose pacifist views seemed strangely anachronistic to many, if not unpatriotic, after December 7. Yet in response to those who wondered what he would say, the Madison Avenue preacher found the answer to be direct and simple. The Church has "but one word—the word of God in Christ." It is a word of redemption and hope, Buttrick declared. "There is only one thing to say—that Jesus, coming from God, has pierced the mystery that hides God's face; that Jesus, by His cross, brings God's forgiveness to sinful men; that Jesus is now and always our torch in darkness, the pledge that God is with us."[26] The only thing more tragic than to be in the war at all, Buttrick said, would be to lose it.[27] So the task of the Church during the war was to include ministries that honor the courage which many will show—both those who fight the battles, and those who by reason of pacifist consciences refuse to fight.[28] And the task of the Church will also include prayer, for that is the only way faith will return.[29]

The luxury of a few thousand miles and an ocean's span from any European, Asian, African, or Pacific Island battlefield meant relative security within New York. The churches of the city were not consumed by war issues. Within a month after Pearl Harbor, Fosdick was making his usual budget appeal.[30] From time to time, a sermon or its preparation might be interrupted by an air-raid alarm.[31] And for a while, congregations in New York feared that their midweek and Sunday evening services might be curtailed by black-out.[32] But what Paul Scherer called the "suicidal insanity" of war[33] was kept at a safe geographical distance from the city.[34]

Emotional and pastoral involvements were great, nevertheless. By the fall of 1942, ninety members of Christ Church, Methodist, were in uniform.[35]   By war's end, more than thirty from Madison Avenue Presbyterian had been killed.[36]   Missionaries from Buttrick's congregation who had been serving at Nanhsuchow, China, were trapped by the encircling Japanese army and were released to come home only through an exchange of Japanese and American civilians.[37]   Among the programs developed by Buttrick's congregation during the war years was a youth group for Japanese-American young people, some of whom were soldiers on leave from Camp Shelby, Massachusetts.[38]   And just before Christmas, 1943, the Church opened its facilities as a hostel for servicemen who were passing through New York on weekends: a place to sleep and a Sunday breakfast were the typical fare; occasionally there was even a chance to call home.[39]

While the Church found ways to be pastoral during the war years, the voice of prophecy stayed alive, too. Henry Luce, formerly one of the Madison Avenue Presbyterian's pillars, was sharply criticized by Paul Scherer for his projection that the end of the war would mean American control of the Asian economy and a windfall of perhaps ten billion dollars for American business. "So do the tragedies of yesterday reappear in new editions!" Scherer complained.[40]   In March, 1944, Buttrick, Fosdick, Scherer, and Sockman were among those who signed a Fellowship of Reconciliation document protesting the obliteration or saturation bombing of German cities.[41]   By 1945, Scherer felt that such principled outrages had been vindicated, pointing out how those preachers who compromise with evil end up, like the German Bishops, labeled as "collaborators," while those who seemed to stand alone in utopian opposition are hailed as "martyrs" for truth.[42]

Certainly the impact of the war managed, for the most part, to disabuse Manhattan's great preachers of any easy optimisms yet remaining with them. Sockman had to admit to his Yale audience, for instance, that Beatitudes cannot stop a blitzkrieg.[43]   And Fosdick said that the transition had to be made "from that old optimism to this terrific world situation where easy-going optimism has not a leg to stand on.[44] The war, said Paul Scherer, is a fact, "and the only way to confront a fact is with a faith that can bring other facts to birth."[45]   Despite our assumptions that we don't need God, "that we can be secure without Him, that we have the last word,"[46] what we know from the objective revelation of God in Christ is that we cannot possibly escape the reality of the Lord. "The hard facts of human life mean God."[47]

The fact of war and the fact of God did not always lead to the same sensitivities among Manhattan's preachers, however. For example, the sufferings of the European Jews did not arouse a uniform level of concern. Buttrick, drawing upon biblical imagery, found the Hebrews in exile again, with millions of Jews in Nazi camps.[48] Fosdick grieved over reports of two million Jews having been slain by Hitler.[49] But Scherer, in what might be generously described as a careless string of anti-semitisms, seemed to delight in referring to Paul as "a little Jew,"[50] "a ridiculous little Jew,"[51] "a bandy-legged little Jew,"[52] and "a crazy little Jew."[53]

Whatever might be concluded from that, some leading New York preachers seemed to find, in the racial and ethnic injustices of the war years, a mirror against which to view American racism. Scherer, for instance, found complaints about the Aryan heresies of Nazism to be rather hollow, and felt that Germans and Japanese would consider them impotent, given America's own grim treatment of blacks and Asians.[54] Fosdick acknowledged the effectiveness of Japanese propaganda against America's racist history.[55] And, though not inclined to overlook Nazi behavior on the pretext of American imperfections, Fosdick and Sockman did frequently deplore the attitudes and actions of white America against non-white citizens.[56]

If the war helped make the faults and the freedoms of America and her churches clearer, it also helped to define more sharply the particular trends in thought and doctrine of individual preachers. Scherer's orthodox, evangelical point of view surfaced in the last Sunday of 1941. "Some obscure and unknown person or persons among the common people must have passed up a chance thirty or forty years ago of making an honest Christian out of Hitler."[57] Sockman's proclivity for psychological rather than theological sensitivities appeared in his reaction to Rosenberg's plan to replace the Bible in German churches with *Mein Kampf*: "a sign," he said, "that the Fuehrer's ego has overreached itself in fanaticism."[58] Fosdick's stress on human effort was manifest in his persistent appeals for an international organization to be created after the war as an instrument of peace: a cooperative world community was essential not only for harmony among nations,[59] but also to prevent "America's becoming a totalitarian militarized state."[60]

Sockman shared Fosdick's enthusiasm for a post-war consortium of nations.[61] And Buttrick, in his own way, did too. But he hinted that popular enthusiasm for this idea whose time had come was overlooking the considerable defects in the proposed United Nations plan.

The customary answer nowadays is that there must be a world order. So there must. [But] the plan suggested at Dumbarton Oaks is feeble and even mildly menacing, but if nothing worthier is forthcoming we had better try to use it. The alternative is inter-national anarchy.[62]

Buttrick's objections were both political and theological: first, he said the plan bestowed too much power on the "Big Four" and distributed Security Council votes in such a way that the power of tiny Portugal was made equal to that of India's "teeming millions";[63] second, his theological concerns found the flaws in the Dumbarton Oaks plan to be symptomatic of a larger reality, namely the failures inherent in human choice. Nothing we choose can make the world one, Buttrick said. "The world is one, not in our choosing, but in something that chooses us. . . . It is already made one in Him."[64]

Thus, the war years clarified the doctrinal positions of New York's pre-eminent preachers, and in some ways alerted them to aspects of doctrine which had not heretofore captured their attention. Scherer grew skeptical about the newly rising popularity of religion: twelve major Protestant denominations had lost two-and-a-half million members between 1926 and 1936, and since then the crowds had been returning to churches; "but it's hardly religion!" Scherer declared.[65] A formal faith, properly affirmed and grandly sung and elegantly housed, is still not true faith. Something more personal is needed. "All the theology that adds up to anything, all the creeds, all the hymns ever written, are nothing but the attempts men have made to point the road to Him."[66]

If Scherer was trying to warn against the hollowness of affirmed doctrine, Fosdick rediscovered the hallowedness of it. He described "the central problem of mankind" in 1944 as the struggle between Christ and anti-Christ, and the need to recognize that "the world cannot endure half-sacred, half-secular."[67] Christian doctrine had to prevail, he said, or some other doctrine would. "Now we Christians have commonly thought of Christ's teaching about God and man as lovely, an idealistic view of life beautiful to hold. We have discussed his doctrine as though we could merely accept it or not, as we pleased . . ."[68] Fosdick understood the historical antecedents of that attitude, for he had helped shape it.

For many persons the religious struggle of youth was to get rid of dogma, break its intellectual bondage, and achieve freedom. So we scrapped authoritative creeds, minimized doctrine, made belief a matter of as you like it, and called Christianity a practical way of life. Now, however, we find ourselves in a new generation with multitudes who never have had doctrine, whose problem is not at all to free themselves from dogma but rather to find somewhere some

> steady truth that they honestly believe in and tie to. It is as though a
> whole generation had rebelled against some political tyranny and
> smashed it, but now, facing in consequence a chaotic society whose
> problem is not to escape from tyranny but from confusion, they cry
> out for government, some government that can bring order and
> claim allegiance.[69]

In November of the same year, Fosdick said that liberals of forty years
earlier had tried to adjust Christianity to modern science whereas "now
we face the desperate need of accommodating our scientific civilization
to Christ."[70] And he added, "Our intellectual formulations can never be
an ultimate standard."[71]

Buttrick would have concurred with that, too, but from a
different perspective and for different reasons. A year before Fosdick's
re-affirmation of doctrine, Buttrick confessed that war-time doctrinal
discoveries like Fosdick's could be more tainted by form than cleansed
by faith. He sensed a deeper ambivalence: "There is a new helplessness,
a new hopelessness, a new hope; a waiting and a watching."[72]

Scherer, near the war's end, did not feel tempered by any such
ambivalence. His views were more rigid. "I have it in for us
[Protestants]," he said, "with our lovely and idyllic gospel, the offence of
the Cross hidden away under the flowers, the gentle Jesus, that mild
friend of man, and a God who is the superlative of humanity, a Father
Who couldn't possibly be hard on anybody."[73] Scherer suspected that the
only direction Protestants could constructively take would be to withdraw
from the world and become a minority again, where in isolation the true
faith could be cultivated once more.[74]

So pulpits churned with theological turbulence during the early
forties, even as the world yielded to its own efficient devices for violence.

CHAPTER IX
THE EFFORTS OF FAITH

It is not unusual for preachers to disparage their early homiletical efforts, and Sockman followed the pattern. When he observed the twenty-fifth anniversary of his ministry in New York, he said he could avoid any nostalgic temptation to deliver again the first sermon he had preached in 1917; in what he called a "mercy killing," he had destroyed all of the sermons from his first ten years at the Church.[1]

Nevertheless, he did remember the biblical text for that first message. It was I Corinthians 2:2—"I determined not to know anything among you save Christ and Him crucified." Its indelible place in his memory is the sort of evidence that may be used to corroborate Robert Bruce Hibbard's view of Sockman as "a biblical preacher."[2] And Sockman took the anniversary as an occasion to say that his homiletical goal, announced a quarter-century earlier with that text, remained unchanged. "I still use it today not as a mark of something achieved but as the ideal to which I strive in this ministry. . . . My ideal is still to preach Christ and Him crucified."[3]

Moreover, Sockman's anniversary text makes a point about the content of his doctrinal perspective: that Jesus is not a gnostic or subjective pattern of thought but "'an objective, historical revelation of the personality and purposes of God.'"[4] Elsewhere, Sockman had declared that God is revealed in human life,[5] in nature and human history, and in Christ.[6] And through this self-disclosure in Jesus, God had given us a story not merely of someone "who once lived a life worthwhile."[7] Rather it is a story of one "who makes living seem worthwhile." For Christ, according to Sockman, co-ordinates the impulses of life and transforms the chaos of existence into unity.[8]

If this suggests that Sockman during the war years developed a new-found appreciation for the drama of salvation victoriously wrought by God, or (to say it another way) that war-time helped Sockman rediscover his evangelical roots, then further examination is necessary. In the first place, Sockman expressed candidly his disaffection for personal evangelism as a way to tell the story: it is "too slow" and "inadequate in quality," he said; for "the conversion of the will" under the sway of an evangelist is generally not followed by "a cultivation of taste and thought" into the character that mark one as a Christian.[9] In the second place, Sockman wanted no retreat from the goals of the social gospel.[10] Yet he knew that the social gospel alone was not enough, for "garments do not make a Christian society" any more than Prohibition made "a sober citizenry."[11] So, in the third place, Sockman said religion had to borrow the strategy of the war effort and "control the air"—that is, the Church had to dominate the spirit of the times, the passions of the age.[12] In other words, Sockman apparently wanted Christian forces to spread the story of Jesus by exercising hegemony over the culture, by ruling society's tastes. Which suggests, in short, that Sockman wanted the powers of religion to create and impose the Kingdom of Heaven.

However, the war years had fostered an age when spiritual influences seemed to be in retreat. Sockman lamented at Yale that the sense of America as God's country was gone.[13] He gave assurance early in the war that, if democracy should fall, Christianity would not crumble but would "find another medium" in which to grow.[14] And yet, near the end of the conflict, he was persuaded that the growth would come only with great difficulty: in the area of preaching alone, he said, many voices now competed for public attention. In the days of Henry Ward Beecher and Phillips Brooks, the voice in the pulpit was the only one raised in the village, whereas the modern preacher had to vie with many others.[15]

The hinge on which Sockman held out hope for the power and priority of the Christian message was its political utility, its functional quality, its attractive logic, and its psychological benefits. Christianity may be able to survive without democracy, but democracy cannot endure without its religious and moral base, Sockman believed. Therefore, within weeks of Pearl Harbor, Sockman argued that it is in the interest of democratic nations to safeguard and encourage the forces of religion.[16] So Christianity is politically useful. It also confers psychological benefits: the person who is trying to "find his life must lose it in some cause larger than himself. Christ came to enlist men in such causes."[17] Thus the Christian acquires a sense that life really is worth living. Again, Christianity offers a satisfying rationale: "for me it is easier to account for evil in God's world," Sockman said, "than to account for good in a godless world."[18] In the last analysis, Christianity works; and that is the prime concern to respond to a world whose troubles offer essentially "a challenging task of spiritual and social engineering."[19]

The crisis of war, it seems, fostered no marked departure from Sockman's prevailing views during the thirties. He may have disparaged his very early sermons, and he may even have placed slightly different shades of emphasis on some doctrinal matters in the forties. But his theological instincts during the war still lay with those liberal notions which had animated him in the past. The moral man *can* change immoral society, he asserted.[20] Individuals *can* take steps to solve our social problems.[21]

So, as he observed his twenty-fifth anniversary in ministry during the early months of America's involvement in the war, he put the issue boldly.

> Our Christian philosophy of life is at stake. . . . We are in a revolution greater than the war now in progress, and it is possible that the nation or nations which win the war might lose the revolution and the peace. The nations with the soundest philosophy of life will be the ultimate survivors and winners.[22]

In effect, Sockman had drawn the kingdoms of heaven and earth close together once more. To see Christianity in functional terms, offering political and psychological benefits, was to ally it doctrinally with the forces of democracy in war and peace. The conflict was not yet a year old when he told his congregation

> The eternal value and dignity of the human soul is at stake. . . . The soul of America is at stake. . . . In going "all out" for this war, let us so live that we shall not be "all in" when the victory is won.[23]

At the time Sockman was pressing his point of view, he was approaching the height of his influence and power. Since his assumption of the Manhattan pulpit that became Christ Church, Methodist, his congregation had grown from 450 members to more than 2000, with a tenfold increase in its budget.[24] About half of the people in the pews before him on Sundays in New York were visitors who wanted to see the face behind the voice that millions heard on radio each week.[25] He was being courted by the Methodist Church for episcopal office.[26] Nearing the pinnacle of his career, he was to remain a man of prestige for almost two decades to come.

Yet as he approached the heights of his profession in the early years of the war, he also plunged to the depths of his personal life. His son William, a Latin scholar, a poet, a graduate of the Hill School who had studied at Harvard and Columbia, died at the age of 21 in the spring of 1941—apparently the victim of a suicide. Sockman's published Beecher lectures at Yale were dedicated to William's memory. The painful shock and tragedy of it all had the effect, Sockman believed, of providing his sermons with a lessened social emphasis and a deepened pastoral feeling.[27] In any case, it did not mitigate his theological concern for the human effort that rises to meet a challenge and works to gain peace.

> I know a father whose son died young. That father feels that he must somehow carry on his son's work, and he does double duty rendering seemingly almost superhuman tasks.[28]

A. Justification by Faith

The evidence is ample that Sockman's war-time sermons had an enlarged sense of the objective work of divine grace. He called it "the heavenly gift"[29] and he spoke clearly about the place and the form of its appearing.

> The goodness of God's grace came along and with that grace and person of Jesus came a power, a mysterious power. . . . He came down and identified Himself with the poor, the oppressed, the slave, and out of that unity with people, Christ gave us the power of community.[30]

But the gift was not simply some temporal manifestation: "Christ is more than a historical figure. He is an internal force."[31] And on Christmas Eve, 1944, Sockman said plainly that we are saved by the grace of God in Christ.[32] No other power but "that spirit which comes down from heaven" can create the human community or "make us brotherly."[33] To the extent that there are natural dispositions in humanity toward unity, or natural inclinations toward God, it is grace revealed in Christ that stirs up such natural gifts.[34] In that same 1944 Nativity sermon, Sockman told his congregation: "Bethlehem is the place where the human spirit catches a glimpse of its homeland."[35]

Yet it is in precisely such moments as his Christmas comment that Sockman suggests this grace is not some "other" power at all but is the appropriate management of what is already available to humanity. The "gift" of Christ is not so much to alter our human constitution, or the structure of our relationship with God, as it is to "co-ordinate our resources"[36] and "awaken" our dormant "desires."[37] Jesus shows us scars we had never noticed[38] and human potentialities that allow us to dream of our higher selves and discover what we can become.[39] And if Christ ignites a flame, it is fueled "by the deepest things in human nature" and by the noblest human motives, as well as a divine source.[40] Thus, for Sockman, divine grace is that impulse which kindles what human life has neglected or forgotten, but which it nevertheless has had and has never lost; with the "pattern and will" of Christ, however, it can be discovered again.[41]   The effort to be near Him in thought may be enough: "When we focus our thoughts on Christ, we begin to fall in love with him."[42]

From this standpoint, then, despite all of Sockman's references to the objective reality of God's grace, he seems to present an image of Christ as a remedial instructor or enabler, rather than a redeemer. It is as if all of the tools necessary for humanity's right relationship with God had been available all of the time, but that Jesus was needed to organize the equipment and assemble the parts. And in fact, Sockman comes close to suggesting that very image of the Messiah: to Protestants, he said in the fall of 1942, Christ is not a crucified body to arouse pity, or a martyr, but a Teacher and Master and Lord of Life[43] who provides "an atmosphere of understanding and insight."[44]   One of the central bits of instruction given by Jesus was the principle of vicarious sacrifice. "Not only is that the deepest law of Christ, it is the deepest law of society."[45] Specifically, Sockman pointed to the price paid in human blood "at Valley Forge and Gettysburg" and "Calvary" as well as the battlefields of the current war.[46] They were all, he seems to be saying, of the same qualitative dimension, and they all demand from us the same moral accountability. "It is a long hard pull to become a good soldier or sailor in the United States. How easy we make it to be a soldier of Jesus Christ."[47]

In the end, the effort seems to be the key to Sockman's pulpit theology. Whether it be the effort to be near Christ and learn to love Him, or the effort to become a good soldier and follow Him, or the effort to use the natural human potentialities which have been awakened by Him—a right relationship with God according to Sockman's war-time message seems to be not so much a bestowal as an achievement, not simply by faith but by works.

Faith is a nebulous human commodity that can be invested in oneself or in others or in God: we choose which one, by our work and our decision.[48] "We get faith *in* God by keeping faith *with* God," was the way he rendered it in one of his maxims.[49]   And, in an interesting restatement of the medieval theology against which Luther rebelled, Sockman said, "God does fulfill our efforts, but He always adds to our efforts, when we have done our best."[50] When Sockman delivered those words from his pulpit, the war was more than a year from its end. But theologically, at least, he left no doubt as to what God expected if Christians were to endure to the end and overcome the current adversity with hope: if "you would meet the promises of God on God's terms, the first of those terms is *work*. The second is *faith*."[51]

B. The Authority of Scripture

On a Sunday in New York, late in 1944, Sockman illustrated one of his sermons with a story about the daughter of a minister who wanted her father to read her the newspaper comics. The preacher demurred, however, saying that he had to write his sermon. She replied that she thought his sermons came from books. But he said they came from his mind, after studying books, for the congregation expected to hear what he had to say. To which the persistent little girl responded: "Why don't you fool them this time and get it out of the Bible?"[52]

It is almost certain that Sockman told this story on himself. His daughter did have a habit of interrupting him on a Saturday at home when he was trying to write.[53]   And, more to the point, he had been chiding himself and others about the lack of biblical authority in his ministry.

> You may be reading your Bibles at home, but I doubt it. No we are
> not studying the Scriptures.   Maybe I don't preach it enough. . . .
> Maybe I don't get my sermons enough out of the Bible.[54]

Of course, his homiletical forte (like that of his mentor, Harry Emerson Fosdick) was "life-situation preaching."[55]   And yet in his Beecher lectures in 1941, Sockman cautioned his listeners: "Life situation preaching should be blended with biblical exposition and doctrinal preaching."[56]   Moreover, he saw no discontinuity between his normal pulpit approach and the need for authentic Christian doctrine to be proclaimed.

> Various Lyman Beecher Lecturers through the years have noted that
> doctrinal sermons were not popular.   Doctrinal labels are no more
> popular today.   But life situations can be so treated that they lead
> into the great formative doctrines of our faith. . . . We have assumed
> that doctrinal preaching is too heavy for our stream-lining spiritual
> diet. . . . The great historic doctrines of the faith, like the filament of
> the electric light, serve as the medium of incandescence.[57]

This insight into the significance of doctrinal authority in general and biblical authority in particular was something Sockman seems to have found increasingly compelling during the war years. Lynn Harold Hough and Sockman's college president, Bishop Herbert Welch, both felt that his sermons over the years tended toward a more biblical foundation.[58]   In February, 1945, for instance, he lamented the popular handling of the Bible: "we don't take it and don't use it."[59]   The previous week he had used a sermon given originally in March, 1939, to which he added a reference to the "moral and spiritual health" that includes disciplined Bible reading.[60]

Yet this hardly represents a new trend in Sockman's preaching. For in 1934 he had deplored the modern penchant for "making nothing of the Bible at all."

> Many church goers treat the Bible very much as sentimental maidens treat wedding cake—i.e., they break it in small pieces and sleep on it. . . . Many preachers, especially the younger, seem to steer away from scriptural preaching and give topical sermons on all sorts of secular subjects . . . but very little of the Bible. The result is that we have church congregations which have drifted almost out of contact of their biblical base.[61]

Thus, rather than a trend in his thought, the issue of biblical authority seems to have been a concern that caught Sockman's attention from time to time without becoming a dominant issue. He spoke of a change in the tide of biblical interpretation away from the human search for God to the holy search of God for man.[62] But he also said that "the Scriptures are not a doctrinal protocol" for defining the limits and order of Christian life.[63]

In the long run, Sockman seemed unclear about the precise status of scriptural authority. He dismissed a critic's charge that Protestants had abandoned all of their bases of authority, including the Bible; but, he cautioned his fellow Protestants, "let us not allow the irritating inaccuracy of such a charge to lessen our determination to recover whatever solid bases of authority may have been lost."[64]

In fact, Sockman seemed intent on keeping a safe distance between himself and the principle of *sola scriptura*. The Christians' appeal to an inheritance as "sons of God" includes a certainty that God will not disown or disinherit His children.[65] But the certainty of the bequest relies on more than a biblical testament.

> We are heirs of God not simply from the promises of the Word. We are heirs of God because we are linked to forerunners who did not live merely for themselves, but who lived with a surplus they passed on to us.[66]

Which sounds more like the treasury of merit that the sixteenth-century Reformers opposed than anything they upheld.

So it was with the authority of Scripture, also. Sockman found acceptable only those bases of authority that are "rational,"[67] that are "acceptable to free and enlightened minds,"[68] that maintain "faith in the biblical doctrine of the divine right of man."[69] Perhaps he embraced a shift in biblical interpretation to the premise that "God is in the hunger that sets men searching for Him."[70] But that was not to say that this or any other biblical perspective would authorize his doctrinal positions.

> To me the most convincing proofs [sic] that there is a promise and a
> pattern in life isn't from what I see in the heavens or in the
> microscope, or even in the Bible. . . [but] in the eyes of people who
> are looking for God. . . . There is a promise written in us.[71]

It is, therefore, at the very least true of Sockman's war-time preaching that, for all his sensitivity to the importance of Scripture, he did not avoid the compromises that make the Bible less than authoritative. He still trusted the authority of human personality to find and follow the presence of God, a presence which he was confident could be found cogently in more places than the Bible.

C. The "Freedom" of the Will

One of the practical concomitants of war was the freedom it took away from people. A system of rationing exercised control over patterns of travel, eating habits, and clothing purchases. The censorship of mail imposed certain constraints upon communications between people. Ralph Sockman found, in the war-time experiences of unfreedom, a testimony to freedom. "War, though it temporarily and tragically limits man's liberty, is itself born of belief in man's moral freedom and responsibility."[72] So, for Sockman, freedom is one of the axioms of human life, and remains so, even in circumstances of least liberty.

However, he qualified the premise of freedom with the understanding that human life is not absolutely free: "We are free within a framework of purpose," he told his congregation.[73] Therefore, mere human will power in pursuit of ideals does not have the power or substance to cope with life's crises. "Using individual will power to follow ideals," Sockman wrote, "is something less than being used of God in purposes which run beyond oneself."[74] The human will, no matter how courageous, must draw upon the heights and depths of God,[75] and "without the presence of the Great Lover" it is impossible to practice great love.[76]

Knowing that, Sockman said, some people sketch the blueprints of their own desires and then stamp them with the authority of God by trying "to conceal their autographs under the initials of divinity."[77] They pretend, thereby, to presume a pattern of determinism over all of life; but they are self-deceived. For the supposedly pre-ordained plans are not God's, but their own fantasies. And, anyway, in God's realm of promise, "we are not helpless pawns moved across the chessboard of life by an invisible Player"; instead, we are "workers together with Him."[78]

As a result, the exercise of the free human will is of fundamental importance for Sockman's view of the Christian faith. "If we are to receive Christ, our wills must be involved," Sockman explained in the early months of the war. "Christ must have our vote as well as our vision."[79] And a key to that lies in the human decision to draw close to Him: "We must first learn to like what Christ liked."[80] Moreover, the will to do the will of God "must have action."[81] Without free choice and deliberate action, Sockman believed, all questions of value must be set aside: "Virtue, to be virtuous, must be born of free choice," he wrote.[82] All questions of human redemption and deliverance would have to be waived also, were it not for our freedom to make something of the heredity and environment provided for us, and to establish the goals toward which we will press ourselves.[83]

Such a view of freedom must have seemed generously open-ended, even to Sockman, who admitted that he may have sounded like a man proposing that human choice and human effort build the Kingdom of Heaven. "There are those who regard those expectations," he said, "as the rubbish of a discarded liberalism."[84] Yet he insisted in the summer of 1944 that Jesus taught us to "Choose the kingdom of God here on earth, trust God in this world. Do your duty as you see it. God will take care of you. That was His philosophy."[85] On Palm Sunday, 1945, Sockman declared that Christianity has to continue to accomplish in the world what it has already begun: "Christianity has lifted nations from savagery to the sciences," he said, but now it must help "to curb the power it creates."[86] And lest the Church be daunted by the task of continuing to construct the Kingdom, it should consider the alternative facing the world.

> If Jesus Christ's principle of rule cannot be established in the earth,
> we will go on having wars and revolutions to turn the ins out and the
> outs in . . . changing the hands but not changing the hearts.[87]

Sockman was aware of the obstacles in the way, not the least of which was the imperfect humanity to whom he was appealing: "within we remain selfish," he confessed.[88] But he did not consider that to be an insurmountable challenge to his position. "Perfection cannot be attained existentially. But it is an 'impossible possible'; aye, rather it is an *impossible necessary*."[89] He was not eager to put a limit on the humanly possible. Indeed, war-time stories of heroism showed dramatically "'the almost unbelievable possibilities resident in human life.'"[90]

If we use our wills to enlist our imaginations which are more
powerful than our wills, then there is almost no limit to the truth that
where there's a will, there's a way.[91]

As the end of the war drew nearer, Sockman expressed in his
pulpit a theological freedom of the will that he hoped would be relied
upon to make a difference in the postwar world. It would be a time in
need of healing,[92] during which a "'spiritual *underground* to spread good
will'" would be beneficial.[93]   The alternative to America's willful,
Christian dominance of the post-war world, he said, is that "'Russia will
shape the culture of the countries emerging from the heel of Hitler.'"[94]

From the perspectives of social and political (as well as
theological) history, it now seems naive indeed for Sockman to have held
the free human will in such high esteem during the war years. And yet he
remained persuaded that the only way to appeal for virtuous human
behavior was to trust doctrinally in a human will free enough to choose
virtue and create peace.

There was ample precedent for his position, he believed. As he
put it in the opening months of the war, the "ancients. . . had an
unquenchable faith in the world of man and regarded all mankind as
worthwhile." So should moderns. Then "we may redeem man from the
cheapness into which he has been cast by modern materialism, by
modern dictators, and by some modern literature."[95]

CHAPTER X
TIGHTER TENSIONS

Paul Scherer believed that exalted views of the human self and its possibilities were among the very issues against which the Reformation had struck.[1] "The Reformation did its best to resolve the central integrities of being," Scherer wrote; "but it was a losing battle. The impetus of the Renaissance was too strong."[2] In the end, though it represented a divine breakthrough, there were soon theologians making an effort to surround God again and "bring Him within the confines of some roomier doctrine."[3] At times even the broad outlines of Reformation theology were subverted, he said. For instance, the Christian principle of "freedom," so celebrated by the Reformers, has been "irresponsibly transformed into license."[4]

That comment was made near the end of the war,[5] but Scherer's argument was the same earlier in the conflict. The failure of Protestant belief and authority, he said, has allowed nationalism to "become the religion of swarming millions."[6] With sermons on how to relax or how to achieve personality, the Church has failed to "tell the truth" Scherer fumed.[7] And the truth lies not in merging the realms of heaven and earth, but in drawing a clear distinction between the kingdoms of God and of humanity. In "One World at a Time?"—Scherer's most often repeated sermon—he declared "Relax these tensions and you'll rob the universe of the only things that give it any final value."[8]

Scherer first delivered that sermon in late autumn, 1944. But he was making the point in the very earliest period of the war, too. His sermon called "Tighten the Tensions," published by the *Christian Century* in April, 1942, was "written under the first impact of the word that we are at last engaged in active conflict."[9] In it he said that the Church needs to be rid of its ungodly optimisms and "get back to the heart of her message and the center of her history." His goals were a recovered sense of sin, a living theology of Christian life and mission, a supreme concern for persons expressed through personal evangelism, and the social gospel.[10]

> It is the function of the Christian Church, in every area of human
> life, not to relax the tensions that exist between what is and what
> God wants, but to keep them so tight that they may sing![11]

He was not demanding the construction of a just social order—"that we can never have here."[12] But he was appealing for the commitment of "men and women who will nevertheless give themselves to the task of building it" despite their knowledge that it cannot be done.[13]

It was as comprehensive a message as Scherer ever delivered during those years. Still, he made clear the doctrinal foundation on which his proclamation of the word was built. "Any religion that boasts of being creedless is either misrepresenting the facts or writing its own epitaph," he observed.[14] To him, that meant preaching must ultimately be an articulation of doctrine.[15] The appropriate theological accents for a preacher, according to Scherer, are the greatness of divine sovereignty, the tragedy of the human soul as witnessed by the Bible, and the hope given humanity by the invasion of Eternity into Time.[16] The homiletical consequences of these principles make the structure of the sermon clear, he added.

> A sermon without exposition, with nothing which leads to a clearer
> understanding of God's Word, is without its highest sanction. A
> sermon without doctrine, with nothing which leads to a clearer
> understanding of the cardinal tenets of the Christian faith, is without
> foundation. A sermon without the ethical is pointless. . . . A sermon
> without the pastoral is spiritless. And a sermon without the
> evangelistic is Christless and useless altogether.[17]

Despite the sharp focus which Scherer felt could be brought to bear on the relationship between theology and preaching, he insisted that the ecclesiastical efforts of recent decades had a very poor vision of the truth. Modernism had tried to organize everything around the authority of reason, and Fundamentalism tried to organize everything around "a slavery to the letter" which stopped the Bible "dead in its tracks."[18] The rationalizing reductionism of theological liberals and the impenetrable intellectual imprisonment of the Bible by theological conservatives missed the point that God is beyond us and cannot be reduced to reason.[19]

However, Scherer reserved his most caustic, critical words for the liberal theology which seemed to demand a new formula, a new gadget, a new revelation by which to know God—a liberalism that "insisted on going to seed," he said,

> scrapping creeds and boasting of it, substituting for them innocuous
> statements of a gentle purpose; plunging into social action as a
> refuge; turning perfectionist; piling up one ethical meringue on
> another along the road of inevitable progress; accommodating

religion to the demands of science, nervously adjusting its clothes at
every new discovery.[20]

The liberals and fundamentalists had dissected the doctrines of the faith
as if to decide that "Life was either fundamentally vertical, with the tips
of its fingers together," as he put it; "or it was fundamentally lateral and
horizontal." Thus, by either religious ideology, "The two sides of the
coin were reduced to one!"[21]

Returning from vacation in the fall of 1943, Scherer told his
congregation that two fallacies seemed to prevail—one was a notion that
reason will be victorious, and the other is the notion that we can "fall
back on . . . the sheer force of the human will" to be victorious.[22]
Strangely enough, he had expressed optimism that "a rebirth of the
human spirit [and] of genuine religion" was at hand,[23] and that a local
congregation was the arena where it could occur.[24] But, as the war in
Europe was just days from its end, Scherer lamented the Church's
situation. "Everything we've been relying on in the past has let us down:
the kind of Science we've had, the kind of Philosophy, . . . the kind of
morals, . . . the kind of Christianity."[25] And he appealed to the Easter
crowd gathered before him on that Sunday in New York "for some
workable measure of confidence in the Christian gospel."[26] The crisis of
war was not over, but it soon would be. The crisis facing the Church and
its doctrines remained—if anything, its proportions were larger than ever.
"The crisis we are facing is a crisis for faith. . . . It has to do with God
first and prices afterwards; with the meaningfulness of human life and
dignity of the human soul and the brotherhood of the human race."[27]

A. Justification by Faith

At least one thing seemed certain to Paul Scherer—the needed
rebirth of genuine faith in God would not come about by "all our loose
talk about seeking Him,"[28] as he put it in his 1943 Beecher lectures. He
had told his congregation the same thing a year earlier. "In some of our
religious circles, we've been carrying on loose conversations about
seeking Him; I've never heard He was lost!"[29] However, Scherer noted
three years afterward, God sometimes hides and waits—not for us to
catch up in our pursuit, but for us to let God do something for us.[30] "You
don't have to seek the truth in the Bible," he said a little later; "it will
seek you."[31]

Faith does involve responding to God's gift for Scherer,[32] but
never more of a response than our passive permission for God to cleanse

us, to lift us up, to redeem us. Faith is only possible because divine love offers faith as a gift to us, he declared at the 1944 Christmas candlelight service.[33] Therefore, a right relationship with God is thoroughly a matter of accepting the embrace of the grace of God. "All He says is that we have to bring Him some kind of container—the Bible calls it faith—big enough to hold what He has for us."[34] The "container" may be no more than "a brave leap with your eyes open,"[35] or a "defenseless confidence";[36] but, however fragile it seems, faith begins "with a kind of invincible surmise" when a person "starts to live as though God were."[37] For faith is "not a philosophy of life built up from underneath"[38] but a trusting response to the promptings of God.[39]

In Scherer's account, then, faith seems at once to be both delicate and invulnerable; a triumphant power in human life bears "the weight and the pressure itself of a life beyond our own."[40]

Of course, to Scherer, neither faith nor the God in whom faith trusts is amenable to logic. Faith is prior to any "understanding" of God, he wrote.[41] For God "moves across the edges of life, not as a surprise conclusion to some process of reasoning, but as the fact which prompts the reasoning."[42]

It is not, therefore, the mild moral nostrums of liberal theology against which Scherer seemed to rebel. Rather, he challenged the underpinnings of liberalism. More than moralism can "banish God."

> Even the religious consciousness itself, as in Schleiermacher's theology, can get between God and the human soul. . . . It happens when faith instead of God becomes the saving power. There is little to choose between that and the Roman Catholic doctrine of the efficacy of good works. Faith itself becomes for many a sort of intellectual good work.[43]

And we live not by works but by faith, Scherer forthrightly declared at the 1942 observance of Reformation Sunday.[44] "A commanding faith in God and in Jesus Christ is the only thing under the sun that can knit again our disjointed lives and order again our shapeless, ruined civilization."[45]

The next autumn, Scherer was even more insistent, reminding his congregation that Lutherans have consistently been committed to preaching the gospel to individual men and women. Meanwhile, he said, other groups sought to maneuver classes and communities, such as industrial leaders or the labor movement, into altered behavior patterns. "Today it's· even more vital to remind ourselves," he said, "that the Christian gospel doesn't center in Tom and Dick and Harry, or in you and me: it centers in Christ." What little religious faith remains in our time is in jeopardy, he added, "unless we can get these selves of ours out of the way."[46] Specifically, it is pride and anxiety that the self must relinquish: pride as that effort to change the world with what is in oneself; and anxiety as that effort to change the world with what is outside oneself.[47]

That meant to him demolishing the concept of Christ as our "example" and reconstituting our religion around the cross "at the center of the universe."[48] Given humanity's desperate state of need, Scherer had declared in the fall of 1941, God had to provide men and women with more than a fellow traveller and model of behavior. God had to send a redeemer "who could make up our deficits."[49] And, as the last Christmas of war-time approached, Scherer affirmed that the atoning work of Jesus had indeed covered the deficits—and more. "He gathered up this life of ours in His arms and walked off with it through death and set it down on the other side."[50] Thus, in Christ we are a new creation, Scherer proclaimed.[51] And because it happens by God's grace, our only source of pride is in God, not in ourselves. "Our little egos" dominated doctrinal considerations too much in recent years, Scherer said in late 1943.[52] Those influences had to be set aside, he believed—for what we are, and what we do with what we are, depend on God rather than on ourselves. "What we have a right to be proud of is what we are by God's grace, and what He can do with it."[53]

Scherer seems to have been greatly disturbed by those definitions of grace which characterize it as a kind of genteel graciousness, such as Jesus' "charm" or "winsomeness" or "compassion." Grace, he said, is "the sum total of all the varied attributes of God." "It's the depth of His wisdom and the length of His patience. It's the clarity of His justice and the fullness of His mercy. It's the gallantry of His love . . . the steadiness of His power."[54] Especially in the early months of America's war involvement, when those words were spoken, it was clear that no meager concept of divine grace could match the mighty enemies arrayed against faith. "A few little deeds of kindness and little acts of love," as he put it, are hardly enough to cope with—let alone overcome— "the kind of world we're living in."[55] It would be an inadequate force; but, more to the point, it would be an improper rendering of the truth of Christianity. For the faith is not some moral endeavor, in Scherer's view, but a proclamation of the Absolute—under Whose aegis moral discipline is then exercised.[56] When Christians talk of love, it is not about "doing" that they speak: "It's about being."[57] Behavior, morality, and obedience to law neither explain nor exhaust the content of the Christian faith. As Scherer wrote, "God's final word to your life and mine has not to do with everlasting demands: it has to do with everlasting arms."[58]

So, if anything, Paul Scherer's evangelical confidence was firmer and more fully developed during the war years than at any previous time in his Manhattan ministry. What he wrote at the start of the war, he believed at its end, "that the issues are still where they always were, in the hands of God."[59] The testimony of the Christian faith, in which he so profoundly trusted, was that God had chosen to come to His people and that Jesus had decided we were worth dying for: "I wonder what He saw in us?" Scherer wrote.[60]

Never known for his pulpit or personal wit, Scherer was able to flash some homiletical humor. At least when he contemplated the grace and power of God over against everything else, he detected a certain celestial joy. "There is a kind of huge laughter under the sky, as if the heavens themselves were shaking with quiet mirth at all the monstrous, heathen plans of Babylon, spreading their legs apart and trying to stand against God."[61]

No human effort could possibly hope to prevail against such divinity. No human effort would dare imagine itself able to contribute anything to such a Conqueror.

B. The Authority of Scripture

Linn James Creighton has written that Paul Scherer was "pre-eminently an expository preacher."[62] Certainly there was little during the war years to suggest a different conclusion. Structurally, his sermons were without exception built upon a text. And though the range and depth of his thought may have taken him into a fuller development of a text's implications, the characterization of Scherer as a biblical preacher remained valid.

It was more than a matter of organization, too. "Christianity stands or falls" by the story "that the Bible tells," Scherer said at Yale.[63] The Scriptures reveal both God and the kingdom which God is building—but "the one redeeming, decisive fact is just God Himself!"[64] Yet, in addition to providing a glimpse of God, the Bible also affords us an accurate look at ourselves: "The Bible sees us as we are," he said.[65]

So, thematically as well as structurally, Paul Scherer's pulpit theology leaned heavily on the authority of Scripture. He knew *sola scriptura* as a cornerstone of Protestant thought, of course, and on Reformation Day 1943, Scherer declared that while Luther put the Bible at the center of things and made it his very first priority, modern Protestants tended to turn to it last.[66] To recover the content of our faith, he said a few weeks later, we must rediscover the message of Scripture—that "you don't have to seek the Truth in the Bible, it will seek you";[67] that God is striving to reach us and "is hot on our trail."[68]

Yet Scherer resisted the designation of Christianity as a "Book" religion. Too many Christians, he believed, foisted expectations on the Bible that were not relevant to its purpose. For example, the Bible will not show people how to earn a living, or give a "blue-print of the ways of God." It will, instead, bring a person face to face with God and proclaim the good news of God's power, love, peace, and rescue for us.[69] For that reason, what is not a Book religion keeps coming back nevertheless to the Book.

> There's something about it that convinces me. Something about the majesty of it, and the tale it has to tell. Something about the stalwart figures that march through it and leave Time behind. . . . Life isn't futile: that's what it all adds up to. And it adds up to this as well: I have a job to do.[70]

It might be suggested that such a testimony moves not far beyond a romantic appreciation for the Scriptures, but Scherer elsewhere made it clear that he had a rather solid sense of what that "something" was in the Bible. In particular, he wrote that the New Testament put forward a pattern of salvation which consisted of four distinct propositions: first, the New Testament says we are our own greatest problem; second, the only place to see ourselves as we really are is in front of Jesus, with His face looking down on us from the cross, for there our condition of sin becomes visible to us; third, the New Testament tells us to accept ourselves for what we are; then, fourth, the self which is our sinful problem, which we have now accepted, must be handed over.[71] "Don't cherish it, and try to live up to it, or down! Don't defend it and keep patching over the cracks with excuses! Let go in something that's bigger than you are. . . . Christ can do that as no one else can."[72]

In Scherer's approach, such an outline not only lifts up the content of the Scriptures. It also identifies the type of Book with which Christians are dealing: not a philosophy of life or a textbook of therapy for disintegrated and defeated personalities;[73]

> not a guide to discover lost things or to stop bleeding noses; or to decide who is right in a dispute; or to suggest whose side God is on in the War; or to hold out personal favors; or to provide us with prooftexts for prohibition or pacifism; or with the blue-prints of a new social order. It is not given us for its history, so that it can be checked by archeological research; or for its philosophy so that we might have a helpful outlook on life.[74]

146   SUNDAYS IN NEW YORK

Instead, it is a testament that talks "of rescue and release."[75] It declares, in a charter of freedom, "that no yesterday ever has determined, or ever can determine, the shape of any tomorrow."[76] It gives notice that the Kingdom of God is "a present and plain matter of fact."[77]

Only in that sense would Scherer seem willing theologically to close the gap between human history and the realm of heaven. God's work is announced in Scripture as a *fait accompli*, and earth yields to the glory of God's achievement and the authority of God's word.

C. The "Freedom" of the Will

Three weeks after Pearl Harbor, in the days just following the first Christmas of the war, Paul Scherer spoke to his congregation about an assumption imbedded in the gospel authority. "The Christian gospel is based on the primary assumption that the nature of man is twofold," he said. On the one hand, each individual looks out strictly for him- or herself; on the other hand, each forgets the self and is lost in love.[78] That human nature has both capabilities, he added, is a function of God's will; for God has chosen that humanity shall know the Lord not simply through some vague memory of a time when Jesus walked the earth, but also through a living, loving presence.[79] Therefore, a dwindling human recollection of Jesus Christ, which can allow a selfish sinfulness to make inroads, is balanced by the contemporary experience of love, in which selfishness is dissolved.

A few weeks later, the dialectic of selfishness and grace again came sharply into focus. This first winter of the war was an unsettling, disruptive time at best. The prevailing gloom of pessimism seemed to threaten a permanent overcast. Scherer, too, found a reason for pessimism—but not any of the popular ones usually identified by secular commentators. "The Bible dismisses all the others but this: that at the center of every human life there is somehow a demonic will to evil."[80] He admitted that he did not always envision human nature in such stark terms. After all, he had been part of that liberal school which lent much credence to the agenda of human possibilities. "Back in the thirties I used to think we might get well soon. I didn't know how sick we were."[81] The self is not the way to the Kingdom, he realized; in fact, it is in the way of the Kingdom and is an obstacle to its own redemption.[82] The explanation for "this ghastly mess humanity is facing," Scherer declared, "is just human sin."[83] Whether people like the doctrine of the Fall or not is beside the point—"you've got to face the facts of it," he wrote.[84]   And the central fact is that "Man at best is a misfit in this world."[85]   Or, as he put it to the Holy Trinity congregation in the spring of 1943: "Evil isn't an accident. It's fundamental."[86]   And the only way out of the inevitable evil is to be rescued by grace.[87]

Scherer himself felt that his convictions on these matters grew more rigid with the passing years. In one war-time sermon he said that the only way out of the "wreckage of our life and our hope" is through God's "clean and constant will" not our own.[88]   And in another message of the same era, he declared, "The older I get the more confident I am that this religion which we think is so idealistic is stark, naked fact! It isn't Utopian; it's an escape from the Utopia we've been trying to build our own way and making a horrible mess of it."[89]   Scherer's feelings about the direction of his preaching find support in the data from his sermons through the thirties and deep into the war years. Increasingly, he affirms that the human will has not the freedom from evil to contribute to its own rescue. "What God says goes"; and "He said it with a cross."[90]

Through the remaining years of the war, Scherer held strongly to this position. In late June, 1945, he said that "we are up against the way *God* works,"[91] namely the way of gripping individual men and women by an almighty "onrushing sweep."[92]

When compared with the theology from his pulpit even in the early years of the war, such remarks seem to be increasingly bold. It is not that he was discovering at this time some flaw in the human will that he had not noticed before—Scherer had made that adjustment in the thirties. The change during the war years, rather, had to do with the relative degree of theological freedom which he assigned doctrinally to the fallen human will. For instance, just two months after America entered the war, Scherer said on a Sunday in New York that God does not "interfere with our stubborn little wills, but He shapes the over-all course of things."[93]   He believed in the validity and power of "Christian ideals" as long as God was not left out of them.[94]   A few months later, he borrowed an illustration about human freedom from Harry Emerson Fosdick: a lamp post stands on a sidewalk, but people are free to put it to many different uses; a wanderer is grateful for the light; a drunk leans on it; an electrician admires it; a bomber pilot uses it as a target to destroy the city.[95]   The perverse human will is free enough to find good in it or to twist it into evil.

Scherer was dismayed by theologies that spoke of certain "necessities" in life and criticized those who turned in 1941 to a "theology of war" which accepted it as a "tragic necessity." War is only as necessary as the "hell into which we plunge with our eyes wide open," he wrote, condemned by "our own willful and persistent immoralities."[96] Neither evil nor good is imposed on us, he seemed to be saying: God "will not force His bounty on us."[97] What God provides is a context in which human freedom makes its decisions. "Freedom is actually nothing but the ability to choose within a certain framework. God imposes that framework upon Himself . . . . He will not sabotage creation for anybody. He will not ruin us by doing our job for us."[98]

But through the war years a curiously bold, yet subtle, transition seemed to be in process. Scherer spoke of human freedom as "absolute" rather than relative in late autumn, 1943; however, he said that absolute freedom could occur only when "the word and will of God" live in the human heart.[99]   And on the observance of Reformation Sunday the following year, Scherer concluded "What the Reformation meant was that the conscience of a man was as free as the wind: but the wind was God."[100]

What Scherer appears to have done during the war years was to tighten the theology of the freedom of the will, while expanding the area of human freedom, all on a firm evangelical base. The end result was a view of human existence that declared the race to be absolutely free only when absolutely captive to God. Scherer was always distressed by any notion that humanity does not need God.[101]   But he was thoroughly disgusted with the implications of a published poll that indicated the very limited sense people had about the role of God: high school age Sunday School students were asked how Christians differ from other people; the majority said that Christians are more inclined to help strangers across the street. "How on earth did that ever come about?" Scherer exploded.[102]

The "freedom" of the will is boundless—infinite—Scherer believed, because it has meaning only in the hands of the Infinite One who bestows it. The human will is fraught with evil and, in a theological sense, is impotent. The human will, at best, can know only a severely truncated freedom if it rests anywhere other than the everlasting arms of God. But the human will can know limitless freedom if it accepts the embrace of our terrible chosenness,[103] when God's word and will take command of the human heart.

CHAPTER XI
EXPERIENCE AND FREEDOM

The same confidence in reason, experience, and moral suasion, combined with the goal of achieving a well-integrated personality, which had characterized Fosdick's preaching in the thirties, marked his work during the war years also.

Yet the consistency which this suggests must be juxtaposed with some remarkable contradictions in his ministry at Riverside. He was, of course, a self-avowed pacifist who harbored, almost to the end of his career, the suspicion that he might forsake his denominational heritage and become a Quaker.[1] However, at the start of the war, when a number of pacifist ministers in New York announced their intentions to resign rather than even tacitly endorse the aims of battle, Fosdick declared that he would not resign: to do so would be to place his personality above the Church, and he declined any such self-aggrandizement, he said.[2] But that argument was itself a contradiction, inasmuch as the very existence of Riverside was the result of Fosdick's personal stature: one of his conditions for accepting the call to Park Avenue Baptist Church was to demand a new building, away from the world's most elegant neighborhood; and its seven-day-a-week ministry was the result of his insistence on service that touches the full scope of human life. When he finally retired in 1946, one of the obvious questions about "Dr. Fosdick's Church" (as it was called) was whether the congregation could endure "without his strong personality."[3]

The contradictions surrounding his work were not only ecclesiastical and personal but theological as well. He considered himself to be a teacher more than an evangelist,[4] yet as an apologist for Christianity he became the outstanding evangelist of his day, said Charles B. Templeton.[5] Which was not bad for a Christian preacher who did not believe that God was completely revealed in Jesus Christ.[6] Nor did Fosdick's legacy put a high premium on Christian doctrine. On Fosdick's seventy-fifth birthday, John D. Rockefeller III gave $250,000 to Union Seminary to endow the Harry Emerson Fosdick Visiting Professorship at the school. No theological restrictions were placed upon the choice of those who might occupy the chair. In fact, it was not even necessary for the occupant to be a Christian.[7]

Nevertheless, Fosdick's ministry during the war years kept him at the pinnacle of ranking American preachers. His congregation continued to grow and prosper beyond the 3300 or so members it had near the start of the war.[8] His radio audience was unsurpassed. And his books of sermons sold about one-third of a million copies during his career.[9] Fosdick himself felt that "his own greatest sermons" came during World War II.[10] Of course, he was preaching on well-practiced themes, the same ones that had become his trademark in the thirties, dominated by the authority and power of personal religious experience.[11]

Three weeks after Pearl Harbor, Fosdick spoke to the congregation at Riverside about the "great day" that arises when an individual has the "real, personal experience" of discovering what it means not simply to seek God but to be sought by God.[12] With that moment, he said, comes the realization that Christianity is not fundamentally the religious organizations which believers have built, or the creeds that Christians have composed, or their "fabricated, elaborate sacraments"; instead, Christianity comes to be seen as "a way of life."[13] Behind theological formulations lie the experience which, if shared, make dogmatic formulae unnecessary, Fosdick believed.[14] Since the difference between ordinary individuals and Jesus Christ is a matter of degree rather than kind, as he affirmed,[15] personal religious experience can make ordinary individuals the vehicles of deliverance for others in need of salvation. "I believe in Christ—in Christ and some people I have known who have caught his spirit. They are not arguments but incarnations."[16] So the experience of faith can make an individual believer the incarnation of Christ's spirit, even as Christ was the incarnation of God's.

Fosdick was talking about the phenomenon of spiritual experience near the end of the war, also. He suggested that Christ's victory was won "not on the cross first of all" but in the agony of Gethsemane: before Christianity ever involves "a theology . . . an ethic . . . [or] an historic fellowship" called the Church, it involves the experience of wrestling with oneself in crisis.[17] The atonement, then, has meaning in the sense that the Messiah's true triumph is a repeatable experience in the life of an individual. To meet and overcome the prongs of a crisis is to find the glory that was Christ's.[18] "Revelation comes through experience," he believed.[19]

Thus, from the beginning of the war to its conclusion, Fosdick found Christian truth embodied in reproducible spiritual experiences.[20]

And he trusted reason to ferret out its meaning. Among Fosdick's lasting contributions to American preaching, said Deane W. Ferm, was the role of reason in the pulpit.[21] Its impact, though, seemed to be modulated during the later phases of his career. In the thirties, for instance, Fosdick was determined to continue trying to make Christian doctrine amenable to the mind of the modern era. Although that emphasis subsided during the latter part of the decade, it certainly did not disappear. Ideally, "revelation is primary and reason is secondary"[22] for Fosdick; however, in practice, things may not quite come out that way. "A careful, detailed-study of Fosdick's preaching leads to the conclusion that . . . he tends to place reason in the primary role, with revelation occupying a secondary role."[23]

Clearly, the one issue for Christian faith in which Fosdick consistently relied most heavily on reason was the matter of immortality. "In the discussion of the importance and the possibility of immortality," wrote Hardy Clemons, "Fosdick argues almost exclusively from reason."[24] He frequently addressed it in the pattern of his 1944 Easter sermon. "Our deep concern for eternal life springs from . . . our love for other people . . . in whom we see values that a reasonable universe and a just God ought not to throw away."[25] In other words, it would be intellectually unacceptable for immortality *not* to exist. It would be contrary to reason for life to end with earth's final breath. Therefore, to conform logically with all the other divine attributes of God, such as justice and mercy, the heavens must offer immortality.

Besides, immortality was the reasonably appropriate complement to another pivotal theme in Fosdick's preaching during the war years—namely, the goal of an integrated personality. He was persuaded that the greatest thing in life is personality,[26] and, as he put it, "Immortality is the supreme assertion of the worth of personality."[27] Moreover, what eternity affords, earth should imitate: so human life should be the celebration of personality. And in the winter of 1945, Fosdick interpreted that to mean hope for the post-war world. He wanted the earth's people to become a family, "where the fatherhood of God is fulfilled in the brotherhood of man, every personality valued for its own sake."[28]

In the midst of the war came Fosdick's best-seller *On Being a Real Person*. By his own admission, it was not written as an argument for religion or as a rational justification for faith.[29] It was written, as he said in a sermon around the time of publication, with "a deep faith in personality, its rights, its possibilities, its moral obligations, its capacity in a pinch to serve God rather than man."[30] Fosdick believed that Jesus was a seer of the possibilities in the human personality,[31] and that human redemption was, in effect, a matter of laying claim to the possibilities that Jesus has seen in us. "For Fosdick," wrote Katherine A. Bonney, "personality, with its wonderful potentials, is the supreme value in life."[32] Thus, especially under the pressure of the war, Fosdick felt that his sermons had to be more directly supportive of the human personality. His preaching even more intentionally than before became an exercise in personal counseling on a group scale.[33] His homiletical goals more clearly involved the development of well-integrated personalities. What Douglas Lawson said generally of Fosdick's work was specifically true during the early forties: "Personality is the unifying element in Fosdick's philosophy."[34] The premise had a social and civic corollary during the war: democracy is the only political mechanism to preserve the dignity of the human personality, he said;[35] therefore, democracy must prevail.

This style of pulpit theology meant setting aside some other varieties of homiletical handling of doctrine—those that stressed the sovereignty of God, for instance, or the substitutionary atonement. Said Fosdick, "I have very little use for John Calvin's theology."[36] Unalterably opposed to the doctrine of total depravity, Fosdick said, "Calvin's God is my devil."[37]

But he was not without concern for doctrine in general. Especially as the war moved along, Fosdick seems to have intensified his pre-war sensitivity to the need for theological principles on which to rely. "We are not consciously hungry for dogma. And yet in our churches how many now are finding their religion inadequate for these turbulent days?"[38] Christians would not be the first to find their rebirth in doctrine, he argued; communists had already done so.[39] The war years further clarified what the pre-war period had suggested, that if the teachings of the Christian faith did not become dominant, then other ideological principles would.[40]

Still, Fosdick was skeptical of doctrine. He resented the "ecclesiastical ghetto" in which Christian theology had enclosed Christ, preferring instead the broader "moral law of justice, decency, and humaneness."[41] Therein lies the potential of the human personality "to become true sons of God," as Katherine Bonney put it.[42] As a result, the redemptive process which coursed through Fosdick's pulpit theology became manifest in sermons which sought a closeness with persons, who might thereby find closeness to God.[43] This was the path to personal, spiritual experience in faith, Fosdick believed. He felt that "emotional atheism," in which people lacked the conviction born of religious experience, was a far greater threat to the Church than "theoretical atheism," in which people lacked the dogmatic structure of faith.[44] As he analyzed it in the final winter of the war, the resource that will help people cope with a crisis, after all, is not a theory but a deeply felt commitment.

> One feels sorry for some people today. They have never known
> what vital Christianity means, and now they face an emergency.
> And when an emergency comes, there is so little time to get ready.
> One must be ready. Life is a series of ambushes.[45]

So, if there was a growing emphasis in his sermons during the war years on the usefulness of doctrine, there was an even more marked rise in the emotional appeals from his pulpit. Notwithstanding his protests about being an educator rather than an evangelist, he called more frequently for evangelical decisions to be made.[46] The trend toward a more mystical impulse in the late thirties may thus have acquired a new intensity in the deepening years of war.

Meanwhile, Fosdick's personal career came to a significant turning point. Having decided to stay at Riverside when the war began, he approached the time when his contract as Riverside's preacher was about to expire. He was in his middle sixties and wished to retire in 1943 after forty years in the ministry. But the Trustees prevailed upon him to stay until the end of the war, and he consented.[47] By the fall of the year, under the title "After Forty Years in the Ministry," Fosdick declared to his congregation that he would devote the rest of his professional career

> to one major aim—to help put back again where it belongs the truth
> that there is an everlasting right to which our nations, our business,
> our racial relationships, our schools, and churches and our personal
> lives must be conformed if any salvation is to visit us.[48]

A. Justification by Faith

That Fosdick could develop such impressive agenda in the remaining years of war—and appeal for substantive human effort to run the gauntlet—is valuable evidence of his confidence in what humanity is responsible to do. The everlasting righteousness of God, for Fosdick, is something to which human life must conform; as another observer noted, the conformity will happen "only if certain conditions are fulfilled, those laid down by moral law."[49] The cherished principles of moral law were at the center of Christendom. For that reason, he said early in 1943, the hope of the world lies "in the Church of Christ, and what at its best it stands for."[50]   A year later he exhorted Christians to realize that their duty was "to rally around their churches and the principles for which they stand."[51]   To the individual who readily perceives that the Church is not perfect, Fosdick offered counsel nevertheless to "believe in the best he can get his eyes on to believe in, imperfect though it be."[52]   So the road to redemption seemed to turn on moral law and human effort.

Yet, he knew the shortcomings of an approach to religion where everything was reduced "to stress ethical conduct and to follow Christ."[53] He was still confident that modernism's focus on moral obligation was a necessary corrective to sterile old orthodoxies. But he felt that

> something deeply is the matter with a Christian life reduced to laborious duty-doing; it has missed the essence of the New Testament; there Christianity is duty-doing plus, and it is that extra, that radiance and spontaneity and overflow, that gladness and inner sense of victory that have made it contagious even in this obdurate world.[54]

Was this "extra" or "plus" his understanding of "faith"? Clearly he was wary of a religion of mere moralism. He had a formidable concept of grace—universal and prior to all human effort—that reaches to all whether we have "failed morally" or been "conquered by trouble" or have only very ordinary gifts.[55]   But except as a sense of pardon for human imperfections, the grace of which he speaks was not the operative force in human salvation. Strictly speaking, one was not justified by grace through faith; rather, one found justification by faith in its human application.

In the broadest religious terms, "faith is man's response to God" for Fosdick.[56]   Faith is the only way for humanity to apprehend God.[57]   In sharper focus, faith is a natural human aptitude for trust and confidence. It is "a power, solidly grounded in man's constitution,"[58] that has always been present in human nature.[59]   Moreover, "faith is a capacity in human nature that we cannot get rid of."[60]   His parishioner and patron, John D. Rockefeller, Jr., shared with Fosdick the view that religious faith "is the inborn longing of the human soul for God and for companionship with him. It is as fundamental as life itself, as enduring as the human race."[61] As such, faith serves as "the supreme organizer of life."[62]

And yet, in Fosdick's view, faith has no qualities of its own. It is a neutral commodity. It begets nothing; but it can be placed in anything or anyone; and it can be directed to any good purpose, or any evil. Hitler placed his faith in Nietzsche, for instance.[63]   So faith could be an egomaniac's admiration of himself or it could be Luther's commitment to the Word of God as he told the Emperor at Worms. In any case, faith is "a profound ineradicable religious necessity in man to believe in something, belong to something."[64]

To Charles Earl Leininger, Fosdick was simply presenting faith as he had presented reason—in terms of a "response to revelation." The foundation of Fosdick's doctrinal approach was not, in Leininger's view, a natural theology but "a view of general revelation which is essentially Augustinian."[65] This is doubtful, however, since there seems to be lacking any genuine sense of the "graciousness" of faith—that is, the benevolence of God in bestowing faith, and the abiding relationship formed between Giver and believer. And the thought of faith as a *neutral* human capacity for trust seems in keeping with neither Augustinian nor Protestant doctrinal foundations.

Fosdick does say that there is a tremendous, latent, unused reserve of faith in people,[66] the evidence for which he found in correspondence with soldiers and in his experience as a counselor. And he believed that the recovery of positive faith at the center of life was something people could absorb from one another: "Faith is contagious; we catch it from the company we keep."[67] So Fosdick presumed that faith was a human commodity, applicable to daily demands and communicable to others. And he had confidence in the "great faiths" which "put meaning and driving power and hope into work."[68]

He found Christian faith unique to the extent that it met human standards for quality. Christianity, he said early in 1942,

> . . . is the best we've got. It enshrines the noblest spiritual traditions
> of the race. It conserves the most needed faiths of men's souls—in
> God and in the sanctity of human life.[69]

What Jesus did was enjoy an intimacy with God that could be manifestly experienced by other believers. In Hardy Clemons's words, "His divinity discloses a latent divinity in man that is capable of responding to God."[70] Christ's testament or bequest, one might say, was to reveal the human potential for redemptive achievement.

Theologically, Fosdick remained sensitive to the charge that his views amounted to a moral influence theory of the atonement. Thus, from time to time, he would adjust the drift of his doctrine. For instance, late in November, 1944, Fosdick declared, "Christ is nothing that you and I can do. He is a gift, either to be welcomed or refused . . . God is trying to give us something."[71] And just as Christ is a gift, He is a bearer of gifts, said Fosdick; for He brings to the world "a new dynamic force that can and does and will change human life and transform human relationships."[72] That gift, he said, is what makes Christianity real.[73]

So the character of the Christian faith as a gift or a bestowal is not entirely lacking from Fosdick's pulpit theology. Nevertheless, it is actually a course correction in the prevailing direction of his doctrine. He did indeed oppose that notion of religion which relied upon "a genial optimism colored by a belief in the divine."[74] But he opposed it with the conviction that "the foundation of our faith is the greatness, inexorableness, and austerity of a God of moral law."[75] When he proclaimed that "salvation" was "desperately" needed, he called for a recognition of the abiding moral values in the universe.[76] When he exalted the dynamic force which God let loose in the world, he held that its perpetuation and effectiveness in the world "is up to you and me, millions of us, to whom the Christian faith ceases to be a form and becomes dynamically real."[77] Christians have to awaken to it and build a fellowship around it, not as a Church dedicated to preserving outdated forms but as a Church committed to a moving force.[78]

Understood this way, the theology from Fosdick's wartime pulpit amounts to a laborious challenge to satisfy a moral law. Therefore, it is again an exhibition of a doctrine of justification by works. Its hallmarks were a foundation of moral law to which human effort must conform, an application of the latent human commodity called faith, a decision to trust the divine force given to the world, a discovery of human possibilities through the teaching and example of Christ, and a dedication to Church life in tune with the dynamism of God. The test of God's promise, though, was the gallantry of the human performance: the courage to risk it was indispensable.

Just before Christmas, 1944, Fosdick spoke of religious faith as a gamble—"the supreme gamble of the human soul."[79] This sense of risk and venture, in the context of his other theological principles, suggests that Fosdick's view of justification required both human effort and human fortitude. As he put it on the first Sunday of the new year, 1945, "God is calling on each of us for some new attitudes, new resolutions, new ventures of faith and character."[80] The element of risk was no less apparent in a year-end sermon two years earlier, when he defined faith not as "credulity" but as "wagering life on something not fully known and achieved."[81] Thus, the risk implied not only courage and a venturesome spirit, but also a confidence in the prospect of achievement. And even when he said, as he did on a Sunday in New York during the spring of 1942, that "real Christianity is daily personal, practical reliance on God,"[82] he was still not far from transforming Christianity into exercise and function. Creeds and rituals and organizations would die, he said, were it not for the fact that

> millions of individuals, in bearing trouble, facing illness, overcoming resentment, escaping guilt, mastering sin, confronting death, discover that this Christian religion does actually work.[83]

So the truth of Christianity, in Fosdick's pulpit theology, lay in the human experience of putting it to work. Its measuring standard was functional—not, in the classic Protestant sense, faithful. It was a risk toward the earthly achievement of peace and personality, not toward the divine gift which transcends all of the world's standards.

B. The Authority of Scripture

In his review of the central theological themes in Fosdick's career, Hardy Clemons suggests: "It would be difficult to overstate the importance of the Bible for Fosdick."[84] Clearly the Riverside preacher had a sizable personal commitment to Scripture. Steeped in it literally as a child, he became one of its best-known constructive critics. And if his enemies granted him little credit for positive contributions to the understanding of the Bible, he was nevertheless a disciple of the Word. Or, as the *Christian Century* editorialized on Fosdick's eightieth birthday, he devoted himself creatively to that crucial Protestant question of the relationship between the Word of God and words of the Bible.[85]

There were limits to his creativity, of course. Elmer Edwin Burtner, the scholar who has most carefully examined Fosdick's use of the Bible, holds the opinion that his perspective on Scripture remained unchanged after 1933.[86] That perspective, virtually all commentators agree, involved Fosdick's ultimate reliance upon the authority of human experience to validate claims of truth.[87]

Just as Fosdick would find in his sermon preparation a biblical passage with which to verify the big idea he wanted to communicate on a Sunday in New York, he found in the Scriptures a verification for his basic doctrinal stands. The value of the Bible depended on its correspondence to the facts of human experience. On three occasions in the spring of 1942, he asked rhetorically: "Do you suppose the New Testament would have lasted all these centuries if it had not been founded on certain unshakable facts of experience?"[88] Later that same year, and again in the summer of 1944, he repeated the point. "One advantage of knowing the Bible is that in days like these one continually finds one's own experience there."[89] Furthermore, the experiences reflected in

Scripture are those written on both large and small scale: the intimate, personal ones that only affect each of us as individuals; and the gigantic events which impinge upon whole cultures or the entire human race. He found a parallel, for instance, between the news America received from Warm Springs, Georgia, in April, 1945, and the news which the Bible had reported from Gethsemane and Golgotha for twenty centuries: the death of President Roosevelt "has fallen on us all as a tragic blow," he said; but the Scripture shares that sense of moment, for "the New Testament is built on tragedy."[90]

This centrality of experience was not a rival to the authority of Scripture, he believed; rather, it was the very essence of Scripture.[91] Dogmas and doctrines which theologians extract from Scripture miss the heart of the Book, he insisted.

> I do not care a bit whether a man believes in trinitarian dogma . . .
> but I care a lot whether a man has the trinitarian experience . . . . The
> New Testament is full of that experience and there lies the moving
> power of the early church.[92]

In Burtner's assessment, Fosdick's God meets us not primarily in Scripture but in the "actual human experience" to which Scripture bears witness.[93]   And the preacher's job is to "reproduce the abiding experiences in the Bible," Burtner wrote.[94] Or, in the thesis of Joseph Calvin Hall, biblical authority for Fosdick rests upon the reproducible experiences of biblical personalities.[95] It is, therefore, a subjective authority, whose objective content is tangential to truth.

Fosdick's approach submitted the biblical witness to his own peculiar hermeneutic. In his first sermon for 1942, he said that the New Testament anticipates modern psychiatry in the way it seeks to form a healthy human personality.[96] He elaborated the point in his popular writing, arguing that no emotional aspect of human nature is to be despised—for instance, "pugnacity."

> Pugnacity can be "sublimated," that is, channeled in personally
> satisfying and socially useful courses. . . . The New Testament does
> not eliminate pugnacity but sublimates it.[97]

Fosdick frequently referred to "the God of the Bible"[98] and often categorized some matter as the essence of New Testament Christianity.[99] Scripture, to him, was the inevitable touchstone for Christian faith and work, and a return to true religion meant for him a "turn to the inner wealth of New Testament Christianity."[100] But that always meant for him a renewed contact with the personal experience of others in ages past who had discovered and applied their faith. For the Bible is a witness to "radiant, opulent, victorious" living.

> It is the gladdest, most triumphant book in literature. . . . All the
> troubles the world contains are in this book. . . . And yet, even in the
> midst of that unruly and desperate world, like our own today, the
> New Testament's dominant message is the experience of an
> abundant and victorious life.[101]

The evidence clearly suggests that Fosdick had agenda in mind for which he found the theme of biblical authority to be supportive. Scripture was subsumed under the prevailing winds of doctrine in the theology from his pulpit. As Creighton commented, "The preacher does not use the Bible but the Bible uses the preacher. With Fosdick the reverse is true."[102] He trusted the authority of human experience of the Holy Spirit, said Samuel Weaver, because he failed to recognize the Bible as the Word of God.[103]

It is worth noting that much of the documentation by which to judge Fosdick's confidence in the authority of Scripture comes from the early years of the war. As the conflict lengthened and the middle of the decade approached, Fosdick began to take that authority increasingly for granted and to press with greater insistence for the experience of personal decision and moral commitment.

C. The "Freedom" of the Will

On a Sunday in New York in the autumn of 1942, Fosdick spoke from the Riverside pulpit about the terrors of the Nazi menace. Along with the horrible stories of the starvation and execution of hostages and captives, he deplored the loss of freedom—not just political freedom, but intellectual freedom. "The most dreadful thing," he said, "is the Nazi policy of capturing the minds of the people."[104]

In Fosdick's pulpit theology, human freedom was basic; indeed, it was indispensable. The freedom to make moral commitments, the freedom to take personal decisions, the freedom to choose the way of Christ: these were primary components of the redemptive process. And he was dismayed by any force that interfered with human freedom, whether it be doctrinal, political, or economic. The irreducible fact for Christianity was that there had to be room to exercise a choice: and provision for an act of will. "Christianity has not been tried and found wanting, Christianity has been found difficult and not tried."[105]

Fosdick was not so careless theologically as to suggest that human effort alone could subdue every opposing force or every enemy.[106] He felt that his views on human nature were very similar to those of Reinhold Niebuhr.[107] And he even allowed that "there is a kernel of truth in determinism," noting that much of human experience involves the attempt to respond to the forces of the universe which are prior to it.[108]

Yet Kenneth Cauthen was scarcely groundless in his charge that Fosdick was "a modern Pelagian."[109] For, despite any cautions to the contrary, Fosdick held to a fundamental principle of freedom as the quality that makes life human. He knew that there were times in history, perhaps including the current war, when people longed for God to "speak out with all the thundering compulsion of his power." That might remove some temporary threat or end a crisis, he recognized; but the cost would be too high for human existence. "We would be utterly overborne, helpless automatons with no freedom to make our doing of his will a voluntary choice."[110] A legitimate theological position, in Fosdick's view, had to preserve the principle of human freedom. Since the drama of redemption includes the human choice to participate in being delivered, an act of will is required: and it is no act of will if salvation is a compulsion or a necessity laid upon human shoulders. Deliverance cannot occur outside the frame of personal existence. An individual must choose, must decide, must participate voluntarily. Indeed, Fosdick seems to argue, salvation has to begin with the initiative of the free human will.

> Other preachers have conceived faith to be initiated by God in Christ
> through the Holy Spirit who is active, prevenient, compelling. In the
> drama of redemption it is God who is the Actor, and who penetrates
> the world as from above, as the sun penetrated a cloudrack. For
> Fosdick, to all practical purposes, the initiative lies with man.[111]

Sometimes the initiative is expressed in the ability to turn a moral failure to some good result: "The greatest characters of history," he said in November, 1942, "have been, as it were, born out of the travail of the sense of shame."[112] Sometimes the initiative involves a response to tragedy in a way that deepens character. "Sometimes I think that this is why God allows tragedy. He wants depth of character, and even he does not see any other way to get it."[113] Error or evil thus is perceived as a test of the human will to respond, to draw upon resources which God affords human life, to seize the possibilities that exist on the other side of crisis. As he put it in the spring of 1944, "An evil situation can be one of the most stimulating experiences one ever meets."[114]

Therefore, across the years of war, Fosdick held tightly to the principle of free will. His pulpit theology never compromised his confidence in the human ability to respond to a challenge or an offer of hope. In Katherine Bonney's interpretation of Fosdick's argument,

> Man knows he has the ability to respond to life as he will. This is
> his freedom, and his use or misuse of it determines his personality
> . . . . Man is responsible to God for developing the possibilities
> within himself in such a way that he helps in the accomplishment of
> God's over all purpose for mankind.[115]

The ultimate form of response, Fosdick believed, was in the matter of self-sacrifice. Often held out as an ideal, he said, it became real in time of war.[116] "The only way to win peace," he said on November 8, 1942, "is to pay its enormous price."[117] And on the following Sunday, he raised again the issue of self-sacrifice: when motivated by love, he said, it remained "the mightiest power in the world.[118]

Like faith, however, self-sacrifice in Fosdick's approach (even "when motivated by love") seems to be an act of will that is *neutral* in character. That is to say, all kinds of people were sacrificing themselves under the motivations of various sorts of love during the war years. Not least were the 40,000 who served aboard German U-boats, thirty thousand of whom did not survive.[119] The enemy, as well as the ally, could appeal for sacrificial self-giving.

So while Fosdick relied heavily on the freedom of the will, he also had a running confidence in the *positive* qualities of the will to choose noble goals for personal commitment. Yet it was a confidence whose limits he recognized. He shared with the Riverside congregation in late April 1942 (and on radio six month later) the fact that in schools of theology "the liberals are being soundly trounced by the realists" who correctly say "that this world is a much wilder, fiercer place than such superficial liberalism ever took account of."[120] Fosdick's interest reawakened in the topic of original sin, or "human cussedness" as he preferred to call it.[121] In his Palm Sunday sermon for 1945, Fosdick warned his congregation that they should "never expect Christianity to pipe down on the reality and terribleness of sin."[122] It was war, he said two months later, that made Christians "take sin more seriously."[123] He had even, in the middle of the war, gone so far as to say that "our sins" are the reason Hitler rose to power, and therefore "our sins" are the reason young soldiers were dying.[124]

Yet his renewed consciousness of sin left him neither grim nor hopeless at the appalling depravity of humanity. Both Hitler and Christ are human nature, he said, albeit Christ's "human nature [was] illumined with Divine nature and made into a new kind of man."[125] But Christ did not despair over the condition of "the unpromising material" with which He had to work.[126] Rather, He saw great possibilities in humanity,

Fosdick said. And so it is not human nature but human behavior that needs to be changed.[127]

Though there is some reason to suspect that the lengthening years of war tended to make him less patient with human nature and more conscious of the sinful human condition, Fosdick never relinquished his confidence in the human will as the instrument to saving peace. By the later period of the war, he did consider himself to be preaching the gospel of Christ with greater urgency.[128] But the homiletical form of it was to appeal more fervently to an act of the human will: a decision for Christ, an awakening from darkness, or a discovery of the latent reserves of faith, by personal choice. With a regularity never seen in his earlier years, Fosdick's sermons in the final period of the war—after his fortieth anniversary in the ministry—took on the appearance of moral demands disguised as evangelical pleadings.

A human soul, "sunk in doubt and pessimism," can rise in faith and courage to the "greatest heights" in the "flames" of the Spirit, he said on November 28, 1943: "I want that to happen here today."[129] The following month he said, "I want some personal decisions made, some serious self-committals here."[130] On the first Sunday of October, the following year, he said "Some personal consequences ought to come from this service. I want something to happen here. . . ."[131] On the last Sunday of that month the message was "I want something important to happen here this morning in some lives, for our own sakes, for America's sake, and for the world's."[132] That same day on radio he spoke of the "cosmic God" bringing the kingdom of heaven into the human soul: "Today I want this experience to be with someone here a permanent discovery of the soul."[133] At the end of February, 1945, he told the Riverside Church: "I want some choices made here this morning, that years from now, when the trip is done, will land us where we really want to go."[134]

It was an exercise to challenge the free human will, laying moral demands upon those who consider themselves to be the Church, expecting them to choose their destiny. The implication was that the only obstacle to getting "where we really want to go" is that choice. Moral man can veto both immoral society and individual "cussedness," in Fosdick's view.

So the form of Fosdick's pulpit theology may have found new patterns of emphasis during the war years, but the substantive doctrinal presuppositions of his pulpit theology endured. Hardy Clemons's opinion that Fosdick was "heavily anthropocentric . . . but not basically anthropocentric"[135] seems a bit too generous. And Joseph Calvin Hall's conclusion—that he "preaches the saviorhood of Jesus in anthropocentric and moralistic manner" which gives his sermons "little real doctrinal basis"[136]—is more properly targeted but still misleading. The doctrinal basis is there; however, it belongs in the categories of justification by works and Pelagianism which were anathema to his Protestant forebears. Nevertheless, that was Fosdick's way to describe God in meaningful relationship to persons.

Once a year, normally in the middle of May, Fosdick would deliver a sermon "for boys and girls." In the middle of the war, he adapted a 1938 homily for this purpose. In its revised version for 1943, Fosdick's message was that to put Christ in the center of life and "test yourself by him" is "in some degree [to] become like him." He called that process "the secret of real spiritual maturity."[137] The free human will possessed both the power to choose a savior and the capacity to imitate Him. God could become personal and deliverance real by effort and choice.

CHAPTER XII
THE END OF AN AGE

No preacher had a monopoly on the theme of a personal relationship with God, of course. When George Buttrick spoke to his congregation about the homesickness of the soul on December 7, 1941, he assured them that the vastness of the universe, the enormous expanse of time beyond life's tiny years, and the buffetings by "the ruthless forces of our age" are no threat—"if we are sure of a God who is both Friend and Father." "What we need is the sense of Infinite Mystery become our Personal God. What we need is new faith in the Christian Gospel of the Incarnation."[1] However, the need for faith is not cast in the form of an appeal to decide, to act, or to make an effort. Indeed, Buttrick wrote

> It will not come by tongue-lashings from politicians or preachers, nor by organizations, nor by new additions to our embarrassing store of facts. . . . Revival of faith can never come *from us*. It must come *from God*, in us and through us.[2]

Buttrick was in the camp of those who perceived an infinite, qualitative distinction between time and eternity. And his sermons put forward a variety of visual and aural illustrations with which to make the point. In mid-June, 1942, he spoke of the life of Jesus as an "Unfinished Symphony"—not in the sense that humanity has the task to finish the word of Christ, but rather "because the world and time are too small a page for the majesty of the music."[3] That same spring he excoriated the "false faith" in bigness by which we moderns "part company with Jesus." New York City, he said, boasts of "the tallest skyscraper" in the Empire State Building, and "the world's largest theater" at Radio City, and "the world's richest street," namely Park Avenue.[4] But those were the measures of this world only; and there are, in fact, two worlds. In this world of "jumboism," for instance, a candle light is merely a candle light, and it is often and easily blown out. However, in God's world that same candle light "may be a great radiance." The point that mattered, for Buttrick, was that "God's world prevails."[5]

The two realms co-exist, and even touch, though "perhaps we can touch no more than the fringe" of God's mystery.[6] Nevertheless, our inability to touch God does not impede or impair God's contact with us. "God grasps us, though we never held His hand; and He holds us."[7] Thus even the hopeless have hope, and even the homeless have a home, for "we are not alone: whenever our hands honestly seek, another hand grips them in the night."[8] Moreover, neither humanly created darkness nor depth of night can exile the hand of hope. "There is a world above our world. It is untouched by our insanities. It stands serene whatever our chaos and strife."[9]

Within Buttrick's general perception of the two worlds was his specific conviction that the war years meant "the end of an age." He believed that the ideology of isolationism was dead, that race prejudice was "under sentence of death," and that the economic patterns which permitted indifference to "the welfare of the masses" was over.[10] The new age, however, could mean both a new hopelessness and a new hope. Certainly, in the area of race relations, it involved a threat to old hopes, Buttrick said.

> Race prejudice is primarily a matter of our comfort and our pride. If the Negro is ignorant, he must be enlightened; and that is a threat to our comfort. If he is enlightened, he must be a Brother; and that is a threat to our pride, which loves to "lord" it.[11]

The only kind of brotherhood there is, he said during the next month, is the Brotherhood "which overcomes my pride."[12] The coming of a new age meant, therefore, the despair which is humanity's only hope: that is, despairing of its own devices, it is overwhelmed by the ways of God. So in the last, dark autumn of the war he could say, "This is the springtime of a better world, this the springtime of a weary age. Repentance and belief open the gates to the incoming of God."[13] Eight months later, with the end of the war in Europe, he sounded God's reveille. "On this first Sunday after VE Day, hear the Christian bugle at the sunrise. God gives periods of rest. . . . Then He sends a new day, a time when men must break with old ways, and march clothed with light."[14]

It should not be assumed, however, that Buttrick was issuing some appeal or pleading for some turn to a new ideology or effort. He mourned such things, as for instance when the election of 1943 resulted in the selection of a Harlem communist, Benjamin J. Davis, Jr., to the New York City Council.[15] "Does it mean," he wondered, "that Harlem is tired of waiting for the Christian Church and would rather trust the Russian state?"[16] The Church had a mission to spread its doctrine of God and "man," Buttrick argued, and those Christian teachings were superior to any earthbound ideology or religion.[17] For, in the end, such worldly endeavors to seek justice or peace are doomed. "Our search always fails," he said. "God must come to us."[18]

So, for example, he did not share the confidence of his Manhattan colleagues in the efforts to build an international agency for post-war peace. Human labor will not unify the world, he said, and the proof of that lay in the imperfections of what was generated in the proposal for the United Nations. "A partial failure at Dumbarton Oaks is a symptom."[19] For its flaws express the indelible imperfections in human nature. Only "the Purpose of God" not the plans of people can offer genuine hope.[20]

A. Justification by Faith

To Buttrick, that divine purpose was not a hypothesis but a fact. Therefore, it was not something to be tested or judged, but rather something which "calls for our consent."[21] The process by which that consent is granted, in Buttrick's *words* at least, is the one so commonly cited by Fosdick: as a risk or venture of faith. "Faith is inward truth daring the unknown," Buttrick said.[22] "The term venture," wrote Peter Craven Fribley, "is absolutely central in his writings. Faith is venture."[23] So, early in January, 1943, Buttrick told the Madison Avenue Church that the only proof for God is found in the adventure of faith, and the adventure can be had only in the risk of "surrender."[24] What makes the adventure occur is the leap in which one uses no resources except trust in the Lord. Should psychology, for example, try to understand prayer, "it must pray, flinging itself on God."[25] The risk is the only assurance of the objective fact of God. "We must leap by faith beyond ourselves: we must fling ourselves on God. . . . In that objectivity—the objectivity of the Creator—we see truth."[26]

At the core of the difference between Buttrick and Fosdick on this "venture," however, is the clarity with which each of them identifies the inspiration for the risk. Without doubt, Buttrick never salutes faith as a neutral, human commodity which places trust in something or someone. Rather, his sense of the adventure of faith is always as a response: "Faith is man's response to God's self-revealing," he said. "Faith is the leap of our spirit to that sign [of the Cross]."[27]

As Buttrick's pulpit theology molds the issue, faith means the relationship between humanity and God in which both sides are active. There is no "blind" human leap, for God has chosen to be "seen" in revelation.   There is no oppressive divine despotism, binding itself autocratically to individuals, for a person "responds" or "consents" to God's offer of relationship.

> The momentous feature of this Christian change is that neither the beholder nor Christ is passive. Both are agents—Christ in the initiative and the beholder in his response. . . . Therefore as we behold Him a Personal Influence comes out to meet us and changes us by an active grace.[28]

Moreover, faith is not the consequence of some prior knowledge of God. That is, one does not have some understanding of God and on that basis choose to trust God. For Buttrick, faith is the means by which one knows God and knows that God has come. Or, in the interpretation offered by Wayne Blankenship, "Faith, as the basis of knowledge, is always the response to some prior beckoning."[29] Divine invitation, not human comprehension, takes logical and theological precedence over faith.

All of this implies that there is some impairment in humanity which has necessitated the sort of knowledge that only faith can provide. Some rupture in humanity's relationship with God needs repair. Some quality of righteousness is absent in human life, and divine intervention is needed to present it again. What is implicit, Buttrick makes explicit. "We are not saved until we learn to despair—of all human power, and fling ourselves on God."[30]

So faith is both the leap of trust in God which consents to a relationship of righteousness with God, and it is the means of knowing that such a relationship is possible. Clearly, this is a mature pulpit version of the doctrine of justification by grace through faith alone. It is a relationship which requires no sophisticated intellectual might or well-integrated emotional bravery. In fact, Buttrick says the Christian faith becomes conqueror with little more than a surmise.

> The strength of the Church is in the fact that it is for the weakest man—if he throbs to the invincible surmise that what "is highest in spirit," namely the soul of Christ, is "deepest in nature, enthroned in the everlasting.[31]

Thus, the only way to describe faith is in terms of cosmic, divine grace. And that was how Buttrick put it on the Sunday after D-Day. "The coming of Christ, then, is the very grace of God—His free, unmerited, abundant pardon for our sins, His complete identification with us that He may redeem us."[32] To put it succinctly, faith is a gift: not a human attribute by which trust is placed in some authority, but a "bestowal."[33] "Faith in its origin is a gift," Buttrick wrote, and "in its continuance is still a gift."[34]

Through the war years, the implications of this doctrinal insight persisted in Buttrick's preaching. The Christian faith is not fashioned out of a moral imperative or an ideal dream but a historical reality. "Christ Himself is not spun out of consciousness," he said in September, 1943; "He is fact."[35] In faith, one responds to the fact. "God ought to have forgotten us,"[36] but instead was willing "to share our life and bear our sins."[37] Only by "trust" in God's gracious action can we find the peace and joy that grant the experience of redemption.[38] "To believe on Jesus means to trust what He did. . . . To believe on Jesus means to trust what He is."[39]

What is thus conveyed is liberation into a new sense of life's purpose and values. The freedom brought by faith comes with such force and finality that it stands as the fundamental measurement of human integrity. Faith in Christ is not the venture which leads one to a well-integrated personality, for Buttrick; rather, faith is the gift which bestows the only relationship by which one can speak of personal dignity. Therefore, faith is "man's only treasure."[40] "If we lose the faith, we lose everything; if we keep the faith, we are still rich."[41]

If Buttrick's message seemed to cast aside any sense of promise or confidence in human resources, he was not shy to say so. He did not trust the human mind to know God by any channel other than faith. In fact, Wayne Blankenship says Buttrick considered the mind an imprisoning force from which faith brought release. "Apart from faith man is shut up within the confines of his own mind, separated from any possible knowledge of the world or of other minds with whom he can share his knowledge."[42] Our minds cannot save us. Nor can our deeds.[43] Any purely human attempt to behave lovingly is futile, Buttrick believed, because "we can love . . . unswervingly only in faith. . . ."[44] In some forums such theology would provoke a sense of hopelessness. But in Buttrick's pulpit the message was that God does not require what humanity cannot do; instead God provides what only God can offer.

> God does not demand righteousness for our sins: He imparts
> righteousness when we have no righteousness to offer. He does not
> require love: He pours love into hearts become loveless. He does
> what man cannot do. It is all His doing.[45]

This was the foundation of Buttrick's pulpit theology. But if he set aside the prospects for redemption through human resources and actions, he did not fail to see the connections between faith and life. There was the matter of reason, for instance.[46] "Faith is a deeper gift than reason. It is not independent of reason, or ever its enemy. . . . Faith plants the flag: reason can only trudge down the path which faith has blazed, and organize the land which faith has won."[47] Nor can the creeds of the Church be ignored or be allowed to wither in sectarian debate. "Faith frames the theologies," Buttrick wrote. "Creeds are the successive homes of faith."[48] And he added: "a great creed should be sung rather than debated."[49] The intellectual—and presumably liturgical, aesthetic, architectural—forms of faith were not to be discarded. "Without forms God is everywhere but not somewhere."[50] However, the forms into which faith is molded identify God's Presence. And the fullest expression of that Presence is in the Word.

B. The Authority of Scripture

The typical homiletical structure of Buttrick's earlier preaching remained in the war years. Virtually every sermon sprang from a biblical text and developed in relationship to the integrity of the text. The character of Buttrick's sermons makes it clear, wrote Paul W. Stevens, that "Preaching in any age is from the Book in which history and gospel are one."[51] He not only started with a scriptural mandate, he made ample use of biblical imagery, in which he felt "quite at home."[52] In a letter written after his retirement, Buttrick put it clearly if inelegantly: "My bag is the Bible with all that is implied."[53]

From the standpoint of pulpit theology, the Bible was Buttrick's doctrinal source. To take the risk or run the adventure of faith, he said, to "surrender" to God, was the biblical word.[54] What he called "heroic faith" was exalted by the Bible.[55] And when he defined "grace" it was with biblical images that he chose to do so.[56]

This was not a perspective at which he was late to arrive. Though he rebelled against the fundamentalism of his Primitive Methodist father,[57] he did not minimize the claims of Scripture in his preaching. And despite his acknowledgment of the influence that neo-orthodox theology had upon him, he felt that its importance lay not solely in the new insights it afforded him but also in the ways it confirmed his own commitments. Neo-orthodoxy, he wrote, "appealed all the more because of its biblical root!"[58]

What Buttrick seems not to have done in his sermons during the war years is make an issue of his reliance on the authority of Scripture. There appear to be no sermons from the early forties that tackle the question directly, thus leaving one to sample the bits of evidence from scattered sermons and then to draw from a number of possible conclusions. Those conclusions might be four: that he felt the controversies of the previous decades had exhausted what could be said on the matter; that his own views on biblical authority, manifest in sermon after sermon every week, were so clear as to require no further explication; that the early forties pressed so many other concerns so forcefully to the surface that he could not address this one; that he felt the point was best argued indirectly rather than through some forthright presentation. Concerning this last possibility, Buttrick spoke on the Sunday before Christmas, 1943, about Hitler's promise to destroy the churches. Its vanity, he told his congregation, is shown by the fact that the Bible still out-sells Hitler's words: "*Mein Kampf* is a murky flare; the Bible is a spreading dawn."[59]

It is clear that Buttrick criticized those preachers, including his own Manhattan colleagues, who found other authorities besides Scripture on which to rely. He said that Fosdick, for instance, relied too much on natural law.[60]

Yet the war years may have brought a drift in Buttrick's preaching that involved his looking to other authorities, also. The absence of firm defenses of biblical authority is not nearly so significant as the presence of so much material in his war-time sermons on the venture, the risk, the leap, and the thrust of faith. There is no doubt that he placed heavy emphasis on that dimension of Christian spirituality. But did experience supplant the Bible as the authority for the believer? Wayne Blankenship, for example, discussed the relationship between reason and experience in Buttrick's work by saying that "reason can never replace experience . . . as the source of the basic religious data."[61] Moreover, Buttrick noted that existentialism offered a significant tool for apologetics because "the Bible contains basically subjective truth."[62] Did this mean that Buttrick was tending away from the authority of the Bible as objective fact, and more to the sense of its power to provide the images which inform subjective experience? Was he de-emphasizing the biblical datum and stressing spiritual exercises?

It is an intriguing speculation, but one for which the war years offer no convincing evidence. He did publish his powerful volume on *Prayer* in this period, beginning a series of writings on that theme. Yet in its pages he testified to scriptural pre-eminence. "The Bible is *the* Book. It enshrines the genius of the Old Testament insight and the sole glory of the New Testament Christ."[63] The preacher's energy, he wrote in 1943, is in the gospel. "The Beatitudes," for instance, "are dogmas: they are not argument, not a "'point of view,'" but statements of *what is* by eternal decree. When a man preaches dogma with eager belief his words have a double power."[64]   So speculations to the contrary do not mitigate the basic conclusion to which Buttrick's preaching leads—that the biblical word is the unsurpassed and unequalled authority for Christian belief and practice.

C. The "Freedom" of the Will

A few weeks after the Sunday morning attack on Pearl Harbor had revoked America's freedom to stay out of war, George Buttrick was in his pulpit talking about the human freedom to will and to do. "We must still choose. There are no compulsions in Christ. He comes, not as a threat, but as an 'influence' a 'spirit' a quiet presence. We are free, with however limited a freedom, and the choice must be our choice."[65] A few months later he seemed to say the opposite: "Religion chooses us or we are left forlorn."[66]   According to one critic, these divergent views were not in conflict at all, but rather were "two sides of one coin." For Buttrick never saw the relationship between God and the world either in terms of "absolute freedom" or "absolute necessity." In fact, he held the two so clearly together that they could not be separated.[67] What holds them together, one should say, is God.

There remains human freedom. We are not mere photographic plates, on whom God stamps an irremediable image, Buttrick said. "We can cleanse the plate or deliberately fog it." Therefore "we have choice and must exercise the choice."[68] Among the choices is the decision of faith. "We need faith in God; but the faith, because we are free, must be implemented by our own act, even though the act be no more than a prayer in extremis."[69] The choice must involve "the thrust of our will"; otherwise we simply "stumble into heaven,"[70] when in fact we should be trying "to live His life in our daily life." For only in "such a venture can assurance come."[71]   And without freedom, Buttrick wrote, "prayer is folly."[72]

The two remain in gracious unity. After all, there is human freedom solely because God chose to provide it.[73] "God gives a certain range of freedom to our deeds: the range is not wide, but it is real."[74] And whenever one attempts to do good, "our good is helpless without God."[75] There are limits beyond which human effort and choice and will cannot reach. There are things humanity is incapable of doing. "God must do what man cannot do," Buttrick declared.[76] So, in the same sermon which included an exhortation for his congregation to "exercise the choice," Buttrick also told them that "despite our measure of freedom, our power is small; and our faces are veiled."[77]

At issue is what stands between the human freedom to will and the divine grace to deliver. There is a flaw in the human will that separates it by an unfathomable chasm from the perfect will of God. The flaw expresses itself in an abuse of freedom, which from time to time prompts people to wish God would take the freedom away and compel every event to be good.[78] To do so, however, would cause human life to cease being human, and would distort God into something other than the presence of love. Nevertheless, the dilemma of the human condition remains: "it is original sin."[79] In Buttrick's words, "the modern mind is not only stupid, it is diabolically stupid"; the constitution of the human will suffers from "a perverse contradiction."[80] No remedial efforts, no moral appeals, no diligent labor can amend the situation, for we are "ugly and cruel."[81] "Man is not an angel in process of liberation: he is enough of a devil to breed a Hitler. . . . There is a defect in his will. His evil is endemic."[82] Against those older, liberal presumptions that evolution would breed the evil out of the race, Buttrick felt the catastrophe of war was sufficient evidence to the contrary.[83] "In late years we have relied upon ourselves. We needed no other help. . . . What the Church called sin was only a greenness: it would soon pass in the course of evolution . . . . Now our world is in ruins."[84] The truth is that sin infected the human memory, the human will, and the entire world, Buttrick declared.[85] And no human freedom could cure it. The healing had to come in a relationship with God.[86]

In the early months of the war, he had made it clear that no willful attack on the sinful condition could remedy what was ailing the world. Even the noblest human endeavors were certain to fail. He looked askance at a national preaching mission, for instance, claiming that it had become "too organized."[87] "Human love without the love of Christ is corroded, and human love without the hope of Christ is made the more hopeless by its very yearning. . . . By His grace we are stronger than all the assaults of evil."[88]

The significance of that, for Buttrick, is political as well as personal. No charter for a United Nations could unify the world, he said. "The world is one, not in our choosing, but in something that chooses us. . . . It is already made one in Him."[89] The most, and the least, that the people of the world could do is pray. "Our wrongdoing is a limit," he wrote, "but . . . the praying man is cleansed and clothed in unearthly light. Fetters themselves become freedom."[90]

INTERLUDE: Clouds of Peace

Not long after the first world war, Harry Emerson Fosdick vowed that he would never again endorse a war and that he would never again serve a Church which was divided by sectarianism or devoted to less than a seven-day ministry. By 1930 Riverside Church enabled him to keep the second promise. By 1941, he had found the first promise to be a bit more elusive. The war years cast a different shadow over everyone's preaching. Buttrick, for example, encountered trouble with some of his parishioners and colleagues over his pacifist views.[1]

But the war did not alter the basic patterns of pulpit theology among New York's four most prominent preachers. Again, as in the thirties, Fosdick and Sockman sparked a renewed interest in doctrinal preaching, but wrought no permanent change in their doctrinal tendencies. Buttrick's views remained substantially the same in the forties as in the pre-war years. If anything, the war era may have brought a further stiffening of Scherer's position: gone indeed are the old liberal leanings of the twenties and thirties; firm indeed are the evangelical positions to the near exclusion of the social gospel.

Likewise, during the war itself, there were no dramatic shifts of emphasis. Fosdick, and to a lesser extent Sockman, hammered away at the need for a co-operative international organization.[2] Buttrick was alert to its values, too, though he may have been more prescient about its practical failings.

As the war drew to a close, new signs of hope and of sorrow appeared. Fosdick would have his beloved UN and his retirement. Sockman would go to Russia for a look at communism first-hand. And George Buttrick, who spoke in the late spring of 1945 about marching forward "clothed with light,"[3] would look aghast at the ferocious light which human engineering had made possible. For before the summer was over, they would see a brighter light than any preacher had ever imagined could come from human hands. And a more devastating one.

PART FOUR

THE POST WAR DECADE

CHAPTER XIII
THE LAST TURNING POINT

On Sunday, August 5, 1945, Harry Emerson Fosdick told his congregation at Riverside Church that the salvation of the world did not rest on "the application of mere scientific knowledge" to treat the problems of the world. "The cure does not lie in more scientific power to produce more poisoned razor blades, bombs, and corrosive fluids. Salvation lies in another realm altogether . . . namely in the faith and principles of Christ."[1]

By the time his parishioners were sitting down to their evening meal that day, however, a new scientific knowledge *was* applied for the first time as an instrument of war. Hiroshima was exposed to the explosive energy of creation. Two days later, Nagasaki was bombed. And the world mushroomed into a new age. Oddly enough, the atomic secret had been found just around the corner from the site of Fosdick's sermons: the first splitting of an atom had occurred five and a half years earlier in the Pupin Physics Lab at the southeast corner of Broadway and 120th Street.[2] Without knowing it, Fosdick had been just blocks away at the moment of creation.

Historian John Lukacs has written that 1945 "was the last great turning point in the history of the world."[3] Ralph Sockman at Christ Church, Methodist, called the period from April 1945 to April 1946 the most significant twelve months since the birth of Christ; for in that year the world had seen the creation of the United Nations, the destruction of two dictatorships, and the dropping of the atomic bomb.[4] At first, Sockman confessed, he considered the bomb to be just another weapon.[5] He wrote that it was not for him to express an opinion on controlling it.[6] Less than two months after the levelling of Hiroshima, he fretted that "in our anxiety about the atom bomb we may cease to be grateful for the progress of science."[7]

Nevertheless, Sockman shared the anxiety. And he turned his rhetoric to it. "Two centuries ago Jonathan Edwards stirred a revival of religion here in America by picturing sinners in the hands of an angry God. Now, by releasing atomic energy in the form of a bomb, we have the power of God in the hands of angry sinners."[8] Exposure to radiation can cause disease, he said in the same sermon; but people who have been exposed to Christ can in turn radiate spiritual power to others around them.[9] This was not only rhetoric. It was also very much indicative of his theological style, namely to trust greatly in the powers of those who have been influenced by Christ. He exalted the human technique and effort that could redeem civilization from the enormity of the bomb. Programs of compassion and spiritual service to humanity would have to be instituted to atone for the chaos and bloodshed of the twentieth century, he said.[10] And a world government had to be established, one "strong enough to stop wars at the start," for only that could "guarantee against the brutalizing use of that bomb in the future by uncontrolled people."[11]

Meanwhile, George Buttrick received first news of the atomic age at his vacation retreat in Michigan. In later years, he denied that the events of August, 1945, changed his thinking. However, at the time, the Hiroshima blast provoked an intense reaction from him. During his final vacation month at the Sequanota Club,[12] he plunged into writing *Christ and Man's Dilemma*, a blunt exploration of the doctrine of total depravity and a fierce statement of the infinite qualitative distinction between God and humanity. In the following months, he told his Madison Avenue congregation how strangely real the prophecies of the end of the world in the New Testament appear in the atomic age: the bomb has changed our view of the earth, he said;[13] it has changed our understanding of military activities and their role in world affairs;[14] it has "brought a climactic turn in history."[15] In Buttrick's view, atomic power is not power at all, but rather a "chaotic weakness."[16] And the only force that can counteract it and cleanse us of it is the spirit of God.[17]

So the Church was not lacking in responses from some of its leading preachers to the post-war crisis. Whether their voices spoke with any authority, however, is another matter. Henry Steele Commager, for one, apparently believed they did not: "The great moral crises of two world wars failed to elicit any authoritative religious leadership or even to inspire any spiritual interpretation, and not the clergy but the scientists instructed the American people in the moral consequences of the use of the atomic bomb."[18]

To be sure, the nuclear mushroom was not the only cloud on the Church's horizon in the post-war period. Urban Christianity was facing a new set of circumstances, in large part because urban life in general was losing its appeal. Prior to the war, according to William Manchester, the suburban world was symbolized by Greenwich, Connecticut, and Winnetka, Illinois—the preserve of the wealthiest classes, whose education was received at the most exclusive prep schools and colleges, and whose life was an extension of the country club. But after the war, a new suburban existence was born: symbolized by the Levittowns and Park Forests which were an extension not of the country club but the shopping center.[19] The most characteristic residences in America by election day, 1952, were the little white houses in these new suburbs.[20] And the flow of American households to such exurban subdivisions was more like a flood, or a tidal wave: in the period immediately following the war, eighty-five percent of the housing construction in the United States occurred outside of cities.[21]

Thus, the George Washington Bridge and its counterparts on Manhattan's other perimeters became pathways for an exodus away from urban life. During the fifties, "more than a million New Yorkers left the city to live in the post-war communities ringing it." By the end of the fifties, the daytime population of lower Manhattan, south of City Hall, was in excess of a million; but the night-time population, after the departure of suburban commuters, was about two thousand.[22]

With so drastic a drain of its most ambitious, able, and successful constituents, the urban Church was clearly coming to the point of a great adjustment. City Church membership was struggling not to decline. Sunday School enrollment and financial support were already declining.[23] "All is not well with the city church," Frederick Shippey wrote in 1949. "This is Protestantism's anxious hour."[24]

In one sense it was a false alarm. The Evangelical Lutheran Church of the Holy Trinity had grown from 350 members in 1920 to 1000 by 1945,[25] and it apparently was a solid institution when Paul Scherer departed. Christ Church, Methodist, continued and completed its construction in the post-war years, finishing the interior mosaics by the fall of 1949.[26] And it could claim 1750 members.[27] Riverside Church boasted a growing budget and a program of community service that had expanded into some of Manhattan's poorest neighborhoods.[28] The Madison Avenue Presbyterian Church in 1947 increased its budget, too—not as much as Riverside's, but still around twenty-seven percent.[29] Pledges to support it considerably exceeded those of the previous year,[30] and the number of members on the rolls surpassed three thousand.[31] The following year a new chancel chapel was given.[32] A year later, during the dedication of the chapel, Buttrick let it be known that there were discussions underway about air conditioning the sanctuary and other

ideas to improve the physical plant.[33] By spring, 1952, the congregation
had grown to 3200 members, and plans had been drawn for more than a
million dollars worth of remodeling to improve the Church house and
chancel, and to increase the capacity of the sanctuary from one thousand
to about eleven hundred.[34]   In November of that same year, the
congregation was accepting contributions from 1800 individuals and
family units.[35] Yet these impressive data apparently did not forestall
those observers who saw a rather grim future for the congregation. One
published report said that the Madison Avenue Presbyterian Church was
going to leave the neighborhood. And on a Sunday in New York,
Buttrick reacted with a howl of protest,[36] and a proposal to construct
further physical improvements in the building, including an Assembly
Hall on the lower level to seat five hundred people.[37] "I have never heard
a serious hint of our moving," Buttrick said. "This corner is a mid-point
of Manhattan and a vantage point in our nation. . . . We rejoice to bear
our witness for Christ here, in the most needy, the most fortunate, the
most strategic city in the world."[38]

    Notwithstanding the protest, Church life in the city had changed.
The Madison Avenue Presbyterian Church, whose influence had been
used to lift war-time air-raid restrictions in order that Sunday evening
services might continue, ended its program of Sunday evening worship in
the early fifties.[39] It was just one small sign of the great social transition
underway. The growth of the suburbs was another, and much larger,
piece of evidence.

    But more profound, and with even greater implications for the
white Protestant ethos which had dominated American culture and the
great urban Church, was the trend toward egalitarianism which Eric
Goldman has described.

> Once upon a time, white, Protestant, relatively old-stock Americans
> had been the arbiters of the national life. Small-town storekeepers or
> big-city bankers, they were "nice people," the "Best People,"
> expecting and receiving a certain deference. Now the established
> classes were having to make room for groups from the bottom and
> they were feeling uncomfortable, jostled, almost displaced in an
> America which they had assumed belonged peculiarly to them.[40]

The symbols of change appeared in many areas of life. A Major League
Baseball team was desegregated in Brooklyn during the same year (1946)
that the Hall of Fame for Great Americans enshrined its first Black
American.[41]   Labor unions moved beyond their roles as economic
bargaining units and became powerful forces which influenced national
public welfare policy, political power, and Presidential elections.[42]

Meanwhile, after a generation had endured two world wars, an unsuccessful experiment with Prohibition, and the economic dislocations of the great depression, the old authorities seemed to be less than trustworthy. The experiences of the previous thirty years "helped discredit all symbols of authority, from the flag to the cross, from the President in the White House to each father in his house."[43] There was a dramatic move away from authority and toward equality. During war-time mobilization, people had worked co-operatively with others whom they might never have considered their peers. Stratification between social classes, races, ethnic groups, economic levels, and quantities of academic privilege, began to blur.

> In the course of the twentieth-century, the gap between rich and poor, native and foreign-born, Protestant, Catholic, and Jew, gradually narrowed, and during and after World War II the progress toward equality was spectacular. The levelling of standards of living, the increase in income, . . . the cessation of large-scale immigration, the advent of all but universal high school education, and the enormous increase in college and university enrollment, the standardization of consumer products—all of these developments tended to make American society at mid-twentieth-century more egalitarian.[44]

If a strange new cultural unity seemed to be emerging from this levelling process, a strange enemy seemed to threaten it with new power. The specter of communism, which Karl Marx had said was haunting Europe a century earlier, now appeared to be keeping Americans awake at night.[45] Allies in the last war were now enemies in peace. Communism was considered to be arrayed against Christianity, against capitalism, against freedom, against western civilization, against the American way of life, and (before long) against a defenseless would-be democracy in South Korea.

As in the case of every other element of transition in the post-war world, this new polarization had a profound affect upon preachers and their churches. George Buttrick was not persuaded that the contrasts between good and evil should be so sharply drawn in ideological terms. Perhaps, he suggested, the specter of wickedness was something in the soul of America. "If there were no Russia we might have to invent a Russia if only to have an excuse for spending ten thousand million dollars a year on largely obsolete armaments in a world that is hungry and in despair."[46] And he warned his congregation: "Communism does not thrive on its theories; it thrives on the long but bitter patience of the poor."[47]

Ralph Sockman, on the other hand, did perceive the Soviet communists as a threat, and he counseled against any policy of "appeasement." The human remedies he advised were patience and dedication to the principles of one world governed through the United Nations.[48] He believed that the best defense against communism was "a healthy community spirit."[49] And the ideal community spirit flows from the Christian religion. "Communism never infects a country where a vital Christianity has been at work."[50] For that reason, Sockman blamed the Church for permitting tyranny to rise in communist Russia and elsewhere. It was "a certain form of perverted Christianity" which the Russian Church had offered, he said, and the nation "became disillusioned" with it.[51] The Russian Church under the czars and German Church in the twentieth-century "'were so preoccupied with doctrine and ecclesiasticism that they failed to take note of the deteriorating society about them.'"[52] Theological and institutional interests, as far as Sockman was concerned, were impediments to developing that sense of community by which communism could be stopped.

But mixed with these religious sentiments were patriotic ones. In an Independence Day sermon one Sunday in New York, Sockman was unabashed to link his affection for his country with that for his faith.

> The feeling of the writers of Deuteronomy toward their nation should be the feeling of a good American toward his nation. We should so keep the statutes of God that the peoples of the earth will look at us and say "surely this great nation is a wise and understanding people."[53]

Even when Americans take up arms, the world should perceive it as an act of faithful charity. Our motive in Korea, he said, must be seen not as "'merely enlightened self interest but true Christian helpfulness'" in a police action under United Nations auspices for a free Korea.[54]

Sockman openly confessed his patriotic feelings. "A lump rises in my throat when I have been abroad and sail back up and see the flag and the statue of liberty. Who doesn't feel it that's worth the name of an American?"[55] But there were those who questioned the integrity of his sentiments. In the year he served as president of the Federal Council of Churches, he travelled to the Soviet Union during the summer of 1946. After his return, the American Council of Christian Laymen accused him of harboring communist sympathies. Sockman apparently was spared the sting which many persons felt when facing similar accusations because one of his regular radio listeners was F. B. I. Director J. Edgar Hoover. Sockman asked Hoover to investigate the Laymen's Council "lies" about him, and the personal attacks subsided.[56] In the meantime, he appealed for a religious revival out of faith rather than fear, and for a rush to the Kingdom not simply out of terror of the Kremlin.[57] He asked for a mass rally of all religious faiths at some place like Madison Square Garden to unite in spirit against "'the perils which are poisoning our civic and social life.'"[58]

Despite his personal protections and his public appeals, however, he was not indifferent to the perils of the rising anti-communist mood in the country. His sermons during the summer and fall of 1953 continually refer to the charges of communist subversion which were being hurled at clergy and churches. He complained about the pulpits that were being used for "political propaganda."[59] He opposed the torrent of hearings and investigations.[60] He blamed "'little dissatisfied splinter ecclesiastical bodies'" for keeping the Church "'under fire'" when Christianity "'should be on fire' leading Americans to God."[61] He declared that if communists really are trying to infiltrate the Church, that is "a tribute to the power of religion" in America. But if the charges of subversion were to prevent people from joining the Church, "then communism was winning its point."[62]

Fosdick's career did not include a full-time ministry in the era of all these troubles, but he did speak to the situation on Sundays in New York. He deplored the fact that one-and-a-half million New Yorkers claimed to be Protestant but had no affiliation with a congregation: the churches were not successful at converting them; yet communists had "stolen our technique" of personal conversion and were making gains.[63] Like Sockman, he did not believe that people should embrace Christianity as an expression of anti-communism—"'being a Christian for political reasons does not carry anyone into the profundities of the gospel.'"[64] But he still believed communism should be fought, and he was willing to endorse a variety of weapons for doing so.

Fosdick's pacifism was widely known, of course. Nevertheless, he seems to have been ready to renounce it in the face of the Soviet threat: "We need military strength," he said.[65]

> Suppose that communism should sweep the world and submerge us even here. Where would we be? We ought to be in the underground resistance forces. Whether fighting with outward weapons or practicing Gandhi's non-violent resistance, there is where we ought to be. Temporarily conquered, yes, but like the underground forces in Europe when the Nazis were in power.[66]

In fact, Fosdick seems long to have been prepared for such a conflict. His final sermon as pastor of Riverside Church, delivered just two days after his sixty-eighth birthday, contained a warning of a "coming 'head-on collision' between Christianity and communism." The battleground, and its trophy, will be in the human heart, he said.[67]

Apparently "America's preacher"[68] was among those who saw the Christian mission and American policy as allies at least. He held the Church accountable for the moral fabric of the nation and he fretted about a breakdown in personal morality after the war: increases in adultery and divorce will be among the signs of a moral slump and ethical chaos, Fosdick said.[69]

Ralph Sockman seemed to hold the American Church and the American nation accountable for each other. "America was founded on the principle of God's sovereignty," he said.[70] "Religion is an integral part of true Americanism," and it is the force "'that has made America great.'" Insofar as God selects any people, the selected are the Americans, according to Sockman: "'We have an inheritance from God. There is no special chosen people of God, but God made Americans a choosing people.'"[71]

To Sockman, such convictions were no mere patriotic sentiments. They were theological affirmations, too. The Protestant Reformation and the American democracy are blood relatives, he believed, for Luther's movement was a direct ancestor of the values cherished by democracy: human rights, scientific and social progress, and the principle of private judgment.[72]

> Who could have predicted that ... a young monk, in Germany, ...
> [would start a movement] ... and out of it would come a new
> movement of such vitality that it would start an interesting democ-
> racy and right until it became the forerunner and fount of the
> greatest nation of the world, over here on this side of the Atlantic.
> Who could have predicted it?[73]

Sockman's convictions about the matter grew out of political and economic, as well as theological, history. North America, he said, was founded by people looking for God; South America, by people looking for gold. The United States, he affirmed, is based on "the Union between Father, God and Mother, Country."[74]

Paul Scherer, however, looked disapprovingly on all of that. What had become of the Reformation, Scherer believed, was not a development but a distortion; not its political and cultural fruition, but its sterility to the point where "the gospel in a thousand pulpits across the land is allowed to do little more than recommend itself as relatively sound advice."[76] Popular opinion has it, said Scherer, that the Reformation "exaggerated the significance of the individual." In fact, Luther "wanted the Word of God at the center, incarnate in a Person, bearing witness to the Christ who is its judge." But instead of having the Word as our first recourse, Scherer declared, "it is hardly even the last with us."[77]

The blame for this distortion of the Reformation, in Scherer's view, belongs to the Protestant tradition which had been invested with Luther's discoveries. "One by one, the generations that refused to be bound by the Pope, and refused to be bound by the Church, decided in an ecstasy of freedom that they would not be bound by anything—not by the Bible, not by conscience, not by God Himself."[78] It was a perversion of Protestantism and—not just in America but throughout the western world—Protestantism itself is largely responsible for the decline.[79]

Thus the very phenomena that impelled Sockman to dream of a revived and benevolent America, and led Fosdick to endorse spears and swords against the enemies of freedom, led Scherer to mourn the failures of Protestants to adhere to the doctrines of reform that spawned them. He felt that there had been too much confusion of the Reformation with the Renaissance. They may have been historical twins, but they were not identical—more like Jacob and Esau, in Scherer's view.[80]

To compound the tragedy, he believed, society was even deceived about what had been threatened or what may already have been lost. There was a fear that Christian culture may be doomed.

> The collapse which we have been witnessing in our generation is not by a long sea mile the collapse of a Christian culture. . . . It is the collapse of a culture that wanted to call itself Christian and was hardly ever in sight of either the Christian gospel or the Christian ethic.[81]

True freedom is biblical, Scherer insisted, not political or economic. "The debacle of freedom is the debacle of a faith that has been leaning back on its chair with its feet on the table."[82] He accused pulpits of offering no more than "a philosophy of life."[83] However, "it was not Christianity any more."[84] And the substitution of a false Christianity for the truth of the faith was just the foundation on which Hitler arose—not on the ecclesiastical and doctrinal selfishness that Sockman had deplored, but on the deviant forms of faith which Christians embraced.

> The wretchedness of the Church consists not in its weakness, but in its refusal of strength; not in its finitude, but in the pride that sets itself in the way of the Infinite; not in the relativities of its temporal lot, but in its substitution of them for the absolute and the Eternal.[85]

For all its stridency, however, Scherer's was among the rare voices of protest. Religion in America, during the late forties and early fifties, was not in decline but on the upswing. Throughout the post-war decade, the signs of ecclesiastical prosperity and health were abundant.

As Fosdick declared in retirement visits to the Riverside pulpit, Church membership[86] and Church attendance[87] in America were at an all-time high in the early fifties.

And the Revival had not peaked. Church membership was about thirty percent greater in 1956 than it had been in 1930, and it was higher still four years later.[88] From 1926 to 1950, the American population increased 28.6 percent while religious affiliation increased 59.8 percent,[89] more than double the rise in population!

Even beyond the limits of membership in religious institutions, there was a broad base of support in the larger society. A Gallup Poll in 1955 found that 96.9 percent of American adults considered themselves religious—70.8 percent of them as Protestants.[90] In 1954, ninety-five percent said they believed in prayer, ninety-four percent affirmed a belief in God, sixty-eight percent believed in life after death, and sixty-nine percent wanted to add the phrase "under God" to the Pledge of Allegiance. With such a mandate, it was done that very year.[91] And in 1956, "In God We Trust" became the official motto of the United States.[92] *Life* magazine wrote about the "great religious upsurge" in the land, crediting Sockman, Buttrick, and ten other preachers with being its leaders.[93] Hollywood screen stars were interviewed about their religious preferences.[94] And *The New York Times*, in the 1952 presidential election, was careful to ask the candidates how religion would influence them.[95]

Amid all of this overt spirituality, the breadth of Americans' religious convictions was questioned by some, the depth of them by others.

Charles Gilkey stretched his vision from 1951 back to the turn of the century and found a breakdown in the habit of regular Church attendance. Riverside and Madison Avenue Presbyterian were exceptions to the pattern of declining participation, he argued; but those who did come to worship presented their preachers with a less literate audience in matters of Bible and Church history than would have filled the pews a half-century earlier.[96]

Daniel Boorstin, on the other hand, did not dispute at all the quantity of religious expression in mid-century America; just its quality. With Church membership entirely a voluntary matter, the social "pressure to participate leads to more and more nominal membership." So, Boorstin adds, "We wish our membership to be reported. We do not care to participate."[97] H. Stuart Hughes labeled America's religiosity "the latest thing"; in other words, a fad.[98]

The leading preachers, too, had their suspicions. Ralph Sockman reminded his congregation that Church growth did not necessarily mean Church health.[99] Harry Emerson Fosdick complained that too much Church-going was formal, not vital, involvement in a facade of social respectability;[100] he preached and later published a sermon titled "The Dangers of Going to Church."[101] And George Buttrick flatly denied that there was a religious revival in America, "because as yet there is no deep penitence."[102]

Still other pulpiteers not only observed an outpouring of spirituality, but also applauded it.

> The contemporary religious mood is criticized sometimes because of its mass expression. It is alleged that perhaps people go to church because everybody is doing it . . . and that people sometimes commit themselves to the church in the same manner and for the same purpose they join a cultural organization or a service club. Only a few years ago church people lamented because folks did not go to church; now that they go there at best it is only synthetic Christianity. . . . Virtue as well as sin can be popular.[103]

But disclaimers like that ignored the more fundamental critique of America's religious revival, a critique which suggested that even the cautious leaders of the spiritual upsurge were part of the problem. Ralph Sockman, for instance, told his congregation at the start of 1948 about "the vital place for religion" between the extremes of secularism and sectarianism. What Will Herberg would describe sociologically several years later in a negative light, Sockman happily avowed in his pulpit theology.

> Protestant, Catholic, and Jew . . . believe in God the Creator, the Father of all men. All of us believe that God's creation is revealed and his principle is revealed in the literary documents of the Bible in the Old Testament, in nature around us, and in conscience within us. All of us believe in the moral sanctions as given in the Ten Commandments, in the Golden Rule. All of us can join in the Lord's Prayer. That's the basic common faith on which this country is founded and the greatest danger to this country's future doesn't come from some attack by air or atomic bomb across the sea, it comes from the undermining of our traditions and our institutions by issues and ideas and they get in only if we have not kept that tradition alive which made America in the beginning.[104]

For that reason, he said, religion should not be merely elective in the public schools.[105] Four years later, in 1952, he endorsed the effort by the New York State Board of Regents to require prayer in schools.[106] The year after that he appealed for Protestant, Catholic, and Jewish leaders to meet and map a plan for cleaning up public corruption in the city.[107]

It was Herberg's classic study, of course, which described the broad social trends so clearly ingrained in Sockman's approach. Herberg found that Protestants, Catholics, and Jews in America had come to be understood "as three culturally diverse representations of the same 'spiritual values.'"[108] His thesis was that religion in America was actually a "secularism of a religious people" or a "religiousness in a secularist framework": for both secularism and religiousness in America derive from the same sources and are intelligible in the context of sociological forces.[109]

This secular religion, called The American Way of Life, was neither the lowest common denominator of religions nor a synthesis of beliefs from various religions, but rather "an organic structure of ideas, values, and beliefs that constitutes a faith common to Americans and genuinely operative in their lives, a faith that markedly influences, and is influenced by, the 'official' religions of American society."[110] Its affirmations include the supreme dignity of the individual, the merit in activity rather than passivity, self-reliance, the standard of achievement, optimism, and idealism. Its shape draws upon "the contours of American Protestantism," and can be best described "as a kind of secularized Protestantism, a Puritanism without transcendence, without sin or judgment."[111]

In society, Herberg found that this peculiarly American spirituality was of benefit to the persons who were tormented and disoriented by individual crises. "This inner, personal religion is based on the American's faith in faith."[112] But along the way, it devitalized the traditional faiths and left traditional religions thoroughly "Americanized."[113]

Perhaps it is indicative of the situation that one of the best sellers of the age was Rabbi Joshua Loth Liebman's *Peace of Mind*,[114] about which Sockman's opinion ranged all the way from calling it a "great book"[115] to condemning it as an inspirational sedative.[116] Religion's goal, according to Liebman, was to achieve that inner satisfaction which The American Way of Life was so attuned to provide, and which Fosdick had long celebrated as the contentment of a well-integrated personality. It was a touchstone of what was happening in mid-century religious thought in America—and what was not.

Even in the early post-war period, Sockman seemed a bit uneasy about it. At a conference of Methodist World War II veterans, the complaint was voiced "that the church sent out its youth to war without any clear knowledge of its teachings."[117] So on Reformation Sunday, in

1946, he offered a sermon on what he considered the distinguishing beliefs of Protestants and Christians: that God lives, is ever accessible, is Creator and Controller of nature, and is love, all of which are sentiments shared by Catholics and Jews with Protestants; that we approach God by faith alone, without the intervention of legal codes or ceremonies, which was the distinctive discovery of the Protestant Reformation; that Christ is ever present in spirit, in the same way that a distant or deceased relative can be, especially in the sacramental meal which is a memorial (but not a repeated sacrifice) of his death; that the Bible is living and open to all but not infallible; and that personal faith is free for all, unburdened by dependence on some priestly class.[118] It was Sockman's very personal effort in pulpit theology to deepen the channels and clear the muddy streams of doctrine in post-war Protestantism. But it could hardly have been a more apt indication of the tendencies in this new secular religion being enjoyed by Americans. He tried to correct a situation that lacked depth and clarity and only managed to offer another illustration of the problem. Perhaps it could simply be said that he was a victim of his own presuppositions, to which he had confessed a few months earlier: "Whether Jews, Romanists, or Protestants, we all worship the same Heavenly Father and are all members of His family."[119] That was an article of faith not so much in keeping with the classic Protestant commitments to Christian discipleship as with the axioms of The American Way of Life.

          To be sure, Sockman was not the only leading homiletician trying to cope with the problem on Sundays in New York. But his colleagues were fewer. Two of the Church's most distinguished pulpit theologians had departed.

          Paul Scherer moved from the Evangelical Lutheran Church of the Holy Trinity in 1945 to become Brown Professor of Homiletics at Union. In time, he decided that his sermons during twenty-five years in the parish had lacked theological depth; and he wished they had never been published.[120] The doctrinal maturity which developed within him strengthened his commitment to classical Protestant principles. And he came to two unshakable convictions out of his careers in the parish and in teaching: that the Word of God "never has to be made relevant," for it always is relevant; and "that there is not today, there never has been, and there never will be any adequate substitute for preaching."[121]

          If one proposition prevailed above all in Scherer's theology, it was the premise of biblical authority. The Scriptures not only phrased his expressions; they framed his theological approach.   The quest to understand and interpret true human freedom, he wrote, "must begin where the Bible begins, with God."[122]   As the Reformation exalted (against the tyranny of ecclesiastical tradition) the moral and religious authority of the Word which God has spoken and the deed which God has done in Christ,[123] so a modern movement toward biblical Christianity can exalt (against "subjective and individualistic vagueness") the sermon as an act of worship which declares "the authoritative Word not of man but of God."[124]

However, said Scherer, though there is authority in the Scriptures, there is no easy comfort. "It isn't safe to believe in the God of the Bible,"[125] in the sense that there is no protection for our feelings from the approach of God's truth. "The Bible wastes little time on the way we feel,"[126] and it is clearly "not primarily concerned with character and personality."[127]   Rather, it "is what Protestantism calls it, the only rule of faith and practice."[128]

The mature Scherer recognized this as a scandal, certainly in the context of an age that stressed God's cozy desire to grow good personalities and give peace of mind. But Scherer found in that scandal the crux of the Gospel and the clue to the search for human freedom. Jesus always probed to the depth of human need—to the lust beneath the adultery, and to the hate beneath the murder.[129] So the Scriptures confront humanity with the truth, and humanity recoils from it.[130] Nevertheless, the challenge and the hope offered by the Gospel are scandalously clear: "the tension is between the will of God, which is both within history and beyond, and the will of man, which is solidly enough within history to continue doing a great deal of damage."[131]

Therefore, Scherer relied upon the authority of the Scriptures to declare that freedom can be found not in the human will but in the divine will. "Christianity is the only escape possible . . . from the Utopia we have been trying to build *our* way, and making such a horrible mess of it."[132]   Christianity, he said, is not a way of thinking or feeling or living.[133] It is rather the challenge of God—in which is hidden a gift.[134] Into such terms was Scherer's theology cast after he resigned from his pulpit at Holy Trinity.

His departure was followed within a year by the long-postponed retirement of Harry Emerson Fosdick from Riverside Church. Having agreed to remain until the end of the war, Fosdick concluded his pastorate in May, 1946. The retirement did not keep him out of the pulpit, of course. He was named Minister Emeritus and made periodic visits on Sundays in New York. And he continued writing: an autobiography and one last volume of sermons were among his productions after his full-time work ended. No less a prophet than Martin Luther King, Jr., ranked Fosdick as one of "the foremost prophets of our generation." And King considered Fosdick "the greatest preacher of this century."[135]

To the many who, like King, held Fosdick in the highest esteem, the Minister Emeritus of Riverside Church continued proclaiming "the universal profundities of the gospel" in a way the world can hear them.[136] He understood that to mean drawing upon the authority of what is common to all persons, namely human experience. Basically, wrote Harry Black Beverly, Fosdick's was a theology of experience; he could be called "America's Schleiermacher."[137]

Fosdick believed that the religious sensibility was an indelible trait in human existence. "Each of us is instinctively a worshipper," he wrote, "giving himself to something, making a god of it and serving it, so that even when we get rid of God philosophically we never get rid of him psychologically."[138] What he described as "the universal essence of all great religions"[139] lay at the heart of Christianity as well: the Christian faith at its best is a personal experience.[140] When the Bible puts forth a central statement of Christian dogma, he declared quoting Ephesians 2:5,[141] "That's not just theology, that's experience, reproduced again and again across the centuries in redeemed characters."[142] Even the thorniest issues of doctrine were, to Fosdick, really a description of repeatable human experience: "What we call the Trinity was to Paul not primarily theology; it meant a vital, transforming, illuminating experience."[143]

The purpose of preaching, Fosdick believed, was to bring about that same kind of experience in the lives of the hearers. "A sermon should creatively get things done, then and there, in the minds and lives of the audience; it should be a convincing appeal to a listening jury for decision."[144] The goal every Sunday is "personal conversion," Fosdick declared[145] and he repeatedly commanded his audience with words like "I want something to happen here."[146] It was a moral dictate, virtually a direct order, to convert.

After all, Fosdick believed, personal experience was the *sine qua non* of every renewal in the history of the Church. That the just shall live by faith was Luther's illuminating experience, his Damascus road encounter,[147] his "profound personal conversion."[148] It was the same for Wesley, Fosdick said.[149] Justification by faith "achieves a saving personal relationship between the soul and God, as revealed in Christ."[150] Faith in the reality of the spiritual world "is not faith alone," he said, but actually an attitude which "begins with factual experience"; it is "not a leap in the dark, but a conviction often forced on our unwilling minds by the soul's experience."[151]   Accepting Christ, Fosdick argued, is not a matter of faith alone but of the "perceptive insight" gained through experience.[152]   "Nothing spiritual exists outside the realm of the personal," he said.[153]

Fosdick did not abandon faith to the realm of pure subjectivity, of course. That Christ died for our sins is "a law as deeply imbedded in the spiritual world as the law of gravitation is in the physical."[154] As he put it just before Christmas, 1945, "the historic Jesus did perform an objective ministry whose benefits we all share and well may celebrate."[155] However, Christ's objective work alone merely marks Him as the Jesus of history, "a spiritual King Arthur who . . . wrought exploits whose benefits remain."[156] In other words, He who remains a fact of history cannot redeem anyone: He only redeems who is personally experienced by the individual.[157]

Thus did Fosdick push "faith" away from its Reformation definition—as the creation of a right relationship with God, graciously bestowed in Christ, the gift of knowledge and truth. For Fosdick, an authority other than grace obtained: namely, the authority of human experience. And faith, rather than being the gift of knowledge, was merely "the road to knowledge."[158]

That was true, he believed, whether the knowledge one sought was in religion or science or any other endeavor. Faith, to Fosdick, was a subjective, amorphous, ambiguous, ambivalent trust, exercised by human decision, not by divine grace. One could place faith in the Christ who died for our sins, or in atomic bombs; indeed, we could have faith in the human power "to tame the rude barbarity of man so that the atomic age becomes blessing and not curse."[159] There is true atonement, Fosdick wrote: "Christ's life of saviorhood is to be continued in the vicarious sacrifice of his disciples' lives."[160]

What gave inspiration for continuing the saviorhood and sacrifice, said Fosdick, was the Bible.

> I turn to the Bible . . . for spiritual illumination, to share in the most
> influential development of religious ideas in man's history, to watch
> divine deeds that have changed human destiny, to sit at the feet of
> great prophets, to learn from the insights of the seers, to find
> guidance in distinguishing right from wrong, and above all to come
> under the saving influence of Jesus Christ.[161]

Progressing as it does to ever nobler concepts of God, the Bible is "the greatest source of faith."[162] Fosdick recognized the historic significance of the principle of biblical authority for the Reformation: Luther founded

Protestant theology "primarily on the Scriptures,"[163] and held among his affirmations the principle that the Bible is supreme over all ecclesiastical authority.[164] "The sufficiency of the Scriptures as the rule of faith and practice for all Christians is one of the most consistently maintained principles of the Reformation," Fosdick wrote.[165]

Yet, having said that, Fosdick attributed the success of Luther's Reformation not to his theological commitments or to scriptural authority but to his achievement in "focusing social trends and drives precedent to him and now concentrate in him."[166] Fosdick's style was always to seek the abiding experiences in history, no matter what its changing categories may be. As a result, he was quick to see in Luther's work the achievements of a social engineer rather than a biblical theologian. He could see in Jesus, too, the human achiever to whom everyone might aspire: Jesus was an "idealist," he wrote, a man whose animating power derived from his "loyalty to a Personality," that is to God.[167] Samuel Robert Weaver said that to Fosdick Jesus was "only a spirit-filled man."[168] Fosdick's own words about Jesus say so as well: "The sources of [Jesus'] high ideals must be sought in the depths of his own personality and in his idea of God."[169] Christ thus became, for Fosdick, pre-eminently an ethical example.[170]

This reliance on the authority of experience, this confidence in a continuity between Jesus' experience in particular and humanity's in general, allowed Fosdick to see Christ's relationship to the world in reversible terms: our faith in Christ includes Christ's faith in us. "In Christ's basic faiths about God and man, his principles of justice and good will, worked out in human relationships with patience and determination, lies our hope."[171] Fosdick admitted to having a quarrel with Scriptures: "all that is best in us is God in us," he said;[172] "manhood and womanhood at their best are Christ-like," he affirmed;[173] and all of that made it very difficult for him to accept the New Testament's "estimate of man."[174] He knew that mere human kindness was not redemptive enough amid "this blood-soaked, violent mankind today."[175] He was, in the post-war era, more realistic than ever about the sinful human condition.[176] But he still believed that "the ignorant or wicked abuse of our free will"[177] was the cause of most evil; and he continued to trust that "patience, courage, and faith that hangs on when hope fades" could control this human barbarity.[178] By means of prayer, he thought, humanity could "endeavor to put ourselves into such relationships with God that he can do in and for and through us, what he wants."[179]

It is the opinion of Charles Earl Leininger and Samuel Robert Weaver "that Fosdick's experience of Christ and his Baptist evangelical background take him farther than his theological categories logically warrant."[180] Certainly he seems to have been very capable of drawing quite close to the affirmation of the Reformers without sharing their dogmatic principles. He could testify to the authority of Scripture, but not really accept it without filtering it through the authority of experience; he could celebrate the doctrine of justification by grace through faith, yet only by transmuting it into a Schleiermacherian sense of experience; and he could nearly confess with Luther that humanity is *simul iustus et peccator*, but still quarrel with the Bible for saying so. In his personal faith, he drew upon the classic convictions of the Reformation. But in his pulpit theology, he was arguing from new premises altogether.

In the middle fifties, when Fosdick's autobiography was published, the flyleaf legitimately identified him as "minister Emeritus of all America." At the same time, he also was being legitimately criticized as a man who had "made the secular culture paramount and standard."[181] By then, of course, the tendencies of the age had made The American Way of Life the popular, cultural religion. And The American Way of Life, both in its secular and religious institutions, was a thriving success. Churches were prospering right along with society. In New York State, where suicide and starvation had accompanied long unemployment lines into the pit of the depression less than two decades earlier, there were so few unemployed in 1950 that the state compensation division fired five hundred persons from the unemployment office staffs. There simply were not enough people out of work to keep them busy.[182]

Perhaps Fosdick was the nation's pastor emeritus in this flourishing age. Perhaps Ralph Sockman, still active in his pulpit after nearly forty years, exemplified the age as its spokesman. As the first decade after the war was drawing to a close, Sockman offered the opinion that most American churches were materially rich. And he looked forward to Christmas 1955 as "'the most prosperous in the history of America and the most hopeful since the close of the last war.'

CHAPTER XIV
A BLEND OF OPTIMISMS

This prosperity of Christian culture was not, to Sockman, a cause for unmitigated bliss. He felt that religion had been popularized by stressing Christ's promises and ignoring the Lord's demands.[1] "We want the promises of Christ without the sacrifices of Christ," he declared.[2]

Yet Sockman himself was a man who found the promises in most circumstances. He denied that he was a super-optimist; he even insisted that his tendency was to see the dark side of things, to be fooled more often by his fears than by his hopes.[3] However, he considered his positive approach to be a counterforce against prevailing trends in the twentieth-century: the nineteenth-century had been much too optimistic about humanity, he reasoned; the flaw in the twentieth has actually been too much pessimism.[4] He did not want to add to the modern world's foolish cynicism about human possibilities, he said. And he certainly did not want to establish a reputation for being tough on sin by denouncing those sinners and forms of sin not present in his congregation.

> As a minister I'm supposed and consecrated to preach the word of God as best I can see it. But there's no use preaching the word of God unless there's somebody to hear it, and I must make that word of God acceptable and so to make it acceptable, I must win hearers, and it's a very difficult place for a minister to know where his loyalty and interest in his people conflict with his loyalty as a prophet to God. It's so easy to get a reputation for courage in a congregation by attacking absentee sinners. A man would be very safe in a church like this to preach this morning on bad labor leaders (none of them here) . . . [or] bad authors, and very wise to keep silent on unpleasant things.[5]

Besides, what Jesus did was to reveal to people an awareness of the positive values they already had.[6] Christ is remembered beyond all other persons, Sockman said, because he fulfilled "the deep inarticulate longings" of ordinary people.[7] So, to Sockman, preaching in every age and circumstance has to focus on the needs of people[8] and has to offer concrete suggestions for changes in their lives.[9] "Preaching is discourse developed from divine revelation and designed to move men through and toward the divine will. . . . But only by looking to Jesus, the author and finisher of our faith, can we carry others with us."[10] What Jesus offers to the process are multiple insights into noble values: a principle of vicarious love, prophesied in the Old Testament and fulfilled by Him;[11] an enhanced confidence in immortality, even though the integrity of the universe already convinces us of it;[12] an example of how to cope with our own Gethsemanes;[13] and an illustration of gentlemanliness, of which He was the first.[14]

So, essentially as an example to humanity, Christ becomes the instrument of salvation, for He shows us that the world will be saved by "God in man, working through man."[15] The scars of sin that remain in us are flooded by God's grace,[16] and evil is driven out by turning on the flow of goodness.[17]

It was no blind hope that Sockman believed himself to be trusting. He was convinced the signs of its presence lay in the United Nations which replaced "the old war system with an international police force" in Korea,[18] and in the commitment to secure "a higher and richer quality of life among men generally."[19]

A. Justification by Faith

In Sockman's own way, it could be argued, he was presenting the theme of justification by grace through faith. But his was not, it should be added, the classic Protestant formula of justification by grace through faith alone. He distinguished between "belief," which he defined as assent to a proposition such as that God exists, and "faith" by which he meant the consent to trust in God and commit oneself to Him.[20] More specifically, Sockman says "Faith is not a sixth sense by which we apprehend realities for which we have no other evidence." Rather, faith "is our human capacity to appreciate the true significance of the reality we apprehend. It is not a substitute for our other ways of knowing; rather it is our way of unifying what these other methods bring us."[21]

The key issue is faith's character as a human capacity; for it is "exactly the same attitude of mind and the same principle of action that we use in office or home."[22] Faith is "belief plus trust plus consent plus commitment," and it is "hope plus confidence."[23] So, in Sockman's view there is nothing theologically unique to say about faith that could not also be said about trust in and commitment to a military strategy or a corporate marketing plan or a medical treatment procedure or a football play.   "When we speak of faith in connection with religion we're speaking of the same faculty that we use every hour of the day," he told his congregation.[24]

But Sockman did find a special way to describe faith in a religious sense. "The true believer in the Holy Spirit," he wrote, "is one who knows how to hoist the sail of his own spirit to catch the winds of God."[25] In the pages following that remark, Sockman denied that this means faith is a matter of effort to hoist the sail or to copy Christ. Yet he still declared that our growth in Christ requires us to "put ourselves in contact" with the Lord and His words.[26] The unmistakable impression thus created is that faith, at least initially, is a matter of works.

And on Sundays in New York, Sockman surely encouraged the deepening of that impression. He spoke of the nearness of God which results "when a person sets himself solely to seek God's will and not his own," or when one "continues to pay the price of his conscientious convictions."[27] He declared that "the way to life is through a narrow gate of discipline,"[28] affirming that Jesus' philosophy of life was "Choose the kingdom of God here on earth, trust God in this world. Do your duty as you see it. God will take care of you." It all had the flavor of Luther's disciplined effort to work his way to salvation in the monastery, before his illumination.

Sockman's pulpit theology, in effect, turned justification by faith back into an anthropomorphized works-righteousness. We are not to copy Christ, he recognized, but we are to be His comrades: "Salvation comes to us only through trying to save others"; "wherever we go, we take Christ with us."[30] It was in such terms that Sockman understood the Church as a fellowship in Christ which others should be pleased to join for Church membership allows persons "to put their faith into their fellow men because they believe God has faith in them."[31] And not only does the Church affirm that God believes in us, but also that Jesus is "the kind of man I can believe in,"[32] for He displayed a "consistent character," "wisdom," "moral perfection," and "power."[33]

At the very minimum, Sockman seems to have confused justification with sanctification. He wrote, for instance, that justification by faith means "We believe that our infinitely understanding Heavenly Father judges us not by what we are at any given moment but by what we are becoming."[34] Rather than following Paul, who said that "while we were yet sinners Christ died for us," Sockman said that God "can shower his love on us when we become true sons to him."[35]

But what Sockman really avowed was justification by achievement, by becoming, by works. Faith to him was a functional or utilitarian enterprise of the human spirit which breeds "the qualities of industriousness, integrity, and mutual respect."[36] By such fruits is faith measured, Sockman held.

Sockman offered an altogether genteel Christianity in his pulpit theology. It fit nicely into The American Way of Life. Christ "mellows" the heart, he said, and "lightens it by dropping off those sins of yesterday" and Christ "strengthens that higher nature by filling it with good thoughts."[37]

B. The Authority of Scripture

That insight, said Sockman, is the New Testament perspective into which the Scriptures evolved from the primitive conception of the nasty despot who roamed the pages of the Old Testament.[38] Sockman shared the view of biblical evolution which Fosdick had so clearly articulated in his *Guide to Understanding the Bible* a quarter-century earlier.   So, in a sense, the authority of the Bible involved its compatibility with our human preference for a more gentlemanly God. But, Sockman said, the Scriptures also offered a gift to humanity, "a faith above our faith,"[39] something higher than the ordinary faith which sustains us in business, sports, or patriotism.

This "gift" is something which Sockman professed to find frequently in Scripture. "Read your New Testament: the whole Bible in fact and see how often the word 'receive' occurs."[40] This gift of faith brings a certainty of victory and "a confidence which can weather both success and failure," Sockman wrote.[41] "Whence comes such faith? From the Bible."[42] For the Bible tells "a mystery story . . . the mystery of goodness,"[43] and conveys all we need for salvation.[44]

However, to see in Scripture the offer of a gift is not to declare that the Bible is one's sole authority, and indeed Sockman relativized the claims of biblical authority by grouping the Scriptures with other guidelines for living and with other texts of truth. "The Bible has come down to us as containing the Word that God has spoken. . . . And we call it God's Word."[45] But the Bible is only one of the books containing the wisdom of the ages, he said; and God's guiding hand is manifest in other authorities and can be known, for instance, "by the general patterns of history, by the still small voice of conscience, by the luminous insights of our best moments,"[46] or by the Church.[47]

He did seem to cherish a special place for Scripture as "the guidebook of the road" in our "journey of life,"[48] for among other things it leads us to "do away with that easy optimism that has been too much in vogue"[49] and "to look to God for divine help" rather than trust "man's natural goodness."[50] Besides, "'every revival of religion . . . has stemmed from a reawakening of interest in Bible study.'"[51] And any twentieth-century spiritual renewal will have to include a return to expository preaching, with sermons that "start on the sidewalk level where men are living and then lead their thought into the biblical uplands of the soul where men are 'transformed by the renewing of their minds.'"[52] The preacher is "the bearer of a Book," Sockman wrote, and as such can speak with "voices other than his own, voices which haunt us and the ages before us with a heavenly appeal."[53] On one Sunday in New York he declared it to be "the duty of the Christian and the Jewish pulpits to hear the voice of someone not ourselves, to cause others to hear it, and to interpret to them what it says."[54] But on another he seemed concerned that he may not have followed his own advice: "I hope in this church we do keep our biblical basis and not be content with mere opinions from a preacher or mere pep-talks."[55]

The evidence suggests that, despite Sockman's efforts to the contrary, he had in fact woven a tapestry of opinions. At the very least his appeals to get back to the Bible[56] did not amount to an effective restatement of the Reformation commitment to the authority of Scripture. Sockman knew that "the crust of tradition" had been lifted from the Bible by the Reformers, but to him that meant that the Book had come to life in the education and the liberty which were to spread in succeeding generations.[57] He seemed insensitive to such themes as the guidance of the Holy Spirit to make the Bible live with authority. And he appeared ever eager to reduce the Scriptures to principles of life and action which might be equated with other ancient wisdom and be acceptable to non-Christians, too. His were moral appeals to a tradition rather than energetic declarations of biblical dogma. He was more a spokesman for the prevailing American sentiment than for the creative unrest of Reformation doctrine. And he could shape the biblical message to fit his own premises when needed.

C. The "Freedom" of the Will

"The first suggestion which the Bible makes clear as a condition for going God's way," Sockman wrote, "is that we must start with a surrendered will."[58] The problems of a "conditional" salvation aside, this "surrender" of the will is a prominent theme of Sockman's pulpit theology during the post-war years.[59] To become a Christian involves giving "one's will to following the way of Jesus, . . . one's mind to learning the truth about Jesus, and . . . one's life to be linked with the life of Jesus in serving him."[60] Clearly this requires a substantial amount of human effort and a dedicated human initiative: "We cannot get into what Christ called this glorious state of the Kingdom of God by just a kind of mediocre morality"; instead "a man gets Christ ruling in his will and goes all the way."[61] And the first step in the process of getting Christ to reign is to surrender one's will.[62]

Sockman allowed that there are some situations which only the grace of God can cure, such as the arrogance of nations in retaining "their sovereign, so-called, right to make war."[63] He acknowledged that there is a human "bondage to sinful habits" that cannot be shattered by human effort alone.[64] Sin, he said, "is original, it has got to be rooted out by God Himself."[65]

And yet this was surely a shallow concern in Sockman's work, for he had said six months earlier that

> Jesus saw the only way to curb original sin is to cultivate positive virtues. . . . Jesus would say that the only way to eradicate original sin is by original goodness . . . to grow up out of the baseness and bondage of our lower self into that purity and freedom of the higher self . . . to enthrone reason above impulse and beauty above desire . . . to grow out of our narrow selfishness into ever widening sympathies . . . to be kind . . . to like the things that Jesus did.[66]

Then, only a little over four years later, Sockman claimed never to have preached on original sin before.[67]

Yet it was hardly a new issue for him. His professed eagerness to "do away with the easy optimism" of the age[68] and to see original sin as "the inborn predisposition to evil"[69] had been preceded by a warning in the immediate post-war days: "To lose our feeling of sin is worse than to lose our courage in correcting it."[70] In the end of the post-war decade, he preferred to understand the human condition both ways: "We must not underestimate evil"; but we must take care not to "overestimate evil."[71]

Given this mixed picture of the human situation, the question remains about the extent to which Sockman felt the race can arise to seize its own hope: in other words, the "conditional" salvation notion to which he apparently subscribed. Surely he allowed for a significant amount of personal achievement in the adventure of liberation from sin. "Too many think they can hitch-hike their way to a better world here and hereafter."[72] Perhaps we have to provide our own transportation.

And of that Sockman considered humanity to be quite capable: "when a man gets so aligned with God that his will is in the line of God's will, it is difficult to set a limit to what the mind can do over the body," he said less than two years after the end of the war;[73] then, on a Sunday in New York eight years later, he found it "almost impossible to set a limit to what the power of the will can do."[74] If war requires a great deal of effort, peace will be won by an equal labor.[75] If loving our enemies is too high a calling, we should keep "looking up . . . and maybe climbing up, too."[76]

What Sockman presented during the post-war years, therefore, was a very broad doctrine of the freedom of the will. "We can and should choose the direction of our aims," he said,[77] even in the most extreme circumstances. To the modern world, that meant places like Dachau and Buchenwald, which Sockman admitted showed evidence of "unbelievable depravity" but at the same time became areas where "the examples of heroic sacrifice, the glimpses of greatness, the Christlike comradeship often transcending racial and religious barriers" were displayed. That was the crucial thing on which history should focus, Sockman believed, for those episodes "reveal the potential nobility of the human spirit amid the storm clouds of a dark day."[78]

Such willful courage and determination are not owned by the timid or the tired, Sockman knew, and that apparently convinced him to write: "The work of Christ is no place for weaklings. The strong Son of God calls for the strongest sons of men."[79]

So humanity enjoys the capability of a free will and can freely exercise the power to use it, according to Sockman's post-war pulpit theology. Whatever is to be said of God's gift of grace, an individual can use her or his "iron will to stir up God's gift."[80] Sockman was not without caution in these matters: "We recognize that our freedom of choice is not unlimited; but we believe that within our limitations we have the room and the responsibility to make decisions which determine our destinies."[81] And not even God will impair our freedom to do so. "If God interfered with man's right of free choice, he would cease to become a father and become a dictator . . . he has to leave us free."[82]

Even the choice of whether to save the world from its "concentration camps and mass murders" will have to come by the work of God in and through humanity.[83] Sockman felt sorrow when evil arose and appeared to prevail.[84] But he never seems to have doubted that the free human will can alter any situation and decide its destiny.

CHAPTER XV
PROSPERITY AND PERVERSITY

In 1947 George Buttrick was in his middle fifties and was completing his twentieth year as pastor of the Madison Avenue Presbyterian Church. This largest of all the Presbyterian congregations in New York City was continuing to grow under his leadership. His parish chose to honor his two decades of service with an extended leave, a trip around the world, and a published booklet of his sermons which was inscribed as follows.

> His preaching of the Word in sermons and in books, with clarity, honesty, insight, and conviction, has been imaginative and fearless in content, beautiful in expression, dramatic in presentation, and has ever reflected a consuming purpose to represent the redeeming power of Christ. His pastoral ministry, always wise and kind, has evidenced his unabating concern for those in every sort of need. To young and old, in seasons of joy and times of perplexity or sorrow, he has given himself without reserve, and roots of friendship have become strong and abiding. His ministry of prayer, devout and unremitting and ever implying the sovereignty and compassion of God, has brought comfort, courage, and hope to the members of the Church, to the community, and in the wider fellowship of Christ.[1]

Respect for his leadership was not limited to his parish, however. He was selected to be General Editor of *The Interpreter's Bible*, a task which apparently forced him to postpone the five-month leave.[2] And he was popularly identified as one of the twelve preachers most responsible for the "great religious upsurge" in the country.[3]

Nevertheless, the prosperous condition of Christianity in America after the war did not please him. While others observed in the United States a striking growth in spirituality, Buttrick observed a profound absence of it. "The present generation," he said, "is the first not to take faith as the basic axiom of life."[4] Other forces were masquerading as religion. Just as "Liberal theology of the last generation was influenced by boom years in industry,"[5] so the social forces of mid-century were imposing alien values on Christian belief and practice. Prosperity, popularity, and wealth had become the dominant motifs of American Christianity, with the result that the lofty status of the Church in the nation had been bought at great cost: no less than the sacrifice of New Testament authority for the mission of the Church.

> In a world which always asks the reason for pain, Christ tells his followers that to follow him means pain. . . . Men of faith must welcome this pain, for by their witness in an alien world the Cross is lifted high above our proud and rebellious culture. Thus pain in the New Testament is no longer dark judgment or dark mystery: it is vocation and testimony. This public witness in our time is in, three main areas—the issue of peace and war, the issue of poverty . . . and the issue of color and race. . . . Thus rich men in the church have withheld their contributions, not alone in the southern states, when pastors have spoken a brave word for civil rights. They have starved their pastors and plotted against them. The administrative officers of the various denominations have wobbled, when they should have invited these critics to leave the church and take their wretched money with them.[6]

Many years later, Buttrick voiced similar sentiments when a faction within Presbyterianism sought a return to "Bible preaching." What they really sought, in Buttrick's opinion, was to silence the prophets (like Amos, Isaiah, and Jeremiah, who criticized national policy and wealth and ease) and to stifle Jesus' message to the rich man. Of the faction, Buttrick wrote, "They are just *too* rich. They break the bond between the Bible and the life of prayer."[7]

When the pastor is told to "stick to the Gospel," he said, it usually means "that the preacher should be content to take an anemic Christianity for a Sabbath airing in an ecclesiastical baby buggy."[8]

So in the post-war period, Buttrick was unimpressed with the overt religiosity of American society. He found nothing in this country that differed significantly from national perspectives in the Soviet Union or even in the Nazi Reich: Germany extolled "'blood and soil'"; Russia exalts "'proletarian freedom'"; Americans uphold "'success and the high standard of living,'" he said; all three are actually appeals to the evil self of individuals.[9] No religious revival had yet occurred, Buttrick said, "because as yet there is no deep penitence."[10]

In fact, during the post-war decade, Buttrick felt that the condition of the Church in America—both theologically and institutionally—was not better but worse.

Doctrinally the Church had lost contact with the Bible and its profound truth. Pulpits were filled with talk about personality and success, apparently forgetting that Jesus had "died as a common criminal."[11] "A glut of books" on peace of mind descended upon readers, Buttrick said, but the reading public found in them only "a cheap or a deceiving escape."[12] Civic clubs "prove their shallowness" by recommending the Golden Rule without an equally energetic recommendation to pray.[13] All over New York, he said, "happiness cults" abound; but they "never fashioned a soul.[14]

> New York is infested by happiness cults. Books on peace of mind multiply and are eagerly read. There are Christian pulpits that only narrowly escape the banalities of a charm school. But the words of Jesus are not of that stripe. They are stern challenge.[15]

Institutionally, too, Buttrick considered the condition of the Church in America to be suspect. For all the apparent strength of religion, he said society was actually indifferent to it. "Secular New York does not persecute people of faith: it just ignores them; . . . our faith is so tepid that it is not worth persecuting."[16] Even the landscape of the city, its skyline, argued for the same conclusion. For "banks, office buildings, and universities now tower above churches"; the inspiration offered by the medieval cathedral, "that earth is tragic unless dedicated to the Will above the earth," is unknown to the modern world.[17] Were the Savior's presence and power solely dependent on the influence of the Church, Buttrick believed, Christ could not be found. And without Christ, even though crowds descend upon the sanctuaries, joy will be absent; for "even worship will be boring until a man finds Christ."[18]

A. Justification by Faith

Yet, according to Buttrick, no one ever finds Christ. Rather, one is found and beckoned by Him. The finite human mind moves "towards its infinite ground, and the movement itself is drawn by infinite beckonings."[19] The name of that movement, for Buttrick, is "faith." He never understood faith as some human capacity whereby a person chooses what to trust. Rather, faith is a gift which arrives by the beckonings of God.[20] We do not find the beckoning; "it finds us."[21] And the form in which the gift first comes is a "yearning . . . an ache to know ourselves and God, and a hunger to live in Life."[22] Faith is also a courageous reply, "the valor of a response" as Buttrick put it.[23] Besides the hope and the "quickening of the soul" that faith brings, there comes the "act and venture" in answering; and finally, "there is arrival in joy."[24]

To describe faith in terms which make it both the offer and the answer, both the gift and the ache, both the beckoning and the venturing, is to suggest that faith occupies the center of life. Indeed, in Buttrick's pulpit theology, faith is the nexus between grace and courage, between invitation and embrace. Faith is the basis of *all* knowledge, as Wayne

Blankenship noted.[25] Perhaps, in Buttrick's words, it is "the optic nerve without which we are blind to any learning and any truth."[26]

This knowledge includes, of course, the knowledge of God. So there is no discovering God except by the gift of heaven.[27] "God will be found, not by our seeking, but by a response in prayer and life to One of whom we are dimly aware—as a child, half waking, responds to the mother who bends over him."[28] Nor can some outstanding moral performance make a difference. Strictly speaking, as Buttrick said one Sunday in New York, "There are no good works: there are only grateful responses to God's goodness, and these are possible only through God's power."[29]

Buttrick argued the same point in print and pulpit, that faith involves no human initiative and—except as the dimension of response—no human action at all. Faith is simply a gift, one that touches the "primal awe" in the human spirit.[30] And faith is in Christ because He is its test. "Ultimately the proof of Jesus . . . is that by His life and death He quickens in us that vital awe which every man at some time or other gives to God."[31]

Of course, the issue for Protestant doctrine was not to justify faith but to affirm justification by grace through faith alone. Buttrick pointed out that the term justification was "a metaphor drawn from the Roman law courts: we have a Friend in court with rulership of all courts and through him we have unmerited acquittal."[32] So justification by faith does not obviate the law; neither, however, does it require humanity to derive hope from the law. "Without the law we cannot live. But *with* it we cannot live, and there's the rub. For the law shines down with what seems to be eternal light, while we have only temporal powers, and we fail. Then we are haunted by memories of failure."[33]

To Buttrick, only Reformation doctrine has overcome this paradox. "For Romanism still leans on man's works of penance, and Protestantism leans on nothing but the sheer grace of Christ received in faith."[34] Works are very much a part of the Christian life, Buttrick said, but only as the fruit of faith not as the root of it. Besides, "God does not need our gifts. . . . But some of His children need them."[35] What Buttrick sought to do in his pulpit theology was to avoid misinterpreting justification by faith as a doctrine which still impels humanity to strive for righteousness in order to secure a relationship with God. "The striving to be righteous has gone: God's righteousness, now accepted by faith, flows through us."[36]

Moreover, for Buttrick, there was no sense in which the kingdom comes by human effort or initiative. It comes only by God's grace,[37] which he defined as "free unmerited favor" of God: "the love that opens the prison door."[38]

Provided this premise is clear, Buttrick's pulpit theology eagerly spoke of Christian works, fruits, actions, and service. Christ's yoke, he said, is discipline and commitment. God drives "with the whip of unrelenting demand, and what stern ploughing is to be done in this stubborn planet!"[39] It is possible, for those who shirk the yoke, to fall from grace.[40] But, "when men do thus work with God, there is always a touch of heaven on earth."[41]

The constant adversary of faith, to be sure, is doubt. And when faith is described in such radical terms as "gift," one can question whether there is in reality any giver. Buttrick recognized that a solution, adopted by certain theologies, was to speak of faith as an unshakable gift, one so compelled by grace as to be irresistible and therefore indisputable proof of the giver. But to Buttrick, if faith were compelled, it would not be faith. Likewise, one way to dispel doubt would be to have faith circumscribed by those powers of reason which could prove the claims of faith. Again, however, "if you could prove it you would be compelled to believe it." Either way, such "faith" would not be faith at all, "but only a drab compulsion."[42]

Anyway, the contest between faith and doubt is not amenable to being solved by reason.[43] For faith goes beyond reason. Yet faith and doubt shadow each other. Or, more precisely, in Buttrick's words, "If we must be honest enough (as indeed we must) to admit that doubts shadow our faith, we should surely be equally honest to admit that faith at times brightens our doubt."[44] And faith brightens with creative beauty: as Buttrick pointed out, "doubt could never have built Rheims Cathedral."[45]

B. The Authority of Scripture

Whether in architecture, stained glass, or some other medium, Buttrick believed, everyone is given some power to see the light and recognize it.[46] But, he said, "if we would know about Jesus we must study the New Testament: the knowledge will not come of itself through our pores."[47] And the place to begin, he declared, is where the New Testament begins—"with the human Jesus"; and the Mystery will soon break through in splendor.[48]

So the Bible and the people who embrace the biblical faith have the authority of the historical Jesus on which to depend. And, more broadly speaking, the Bible has the authority of history—for it is history, faith history. It differs, therefore, from myths like Hitler's *Blood and Soil* or the American Dream, Buttrick wrote, for in the election of Israel there was no human merit at the bottom of the selection "but only the mystery of God's inscrutable will."[49] Moreover, God's choice did not permit Israel to bask exclusively in divine sunshine, but rather commissioned Israel to be a light to all the nations of the earth. And should God's people disobey that selection, "the choice would become God's stern judgment." In the end, Israel was to learn "that her very suffering might be the fulfillment of her mission."[50]

But if the authority of the Bible is substantiated by the authority of history, there is nevertheless nothing about biblical authority that requires the continuance of history. In fact, wrote Buttrick, "To the Bible, history cries aloud not for continuance or mere renewal but for total change and redemption."[51] This is a paradox, too, he frankly acknowledged. But "wise men accept the fact of paradox."[52] For the Bible clearly makes opposing avowals: God is both our Great Companion, wholly with us, and the Supreme Other, totally apart from us; Jesus Christ is both our judgment and our mercy; history is both the realm where God's purpose unfolds, and the realm that will pass away.[53] And the Bible is, therefore, the authority in history and the authority for what transcends history: it is, in short, our "Ark"[54] to sustain us during the onslaught of truth under which history will be washed away.

Now Buttrick was quite aware that both supporters and critics of biblical authority found it useful at times to describe Scripture in other terms—as literature, as history, as science, and as a textbook of divine dictation. He found none of those to be an adequate critique of, or necessary correction to, the claim of biblical authority. For instance,

> The Bible itself nowhere claims to be literally inspired. . . . A true doctrine of inspiration is that through the Scriptures God Himself has spoken and still speaks to men, because God will give to those who ask, the gift of His own Spirit as interpreter. . . . The Bible is thus a book of good news, now forever inseparable from the good news which it proclaims, and therefore forever essential to man's salvation.[55]

The authority of Scripture does not need to be defended, in Buttrick's view, by voices that make false claims on its behalf. The New Testament is neither argument nor philosophy, but rather it "testifies to an unquenchable joy."[56] The Bible is not vindicated by its propositions about science but rather by the presuppositions of science. "The Faith that the cosmos is one and worthy of study is biblical faith. . . . Thus all science rests on biblical faith."[57] And every time an age or ideology assumes that it can at last shelve all or part of the biblical story, the message lives again. "Bible stories that we thought were dead get up from the grave and invade with living truth the heart of every age."[58]

And as for the doctrines which Scripture proclaims, Buttrick wrote, "Doctrines are true not simply because they are in the Bible: they are in the Bible because they are true, and because the beckonings of our daily life validate them."[59] It is not in some neat package that the teachings of the faith are transmitted, but rather in the tragic and comic encounters of human existence wherein the biblical story becomes our story. Or, in Buttrick's own words, "The Bible offers its truth not in cellophane, but in flashes of drama."[60]

From this standpoint of authority, Buttrick declared the Bible "calls for a choice."[61] But it is not a choice which will determine human destiny or even the continuance of an authoritative Scripture. That issue is already settled: the battle is "already won."[62] In biblical terms, the choice is between victory and failure, and the victory is God's. So "The Bible says . . . the choice in any crisis is between God and (shall we say?) a self-idolatry."[63]

C. The "Freedom" of the Will

It could apply to any crisis, of course, but the most compelling crisis of the post-war decade was posed by the stark drama of atomic power. The knowledge of this mighty secret and its implementation into weaponry had at least put the ultimate issues of life into bold relief. For now, Buttrick believed, humanity could clearly see what "the strange gift" of God's grace had been beckoning the world to notice all along.

> We are ignorant, but aware of our ignorance, yet unable to lighten
> our darkness: we need a revelation. We are wicked, but we know
> our wickedness, yet we cannot overcome it; we need redemption.
> We are mortal, and chained to mortality, though with a long enough
> chain to see it for what it is, yet we cannot break the chain: we need
> deliverance.[64]

When the hydrogen bomb burst onto the scene in the early fifties, it did not alter the crisis, Buttrick said: "it has only made the questions so dramatic that we can no longer evade them"; still, he asked his congregation, "Is there any cure for man's perversity?"[65]

It is this "perversity," Buttrick insisted, that determines the contours of the human condition; for we can never free ourselves from its shattering power. "There is a cleft in our will, and, since the bond with God is now broken, our good will has no power . . . and our evil will prevails."[66] History has demonstrated the fact, Buttrick declared. "Two world wars sandwiching an acute depression, so acute that the world's richest nation went hungry, are evidence of a virus in the blood of mankind."[67]

This virus, this cleft, this perversity—this sin is in the human will, according to Buttrick, so the human will cannot be the means of salvation.[68] With a "crippled will," he said, only "crippledness" could be done.[69] In fact, Buttrick feared, given the perversity of sin and the power of the atom, the likely outcome is that "human nature will obliterate itself unless it is invaded by a higher nature."[70]

So perverse is the human condition, Buttrick said, that Christ "recoils" from it.[71] Yet so "helpless" is the human condition,[72] that Christ is "drawn by man's needs." Buttrick mused, "Perhaps He really died of a broken heart."[73] The Madison Avenue preacher knew there were "still a few incorrigible optimists about human nature, though how they survive is an enigma."[74] But to him the total depravity of the race was evident both in individuals and society: not that any individual or group is perfectly wicked; rather, he said, "total depravity . . . means that history is cankered in every culture and every person."[75] That canker in us is the same disease of "self will" which made Judas betray Jesus.[76] The "crucifiers" of Jesus, too, were "wicked"—not ignorant but wicked.[77] And "the trouble is still in us."[78]

When Buttrick considered the question about the origin of this evil, he again identified a paradox. For, on the one hand, human responsibility for evil cannot be denied; yet, on the other, evil was not a human invention. "Eve did not create the snake," Buttrick wrote. "So we must hold together two facts: We are responsible for evil choice, but evil does not originate with human nature. These two cannot be held together in theory, but they are held together in daily life."[79]

And as to the escape from evil, a similar paradox applies: one must will to surrender to God's will; but not even the surrender can be an act of willfulness. "We cannot renew the weakened will, for the weakened will is all we have with which to renew the weakened will."[80] Thus, there is no real human freedom. And there is for Buttrick no freedom of the will—except "with however limited a freedom" in which "our will is held . . . in the will of God."[81] The only sense in which

human freedom could be exercised in an initiative toward being delivered
might perhaps occur in prayer: "some small act, some initiative on our
part in response to God, is asked of us."[82] People still have that much
freedom—to go the way of Judas in a selfish strategy "to devise their
own clever salvation,"[83] or to surrender to the will of God.[84] "Our
humanness is pathetic without God, and marked for death. . . . The
human cannot save itself. You and I cannot cleanse history . . . : any
other weapon in our world is not power, but only the weapons of
suicide."[85]

However, not even the choice to surrender to God can be made
in absolute freedom. "We have no power, even though we are pricked
with eternity, to choose Christ—unless He chooses us."[86] We can choose
not to worship Him. We can shut Him out of our lives.[87] But the human
role in finding Christ is always that of response: "he chooses us, and then
we must decide if we accept his choice."[88] Only in the sovereignty of the
divine will is the human will free.[89]

That position, for Buttrick, is both a negative comment on
human freedom and a positive statement on human hope. For it is
precisely in knowing the facts of the human condition and in appreciating
the limits of human freedom that one is in touch with the promise of
divinity.

> Wickedness is the mark both of our doom and of our divinity. We
> are wicked: that is our doom. But we are aware of God, and so we
> know our wickedness: that is our divinity. Thus man's dilemma:
> there is a cleft in our nature which we ourselves cannot heal. On the
> one side of the cleft is our perversity, as long as history and as wide
> as the world, which our forefathers, with more realism than our
> supposedly realistic age can boast, called "original sin"; and on the
> other side there is some contact with primal Goodness—a contact
> without which we could not know sin—a bond which our
> forefathers, with more optimism than we have allowed in them,
> called the likeness and image of God.[90]

So both our sense of sin and our taste of hope come from our knowledge
of God.[91] Which suggests that the knowledge which faith brings is not
somehow an addendum to existence, free to be worn for adornment.
Indeed, in Buttrick's words one Sunday in New York, "No religion can
be just chosen: it is not a necktie, but the main artery of a man's neck."[92]

Yet that in turn could imply no freedom at all. For without such
an artery there is no life, only death. Certainly, apart from faith there is
only the way of death in Buttrick's view, but that does not in itself negate
the human freedom to choose it. No force, not even God, compels a
human choice. "Joy is not freedom from good and evil choice," Buttrick

declared, "for we without that choice would be puppets rather than men."[93] Nevertheless, "human freedom is set in the midst of necessity."[94] In fact, true freedom is only found in "the chosen fulfillment of our destined nature."[95] There is no freedom without destiny, Buttrick said: the two are "correlatives."[96]

Here Buttrick recognized the Reformation distinction between necessity and compulsion. Clearly, while he acknowledged the necessity of accepting God's will if we are to be saved, he did not accept any sense of a compelled destiny for humanity. The choice to live by God's light or in the darkness of the world alone is "never coerced,"[97] he said. "You and I choose to follow or to stay. There is no compulsion."[98] After all, "a compelled goodness is not good, but only compulsion; an automatic goodness is not good, but only automatic."[99]

So Buttrick's pulpit theology insisted finally that Christianity is much more than intellectual assent or emotional feeling—"it is an affair of the courageous will"[100] responding to "the beckonings of God."[101] In contrast to Sockman, who pleaded that when God's word seems too high for us we should keep climbing, Buttrick said "if man is finite, creaturely, dependent, contingent . . . how can he hope of himself to 'ascend.' Perhaps he can be lifted, but he can hardly climb."[102] One can only surrender to the Christ who has already chosen to do the lifting. That was both Buttrick's pulpit theology and his personal story.

> It is doubtful if any man ever did choose Christ except as Christ had first chosen him. For myself I did not choose Christ, but tried to avoid Him. I tried not to be a preacher: I could see the glory in Christ but was impatient with the pettiness of the Church and had not then the eyes to see beyond the pettiness. . . . But He chose me for a preacher.[103]

In the uncompelled necessity of it, Buttrick found his destiny. And his freedom.

EPILOGUE: The Main Stream at Its Crest

On its surface the religious situation in America showed every measurable success for which a preacher might hope. Increases in Church membership and attendance, growing financial support for congregations, a broad popular respect for the institutional Church, and a widespread confidence in religious values were hallmarks of the post-war decade. There was a particularly high affinity expressed for Protestant institutions: their growth rate had exceeded that of the Roman Catholic Church—63.7 percent to 53.9 percent-from 1926 to 1950.[1] Of the nearly ninety-seven percent of Americans who considered themselves religious in 1955, 70.8 percent called themselves Protestants.[2] Children were praying every morning in school. They were pledging allegiance to their nation "under God." They were encouraged to think of themselves as the offspring of Father God and Mother Country.

The glory was soon to tarnish, however. Statistically, the peak level of Church participation was reached in the late fifties, when the increase stopped and a numerical plateau became the prelude to a decline.[3] More significant was the skepticism with which the substance of America's spirituality came to be viewed. For it was built upon an altered foundation—not the Protestantism of the biblical dogma which burst forth during the Reformation, but the secular Protestantism of social gentility that was called The American Way of Life. Perhaps the inheritance of the gospel of wealth made it easier to endorse ecclesiastical prosperity as a signal of divine blessings. Perhaps the social pressure of anti-communism suppressed another inheritance, the social gospel. Regardless, the integrity of Christian doctrine in Protestant circles was at stake.

By the mid-fifties, only one of the nation's best-known preachers was still delivering theology from his pulpit on Sundays in New York. Fosdick and Scherer had departed from the parish ministry a decade earlier. In 1955, George Buttrick moved to Harvard as Preacher to the University and Plummer Professor of Christian Morals. Only Ralph Sockman of the four most prominent preachers in the land remained in his Manhattan pulpit. And there he stayed until his retirement in 1961, after forty-four years in the only congregation to which he was ever appointed to serve.

Fosdick continued to write and preach in retirement until physical disabilities forced him into a wheelchair. Scherer left Union Seminary in New York for its counterpart in Richmond, and then later went to Princeton. Buttrick returned to New York from Harvard to assume the Fosdick Professorship at Union in 1960; thence to Garrett and Louisville, where he spent his last years. Sockman continued to travel, preach, and write from his New York home, and to devote more attention to the Hall of Fame for Great Americans of which he had been a director for some years.

PART FIVE

CONCLUSION

CHAPTER XVI
CONCLUSION

A. Transitions

On October 5, 1969, thirty-nine years to the day after the first service at Riverside Church, Harry Emerson Fosdick died at his Bronxville home. In March of that same year, Paul Scherer died in an Ohio nursing home. The following year, death claimed Ralph Sockman. A decade later, on January 23, 1980, George Buttrick died in Kentucky.

Of this last event, Joseph Sittler wrote "George Buttrick's death really closes the book on a memorable period in Protestant preaching in North America."[1] With their demise, perhaps, the last of the true pulpit princes had disappeared. Academic, ecclesiastical, and popular audiences all had held them in highest regard. But now the era of such homiletical royalty seemed to be ended. Henry Steele Commager wrote that "after Phillips Brooks no Protestant churchman spoke with authority."[2] These four men in their pulpit careers offered a reason to give Commager's thesis a second look. For they were homileticians with a wide following among other preachers, professors of theology, and in the general public. They served as models for generations of pulpiteers. Many among their colleagues and listeners found them to be authoritative examples of how to preach and authoritative proclaimers of the truth that must be preached. Surely no individual in the years since has had similar credibility and clout while occupying a parish pulpit week after week. Certainly no group of preachers serving simultaneously in the same city has had as much impact as these men did from their regular pulpits on Sundays in New York.

Perhaps some of their stature was a consequence of the role New York City enjoyed in American society. A veteran of Manhattan ministry for thirty years wrote in the early sixties that American Protestantism expected New York preachers to offer homiletical content and artistry on a high level. "It knows that when a strong Protestant voice no longer resounds from this center of communications, the prestige and influence of the Protestant pulpit will decline even more rapidly than they do and the common cause of the churches suffer."[3] Of course, transitions in urban life, the post-war suburban establishment, and the rise of other centers for communications, entertainment, and cultural influence, all have helped to diminish Manhattan's former dominance. In the early thirties, for instance, New York was the news capital of the nation. But during the Roosevelt presidency, United Press tripled its Washington news staff, and the Associate Press released one fourth of all its wire service copy from Washington.[4]

But perhaps even more than the erosion of their social base was the erosion of the pulpit as an arena for pronouncing Church doctrine. Heiko Oberman has written that "The preaching of the Word in the Reformation is the living *magisterium* and bridge between Church and Scripture."[5] In a sense, the sermon was *the* doctrinal forum. However, in 1953, Reinhold Niebuhr offered the opinion that "the pulpit does not necessarily affect the trends of theology," except in unusual cases like that of Fosdick. Besides, Niebuhr considered the Riverside pulpit to be "on the side" of Fosdick's main professional duties.[6] The pulpit was deemed subordinate to academic theology. By the end of the fifties, wrote Ronald Osborn, homiletical professors who had distinguished themselves first in the pulpit—Fosdick, Scherer, and Buttrick were his examples—had "vanished."[7]

So the prominence of the pulpit in the Reformation era for conducting doctrinal discourse had been lost. The systematic, historical, and personal link between theology and preaching was weakened. Despite Scherer's conviction that "theology students learn more theology in homiletics courses than anywhere else,"[8] the prevailing trend was to minimize the connection. Halford Luccock said "Preaching, if it is to have adequate depth, height, and breadth, must be theological preaching."[9] "Preachers in every productive Christian period know that they are helpless without doctrine," Ray Petry has written.[10]   As Chrysostom implied, "Although a teacher may not necessarily have a public preaching function, a preacher cannot fail to teach Christian doctrine and still be a preacher."[11] Nevertheless, in Ronald Osborn's observation, "Preaching has become less and less theological, more and more occasional in the sense of *ad hoc*."[12]

Even some who study preachers and preaching have been content to set aside the connection. Fabaus Landry wrote a dissertation on Fosdick in the early seventies, intending to "deal only with his preaching" not with his "influence as a popularizer of liberal theology."[13] And Joseph C. Hall, who found Fosdick's presentation of Jesus as Savior to be "anthropocentric and moralistic," concluded that the Riverside preacher operated with "little real doctrinal basis."[14]

But even bad theology is still theology. A misrepresentation of doctrine is still a presentation of it. Willis Stanley Gertner, for instance, complained about the preaching during the twenties and thirties "which centered on the ethical and social but avoided the theological."[15] Yet a more accurate critique would identify the false doctrine present rather than assume that a deficiency means all doctrine is absent. At least Linn James Creighton addressed what he considered "Fosdick's weakness both as a theologian and as a preacher that he emphasized human dynamism so exclusively."[16]

Carl Braaten, writing in 1964, identified John A. T. Robinson's *Honest to God* as "a cry of alarm at the continuing tendency of theology and preaching to drift apart." In Braaten's words, "The problem of the gaping chasm between the work of theology and the word of preaching remains the most important unfinished business of this generation."[17] Preaching and dogmatics are united in the one kerygma from which they come, he said.[18]

B. Foundations

All of which makes the inescapable point that what comes from the pulpit is inevitably Christian doctrine—false or misleading doctrine, perhaps—but nevertheless doctrine. So pulpit theology must be tested against that tradition in which it purports to stand. What claims to be Protestant preaching must be evaluated, therefore, against the fundamentals of Protestant doctrine. In other words, one can ask of Sockman, Scherer, Fosdick, and Buttrick: How Protestant were they?

Dillenberger and Welch warn against attempting to understand Protestantism "by exclusive appeal to the Reformation."[19] Protestantism, they say, is "an historical community"[20] whose identity should not be restricted to "the patterns of its historical origins."[21] Yet they also say that what made Luther a Reformer in senses in which Huss and Wycliffe were not was "the vision of justification by faith as the point around which the life of the Christian and the Church must be understood."[22] Ronald Osborn comes to a conclusion which he says can be supported in theological, historical, and sociological terms: that "preaching will exert no significant influence on the life of the nation except as it stands on some ground of distinctiveness. In the heritage of the Reformation that ground has been the rock of the Holy Scripture."[23] And then there is the question of freedom, aptly illustrated, writes Joseph Ban, in the case of Harry Emerson Fosdick, who proclaimed the human freedom to develop a well-integrated personality and to affect the destiny of society but was himself "captive . . . to the urban culture of his manhood years."[24]

A doctrine of justification made Luther a Protestant while others were not. A doctrine of biblical authority made the Reformation distinctive, and without it latter-day Protestants are not. And a doctrine of freedom, falsely proclaimed, can overlook the bondage in which the first Protestants knew humanity was caught.

C. Doctrines

So, in answering the question put to Sockman, Scherer, Fosdick, and Buttrick—"How Protestant were they?"—there is recourse to the quarter-century of pulpit theology during which they handled the central doctrines of Protestantism: justification by grace through faith alone; the authority of Scripture; and the "freedom" of the will.

1. Justification by Faith

Quite simply, Sockman and Fosdick lost track of the Reformation definition of faith. The concept of a righteous relationship with God made possible exclusively by the gift of divine grace was muted, altered, or absent in their pulpit theology. They saw faith as a human capacity to place confidence in any person or power. Across the entire quarter-century under study here, they had adopted views on faith and justification which were not in keeping with classic Protestant theology. Somewhere they went adrift on a sea of Pelagianism.

Buttrick and Scherer stood much more clearly in the Reformation tradition. At times Buttrick implied the universality of the gift in a way that one might find surprising, given his orthodoxy. He spoke of the "yearning" for God as a "gift to all,"[25] declared that belief in eternal life is ingrained in human nature,[26] said that "every man is given some power to see the light and recognize it as light,"[27] and even described faith in God as "natural" with "great faith" being "hard."[28] Yet such apparently incongruous constructions, when set in the context of his general doctrinal approach, belong in the category of faith that responds to the prior gift and beckoning of God.

Paul Scherer kept his focus narrowly on the gift of faith, received in personal evangelical experience. The place where he failed to stay close to Reformation doctrine lay in his having had too short a vision of the relationship between God's gift of faith and humanity's offer of response in life. His bitter opposition to the social gospel was a harsh truncating of the Lutheran concept of life overflowing with love. And it was, one might add, a blatant unneighborliness, in an urban environment where Walter Rauschenbusch had labored so eminently a generation earlier.

In sum, the pulpit theology of Buttrick and Scherer amounted to authentic and, generally, consistent proclamations of classic Protestant theology on justification by faith. That of Fosdick and Sockman, however, belonged to another trend.

2. The Authority of Scripture

Ralph Sockman always wrote his sermons with a biblical text at the head of each manuscript. Occasionally, he appeared to have written expository sermons. And yet seldom was the Bible the authority for his word. Sockman preached with an almost indefatigable optimism; with a confidence in scientific, political, and moral progress; and with a firm reliance on humanity's common sense. He steadily compromised and confounded biblical authority with these other premises for his work. There was a kind of shallow reasonableness by which he tested his pronounced convictions, and very little evidence in his pulpit theology that he appreciated the profound significance of biblical authority so central to the Reformation.

For Fosdick, at least in the early thirties, the fundamental authority was human reason. It had lifted him out of the rank fundamentalism of his childhood, had put him in contact again with the Christian faith during his young adulthood, and had served him well in tenacious battles with the forces of fundamentalism in the twenties. But as the thirties rolled along, Fosdick came increasingly to value the authority of human experience. The well-integrated personality was celebrated as the goal of life in his writings, and the insistence on the experience of personal change became a driving concern in his sermons. He even transmuted Luther's grasp of biblical dogma into an expression of sixteenth-century experience. Without doubt, Luther went through a dramatic, life-changing experience; but it was by the authority of Scripture that he could interpret the experience rather than by the experience that he interpreted Scripture.

Fosdick's penchant for life-situation preaching, which Sockman shared, elevated all human experience to the potential of authoritative revelation, and diminished scriptural authority. It was his technique in sermon construction, for instance, to start with a great idea, collect experiences around it, and surround it with Scripture. So the Bible illustrated the preconceived truth, but was not the source of its being told. Scripture did not offer God's word to human experience, in Fosdick's preaching. Rather Scripture itself became a compendium of human experience.[29]

Both Scherer and Buttrick rooted their preaching in the Bible, starting with a text, but more importantly drawing upon the text for the content of the sermon. Especially in his earlier sermons, Scherer relied heavily on expository preaching; but even with a more fully illustrated homiletic in succeeding years, he always insisted on the centrality of the Word. The Bible was the meeting place where a person encountered God. Buttrick, meanwhile, showed his reliance on scriptural authority in his own style of preaching and in the way he taught his students to outline theirs. The text, at the beginning, had to be brought to the level of the earth so that the listener could be lifted to the level of divine truth.

And both Scherer and Buttrick were able to accomplish this while shaking off the constraints that said biblical authority had, *ipso facto*, to mean literalism or fundamentalism. Scripture both offered the place for, and mediated the encounter of, God's meeting with humanity, Scherer believed. Buttrick held that the biblical story tells of that encounter in the past and mediates it in the present. So, in the substance of the narrative as well as in the power to make Christ present, the Bible is authority. Moreover, in keeping with Reformation teaching, they understood that it is by the guidance of the Holy Spirit, through this encounter, that the Scriptures are rightly interpreted. The Bible, literally but not literalistically, is God's word.

Thus did the Reformation teaching on the authority of Scripture become manifest in the pulpit theology of Scherer and Buttrick. In Fosdick and Sockman, the Bible was merely one authority among others, and not necessarily the foremost.

3. The "Freedom" of the Will

Not long after the end of the war, Ralph Sockman told his congregation about a luncheon meeting he shared with Martin Niemoller, the German pastor incarcerated during much of the war for his anti-Nazi views. Sockman alluded to the attitudes prevalent in post-war Germany and the needs of the defeated nation. But he suggested that true repentance should involve some form of reparations by the German people to the world.[30]

It was, in Sockman, a typical illustration of the way forgiveness must occur. Theologically, there is imbedded in his argument the notion that some form of human repair work is necessary, desirable, and possible to reconcile the breach between humanity and God. Even when Sockman assessed the human condition in a way that included concern for the fact of sin, he still considered the freedom of the will—not the flaw in the will—to be the crucial element.

Translated into the political arena, he offered an interpretation of history that traced a direct line from Wittenberg in 1517 to Philadelphia in 1776. He saw the issue of freedom as paramount for both Reformation Protestantism and American democracy. It also meant that Sockman could place great trust in enterprises like the United Nations to correct human frailties. And in science, it meant for Sockman the courage to believe ways could be found to establish a benign mastery over atomic energy.

Because of his confidence in the free human will, Sockman opposed determinism in any form—theological or ideological. So he opposed communism and Calvinism with nearly equal fervor. The answer to communism, he believed, was a healthy human spirit of community. No bondage of the will could prevent any liberating achievement if the proper commitments were made.

There was a similar vitality in Fosdick's handling of the freedom of the will. Though his divinity thesis near the turn of the century on the doctrine of the atonement gave him enough theological acumen to deny that he embraced the moral influence theory of that doctrine, it nevertheless had a high profile in his work. In no significant way did he seem to relate to the classic Reformation view of atonement in terms of Christ's victory on the cross. His pronounced sympathy for the psychological healing made possible through a well-integrated personality was a key example of Christ's "influence" as the means of redemption.

That concern arose especially in the late thirties and during the war years, as his center of authority shifted toward personal experience and away from reason. Nevertheless, Fosdick always seems to have been enamored with the intellectual advances of the modern world and the human capacity for further achievement. He, too, cherished the dreams of the United Nations. He saw no barrier in the will to prevent stupid mistakes from being ameliorated by learning. Even if it required a shift away from his celebrated pacifism toward underground anti-communist activity, Fosdick counted upon the freedom to choose the way that would prevent personal or political bondage. To him, that is what following the Savior meant.

After the early thirties, certainly, there was no such confidence in Paul Scherer's pulpit theology. His deepening conviction was that freedom was impossible except in captivity to God. By his own admission, his attitudes in the twenties and early thirties had been much more optimistic about human capacity to learn and grow and achieve goodness. He rejected secularists like Dreiser, whom he found to be grim determinists; but he was no more pleased at first with those theological doubts about the human condition which Reinhold Niebuhr was expressing. Yet, for most of the depression decade and through the war years, he developed a keen Reformation-style appreciation for the scandal of the Gospel—that the human will is free only when it is enslaved to the divine will.

George Buttrick shared a similar commitment to the principle of Reformation doctrine. The perversity of the will had impaled the human race on its own hopelessness, he believed: humanity suffers not from a correctable but a constitutional fault. If he put it more rigidly in the post-war era, under the atomic cloud, he was no less convinced in the thirties that true human freedom exists only in the destiny in which God holds us. Buttrick never tried to deny human choice, only to say that there is but one human choice which will bring freedom.

That much was apparent in the thirties. In the war years and beyond, it gained new clarification in Buttrick's expression of the difference between necessity and compulsion. God does not coerce human choices. Options exist. And yet humanly devised remedies—for peace, such as the United Nations, or for any other cultural or ecclesiastical goal—offer no real promise. Only the Will that transcends the temporary and ultimately listless deceptions can provide humanity peace. So there is no compulsion to follow God's will, but it is necessary to do so for the sake of hope.

D. Summary

The pulpit theology developed and proclaimed by Buttrick and Scherer was, in sum, a twentieth-century statement of classic Protestant orthodoxy. Both stood authentically in the heritage of the Reformers. And their work made two things abundantly clear: Reformation theology is not an artifact of the sixteenth-century, but vital and preachable Christian doctrine across the ages; and the pulpit remains a worthy forum in which that doctrinal message can resound. How Protestant were they? Very thoroughly.

The pulpit theology articulated so effectively by Sockman and Fosdick, however, was a set of doctrinal propositions that contradicted the fundamental tenets of Protestantism. In effect, they carried forward a popular and prosperous counter-Reformation, filled with misplaced confidences in works, in flawed wills, and in transient authorities. How Protestant were they? Very tangentially.

No one can claim that the rise of secularized Protestantism in American life was wholly due to this theological confusion. That was clearly the consequence of many powerful social and institutional forces. A variety of fierce influences affected the fall and rise of Christianity in America between 1930 and 1955: the depression, a world war, the unleashing of the atom, anti-communist concerns, Korea, the dual heritage of the gospel of wealth and the social gospel. Perhaps the social gospel had been safely domesticated into a notion that everyone would be happy if melted into The American Way of Life. Perhaps the gospel of wealth had been effectively revived into a pursuit of pleasant institutional prosperity.

But, as Dillenberger and Welch note, "the thesis that the life of the religious community is simply determined by social and cultural factors" is to be rejected.[31] Theological issues matter. And, in the case of the turbulent quarter-century from 1930 to 1955, the care and management of Protestant doctrine mattered. In the pulpit theology of its most celebrated purveyors, the neglect of Reformation theology opened a doctrinal vacuum. And that certainly had something to do with the doctrinal condition of Protestant Christianity in the fifties and beyond.

Fosdick and Sockman far exceeded Buttrick and Scherer in the scope of their influence: they published more, had longer preaching careers, gave more radio sermons, and (in Sockman's case) travelled more widely than the pastors at Madison Avenue and Holy Trinity. But Protestant doctrine was diminished by them. The loss of scriptural authority was a crushing burden for non-fundamentalist Protestants to carry, for no substitute could sustain them. The reduction of faith to human trust and human effort robbed Protestants of their appreciation of grace: perhaps it put upon them a works-righteousness infectious with unremittable guilt. The view of freedom which failed to recognize a prevailing, perverse fault in human existence encouraged naive dreams about the possible achievements to be won through prosperity at home and "police actions" abroad. Ignoring the brokenness of the human will put a doctrinal seal of approval on false expectations about the human capacity to liberate individuals and society. Protestantism was without an authoritative theological structure to know where genuine confidence could be placed.

In 1954, Louis Kronenburger wrote, "'The trouble with us in America isn't that the poetry of life has turned to prose, but that it has turned to advertising copy.'"[32] Perhaps that is what happened in the abandonment of Protestant doctrine: the pulpit theology of Sockman and Fosdick on Sundays in New York, and that of their imitators across the land, became shallow offerings of false doctrine; thereby, theological consent was granted to The American Way of Life. Meanwhile, those who imagined themselves to be the heirs of Luther and Calvin lost a firm grip on their Protestant heritage. And the truth of the Reformation could scarcely be heard amid the cacophony of noisy gongs and clanging cymbals.

ENDNOTES

CHAPTER I

1. *New York Times*, October 6, 1930, p. 11 (hereafter cited as *TNYT*). This was not the first time church-goers lined up early to hear Harry Emerson Fosdick. Hundreds overflowed from Park Avenue Baptist Church when the pastor elect delivered his first sermon (Robert Moats Miller, *Harry Emerson Fosdick: Preacher, Pastor, Prophet* [New York: Oxford University Press, 1985] p. 163). A line four-abreast from Park Avenue and Sixty-fourth Street stretched all the way to Lexington Avenue on October 3, 1926, when Fosdick preached his first sermon at Park Avenue Baptist Church after returning from a sabbatical leave (Loral W. Pancake, "Theological Liberalism in the Life and Ministry of Harry Emerson Fosdick," [M.A. Thesis, Drew University, 1946], p. 47).

2. *TNYT*, October 5, 1930, sec. 2, p. 5. *TNYT*, October 6, 1930, p. 11.

3. That is the estimated construction cost reported by *The New York Times* (October 5, 1930, sec. 2, p. 5) apparently from information supplied by Riverside. The figure does not include the cost of the Laura Spellman Rockefeller Memorial Carillon, which was a direct gift by John D. Rockefeller, Jr., in memory of his mother and most of which had originally been in the Park Avenue Baptist Church. Besides the carillon, Mr. Rockefeller donated an additional $1.5 million and a similar amount was realized from the sale of the Park Avenue property (Pancake, p. 50; *TNYT*, February 27, 1927, p. 18).

4. If so, they would have been disappointed. Mr. Rockefeller had resisted the pleas of his ministers to attend the opening service and had sailed instead on a trip to Europe a few days earlier. The *New York Times* saw a positive aspect to his absence: "Attention concentrated, therefore, on Dr. Fosdick's first message from the pulpit of the new church" (October 6, 1930, p. 11). Mr. Rockefeller was present, however, on the day of the dedication service, and *The New York Times* bothered to note that he

"took up the collection on the right side of the middle aisle" (February 9, 1931, p. 19).

5. Sydney Ahlstrom, *A Religious History of the American People* (New Haven: Yale University Press, 1972), p. 911. A similar assessment was made by the editor of *Harper's Magazine* in a 1929 editorial (*Harper's Magazine*, April 1929, p. 525). Fosdick accumulated many labels over the years, not the least of which identified him as "the da Vinci of Protestantism in the first half of the twentieth-century" (Graham R. Hodges, "Fosdick at 90: Tribute to a Man for All Seasons," *Christian Century*, May 22, 1968, p. 684).

6. Physically, Riverside was to be "the largest church structure in the United States" except for the incomplete Cathedral of St. John the Divine (*TNYT*, December 27, 1926, p. 1). However, Riverside's membership did not exceed one thousand until the thirties; in the forties, it approached 3500 (Pancake, p. 55 n.). Yet up to fifteen thousand persons passed through its doors each week, even in the period shortly after its founding (Harry Emerson Fosdick, *The Living of These Days* [New York: Harper and Bros, 1956], p. 207).

7. *TNYT*, October 6, 1930, p. 11. The manuscript is located in the archives of Union Theological Seminary in New York.

8. Its tower exceeded by a few feet the tower of the Cathedral of St. John the Divine nearby. The carillon is described in *The Riverside Church in the City of New York: A Handbook of the Institution and Its Building* (New York: Riverside Church, 1931), pp. 42-43. When the carillon was moved from the Park Avenue Baptist Church to Riverside, nineteen new bells were added to the fifty-three already in place. The new carillon, housed in its 28-story (392 feet) tower, also became the world's heaviest carillon at two hundred tons. The carillon was silent on the day of the opening service and was to remain so until a scheduled Christmas Eve recital that year. It fell victim to an unplanned silence on the day of dedication: a storm hit New York that weekend; snow and ice froze the mechanism (*TNYT*, October 5, 1930, sec. 2, p. 5; *TNYT*, February 9, 1931, pp. 1, 19).

9. The Park Avenue Baptist Church building, known as the "Little Cathedral," had only recently been completed, in 1922. Fosdick himself

suspected that opposition would arise to the notion of another new building so soon (*The Living of These Days*, p. 178; Pancake, p. 46). And in fact there was "much opposition" at first from within the congregation (*TNYT*, May 23, 1925, p. 1) and from some of the apartment owners who faced potential displacement if Rockefeller's originally chosen site just below the present Interchurch Center had been insisted upon. As it was, some tenants did have to relocate elsewhere anyway (*TNYT*, July 25, 1925, p. 22). There was also opposition to the Rockefeller-Fosdick alliance in the larger Baptist family (*TNYT*, June 8, 1925, p. 5).

10.   The fire occurred on December 21, 1928. "The main auditorium, which had been turned for hours into a colossal furnace, became an ice-covered shell strewn with water-soaked wreckage." The contractor found replacement stone and began repairs immediately. The two-million dollar loss was covered by insurance (Pancake, p. 52).

11.   Andrew Carnegie, "Wealth," *North American Review*, vol. 148, no. 391 (June 1889), p. 664. Ralph Henry Gabriel in *The Course of American Democratic Thought: An Intellectual History Since 1815* (New York: The Ronald Press, 1940) notes that persons of questionable character were also devoted to the Carnegie ideology or to variations of it, and that they bestowed their benevolence upon the Church as well. Raymond B. Fosdick, in *A Philosophy for a Foundation* (New York: The Rockefeller Foundation, 1963), pp. 6-7, links the Carnegie and Rockefeller strategies for the stewardship of wealth and considers them the formative personalities in the development of this concept of benevolence. Ralph Sockman believed that the early thirties represented the end of the gospel of wealth era (*TNYT*, January 1, 1934, p. 27).

12.   Paul E. Scherer, *The Plight of Freedom* (New York: Harper, 1948), p. 98.

13.   Henry Steele Commager, *The American Mind: An Interpretation of American Thought and Character Since the 1880's* (New Haven: Yale University Press, 1950), p. 8.

14.   Ralph W. Sockman, *The Fine Art of Using* (New York: Joint Division of Education and Cultivation, Board of Missions and Church Extension, The Methodist Church, 1946), p. 72. Cf. Ralph Sockman, *The Paradoxes of Jesus* (New York: Abingdon Press, 1936), pp. 144-45.

15. William Manchester, *The Glory and the Dream: A Narrative History of America, 1932-1972* (New York: Bantam Books, 1979), p. 44.

16. Manchester, p. 25. Cf. Ahlstrom, p. 905. Barton, himself in the advertising business, was later elected to Congress. He attended the Madison Avenue Presbyterian Church in New York.

17. *TNYT*, February 4, 1931, pp. 1, 5.

18. Gabriel, pp. 149-50.

19. Ibid., p. 151. That lecture was delivered six thousand times before Conwell died in 1925. It brought him wealth, and he turned to philanthropy. (Cf. Ahlstrom, p. 905.)

20. Robert M. Miller, "Harry Emerson Fosdick and John D. Rockefeller: The Origins of an Enduring Association," *Foundations (Baptist)* 21 (October-December 1978): 292. A final reckoning actually put the total over $32 million. (Miller, *Harry Emerson Fosdick: Preacher, Pastor, Prophet*, p. 212.) But even that sum was only a small fraction of his total benevolence. He gave away four hundred million dollars in his lifetime (Raymond B. Fosdick, *John D. Rockefeller, Jr., A Portrait* [New York: Harper and Bros. 1956], p. 433).

21. Fosdick, *The Living of These Days*, p. 179.

22. "God of Grace and God of Glory," a dedicatory hymn written by Fosdick for the occasion, and sung to the tune "Regent Square" (Pancake, p. 53 n.). Raymond B. Fosdick calls Riverside Church "the most complete expression of Rockefeller's ideal of a united church" (*John D. Rockefeller, Jr., A Portrait*, p. 223). Cf. Rockefeller's universalist religious views, ibid., p. 224.

23. Fosdick, *The Living of These Days*, p. 177.

24. Ibid., pp. 177-78. They were called "startling stipulations" at the time (*TNYT*, May 16, 1925, p. 1). Miller (*Harry Emerson Fosdick*, pp. 159-172) gives a detailed review of the process.

25. Fosdick, *The Living of These Days*, p. 178. Pancake, p. 46.

26. Harry Emerson Fosdick, *The Modern Use of the Bible* (New York: Macmillan 1924), pp. 98-99.

27. Ibid., p. 104.

28. Ibid., p. 262.

29. Fosdick, *The Living of These Days*, pp. 144ff. Pancake reproduces the correspondence related to this issue. Cf. Norman F. Furniss, *The Fundamentalist Controversy: 1918-1931* (New Haven: Yale University Press, 1954), pp. 181ff.

30. Fosdick, *The Living of These Days*, pp. 211-22.

31. Manchester, p. 98.

32. Harry Emerson Fosdick, "The Minister and Psychotherapy," *Pastoral Psychology* 11 (February 1960):   12; "Personal Counseling and Preaching," Pastoral Psychology 3 (March 1952): 15.

33. Harry Emerson Fosdick, "How I Prepare My Sermons," in *Harry Emerson Fosdick's Art of Preaching: An Anthology* (Springfield, Ill.: Charles C. Thomas, 1971) ed. Lionel G. Crocker, p. 42. Harry Emerson Fosdick, "What Is the Matter with Preaching?" *Harper's Magazine* (July 1928), pp. 134, 140.

34. Fosdick, "Personal Counseling and Preaching," p. 15. Among the negative views of Fosdick's approach is A. B. McDiarmid, "A Critique of Harry Emerson Fosdick's Conception of Preaching as Personal Counseling on a Group Scale," (Th.D dissertation, Pacific School of Religion, 1961).

35. Joseph D. Ban, "Two Views of One Age: Fosdick and Straton," *Foundations (Baptist)* 14 (April-June, 1971): 169f. Manchester, p. 5.

36. Manchester, p. 5.

37. *TNYT*, February 4, 1931, p. 48.

38. Edward Robb Ellis, *The Epic of New York City* (New York: Coward McCann, 1966), pp. 552f.

39. Manchester, p. 61. Ahlstrom, p. 735, makes the same point.

40. Fosdick, in his pre-pacifist days, had opposed Hughes's candidacy because the Republican refused to pledge that America would enter the war should he be elected. (Robert D Clark, "Harry Emerson Fosdick The Growth of a Great Preacher," in *Harry Emerson Fosdick's Art of Preaching*, p. 143; John B. Macnab, "Fosdick at First Church," *Journal of Presbyterian History* 52 [Spring 1974]: 65).

41. Harry Emerson Fosdick, "What Can the Minister Do?" *Review of Reviews* 86 (December 1932): 45-46.

42. Fosdick, *The Living of These Days*, p. 172.

43. Harry Emerson Fosdick, "A confession of personal loyalty to Christ suffices." *The Riverside Church in the City of New York*, p. 9.

44. Ahlstrom, p. 739.

45. *Christ Church, Methodist: An Achievement of the Christian Faith* (New York: Christ Church, 1951). The decision to seek a new location was made in 1927, but necessary property transfers delayed the start of construction for four years.

46. Fosdick, *The Living of These Days*, p. 84.

47. The dedication was held in November 1933, but the building was not completed until the fall of 1949.

48. "Most Lavish Church is the Most Democratic," *Literary Digest*, (March 17, 1934), p. 20.

49. Robert Bruce Hibbard, "The Life and Ministry of Ralph Washington Sockman" (Ph.D. dissertation, Boston University School of Theology, 1957), p. 60. It is not irrelevant that Cram had submitted proposals for the design of Riverside, but his work had been rejected apparently in a

dispute with Rockefeller over the techniques of Gothic construction, whether to use stone on a steel skeleton, as Rockefeller preferred, or simply stone, as Cram preferred (*TNYT*, February 12, 1926, p. 1). The episode suggests that Christ Church became Cram's opportunity for one-upmanship, by saying that Gothic is wrong for New York anyway. Sockman supported Cram with the argument that Cram's Christ Church design returned to the style of "the early church" (*Christ Church Methodist: An Achievement of the Christian Faith*, n.p.).

50. One of Sockman's later books reached virtually every library in the country, when Alfred P. Sloane of General Motors and a member of Christ Church paid for copies to be distributed where everyone could borrow and read it (Hibbard, pp. 131-32; the story was confirmed in a personal interview with Sockman's secretary, Geneva Helm, on August 27, 1981).

51. Paul W. Stevens, "A Critical Examination of the Preaching of George Arthur Buttrick" (Th.D. dissertation, New Orleans Baptist Theological Seminary, 1972), pp. 12-13.

52. Morgan Phelps Noyes, *Henry Sloane Coffin: The Man and His Ministry* (New York: Charles Scribner's Sons, 1964), pp. 89f.

53. The Madison Avenue Presbyterian Church *Weekly*, January 7, 1938, p. 3.

54. George A. Buttrick, "Our Church—Today and Tomorrow," sermon for March 13, 1932, manuscript at Harvard number MA 414, pp. 5-6.

55. George A. Buttrick, *Jesus Came Preaching* (New York: Charles Scribner's Sons, 1931), pp. 18-19.

56. Ibid.; he later participated in a second Beecher series, published as *Preaching in These Times* (New York: Charles Scribner's Sons, 1940).

57. George A. Buttrick, *Sermons Preached in a University Church* (New York: Abingdon Press, 1959), p. 79.

58. Peter Craven Fribley, "The Pulpit Ministry to Alienation: A Dialectical Study of Alienation and the Preaching Ministries of Gerald

Kennedy and George Arthur Buttrick, Using Sociological Criteria from Paul Tillich and H. Richard Niebuhr, with Particular Emphasis Upon 'Redemptive Alienation' as a Positive Heuristic for the Understanding of Sermonic Discourse" (Ph.D. dissertation, Princeton, 1974), p. 416.

59.   Personal interview with Mrs. Francis Neidick at Holy Trinity Church, October 30, 1981.

60.   Linn James Creighton, "Reconciliation in American Protestant Preaching" (Th.D. dissertation, Princeton Theological Seminary, 1972), p. 230. Scherer was called to Holy Trinity in the summer of 1920 and was installed as pastor on November 7, 1920. He was a fourth generation preacher, in an unbroken succession of ministerial service totalling 136 years prior to his ordination (*Trinity Tidings*, vol. 8, no. 3, September 1920).

61.   Melancthon Gideon Groseclose Scherer, *Christian Liberty and Church Unity* (New York, 1932).

62.   Willis Stanley Gertner, "Paul Scherer: Preacher and Homiletician" (Ph.D. dissertation, Wayne State University, 1967), pp. 14-15. His ministry was not a social gospel but a "gospel with social implications" (Ibid., pp. 17-18).

63.   Buttrick, *Jesus Came Preaching*, p. x.

64.   Scherer, "Yet Much Land," sermon for January 4, 1931, manuscript at Union Theological Seminary, vol. xii, pp. 107-8.

65.   Fosdick, for example, admitted that the congregation was "lucky" to have completed Riverside before the full impact of the depression fell ("The Church Is Dead: Long Live the Church," sermon for April 11, 1937, manuscript at Union Theological Seminary). And Sockman confided that he would not have supported the building plans for Christ Church had he imagined the depth of the impending depression (interview with Geneva Helm, August 27, 1981).

66.   Ralph W. Sockman, *The Highway of God* (New York: Macmillan, 1942), p. 47.

67. Harry Emerson Fosdick, *Adventurous Religion and Other Essays* (New York: Harper and Bros., 1926), p. 75.

68. "Creative business which produces wealth in which the people share is a far more fundamental public service than charity. Business so run is the underpinning of society" (Harry Emerson Fosdick, "Conventionality Versus Heroism," sermon for March 20, 1932, manuscript at Union Theological Seminary, p. 9).

69. Most churches did not try to "balance" the issues (Ahlstrom, p. 804).

70. Gabriel, p. 330.

CHAPTER II

1. Gertner, p. ii; cf. Carl Braaten, "The Interdependence of Theology and Preaching," *Dialog, A Journal of Theology* 3 (Winter 1964): 12, passim.

2. Ralph W. Sockman, *Men of the Mysteries* (New York: Abingdon Press, 1927), p. 36.

3. Reinhold Niebuhr, "The Significance of Dr. Fosdick in American Religious Thought," *Union Seminary Quarterly Review* 8 (May 1953): 3-4.

4. Harry Black Beverly, *Harry Emerson Fosdick's Predigtweise: Its Significance for America, Its Limits, Its Overcoming* (Winterthur, Switzerland: P. G. Keller, 1965), pp. 8-9.

5. Harry Emerson Fosdick, "A Modern Preacher's Problem in His Use of the Scriptures," Inaugural Lecture as Jessup Professor (New York: Union Theological Seminary, 1915), p. 7. In the 1930s Fosdick reduced his teaching load to part-time work. Buttrick was then named Jessup Lecturer.

6. Until age eight, Scherer's education was at home. His mother, who loved to quote the classics herself, had him reciting Shakespeare by the time he was four. The love of words took deep root in him. He wrote an M.A. Thesis at the College of Charleston on "The Use of the Infinitive in

Horace." His father had introduced him to Latin and Greek, and at Charleston he studied classical languages under Thomas della Torre, an Italian nobleman and Jesuit priest who exercised his students by having them read aloud at first sight a passage in Greek, immediately thereafter translating it into Latin (Gertner, pp. 4-7).

7. Ibid., p. 8.

8. Ibid., pp. 21f.

9.   Eberhard Bethge, *Dietrich Bonhoeffer: Man of Vision, Man of Courage* (New York: Harper and Row, 1970), p. 562, quotes Bonhoeffer's dislike of the preaching he heard while he was a student at Union. Brunner was one of Fosdick's students (Fosdick, *The Living of These Days*, p. 265).

10. Ahlstrom, p. 467.

11. Ibid., pp. 939-40.

12. Sockman wrote the Exposition of I Kings, Scherer the Exposition of Job and Luke 19-24, and Buttrick contributed a general article on the study of the Bible and the Expositions of Matthew, Luke 13-18, and Philemon. Fosdick was in retirement by this time.

13.   George A. Buttrick, *The Parables of Jesus* (Garden City, N.Y.: Doubleday, 1928), p. 173.

14.   Paul E. Scherer, *For We Have This Treasure* (New York: Harper and Bros., 1944), p. 162.

15. Fosdick, *The Living of These Days*, p. 84.

16. From a personal interview with Sockman's daughter Betty, October 9, 1981. Cf. Ralph W. Sockman, "Fifty Years of Fosdick," *Religion in Life*, vol. 26, 1956-1957, pp. 289-94.

17. William McLeister, "The Use of the Bible in the Sermons of Selected Protestant Preachers in the United States from 1925 to 1950," (Ph.D. dissertation, University of Pittsburgh, 1957), pp. 12-14. Cf. Kyle

Haselden, "An Honor Roll of American Preachers, *The Pulpit* 35 (October, 1964): 18. Haselden compiled a homiletical "honor roll" and only four twentieth-century figures made the list—Buttrick, Fosdick, Scherer, and Sockman.

18. Commager, p. 426.

19. *Christian Century*, October 15, 1930, p. 1239.

20. Ban, "Two Views of One Age," pp. 163-64. Cf. Winthrop S. Hudson, *Religion in America* (New York: Charles Scribner's Sons, 1965), p. 369.

21. Paul W. Stevens, "A Critical Examination of the Preaching of George Arthur Buttrick," (Th.D. dissertation, New Orleans Baptist Theological Seminary, 1972), pp. 3-4.

22. Gertner, pp. 10f. *Trinity Tidings*, vol. 8, no. 3, Sept. 1920.

23. Hibbard, pp. 13-14. Cf. Clyde E. Fant and William M. Pinson, Jr., eds., *Twenty Centuries of Great Preaching* (Waco, Texas: Word, 1971), vol. X, p. 170.

24. Fosdick, *The Living of These Days*; p. 33. Cf. "Morals Secede from the Union," *Harper's Magazine*, May 1932, pp. 682-84.

25. George A Buttrick, "The Sign of a Savior," sermon for December 23, 1928, in the MAPC *Weekly*, January 4, 1929, p. 3.

26. George A. Buttrick, "The Creation," sermon for January 15, 1939, in *MAPC News*, February 3, 1939, p. 4.

27. Fosdick, *The Living of These Days*, pp. 249-50.

28. Quoted by Kenneth Cauthen, *The Impact of American Religious Liberalism* (New York: Harper and Row, 1962), p. 27.

29. Charles M. Davidson, "George Arthur Buttrick: Christocentric Preacher and Pacifist," *Journal of Presbyterian History* 53 (Summer 1975): 151. Davidson found plenty of that discarded liberalism in

Buttrick's preaching, especially in the period before his coming to Manhattan (cf. ibid., p. 146).

30. Pelikan, "Foreword," in Cauthen, p. viii.

31. Cauthen, pp. 6-25.

32. Ibid., p. 25.

33. Jaroslav Pelikan, "Foreword," in Cauthen, p. vi.

34. Henry Pitney Van Dusen, "The Liberal Movement in Theology," *The Church through Half a Century* (New York: Scribner's, 1936), p. 84.

35. Harry Emerson Fosdick, "The Church Must Go Beyond Modernism," sermon for November 3, 1935, in *Successful Christian Living: Sermons on Christianity Today* (New York: Harper and Bros., 1937), pp. 163-64.

36. Ban, "Two Views of One Age," p. 169.

37. Sockman, "Forty Years of Fosdick," p. 292.

38. *TNYT*, May 16, 1925, p. 1.

39. *TNYT*, June 8, 1925, p. 5.

40. *TNYT*, March 22, 1937, p. 15.

41. Harry Emerson Fosdick, "The Church Must Go beyond Modernism," *Successful Christian Living*, pp. 163-64.

42. Ahlstrom, p. 919.

43. Edward Robb Ellis, *The Epic of New York City* (New York: Coward-McCann, 1966), p. 534.

44. George A. Buttrick, *The Christian Fact and Modern Doubt* (New York: C. Scribner, 1935), p. ix.

45. Quoted by Cauthen, p. 3.

46. Paul E. Scherer, "How Are Your Securities?" sermon for November 29, 1931, manuscript at Union Theological Seminary, vol. 1, series II, pp. 116a-116b.

47. Davidson, p. 151.

48. Harry Emerson Fosdick, "Be Thankful for the Enemies of Christianity," sermon for December 18, 1932, manuscript at Union Theological Seminary, p. 1.

49. Ralph W. Sockman, *Live for Tomorrow* (New York: Macmillan, 1939), p. 93. Buttrick cited similar figures in a sermon on December 5, 1937 (The MAPC *Weekly*, January 7 1938).

50. Harry Emerson Fosdick, "Fares Please," sermon for April 17, 1932, manuscript at Union Theological Seminary, p. 10.

51. MAPC *Weekly*, March 8, 1935, p. 8.

52. Ibid., November 25, 1938; also April 10, 1935; and January 7, 1938, p. 3.

53. Ibid., January 7, 1938, p. 3. Cf. Ellis, *The Epic of New York City*, p. 554; Ira Rosenwaike, *Population History of New York City* (Syracuse: Syracuse University Press, n.d.).

54. Gay Talese, *The Kingdom and the Power* (New York: World Publishing Company, 1969), p. 61.

55. A letter to *The New York Times* from a reader named Morris Friedman was published on March 5, 1931, thanking the paper for including "almost every religious point of view . . . so fairly and impartially . . . that one felt he got the essence of the thoughts of our most prominent ministers in a short time."

56. Personal interview with George Dugan, September 28, 1981.

57. Interviews with George Dugan and with Geneva Helm, Sockman's secretary, outlined the practice of planting sermon excerpts in the

newspaper's religion office. Sockman might call his secretary on Saturday afternoon with something he wanted to get into the paper. She would transcribe it and deliver it to Dugan, who would then work it into the Monday church page. The files of Fosdick's sermon manuscripts at Union Theological Seminary include a number of typewritten sermon "Abstracts" which may have been prepared for this purpose. The Sockman manuscripts at Syracuse contain similar news releases, some in his own hand.

58. Talese, p. 275.

59. For example, in 1938, Fosdick's sermons were quoted eighteen times and he was the subject of an editorial once. Sockman's sermons were also cited eighteen times during the year, with five reports on Scherer and four on Buttrick.

60. The MAPC *Weekly* April 5, 1929.

61. Personal interviews with Ethel King, former secretary to Buttrick, and with Dr. Charles Hattauer, a long-time friend of the Buttrick family, on October 15, 1981.

62. Interview with George Dugan, September 28, 1981.

63. *TNYT*, December 27, 1954, p. 14, December 26, 1955. One half of the page or less was given to sermon reports.

64. *TNYT*, December 31, 1956, p. 29.

65. *TNYT*, December 30, 1957, p. 29.

66. *TNYT*, January 2, 1956, p. 18.

67. *TNYT*, January 6, 1953, p. 34.

68. For a time in the thirties, it had also been the case that the heading "sermons" had dropped out of use, but that may have been because the category would have proved to be too broad for the number of sermons included. Coverage given to individual preachers was quite extensive and each was given a personal name index. In the fifties, when the "sermon"

category lapsed, individual preachers' names were indexed—but rarely for a regular Sunday sermon. Holiday messages might be noted, but otherwise the coverage was for secular events such as commencement addresses and appearances at ground-breaking ceremonies.

69. Manchester, p. 733.

70. Will Herberg, *Protestant-Catholic-Jew: An Essay in American Religious Sociology* (Garden City, N.Y.: Doubleday, 1956), p. 64.

71. Ahlstrom, p. 954.

72. Raymond B. Fosdick, *John D. Rockefeller, Jr.*, p. 233n.

73. Ibid., p. 226.

74. Manchester, pp. 772, 783.

75. Herberg, p. 15.

76. Edward L. R. Elson, "Evaluating Our Religious Revival," *Journal of Religious Thought* 14 (Autumn-Winter, 1956-1957): 56f.

77. Frederick W. Schroeder, *Preaching the Word with Authority* (Philadelphia: Westminster Press, 1954), p. 35.

78. John Dillenberger and Claude Welch, *Protestant Christianity Interpreted Through Its Development* (New York: Charles Scribner's Sons, 1954), pp. 26-27, 31.

79. A contemporary discussion of the issues shows that the basic dispute remains. See Wolfhart Pannenberg, "Freedom and the Lutheran Reformation," and a reply by Richard P. McBrien, "The Reformation: A Catholic Reflection," in *Theology Today* 38 (October 1981): 287-304. Cf. George A. Buttrick, *The Interpreter's Bible*, vol. 8, p. 299.

80. Dillenberger and Welch, p. 45.

81. Ibid., p. 58.

82. Harry Emerson Fosdick, *Great Voices of the Reformation: An Anthology* (New York: Random House, 1952), p. 125.

83. "Authority in the pulpit can scarcely be conveyed unless there is evidence that the minister himself has come under the Authority of the divine Word" (Schroeder, *Preaching the Word with Authority*, p. 119).

84. Erasmus, *The Freedom of the Will*, in *The Library of Christian Classics*, vol. 17 (Philadelphia: Westminster Press, 1969). Martin Luther, *The Bondage of the Will*, in Luther's *Works*, vol. 33 (Philadelphia: Fortress Press, 1972).

85. Heiko Oberman, *The Harvest of Medieval Theology* (Grand Rapids: Eerdmans, 1967), passim.

86. Pannenberg, "Freedom and the Lutheran Reformation," p. 293.

87. Ibid.

88. McBrien, "The Reformation: A Catholic Reflection," p. 302.

89. Dillenberger and Welch prefer to think of Protestantism as an historical movement, not to limit it to the theological outlines drawn in the sixteenth-century. See, for instance, p. 305.

90. Paul E. Scherer, *The Place Where Thou Standest* (New York: Harper and Bros., 1942), p. 42.

91. For example, "Protestantism: Its Assets and Liabilities," sermon for November 1, 1942, manuscript at Union Theological Seminary, vol. 51, series II, p. 282a.

92. Ralph W. Sockman, *The Highway of God* (New York: Macmillan, 1942), pp. 88-89.

93. Harry E. Fosdick, *Great Voices of the Reformation*, p. 40; *Martin Luther* (New York: Random House, 1956).

94. George A. Buttrick, *The Christian Fact and Modern Doubt* (New York: C. Scribner, 1935), pp. 170-71; *Faith and Education* (New York: Abingdon-Cokesbury Press, 1952), p. 54.

95. Paul E. Scherer, *The Word God Sent* (New York: Harper and Bros., 1965), pp. 11, 76.

96. Paul E. Scherer, "Preaching as a Radical Transaction," *Review and Expositor* 54 (October 1957): 560.

CHAPTER III

1. Manchester, p. 23.

2. Fosdick, "What Can the Minister Do?" *Review of Reviews* (December 1932), p. 46.

3. Edward Robb Ellis, *The Epic of New York City* (New York: Coward-McCann, 1966), p. 533.

4. Ibid., p. 535. With followers called "angels" (who likely surrendered all of their material resources to him) and operating out of community centers called "heavens," Father Divine presided at gargantuan feasts. For fifteen cents, one could enter the main "heaven" at 152 West 126th Street and choose a meal from twenty kinds of meat, five salads, eleven relishes, fifteen kinds of bread, six desserts, six beverages, and cheese wheels "as big as automobile tires." Ralph Sockman attended one such feast. (Ralph W. Sockman, "When Life is too Complex," sermon for January 17, 1943, manuscript at Syracuse University.)

5. Gertner, p. 18. In his Beecher lectures, Scherer admitted that he saw no point in churches' spending time painting apartments or fixing the plumbing of less fortunate city residents: "There is no such thing as a social gospel. There is a gospel with social implications" (Scherer, *For We Have This Treasure* [New York: Harper and Bros. 1944], p. 188).

6. "Yet Much Land," sermon for January 4, 1931, manuscript in the Archives of Union Theological Seminary, New York. The Board at Holy Trinity rejected the idea because, in Scherer's opinion, the physicians on

the Board "could not see what they would get out of it" (Gertner, pp. 20-21).

7. For instance, he made that point in two sermons during the early thirties: "The Compassion of Christ," sermon for November 9, 1930 (The Madison Avenue Presbyterian Church *Weekly*, February 6, 1931), p. 5; "At the End of Emmaus Road," sermon for April 3, 1932, manuscript at Harvard University, number MA 420.

8. Peter Craven Fribley, "The Pulpit Ministry to Alienation" (Ph.D. dissertation, Princeton, 1974), p. 397. Also Miss Ethel King, formerly a social worker at the church and later a secretary to Buttrick, described the program in an interview. Cf. the *Weekly* of the Madison Avenue Presbyterian Church for January 27, 1933, p. 1. Fribley wrote that Buttrick believed "in a parish deeply caring for its members spiritually and physically" and "in the responsibility of Christians to work and to bring about a just society" (pp. 412-13). Buttrick described the congregation's social service program as superior to "the best social service agencies" in the area (*Weekly*, April 5, 1935, p. 3).

9. Buttrick, "Jesus and the Home," sermon for May 8, 1932, manuscript at Harvard University, number MA 427.

10. Sockman, *The Morals of Tomorrow*, (New York: Harper, 1931) pp. 232f; *Recoveries in Religion*, (Nashville: Cokesbury, 1938) pp. 20-21.

11. Fosdick, "Union and Liberty in the Churches," *Outlook*, Nov. 13, 1929, p. 423.

12. *TNYT*, April 16, 1934, p. 13. Of course, he saw the connection between the pulpit and the program of the church, advocating unemployment compensation in a sermon for November 16, 1930 "Christianity and Unemployment" (manuscript at Union Theological Seminary). He threatened to make such social services a condition of his continuing to preach at Riverside.

13. On Easter Sunday, 1936, for instance, the church doors were locked at 11:25 before the start of the 11:30 service, when the crowd filled "the nave, the first and second balconies, the triforium, the chancel, the

chapel, the assembly hall, and even the bowling alley clubroom" (*TNYT*, April 13, 1936, p. 12).

14. The Evangelical Lutheran Church of the Holy Trinity, *Trinity Tidings*, September 1920.

15. The Sunday afternoon services were discontinued in the mid-thirties, but the Sunday evening services endured until the early fifties. Two or three full-time assistants shared Buttrick's pastoral and preaching load, in addition to a lay staff that included social workers and religious education specialists (one of whom was Hilda Niebuhr, the sister of Reinhold and H. Richard). Several students from Union Seminary also served the church each year, and in the late forties Langdon Gilkey and Robert McAfee Brown were among them. Nevertheless, Buttrick was the preacher to the congregation, and on the tenth anniversary of his installation as pastor he preached his 750th sermon at Madison Avenue Presbyterian (*TNYT*, April 27, 1937, p. 20).

16. Fosdick, "The Christian Ministry," in Lionel G. Crocker, ed., *Harry Emerson Fosdick's Art of Preaching*, pp. 26, 61; see also his "Introduction" in McComb, *Preaching in Theory and Practice* (New York: Oxford University Press, 1926), p. xi.

17. Fosdick, *The Modern Use of the Bible*, pp. 60-61.

18. Ibid., p. 173.

19. Fosdick, "What Is the Matter with Preaching?" p. 141.

20. Sockman, "Mistakes of Moralists," *Harper*, vol. 162 (December 1930), p. 79.

21. Buttrick, *Jesus Came Preaching*, p. 128 (italics his).

22. Preaching needs to stress "*moral earnestness . . . a new and more vigorous concept of duty . . . a mood of compassion . . . a note of cheer and challenge . . . a sursum corda . . . the mediation of a Presence*" (ibid., pp. 131-39, italics his).

23. Sockman, "Morals in a Machine Age," *Harper*, vol. 162 (February 1931), pp. 371-72.

24. Fosdick, "What Matters in Religion," p. 1, sermon for October 5, 1930, manuscript at Union Theological Seminary. Cf. *TNYT*, October 6, 1930, p. 11.

25. *TNYT*, October 6, 1930, p. 11.

26. Sockman, "Juts on the Social Skyline," *The Rotarian*, vol. 48, May 1936, pp. 6-10.

27. Scherer, "Getting Mixed Up," sermon for October 19, 1930, manuscript at Union Theological Seminary.

28. Buttrick, "Why Does God Hide Himself?" sermon for September 28, 1930, manuscript at Harvard University.

29. Buttrick, "Thoughts Out of Many Hearts," sermon for December 21, 1930, published in the *Weekly* of the Madison Avenue Presbyterian Church, January 2, 1931, p. 6.

30. Buttrick, "How We Know the Love of God," sermon for November 16, 1930, manuscript at Harvard University.

31. Ibid., p. 1.

CHAPTER IV

1. *TNYT*, March 30, 1931, p. 26.

2. *TNYT*, October 6, 1930, p. 26.

3. *TNYT*, October 20, 1930, p. 16.

4. *TNYT*, March 30, 1931, p. 26.

5. *TNYT*, October 20, 1930. p. 16.

6. Sockman, *Morals of Tomorrow*, pp. 232-33.

7. Ralph W. Sockman, "Vanishing Sinner," *Harper's*, November 1930, p. 680.

8. Sockman, "The Pew Talks Back," sermon for November 22, 1931, manuscript in the Syracuse University archives.

9. *TNYT*, November 3, 1930, p. 28. He stressed the same theme seven months later (*TNYT*, June 15, 1931, p. 17).

10. Sockman, *The Suburbs of Christianity* (New York: Abingdon, 1924), p. 126.

11. *TNYT*, November 24, 1930, p. 24.

12. *TNYT*, September 21, 1931, p. 11.

13. *TNYT*, December 28, 1931, p. 15.

14. Sockman, "Where Wise Men Meet," sermon for Christmas 1932, pp. 5-6, manuscript in the Syracuse University archives.

15. Sockman, "The Dawning Decencies," sermon for March 26, 1933, p. 1, manuscript in the Syracuse University archives.

16. *TNYT*, September 28, 1931, p. 15.

17. *TNYT*, April 11, 1932, p. 13.

18. *TNYT*, March 7, 1932, p. 15.

19. *TNYT*, November 21, 1932, p. 22.

20. *TNYT*, September 19, 1932, p. 12.

21. Sockman, "The Dawning Decencies." (The quotation is from the text used for radio and does not appear in the version written for delivery at Madison Avenue Methodist Episcopal Church.) The manuscript is at Syracuse University.

22. *TNYT*, March 20, 1933, p. 13.

23. *TNYT*, May 8, 1933, p. 13. In his sermon on the following Sunday, without mentioning Sockman by name, Scherer denounced "one of our ministers" who "had enough enthusiasm left for common sense to preach about it. I haven't any. It's God's common sense that thrills me, and that's nonsense to us." (Scherer, "This Unpopular Life," sermon for May 14, 1933, manuscript at Union Theological Seminary, vol. I, series II, p. 211b.)

24. *TNYT*, March 26, 1934, p. 20.

25. Sockman, "The Eternal Contemporary," (also titled "The Undying Ally") sermon for September 15, 1935, manuscript at Syracuse University archives, p. 7.

26. Sockman, *The Paradoxes of Jesus*, p. 59.

27. *TNYT*, October 28, 1935, p. 15.

28. *TNYT*, December 9, 1935, p. 16.

29. Sockman, "Juts on the Social Skyline," pp. 6-10.

30. *TNYT*, December 23, 1935, p. 22.

31. Sockman, "Juts on the Social Skyline," p. 10.

32. Sockman, *The Paradoxes of Jesus*, p. 151

33. Ibid., pp. 193-94.

34. *TNYT*, January 22, 1934, p. 9

35. *TNYT*, March 28, 1938, p. 16.

36. *TNYT*, May 7, 1934, p. 14

37. *TNYT*, March 23, 1936, p. 17.

38. *TNYT*, December 28, 1936, p. 10.

39. *TNYT*, February 15, 1937, p. 20.

40. Sockman, "Drifting into Danger," sermon for December 5, 1937, p. 14, manuscript in Syracuse University archives. He had to some extent sensed such a "drift" three years earlier at Christ Church and admitted that "the blame rests on the pulpit as well as on the pew." (Sockman, "Lives Adrift," sermon for December 9, 1934, p. 14, manuscript in Syracuse University archives.)

41. *TNYT*, November 1, 1937, p. 17.

42. *TNYT*, May 3, 1937, p. 28.

43. *TNYT*, July 12, 1937, p. 13.

44. *TNYT*, December 6, 1937, p. 28.

45. Sockman, "Live for Tomorrow," Sermon in July 1939 (n.d.), pp. 16-20. Also, "The Value of Vows," sermon for October 8, 1939, pp. 3-4, manuscripts in Syracuse University archives.

46. *TNYT*, December 12, 1933, p. 14.

47. Sockman, "Children of Wisdom," sermon for January 5, 1941, p. 2, manuscript in Syracuse University archives.

48. Sockman, "Life's High Threshold," sermon for March 19, 1939, pp. 7-8, manuscript in Syracuse University archives.

49. Sockman, "Life's Closed Exits," sermon for November 6, 1938, manuscript in Syracuse University archives, Box 20.

50. Sockman; "Highways to God," sermon for October 27, 1940, p. 1, manuscript at Syracuse University archives.

51. *TNYT*, July 29, 1940, p. 11

52. *TNYT*, December 9, 1940, p. 16.

53. *TNYT*, January 6, 1941, p. 18.

54. *TNYT*, November 24, 1941, p. 14.

55. Sockman, "The Price of Privilege," sermon for November 3, 1940, p. 6, manuscript in Syracuse University archives. Cf. *TNYT*, November 4, 1940, p. 16.

56. Sockman, "Where Is Thy God—Now?" sermon for September 25, 1938, p. 5, manuscript in Syracuse University archives. In his *Recoveries in Religion*, Sockman says, "Man's searching for God is the pull of an impulse planted in him by God, and man's finding is a response to the divine desire to be discovered" (p. 63).

57. Sockman, "Longing and Belonging," sermon for May 19, 1940, p. 4, manuscript in Syracuse University archives.

58. *TNYT*, March 18, 1940, p. 20.

59. *TNYT*, December 30, 1940, p. 15.

60. *TNYT*, March 17, 1941, p. 14. He considered Barthian theology to be "intellectual defeatism" (Sockman, *Recoveries in Religion*, p. 37). And he wanted no part of "'the medieval doctrine of man's total depravity'" (*TNYT*, June 23, 1941, p. 20).

61. Sockman, "The Mercy of Justice," sermon for January 19, 1941, p. 6, manuscript in Syracuse University archives.

62. *TNYT*, September 28, 1931, p. 15.

63. *TNYT*, April 11, 1932, p. 13.

64. Sockman, "To Confused Christians," sermon for September 10, 1939, p. 1, manuscript in Syracuse University archives.

65. *TNYT*, November 28, 1932, p. 13.

66. *TNYT*, April 5, 1937, p. 15.

67. *TNYT*, September 19, 1938, p. 20.

68. *TNYT*, December 30, 1940, p. 15

69. *TNYT*, March 21, 1938, p. 16.

70. *TNYT*, June 30, 1939, p. 6. Sockman, *Live for Tomorrow*, p. 117.

71. George Buttrick was the Protestant panelist.

72. *TNYT*, January 8, 1940, p. 12.

73. *TNYT*, January 20, 1941, p. 20.

74. *TNYT*, July 19, 1937, p. 10.

75. Sockman, "Life's Closed Exits," sermon for November 6, 1938, pp. 5-7, manuscript in the Syracuse University archives.

76. *TNYT*, December 30, 1940, p. 15.

77. Sockman's sermon "Drifting into Danger" (December 5, 1937, Syracuse University archives) is written on hotel stationery from South Bend, Indiana; Zanesville, Ohio; and Utica, New York. The manuscript of "Down to Earth" (May 1, 1951, archives) is on hotel letterhead from Rochester, Syracuse, Kingston, and Mohonk Lake, New York; Duluth, Minnesota; and the New York Central Railroad.

78. From an interview with Geneva Helm.

79. Sockman, *Recoveries in Religion*, p. 21.

80. Sockman, *The Paradoxes of Jesus*, pp. 93-94.

81. *TNYT*, December 23, 1940, p. 17.

82. Sockman, *The Paradoxes of Jesus*, p. 121.

83. *TNYT*, November 23, 1936, p. 18.

84. Robert Bruce Hibbard, "The Life and Ministry of Ralph W. Sockman" (Ph.D. dissertation, Boston University School of Theology, 1957), p. 95.

85. This description is contained in a congregational letter which Sockman wrote on May 9, 1923, to "the Members and Friends" of his parish. Sockman had used the back of one of the leftover copies of the letter to draft his sermon "Drive without Direction." It was found in his archival material at Syracuse.

86. Sockman, *The Suburbs of Christianity*, p. 97.

87. Sockman, *The Morals of Tomorrow*, p. 235.

88. *TNYT*, January 5, 1931, p. 26.

89. *TNYT*, May 8, 1933, p. 13.

90. *TNYT*, November 30, 1931, p. 22.

91. Sockman, "Lives Adrift," sermon for December 9, 1934, pp. 10-11, manuscript in Syracuse University archives. Cf. *TNYT*, December 10, 1934, p. 18.

92. *TNYT*, March 23, 1936, p. 17.

93. Sockman, "Lives Adrift," sermon for December 9, 1934, p. 12, manuscript in Syracuse University archives.

94. *TNYT*, July 20, 1936, p. 16.

95. *TNYT*, November 23, 1936, p. 18.

96. *TNYT*, December 28, 1936, p. 10; May 31, 1937, p. 28; November 1, 1937, p. 17.

97. *TNYT*, July 17, 1939, p. 17.

98. Sockman, "Prophets—Old and New," sermon for January 29, 1939, pp. 4-5, manuscript in Syracuse University archives.

99. Ibid., p. 6.

100. Sockman, *Recoveries in Religion*, p. 62.

101. Sockman, "The Salt of the Earth," sermon for October 19, 1941, p. 7, manuscript in Syracuse University archives.

102. *TNYT*, September 29, 1941, p. 11.

103. Sockman, *Recoveries in Religion*, pp. 60-61.

104. Sockman, *Recoveries in Religion*, p. 64.

105. Sockman, "Fixed Points in Faith," sermon for March 16, 1941, p. 1, manuscript in Syracuse University archives.

106. Sockman, *Recoveries in Religion*, pp. 66-68.

107. Sockman, *The Morals of Tomorrow*, p. 71

108. *TNYT*, February 12, 1940, p. 12. That is why "God as revealed by Jesus is the bulwark of democracy."

109. Sockman, *The Morals of Tomorrow*, p. 78.

110. Sockman, *The Suburbs of Christianity*, p. 28.

111. Ibid., p. 28.

112. Sockman, *The Paradoxes of Jesus*, p. 92.

113. Sockman, *Men of the Mysteries*, pp. 57, 63-64.

114. Ibid., p. 64.

115. Ibid., p. 64.

116. Sockman, "The Vanishing Sinner," *Harper,* (November 1930), p. 680.

117. Ibid.

118. Sockman, *Men of Mysteries*, p. 67.

119. Sockman, *The Unemployed Carpenter* (New York: Harper, 1933), p. 83.

120. Ibid., p. 83; Sockman, *The Paradoxes of Jesus*, p. 89.

121. Sockman, *The Paradoxes of Jesus*, p. 90.

122. Sockman, *Suburbs of Christianity*, pp. 45, 46-47.

123. Sockman, *Live for Tomorrow*, p. 45.

124. Ibid.

125. Sockman, *Unemployed Carpenter*, p. 83.

126. *TNYT*, June 13, 1932, p. 18.

127. *TNYT*, September 18, 1933, p. 15.

128. *TNYT*, April 10, 1933, p. 11.

129. *TNYT*, November 3, 1930, p. 28, and June 15, 1931, p. 17.

130. *TNYT*, December 24, 1934, p. 8.

131. *TNYT*, March 22, 1937, p. 15.

132. *TNYT*, April 10, 1933, p. 11.

133. *TNYT*, October 26, 1936, p. 14.

134. Sockman, "Destiny: What Part Does It Play?" sermon for November 15, 1936, pp. 4f, manuscript in Syracuse University archives.

135. *TNYT*, July 25, 1938, p. 13.

136. *TNYT*, February 27, 1939, p. 9.

137. *TNYT*, March 18, 1940, p. 20. (The overtones of Niebuhr's thesis about moral man and immoral society should not be overlooked here.)

138. *TNYT*, December 30, 1940, p. 15.

139. *TNYT*, November 11, 1940, p. 15. At the service on November 10, the seventh anniversary of Christ Church was celebrated with the dedication of memorials that included mosaics which had been shipped out of Italy just before the British blockade of Italian ports began.

140. Sockman, "A Voice Not Our Own," sermon for December 31, 1939, p. 7, manuscript in Syracuse University archives.

141. *TNYT*, July 29, 1940, p. 11.

142. *TNYT*, March 17, 1941, p. 14.

143. Sockman, "Guarantees of God," sermon for April 27, 1941, pp. 3-4, manuscript in Syracuse University archives.

144. *TNYT*, May 26, 1941, p. 22.

145. Sockman, "Self-Possession," sermon for June 22, 1941, pp. 7-8, manuscript in the Syracuse University archives.

146. Ibid.

147. *TNYT*, November 17, 1941, p. 16.

CHAPTER V

1. Creighton, "Reconciliation in American Protestant Preaching" (Th.D. dissertation, Princeton Theological Seminary, 1972), p. 67.

2. Gertner, p. 10.

3. *Trinity Tidings*, vol. vii, no. 3, p. 5, September, 1920.

4. Gertner, p. 23.

5. Ibid., pp. 21f. Also "They That Were Ready," sermon for November 23, 1930, manuscript in the Union Theological Seminary archives, vol. xii, p. 39.

6. Such a rare moment came in his observation that both Fosdick and Sockman were more popular in their day than was Jesus Christ in His! ("Minds Made Up," sermon for May 10, 1937 manuscript at Union Theological Seminary archives, vol. xii, pp. 288-89.)

7. Scherer, *Facts That Undergird Life* (New York: Harper, 1938), p. 109.

8. *TNYT*, June 1, 1931, p. 13.

9. Paul E. Scherer, "The Third Mile," sermon for September 13, 1931, manuscript at Union Theological Seminary archives, vol. xiv, p. 80.

10. Paul E. Scherer, "The Friendly Dark," sermon for January 10, 1932, manuscript at Union Theological Seminary archives, vol. xiv, p. 271.

11. Paul E. Scherer, "Pentecost and Its Substitutes," sermon for May 15, 1932, manuscript at Union Theological Seminary archives, vol. xv, p. 140.

12. Paul E. Scherer, "Was the Reformation a Success?" sermon for October 28, 1934, manuscript at Union Theological Seminary archives, vol. ii, series II, p. 39a. That he misread the seriousness of the social crisis can be seen from sermons in the early forties where he expresses surprise at the crime rates in the Hell's Kitchen neighborhood near his church ("My Brother Cain," sermon for June 29, 1941, manuscript at Union Theological Seminary archives, vol. v., series II, p. 63a).

13. Gertner, p. 14. Scherer was a bit of a highbrow himself. On one occasion he said that at the very least Jesus had to be recognized as a "gentleman" (*Facts That Undergird Life*, p. 61). On another occasion, he deplored the "levelling" process of the middle-class mind, pointing out that popular opinion once preferred Barrabbas to Jesus (*When God Hides* [New York: Harper and Bros., 1934], p. 51).

14. Paul E. Scherer, "The Hero in Your Soul," sermon for April 13, 1930, manuscript at Union Theological Seminary archives, vol. xii, p. 132.

15. Paul E. Scherer, "Adventures with the Sacred Fire," sermon for January 18, 1931, manuscript at Union Theological Seminary, vol. xiii, p. 139.

16. Paul E. Scherer, "A Religion that Works," sermon for April 3, 1932, manuscript at Union Theological Seminary archives, vol. xv, pp. 84-85.

17. Paul E. Scherer, "God and Man in Search of One Another," sermon for April 30, 1933, manuscript at Union Theological Seminary archives, vol. vi, Series II, p. 201a.

18. *TNYT*, March 23, 1931, p. 19.

19. *TNYT*, March 23, 1931, p. 19.

20. Paul E. Scherer, "Such a Man as I," sermon for March 5, 1939, manuscript at Union Theological Seminary archives, vol. iii, series III p. 435b.

21. *TNYT*, December 30, 1940, p. 15. Cf. *TNYT*, October 19, 1931, p. 19, and February 22, 1932, p. 20, where Scherer is reported to have filed protests at the pre-eminence of business over religion, declaring that nothing in this world is as rich as what God gives.

22. *TNYT*, November 25, 1940, p. 13.

23. Scherer, *Facts That Undergird Life*, p. 106. Also, "The Christian Life as Poetry," sermon for May 25, 1930, manuscript at Union Theological Seminary archives, vol. xii, p. 195.

24. Paul E. Scherer, "The Savior of Life," sermon for January 28, 1940, manuscript at Union Theological Seminary archives, volume of Miscellaneous Sermons, p. 186b.

25. Paul E. Scherer, "Whatsoever Things are Lovely," sermon for June 10, 1934, manuscript at Union Theological Seminary, volume B of Miscellaneous Sermons, p. 486a.

26. Scherer, *Facts That Undergird Life*, p. 104.

27. Paul E. Scherer, "The Lord's Song in a Strange Land," sermon for December 26, 1937, manuscript at Union Theological Seminary archives, vol. v, series II, p. 185b.

28. *TNYT*, September 21, 1931, p. 11.

29. Paul E. Scherer, "Caravans That Turn Away," sermon for April 2, 1933, manuscript in Union Theological Seminary archives, Miscellaneous Sermons, p. 177b.

30. Paul E. Scherer, "The Hope and Power of the Christian Life," sermon for September 8, 1940, manuscript at Union Theological Seminary archives, vol. vi, series II, p. 308b.

31. Paul E. Scherer, "The Direction Protestantism Must Take," sermon for June 2, 1940, manuscript at Union Theological Seminary archives, vol. v, series II, pp. 282a-83a.

32. *TNYT*, April 10, 1933, p. 11. A month earlier he referred to reports out of Germany about "horror stories" which prompted the Federal Council of Churches and the Jewish Congress to demand an investigation; but the reports, in his opinion, generated a "nauseating" amount of "hysteria" over what he felt would prove to be fault "on both sides." ("No More Wizards," sermon for March 26, 1933, manuscript at Union Theological Seminary archives, vol. i, series II, pp. 171a-71b.)

33. *TNYT*, August 14, 1933, p. 16.

34. *TNYT*, May 18, 1936, p. 13.

35. *TNYT*, October 19, 1931, p. 19.

36. *TNYT*, October 8, 1934, p. 13. He admired FDR for being a church-goer ("Wilderness Experiences," sermon for March 5, 1933,

manuscript at Union Theological Seminary archives, vol i, series II, p. 147b). And he deplored those ministers and churches who turned from the slow, hard work of saving souls to spectacular social reform actions, such as organizing strikes, or headline-grabbing sermons on scientific or ethical problems ("The Future of Christianity," sermon for March 23, 1930, manuscript at Union Theological Seminary archives, vol. xii, p. 98).

37. Paul E. Scherer, "Is Christianity Coming to Christ?" sermon for June 16, 1935, manuscript at Union Theological Seminary archives, vol. ii, series II, p. 197a.

38. Creighton, pp. 239, 260.

39. Scherer, *Facts That Undergird Life*, p. 77.

40. Ibid., p. 77.

41. *TNYT*, June 1, 1931, p. 13.

42. Paul E. Scherer, "People We Can't Spare: The Man Who Will Try," sermon for February 4, 1934, manuscript in Union Theological Seminary archives, vol. ii, p. 264.

43. Ibid., p. 264. This quotation in particular poses an interesting textual question. The sermon ("People We Can't Spare: The Man Who Will Try") was, according to Scherer's sermon manuscript logs, delivered on December 2, 1923, and February 4, 1934, at Holy Trinity. The second sentence quoted here ("That's why He gave us faith") appears in the margin of the bound manuscript volume. One wonders: was this sentence an addition to the text for second delivery in 1934, revealing thereby that he was more concerned to stress the "gift" of faith in the thirties than he was in the twenties? Was it part of the sermon all along, serving only to make explicit what Scherer held implicitly to be true? There is no apparent way to answer such questions. That they exist, however, is one reason the debate (between Creighton and Gertner) remains unresolved about the degree of Scherer's liberalism in the twenties.

44. Ibid., pp. 264-65.

45. Paul E. Scherer, "Is Jesus Christ Recognizable?" sermon for May 14, 1931, manuscript at Union Theological Seminary archives, vol. viii, p. 129.

46. Paul E. Scherer, "Digging Again the Wells," sermon for November 8, 1931, manuscript at Union Theological Seminary archives, vol. xiv, p. 156.

47. Ibid., p. 160.

48. Paul E. Scherer, "Facts That Undergird Life," sermon preached on May 23, 1937, manuscript at Union Theological Seminary archives, vol. iii, series II, pp. 37a, 38b. This became the title sermon of a volume.

49. Paul E. Scherer, "Shall It Be Christ?" sermon for November 27, 1938, manuscript at Union Theological Seminary archives, vol. iii, series II, p. 363a.

50. Paul E. Scherer, "Speaking from Experience," sermon for June 12, 1932, and April 8, 1934, manuscript at Union Theological Seminary archives, vol. xv, pp. 171-72.

51. Paul E. Scherer, "Is Christianity Childish?" sermon for February 19, 1939, manuscript at Union Theological Seminary archives, vol. v, series II, p. 245b.

52. Paul E. Scherer, "How to Keep Religion from Becoming a Burden," sermon for October 31, 1937, manuscript at Union Theological Seminary archives, vol. v, series II, p. 149b.

53. TNYT, February 12, 1940, p. 12.

54. TNYT, April 15, 1940, p. 14.

55. Paul E. Scherer, "The Task of the Christian Church," sermon for October 5, 1941, manuscript at Union Theological Seminary archives, vol. v, series II, p. 30a.

56. Ibid., p. 31b.

57. Paul E. Scherer, "The Church in a Bankrupt World," sermon for January 17, 1932, manuscript at Union Theological Seminary archives, vol. xiv, p. 280.

58. Paul E. Scherer, "Moral Confusion and the Christian Faith," sermon for March 20, 1938, manuscript at Union Theological Seminary archives, vol. iii, series II, p. 238b.

59. Ibid., p. 235b.

60. Paul E. Scherer, "Jesus and the Outsider," sermon for March 1, 1931, manuscript at Union Theological Seminary archives, vol. xii, p. 202.

61. Ibid., p. 206.

62. Paul E. Scherer, "Simplifying Life," sermon for June 29, 1930, manuscript at Union Theological Seminary archives, vol. iii, p. 215.

63. Paul E. Scherer, "Moral Confusion and the Christian Faith," sermon for March 20, 1938, manuscript at Union Theological Seminary, vol. iii, series II, p. 238b.

64. Paul E. Scherer, "The Gist of Christianity," sermon for February 1, 1931, manuscript at Union Theological Seminary archives, vol. xii, p. 159. Again a matter of minor textual interest arises here. Scherer first wrote, "how silly it is to talk of dispensing with creeds." Then he crossed out "silly" and wrote "futile."

65. *TNYT*, October 31, 1938, p. 10.

66. Paul E. Scherer, "Was the Reformation a Success?" sermon for October 28, 1934, manuscript at Union Theological Seminary archives, vol. ii, series III p. 38b.

67. Ibid., p. 39a.

68. The change seems to have begun occurring roughly around the time Fosdick's article, "What Is the Matter with Preaching?" appeared in *Harper's* in 1928.

69. Scherer, "The Book of the Ages," in *Facts That Undergird Life*, p. 155.

70. *TNYT*, June 13, 1932, p. 18.

71. *TNYT*, September 23, 1935, p. 12.

72. *TNYT*, April 20, 1931, p. 26.

73. *TNYT*, April 18, 1938, p. 16.

74. *TNYT*, April 20, 1931, p. 26.

75. *TNYT*, November 7, 1932, p. 15.

76. *TNYT*, May 22, 1933, p. 13.

77. Paul E. Scherer, "The Groundwork of Christianity," sermon for January 19, 1930, manuscript at Union Theological Seminary archives, vol. xii, p. 17.

78. Paul E. Scherer, "Was the Reformation a Success?" sermon for October 28, 1934, manuscript at Union Theological Seminary archives, vol. ii, series II, pp. 37b-38a.

79. Ibid., p. 38a. In a December 1923 sermon delivered at Holy Trinity during the height of the controversy over Fundamentalism involving Fosdick and the Presbyterians, Scherer took his stand against the Fundamentalists. "No one denies that there are discrepancies in the book. No one denies that there is a progressive revelation, so that the morality of the New Testament is ineffably higher than the Old. No one intelligently claims that the Bible was dictated word for word with an eye to the intricacies of science or denies that the personal element in the authors entered into the composition of the work." ("Modern Fundamentals," sermon for December 23, 1923, vol. i, p. 38.) An unidentified news clipping in his sermon files indicates that he proposed, at a convention of the United Lutheran Church, a resolution from the "Commission on the Relationship between Science and Religion," which sought to declare that "harmony does exist between the Bible, correctly

interpreted, and the established results of science" even though the mechanistic views of modern science are unacceptable. (Filed with "When Jesus Followed," sermon for November 25, 1928, repeated on April 13, 1933, manuscript at Union Theological Seminary, vol. x. Comic strip markings on the reverse side of the clipping indicate it dated from 1928.)

80. Gertner, p. 88.

81. Scherer, "The Book of Ages," in *Facts That Undergird Life*, p. 156.

82. Gertner, p. 85.

83. Ibid., p. 87.

84. Ibid., pp. 85, 90.

85. Scherer, "When God Hides," in *When God Hides*, p. 6.

86. Paul E. Scherer, "Things We Fight for—and Neglect," sermon for October 30, 1932, manuscript at Union Theological Seminary archives, vol. i, series II, p. 27b.

87. Ibid., p. 27a. Also, "Was the Reformation a Success?" sermon for October 28, 1934, manuscript at Union Theological Seminary archives, vol. ii, series II, p. 36b; and "The Direction Protestantism Must Take," sermon for June 2, 1940, manuscript at Union Theological Seminary archives, vol. v, series II, p. 283a.

88. Paul E. Scherer, "The Protestant Reformation and the World Today," sermon for October 30, 1938, manuscript at Union Theological Seminary archives, vol. iv, series II, p. 343a. Cf. *The New York Times*, October 31, 1938, p. 10.

89. Scherer, "The Protestant Reformation and the World Today," p. 344b.

90. Ibid., p. 346a.

91. Paul E. Scherer, "Why Should I Become a Christian," sermon for June 23, 1935, manuscript at Union Theological Seminary archives vol. ii, series II, p. 204a.

92. Scherer, "The Third Mile," in *Facts That Undergird Life*, p. 96.

93. *TNYT*, September 23, 1935, p. 12.

94. Scherer, *Facts That Undergird Life*, p. 83.

95. Ibid., p. 118. In several unpublished sermons, the significant role of the will is stressed: "The Will to See," (undated, vol. i), "How Can These Things Be?" (June 15, 1924, and March 26, 1930, vol. iii), "Open for Discussion," (March 30, 1930, vol. xii), and "The Third Mile" (September 13, 1931, vol. xiv), all of whose manuscripts are in the archives at Union Theological Seminary.

96. Gertner, pp. 43-44.

97. Scherer, "Accepting Yourself," in *Facts That Undergird Life*, p. 64.

98. Scherer, "When God Stands By," in *Facts That Undergird Life*, p. 118.

99. Paul E. Scherer, "Ye Seek Jesus of Nazareth," *Lutheran Church Quarterly* 1 (April 1928): 132.

100. Ibid., p. 136.

101. Paul E. Scherer, "Overcoming Temptations," sermon for March 6, 1927, February 12, 1933, and July 25, 1937, manuscript at Union Theological Seminary archives, vol. viii, p. 16.

102. Paul E. Scherer, "Light for Our Darkness," sermon for November 29, 1931, manuscript at Union Theological Seminary archives, vol. xiv, pp. 194-95.

103. Paul E. Scherer, "How Are Your Securities?" sermon for January 22, 1933, manuscript at Union Theological Seminary archives, vol. i, series II, pp. 116a-16b.

104. Ibid., p. 116b.

105. Creighton, p. 233.

106. *TNYT*, October 28, 1940, p. 12.

107. Paul E. Scherer, "The Invitation and the Challenge; sermon for June 22, 1941, manuscript at Union Theological Seminary archives, vol. v, series II, p. 522a.

108. Paul E. Scherer, "One Vote for Jesus," sermon for Good Friday, March 30, 1934, manuscript at Union Theological Seminary archives, vol. iv, series II, p. 408b.

109. Paul E. Scherer, "An Ideal Religion in an Unideal World," sermon for January 11, 1925 (also "Does Jesus Fit?" for December 27, 1931) manuscript at Union Theological Seminary archives, vol. iv, pp. 113-14.

110. Paul E. Scherer, "Does Jesus Fit?" sermon for December 27, 1931, January 11, 1925, and May 21, 1936, manuscript in Union Theological Seminary archives, vol. xiv, p. 253-54.

111. Paul E. Scherer, "God's Pageant," sermon for April 10, 1938, manuscript at Union Theological Seminary archives, vol. v, series II, p. 260a.

112. Paul E. Scherer, "Hath God Indeed Said," sermon for June 27, 1937, manuscript at Union Theological Seminary archives, vol. v, series II, p. 65.

113. Paul E. Scherer, "Have You Any Illusions Left?" sermon for September 24, 1939, manuscript at Union Theological Seminary archives, vol. v, series II, p. 87a.

114. Paul E. Scherer, "Digging Again the Wells," sermon for November 8, 1931, manuscript at Union Theological Seminary archives, vol. xiv, p. 156.

115. Paul E. Scherer, "The Road Godward," sermon for April 11, 1937, manuscript at Union Theological Seminary archives, vol. iii, series II, p. 10b.

116. Ibid., p. 11a.

117. Paul E. Scherer, "Some Fleeting Good," sermon for October 23, 1938, manuscript at Union Theological Seminary archives, vol. iv, series II, p. 337b.

118. Ibid., pp. 339b-40a.

119. Paul E. Scherer, "An Ideal Religion in an Unideal World," sermon for December 25, 1931, manuscript at Union Theological Seminary archives, vol. iv, p. 110.

120. Ibid., pp. 113-14.

121. *TNYT*, April 15, 1940, p. 14.

122. Scherer, "An Ideal Religion in an Unideal World," p. 118.

123. He was, no doubt, most directly concerned with the contemporary forms of this doctrine. But we can assume that he was at least somewhat familiar with its place in medieval theology as well in the background of Reformation thought. (Heiko Oberman, The *Harvest of Medieval Theology*, passim.)

124. Paul E. Scherer, "The Christian Life as Poetry," sermon for May 25, 1930, manuscript at Union Theological Seminary archives, vol. xii, p. 193.

125. *TNYT*, October 19, 1931, p. 19.

126. *TNYT*, June 1, 1931, p. 13.

127. Paul E. Scherer, "On Recovering Our Religious Experience," sermon for May 10, 1934, manuscript at Union Theological Seminary archives, vol. vi, series II, pp. 468a-68b.

128. Paul E. Scherer, "On Giving God Another Chance," sermon for March 1, 1936, manuscript at Union Theological Seminary archives, vol. ii, series II, p. 353b.

129. Ibid., p. 352b.

130. *TNYT*, June 22, 1931, p. 26.

131. Paul E. Scherer, "The Eagerness of God," sermon for September 21, 1941, manuscript at Union Theological Seminary archives, vol. iv, series II, p. 21a.

132. Paul E. Scherer, "Hath God Indeed Said," sermon for June 27, 1937, manuscript at Union Theological Seminary archives, vol. v, series II, p. 65.

133. *TNYT*, January 7, 1935, p. 15.

134. Quoted by *TNYT*, May 14, 1934, p. 14.

135. Paul E. Scherer, "The Eagerness of God," sermon for September 21, 1941, manuscript at Union Theological Seminary, vol. iv, series II, p. 23a.

136. Paul E. Scherer, "On Being Equal to Life," sermon for March 19, 1939, manuscript at Union Theological Seminary, vol. v, series III p. 441b.

137. Paul E. Scherer, "Cripples with Queer Remedies," *Homiletic Review* 108 (November 1934): 371.

138. Gertner, p. 46.

139. Paul E. Scherer, "These Days of Reconstruction," sermon for February 14, 1932, manuscript at Union Theological Seminary archives, vol. xv, pp. 24-25.

140. Over the years, Scherer modified the terms in which he expressed appreciation for the Reformation. In the twenties he lauded several great sixteenth-century Protestant principles, which he felt Protestantism had

come to ignore: freedom of thought; an open Bible, whose renewed presence and study would give Christianity its "power" back again; the sense of "immediate access to God"; and "faith" as trust in, and fellowship with, the Savior. (Paul E. Scherer, "Do We Need Another Reformation?" sermon for November 1, 1925, manuscript at Union Theological Seminary archives, vol. v, pp. 234-38.) A year later, still exalting personal freedom, he said that nothing is "more difficult than learning how to submit *your* will to the will of *another*," however that difficulty had been overcome, for the "Reformation [discovered] that this will for you and for me is discoverable." (Paul E. Scherer, "The Art of Living," sermon for October 31, 1926, manuscript at Union Theological Seminary archives, vol. vii, pp. 92-93.)

But by 1928, Scherer seemed concerned about the excesses of freedom in a Protestantism "gone to seed." He saw Protestants in an "unreasoning revolt against everything that even savors of authority," and he lamented the "tragic penchant for adopting *opinions* and calling them *beliefs*." (Paul E. Scherer, "The Protest Against Protestantism," sermon for November 4, 1928, manuscript at Union Theological Seminary archives, vol. x, p. 65.) "Freedom is a dangerous thing until you've learned how to manage it," he declared in June, 1930. (Paul E. Scherer, "Is Lutheranism Christian?" sermon for June 22, 1930, manuscript at Union Theological Seminary archives, vol. xii, p. 229.) In September of that same year, he pronounced freedom to be "an idolatrous cult." (Paul E. Scherer, "Jesus Looks at Our Best People," sermon for September 27, 1930, manuscript at Union Theological Seminary archives, vol. xiv, p. 112.) A year later, he drew those implications further, with the opinion that the Church "has lost vitality for us because of a too great reliance on ourselves." (Paul E. Scherer, "Digging Again the Wells," sermon for November 8, 1931, manuscript at Union Theological Seminary archives, vol. xiv, p. 156.) Protestantism had betrayed its heritage, for it had reduced the Reformation to "freedom of conscience." (Paul E. Scherer, "Was the Reformation a Success?" sermon for October 28, 1934, manuscript at Union Theological Seminary archives, vol. ii, series II, pp. 36b-37a.)

Yet in the early months of 1938 (perhaps under the pressure of changing world events?) he wanted to reclaim again the principle of "freedom." A philosophy of rugged individualism displeased him, but a rediscovery of the dignity and "sovereign worth" of the individual was indeed what the Reformation "had tried to revive" and what Jesus had stressed for all persons. (Paul E. Scherer, "This Tired World," sermon for February 20, 1938, manuscript at Union Theological Seminary archives, vol. ii, series II, pp. 217b-18a.)

CHAPTER VI

1. Harry Emerson Fosdick, "What Is Religion?" *Harper's*, March, 1929, p. 425.

2. Ibid., p. 429.

3. Ibid., p. 434.

4. Leininger, "The Christian Apologetic of Harry Emerson Fosdick" (Th.D. dissertation; Southern Baptist Theological Seminary, Louisville, 1967), p. 58.   Leininger quotes a letter from Fosdick, confirming Fosdick's own belief that the description of him as "apologist" most accurately suited his intentions and the impact of his career.

5. Harry Emerson Fosdick, "The Sermon on the Mount," sermon at Park Avenue Baptist Church on March 31, 1926, published in *The Hope of the World*, p. 149.

6. Harry Emerson Fosdick, "What Liberal Christians Are Driving At," in *Adventurous Religion*, pp. 241-42.

7. Harry Emerson Fosdick, "The Church Must Go Beyond Modernism," sermon for November 3, 1935, in *Successful Christian Living*, p. 154.

8. In his *A Guide to Understanding the Bible, The Development of Ideas within the Old and New Testaments* (New York: Harper Bros., 1938) Fosdick outlined the development of the knowledge of God from early, primitive views to later, more sophisticated understandings.   His articulate interpretation of Scripture in an evolutionary model was, according to Walther Eichrodt, the culmination of the liberal hermeneutic (*Journal of biblical Literature*, vol. 65 [June 1946]: 205-17).

9. *TNYT*, November 3, 1930, p. 28.

10. A Christian is the free Lord of all, subject to none; a Christian is the free servant of all, subject to everyone (Harry Emerson Fosdick, "The New Religious Reformation," in *Adventurous Religion*, pp. 312-13).

11. Harry Emerson Fosdick, "The Appeal from Christianity to Christ," sermon for December 25, 1932, manuscript in Union Theological Seminary archives, pp. 6-7. The sermon was written by Fosdick but never delivered at Riverside by him. He was forced to remain at home with a bad throat on the Sunday for which he had written the sermon. Late on Saturday night, his associate, Dr. Eugene Carder, was summoned to deliver the Sunday sermon. Carder wondered if a full manuscript were ready; and, upon learning that one was, he decided to preach Fosdick's sermon to the congregation.

12. Ibid., p. 7.

13. *TNYT*, October 6, 1930, p. 11.

14. Harry Emerson Fosdick, "Truth through Personality," sermon for December 20, 1936, manuscript in Union Theological Seminary archives, pp. 7-8. Also, "What Does the Divinity of Jesus Mean?" sermon for March 26, 1939, in *Living Under Tension: Sermons on Christianity Today* (New York: Harper and Bros., 1941) p. 157.

15. *TNYT*, October 27, 1930, p. 26.

16. Harry Emerson Fosdick, "The Towering Question: Is Christianity Possible?" sermon for October 29, 1933, and April 30, 1939, in *The Secret of Victorious Living: Sermons on Christianity Today* (New York: Harper and Bros., 1934), p. 50.

17. Fosdick, "The Appeal from Christianity to Christ," sermon for December 25, 1932; manuscript at Union Theological Seminary, p. 8.

18. Harry Emerson Fosdick, "The Contemporary Prevalence of Polytheism," sermon for November 15, 1936, in *Successful Christian Living*, p. 58.

19. Fosdick, *As I See Religion* (New York: Harper and Bros., 1932), p. 151. Cf. *The Living of These Days*, p. 230. Fosdick accepted the critique

as probably legitimate, if by "theology" one means the transient doctrines through which an attempt is made to articulate eternal truth.   But he considered himself to be very serious about the truth which lies at the base of the transient categories.

20.   Hall, "The Basic Theological and Ethical Concepts of Harry Emerson Fosdick", (Th.D. dissertation, Southern Baptist Theological Seminary, Louisville, 1958), pp. 215ff.

21. McDiarmid, "A Critique of Harry Emerson Fosdick's Conception of Preaching as Personal Counseling on a Group Scale", (Th.D. dissertation, Pacific School of Religion, 1961), pp. 76ff.

22. Harry Emerson Fosdick, "The Fine Art of Making Goodness Attractive," sermon for October 16, 1932, in *The Hope of the World: Twenty-Five Sermons on Christianity Today* (New York: Harper Bros., 1933), pp. 195-96.

23. Robert T. Handy, *A Christian America:Protestant Hopes and Historical Realities* (New York: Oxford University Press, 1971), pp. 184ff, points to the year of that sermon as the watershed of the "second disestablishment" of Protestantism in America.   Martin E. Marty, *Righteous Empire: The Protestant Experience in America* (New York: Dial Press, 1970), pp. 238f, sets Fosdick in the context of a decade when liberals were using the pages of *The Christian Century* to explain "How My Mind Has Changed."   Creighton, "Reconciliation in American Protestant Preaching," p. 64, says the sermon flowed with "the prevailing wind of doctrine through the 1930's."

24.   Fosdick had had surgery to remove a bladder tumor in March of 1935 and did not preach until the following September. Three of the four preachers in this study had similar forced absences—Buttrick was seriously injured in an automobile accident in the Poconos on August 23, 1940, and did not return to his pulpit until November; Scherer suffered a throat ailment in 1937 that required him to refrain from all speech for six months. Sockman, however, never missed a day when he was scheduled to preach in the forty-four years of his ministry in New York City.

25. Fosdick, *Successful Christian Living*, p. 154.

26. Ibid., p. 163.

27. Ibid., p. 158.

28. Ibid., p. 159.

29. It enjoyed an unusually wide distribution. Besides the radio broadcast which carried Fosdick's voice around the world, and besides the Monday morning report in *TNYT* (November 4, 1935, p. 18), the sermon was published in the *Christian Century* the following month (December 4, 1935) and in a volume of sermons within two years afterward. Still, this was not nearly as widely distributed as "Shall the Fundamentalists Win?" which publicist Ivy Lee had printed in pamphlet form.

30. *TNYT*, October 2, 1933, p. 16.

31. Harry Emerson Fosdick, "A Fundamentalist Sermon by a Modernist Preacher," sermon for January 17, 1932, in *The Power to See It Through* (New York: Harper and Bros., 1935), p. 191. (Cf. *TNYT*, January 18, 1932, p. 13.)

32. Ibid., p. 199.

33. Ibid., p. 192.

34. Ibid., pp. 194-95.

35. Ibid., pp. 196-97.

36. Ibid., pp. 195-196.

37. Ibid, p. 193.

38. Harry Emerson Fosdick, "The Modern World's Rediscovery of Sin," sermon for December 18, 1938, and August 13, 1939, in *Living Under Tension*, p. 113. Every summer Fosdick travelled to New York from his summer vacation home in Maine to preach at Riverside on the several Sundays that coincided with the weeks of summer school at Columbia.

His usual pattern was to select six of the sermons he had given during the previous preaching season and to deliver them without revision.

39. Harry Emerson Fosdick, "On Being Level-Headed," sermon for October 26, 1934, manuscript in Union Theological Seminary archives, p. 5.

40. *TNYT*, October 26, 1936, p. 14.

41. Harry Emerson Fosdick, "The World Tries to Get Rid of Religion," sermon for January 1, 1939, manuscript at Union Theological Seminary, p. 3.

42. Quoted by *TNYT*, May 27, 1940, p. 14.

43. Fosdick, "The World Tries to Get Rid of Religion," p. 4. Cf. Harry Emerson Fosdick, "A Great Year for Easter," sermon for April 13, 1941, in *Living Under Tension*, p. 251.

44. *TNYT*, January 2, 1939, p. 42.

45. Fosdick, "The Dangers of Modernism," *Adventurous Religion*, p. 274.

46. *TNYT*, March 22, 1937, p. 15.

47. Fodsick, "The Church Must Go Beyond Modernism," *Successful Christian Living*, p. 164.

48. Fosdick, "The Towering Question: Is Christianity Possible?", *The Secret of Victorious Living*, pp. 50-59.

49. Ibid., p. 50.

50. Harry Emerson Fosdick, "The Need of Brains in Religion," sermon for February 22, 1931, manuscript in Union Theological Seminary archives, p. 4. Cf. *TNYT*, February 23, 1931, p. 15, which quotes Fosdick as saying, "Give us churches where religion is intelligent and intelligence is religious, and the gates of hell cannot prevail against them."

51. Fosdick, "The Need of Brains in Religion," pp. 8-9.

52. *TNYT,* April 27, 1931, p. 19. "Nor is there any way out of this," he said, "except building the basic meaning of religion into people's lives from childhood up."

53. *TNYT*, July 20, 1931, p. 15.

54. Harry Emerson Fosdick, "The High Use of Memory," sermon for May 31, 1931, manuscript in Union Theological Seminary archives, p. 5.

55. Fosdick, *As I See Religion*, p. 6.

56. Harry Emerson Fosdick, "The Way Out from a Dry as Dust Religion," sermon for November 1, 1931, manuscript in Union Theological Seminary archives, p. 10.

57. Harry Emerson Fosdick, "Courage," sermon for November 29, 1931, manuscript in Union Theological Seminary archives, p. 4.

58. Harry Emerson Fosdick, "What Is Life Doing to Your Self-Esteem?" sermon for October 2, 1932, manuscript in Union Theological Seminary archives, p. 9.

59. Quoted in *TNYT*, December 7, 1931, p. 22.

60. Quoted in *TNYT*, April 4, 1932, p. 15. Cf. *TNYT*, March 26, 1934, p. 20, where Fosdick says Christianity is more than the beauty of worship; it is a matter of applying "Christian principles to social life."

61. *TNYT*, January 16, 1933, p. 11.

62. *TNYT*, January 23, 1933, p. 11.

63. *TNYT*, February 20, 1933, p. 13.

64. *TNYT*, February 20, 1933, p. 13.

65. Fosdick, *Adventurous Religion*, pp. 53, 56. Fosdick seems to use the terms "faith" and "religion" interchangeably for the same human phenomenon: namely, the confidence and enthusiasm which form the necessary prelude to moral effort.

66. Harry Emerson Fosdick, "The Meaning of the Incarnation," sermon for December 21, 1930, and December 25, 1935, manuscript in Union Theological Seminary archives, p. 11.

67. *TNYT*, April 17, 1933, p. 11.

68. *TNYT*, May 9, 1932, p. 13.

69. Harry Emerson Fosdick, "The God Who Matters Morally," sermon for December 16, 1934, manuscript in Union Theological Seminary archives, pp. 3-4.

70. Ibid., pp. 5, 8.

71. Harry Emerson Fosdick, "Why Is Religion Indispensable?" sermon for January 4, 1931, manuscript in Union Theological Seminary archives, pp. 3-4.

72. *TNYT*, January 7, 1935, p. 15.

73. *TNYT*, February 3, 1941, p. 20.

74. Leininger, p. 232.

75. McDiarmid, p. 298. One might conclude that his faith was more cultural than Christian. In his sermon for October 6, 1935, "Glorifying the Commonplace" (manuscript in Union Theological Seminary archives) he said, "The creative strength of the world lies in the middle class" (*TNYT*, October 7, 1935, p. 16).

76. Fosdick, *The Meaning of Faith* (New York: Abingdon, 1921), p. 263.

77. Harry Emerson Fosdick, "The Practical Use of Faith," sermon for December 30, 1934, in *The Power to See It Through*, p. 156.

78. Harry Emerson Fosdick, "Every Man a Gambler," sermon for December 30, 1934, in *The Power to See It Through*, p. 156.

79. Fosdick, *The Meaning of Faith*, p. 12.

80. The doctrine of justification by faith, Fosdick wrote in 1929, is not unique to Christianity: "so far from being exclusively Pauline or Lutheran, [it] is being stated today and lived upon with peace and joy by one of the powerful Buddhist sects" (Fosdick, "What Is Christianity?" in *Harper's Magazine*, April 1929, p. 553).

81. Harry Emerson Fosdick, "The Unrecognized God," sermon for June 5, 1938, and July 23, 1939, p. 9, manuscript in Union Theological Seminary archives. (An earlier version, under the same title, is also in the archives: see following note.) Also, "The Prevalence of an Unrecognized Religion," sermon for April 22, 1934, manuscript in Union Theological Seminary archives, p. 11.

82. Harry Emerson Fosdick, "The Unrecognized God," sermon for October 12, 1930, manuscript in Union Theological Seminary archives, p. 11.

83. Cf. Jaroslav Pelikan, "Introduction," in Kenneth Cauthen, *The Impact of American Religious Liberalism*, pp. viiff. Pelikan writes: "it must be conceded that some of the spokesmen for liberalism went far beyond medieval works-righteousness in their glorification of what man could do by his own efforts to win a right relation to God. The eternal qualitative difference between God and Man, or between God and creation, or between God and natural process, seems to have been blurred into a merely temporary separation, soon to be transcended by man's moral progress. . . . Few have seen this self-righteousness more clearly . . . than Walter Rauschenbusch or Harry Emerson Fosdick."

84. Harry Emerson Fosdick, "A Religious Faith for a Discouraging Year," sermon for February 28, 1932, manuscript in Union Theological Seminary archives, p. 12.

85. Harry Emerson Fosdick, "The Cross Confronts Our Easy-Going Christianity," sermon for April 2, 1939, manuscript in Union Theological Seminary archives, p. 9.

86. Harry Emerson Fosdick, "The Major Fault of Religious Liberalism," sermon for November 19, 1939, manuscript in Union Theological Seminary archives, pp. 1-2.

87. Ibid., p. 9.

88. Harry Emerson Fosdick, "On Not Being Able to Escape God," sermon for February 9, 1936, manuscript in Union Theological Seminary archives, p. 1.   A similar phrase, "laid hold on by faith in God," appears in "Resources for a Courageous Life," sermon for October 31, 1937, manuscript in Union Theological Seminary archives, p. 12.

89. Harry Emerson Fosdick, "Steadfastness Under the Highest Leadership," sermon for November 7, 1937, manuscript in Union Theological Seminary archives, p. 1.

90. Harry Emerson Fosdick, "The Life that Keeps Its Savor," sermon for January 7, 1940, manuscript in Union Theological Seminary archives, p. 8.

91. Harry Emerson Fosdick, "Do We Really Want God?" sermon for February 11, 1934, in *The Secret of Victorious Living*, pp. 174-75.

92. *TNYT*, June 5, 1933, p. 13.

93. Harry Emerson Fosdick, "The Recovery of a Powerful Religion," sermon for October 25, 1936, manuscript in Union Theological Seminary archives, p. 1.   Cf. *TNYT*, October 26, 1936, p. 14.

94. *TNYT*, February 7, 1938.

95. Harry Emerson Fosdick, "Does the Present World Situation Refute or Confirm the Christian Faith?" sermon for October 22, 1939, manuscript in Union Theological Seminary archives, p. 7.

96. Harry Emerson Fosdick, "The Present State of the World as an Argument for Christian Faith," sermon for September 6, 1937, manuscript in Union Theological Seminary archives, p. 7.

97. Harry Emerson Fosdick, "This Is a Good Year for Christmas," sermon for December 24, 1939, manuscript in Union Theological Seminary archives, p. 5.

98. Fosdick, "Does the Present World Situation Refute or Confirm Christian Faith?" p. 10.

99. *TNYT*, December 6, 1937, p. 28.

100. Harry Emerson Fosdick, "Conquering Fear," sermon for October 5, 1941, manuscript in Union Theological Seminary archives, p. 11.

101. Harry Emerson Fosdick, "Don't Lose Faith in Human Possibilities," sermon for October 8, 1939, and July 14, 1940, in *Living Under Tension*, p. 17.

102. *TNYT*, January 8, 1940, p. 12.

103. Leininger, p. 149.

104. Ibid., p. 33.

105. Ibid., p. 55.

106. Fosdick, "What Is Religion?", *Harper*, March 1929, p. 434.

107. Fosdick, "The Contemporary Prevalence of Polytheism," *Successful Christian Living*, pp. 63-64.

108. Harry Emerson Fosdick, "The Possibility of Transformed Personality," sermon for November 13, 1938, manuscript in Union Theological Seminary archives, p. 7.

109. *TNYT*, May 16, 1938, p. 18.

110. Harry Emerson Fosdick, "The Contemporary Movement Back to Religion," sermon for January 8, 1939, manuscript in Union Theological Seminary archives, p. 9.

111. *TNYT*, October 26, 1936, p. 14.

112. *TNYT*, February 8, 1937, p. 11.

113. Harry Emerson Fosdick, "The Springs of Surplus Power," sermon for October 17, 1937, manuscript in Union Theological Seminary archives, p. 11.

114. Quoted in *TNYT*, May 26, 1941, p. 22.

115. Cf., for instance, Harry Emerson Fosdick, "When Each Man Cleans Up His Own Life," sermon for March 8, 1936, in *Successful Christian Living*, p. 140.

116. Harry Emerson Fosdick, "How We All Miss the Bus," sermon for January 5, 1941, manuscript in Union Theological Seminary archives, p. 12.

117. Harry Emerson Fosdick, "The Past Speaks to Our Present," sermon for February 9, 1941, manuscript in Union Theological Seminary archives, p. 14.

118. Harry Emerson Fosdick, "Achieving Personal Integrity," sermon for November 2, 1941, manuscript in Union Theological Seminary archives, p. 1.

119. Fosdick, *A Modern Preacher's Problem in His Use of the Scriptures*, pp. 12-13.

120. Ibid., p. 29.

121. Fosdick, *The Living of These Days*, p. 51.

122. Eugene May, "How Dr. Fosdick Uses the Bible in Preaching," in Crocker, p. 85. The article originally appeared in *The Pulpit* 21 (1950): 118f.

123. Ibid., p. 84.

124. Ibid., p. 84.

125. "In no instance did I notice that he used the Bible authoritatively." H. Gordon Clinard, "An Evangelical Critique of the Use of the Classic biblical Solutions to the Problem of Suffering by Representative Protestant Preachers" (Th.D. dissertation, Southwestern Baptist Theological Seminary, 1958), p. 179.

126. R. M. Shelton, "The Relationship Between Reason and Revelation in the Preaching of Harry Emerson Fosdick" (Th.D. dissertation, Princeton Theological Seminary, 1965), p. 287-88.

127. Samuel Robert Weaver, "The Theology and Times of Harry Emerson Fosdick" (Th.D. dissertation, Princeton Theological Seminary, 1961), pp. 78-79.

128. Fosdick, "What Is the Matter with Preaching?", *Harper's Magazine*, July 1928, p. 141.

129. Fosdick, *The Modern Use of the Bible*, pp. 60-61.

130. Ibid., p. 103.

131. Ibid., p. 95.

132. Fosdick, *The Living of These Days*, p. 95.

133. Hall, p. 38.

134. Weaver, p. 306.

135. Fosdick, *The Living of These Days*, p. 231.

136. Harry Emerson Fosdick, "Victims of Fate or Masters of Destiny," sermon for October 11, 1931, manuscript in Union Theological Seminary archives, p. 2.

137. Harry Emerson Fosdick, *A Guide to Understanding the Bible: The Development of Ideas within the Old and New Testaments* (New York: Harper and Bros., 1938), pp. 139ff. Fosdick had written his B.D. thesis at Union on the history of the doctrine of the atonement, but he professed to see no abiding value in any juridical views of atonement. Rather he saw the principle of vicarious sacrifice in Isaiah and in the New Testament witness to Christ; therefore he saw the Christian's role as the need to follow the pattern of suffering for the sake of others.

138. Harry Emerson Fosdick, "Beyond Reason," sermon for March 11, 1928, at Park Avenue Baptist Church. *Religious Education* 23 (May 1928): 471-77.

139. Harry Emerson Fosdick, "Religious Faith: Privilege or Problem," sermon for March 1, 1931, and July 10, 1932, in *The Hope of the World*, p. 184.

140. Fosdick, *The Meaning of Faith*, p. 25.

141. Harry Emerson Fosdick, "Animated Conversation," in Crocker, p. 49.

142. Fosdick, *As I See Religion*, p. 35.

143. *TNYT*, October 31, 1932, p. 20. Cf. "Six Ways to Tell Right from Wrong," sermon for October 30, 1932, in *The Hope of the World*, pp. 129-34.

144. Fosdick, "How I Prepare My Sermons," in Crocker, pp. 50-54.

145. Harry Emerson Fosdick, "The Peril of Privilege," sermon for February 21, 1937, in *Successful Christian Living*, p. 126.

146. Harry Emerson Fosdick, "This Is a Miraculous World," sermon for December 12, 1937, manuscript in Union Theological Seminary archives, p. 6.

147. How much of an impact is open to some debate. Leininger implies that neo-orthodoxy was an important, though not exclusive, source of Fosdick's deepening conception of sin (pp. 142-43). Katherine A.

Bonney concludes that Fosdick had a deeper awareness of sin after the middle thirties than he had earlier; but Fosdick expressed, in an interview with her, that he did not believe neo-orthodoxy contributed to his concept of sin (Katherine A. Bonney, "Harry Emerson Fosdick's Doctrine of Man" [Ph.D. dissertation, Boston University, 1959], pp. 66-68).

148. Harry Emerson Fosdick, "The Meaning of Reverence," sermon for May 16, 1937, manuscript in Union Theological Seminary archives, p. 8.

149. Harry Emerson Fosdick, "Christian Faith—Fantasy or Truth?" sermon for March 16, 1938, and July 27, 1941, in *Living Under Tension*, p. 31.

150. Harry Emerson Fosdick, "On Being a Rugged Individual," sermon for December 15, 1935, manuscript in Union Theological Seminary archives, p. 8.

151. Fosdick, "The Modern World's Rediscovery of Sin," *The Pulpit*, March 1939, p. 119.

152. Harry Emerson Fosdick, "The Principle of Released Power," sermon for November 20, 1938, manuscript in Union Theological Seminary archives, p. 10. (It should be noted, however, that this power will come only by our effort to create the conditions which will make its coming possible.)

153. Fosdick, *A Guide to Understanding the Bible*, pp. 193-95.

154. *TNYT*, January 7, 1935, p. 15.

155. Harry Emerson Fosdick, "When Spiritual Forces Confront a Brutal World," sermon for October 20, 1940, manuscript in Union Theological Seminary archives, p. 10.

156. *TNYT*, February 3, 1941, p. 20.

157. Hitler's moves to nationalize the German Church, for instance, were derided as "stupid" (*TNYT*, April 10, 1933, p. 11).

158. *TNYT*, January 17, 1938, p. 20, and February 3, 1941, p. 20.

159. *TNYT*, December 18, 1939, p. 26.

160. Harry Emerson Fosdick, "What Are You Doing with Your Imagination?" sermon for December 17, 1939, manuscript in Union Theological Seminary archives, p. 4.

161. Harry Emerson Fosdick, "How to Stand Up and Take It," sermon for December 29, 1940, in *Living Under Tension*, p. 95.

162.   Of course, "determinism" in Fosdick's usage here did not necessarily exclude from his condemnation the Calvinists' predestinarian views.   But mainly his reference to "determinism" encompassed a secularized philosophy of materialism, built upon the view that the universe is an evolving collection of atoms whose collisions chanced to develop the cosmos as we know it (*TNYT*, July 13, 1931, p. 15, and November 28, 1932, p. 13). In "Why Not Live the Good Life without Religion?" he said a magician could "get a character like Christ or like my mother from the fortuitous play of atoms" (manuscript in Union Theological Seminary archives, sermon for January 19, 1936, p. 5. Cf. *TNYT*, January 29, 1936, p. 17).

163. Fosdick, "Preventive Religion," *The Power to See It Through*, pp. 70-71.

164. Fosdick, *The Meaning of Faith*, p. 263.

165.   Fosdick, *The Manhood of the Master* (New York: Association Press, 1913), p. 48.

166. Ibid., pp. 92-93.

167. He was well-versed in the history of the doctrine of the atonement, having submitted his Bachelor of Divinity Thesis at Union on the topic "The Significance of Christ's Death in Christian Thought: An Inquiry into the Reasons for the Pre-eminence of the Crucifixion of Christian Consciousness" (Douglas Miller Ranson, "The Idea of Progress in the Theology of Harry Emerson Fosdick" [Ph.D.   dissertation, Duke University, 1963], p. 15).

168. Harry Emerson Fosdick, "Through the Social Gospel into Personal Religion," sermon for November 27, 1932, in *The Hope of the World*, p. 38.

169. Harry Emerson Fosdick, "Truth through Personality," sermon for December 20, 1936, manuscript in Union Theological Seminary archives, p. 10.

170. Fosdick, "The Possibility of Transformed Personality," sermon for November 13, 1938, manuscript at Union Theological Seminary, p. 7. Cf. *TNYT*, July 31, 1939, p. 14.

171. Harry Emerson Fosdick, "The Peril of Worshipping Jesus," sermon for October 26, 1930, in *The Hope of the World*, p. 104.

172. Fosdick, "The Contemporary Prevalence of Polytheism," *Successful Christian Living*, pp. 63-64.

173. Harry Emerson Fosdick, "On Being Indifferent to Religion," sermon for January 17, 1937, and April 12, 1942, in *Successful Christian Living*, p. 198.

174. Harry Emerson Fosdick, "The Meaning of Trust in God," sermon for November 23, 1930, manuscript in Union Theological Seminary archives, p. 8.

175. Harry Emerson Fosdick, "The Life of the Spirit," sermon for March 18, 1931, manuscript in Union Theological Seminary archives, p. 8.

176. Harry Emerson Fosdick, "Being Good without Trying," in *The Hope of the World*, p. 213. No date has been identified for this sermon, except, of course, that it was delivered prior to 1933 when the volume was published.

177. Fosdick, "Why Is Religion Indispensable?", sermon for January 4, 1931, manuscript at Union Theological Seminary, p. 8.

178. Harry Emerson Fosdick, "The God Who Matters Morally," sermon for December 16, 1934, manuscript in Union Theological Seminary archives, pp. 3-4.

179. Fosdick, *Pilgrimage to Palestine* (New York: Macmillan, 1949), p. 136.

180. *TNYT*, August 10, 1931, p. 13.

181. Harry Emerson Fosdick, "Putting Manhood First," sermon for January 12, 1936, manuscript in Union Theological Seminary archives, pp. 7, 11.

182. Therefore, democracy should be the spiritual, not just the civic or political or constitutional, aim of America.   Harry Emerson Fosdick, "How Much Do We Want Democracy?" sermon for February 23, 1936, manuscript in Union Theological Seminary archives, pp. 6, 10.   The same sermon, retitled as "Rededication to Democracy," was delivered on Thanksgiving Day, November 26, 1937.   Cf. *TNYT*, February 24, 1936, p. 13.).

183. Harry Emerson Fosdick, "Moral Independence," sermon for October 19, 1930, manuscript in Union Theological Seminary archives, p. 2.

184. Harry Emerson Fosdick, "The Need of a Dependable Character," sermon for January 10, 1932, manuscript in Union Theological Seminary archives, p. 7.

185. Fosdick, "The Need of Brains in Religion," sermon for February 22, 1931, manuscript in Union Theological Seminary archives, pp. 8-9. Cf. *TNYT*, February 23, 1931, p. 15.

186. *TNYT*, January 19, 1931, p. 20.

187. Fosdick, "What Is Life Doing to Your Self-Esteem?" sermon for October 2, 1932, manuscript in Union Theological Seminary archives, p. 4. The mayor was Jimmy Walker.

188. Ibid., p. 9.

189. *TNYT*, October 12, 1931, p. 19.

190. Fosdick, "Victims of Fate or Masters of Destiny," sermon for October 11, 1931, manuscript in Union Theological Seminary archives, p. 12.

191. Harry Emerson Fosdick, "Regaining Faith in the Worth of Life," sermon for October 20, 1935, manuscript in Union Theological Seminary archives, pp. 3-4.

192. Harry Emerson Fosdick, "Personality Changes the World," sermon for December 22, 1935, manuscript in Union Theological Seminary archives, pp. 3-4.

193. Harry Emerson Fosdick, "The Gospel of Hope," sermon for Easter Sunday, April 5, 1931, manuscript in Union Theological Seminary archives, p. 12.

194. Harry Emerson Fosdick, "No Man Need Stay the Way He Is," sermon for November 25, 1934, in *The Power to See It Through*, pp. 59f.

195. *TNYT*, October 12, 1936, p. 25.

196. Fosdick, *The Modern Use of the Bible*, p. 110.   Fosdick, "A Religious Faith for a Discouraging Year," sermon for February 28, 1932, also delivered on radio April 17, 1932, manuscript in Union Theological Seminary archives, p. 12. Harry Emerson Fosdick, "Man's Critical Need of Interior Stability," sermon for October 3, 1937, manuscript in Union Theological Seminary archives, p. 9.

197. Harry Emerson Fosdick, "The Secret of Victorious Living," sermon for March 4, 1934, in *The Secret of Victorious Living*, p. 6.

198. Harry Emerson Fosdick, "The Use and Misuse of Power," sermon of unknown date in *The Secret of Victorious Living* (1934), p. 77.

199. Fosdick, "Do We Really Want God?", sermon for February 11, 1934, in *The Secret of Victorious Living*, p. 177.

200. Dr. Francis Townsend and his adherents, in an attempt to assist the aging while at the same time stimulating the economy, proposed an old

age pension plan that would contribute $200 a month to persons over 50 with the stipulation that they agree to spend those funds within 30 days.

201. *TNYT*, February 17, 1936, p. 13.

202. Harry Emerson Fosdick, "Basic Conditions of Spiritual Well-Being," sermon for February 3, 1935, in *The Power to See It Through*, p. 140.

203. Harry Emerson Fosdick, "Basic Conditions of Spiritual Well-Being," sermon for May 2, 1937, manuscript in Union Theological Seminary archives, p. 9.

204. Harry Emerson Fosdick, "The Miracle of changed Lives," sermon for October 4, 1936, manuscript in Union Theological Seminary archives, p. 11. Harry Emerson Fosdick, "Our Moral Muddle," sermon for March 8, 1931, manuscript in Union Theological Seminary archives, p. 10.

205. *TNYT*, October 15, 1934, p. 13.

206. *TNYT*, October 20, 1930, p. 16.

207. Fosdick, "Union and Liberty in the Churches," *Outlook*, November 13, 1929, p. 423.

208. *TNYT*, April 10, 1933, p. 11.

209. Harry Emerson Fosdick, "Crucified by Stupidity," sermon for April 9, 1933, in *The Hope of the World*, pp. 226, 230.

210. Ibid., p. 226.

211. Fosdick, "No Man Need Stay the Way He Is," sermon for November 25, 1934, *The Power to See It Through*, p. 58.

212. Fosdick, "Being Good Without Trying," *Hope of the World*, pp. 210, 213.

213. Ibid., p. 213.

214. Harry Emerson Fosdick, "The Unknown Soldier," sermon for November 12, 1933, in *The Secret of Victorious Living*, p. 95.

215. Ibid., p. 97.

216. Ibid., p. 98. Cf. *TNYT*, November 13, 1933, p. 13. On some later occasion, Fosdick repeated these remarks. Wider publicity was given to this second presentation, with the result that an "endless stream" of responses came to him, ninety-nine percent of them in support of his views (*TNYT*, May 21, 1934, p. 13). Meanwhile, of the 20,000 ministers responding to a questionnaire, 13,000 signed or agreed to sign a statement renouncing war. "We mean precisely what we say," Fosdick declared; "we will meet you in prison first" ("An Interpretation of Pacifism," sermon for May 20, 1934, in *The Secret of Victorious Living*, p. 109).

217. *TNYT*, January 4, 1937, p. 30. The following Sunday, however, he confessed that he expected to die with "his eyes looking on a world, however much improved, still in danger of war" (Harry Emerson Fosdick, "Five Sectors of the Peace Movement," sermon for January 10, 1937, manuscript in Union Theological Seminary archives, p. 11.) Fosdick died in 1969, at the height of American involvement in, and controversy over, the war in Vietnam.

218. Harry Emerson Fosdick, "How Much Do We Care for Our Children?" sermon for October 2, 1938, manuscript in Union Theological Seminary archives, p. 5.

219. Harry Emerson Fosdick, "The Christian Church's Message to the World Today," sermon for October 1, 1939, manuscript in Union Theological Seminary archives, p. 1.

220. Harry Emerson Fosdick, "The Ethical Problems of Neutrality," sermon for October 15, 1939, manuscript in Union Theological Seminary archives, p. 1.

221. Harry Emerson Fosdick, "I Want My Own Way," sermon for May 5, 1940, manuscript in Union Theological Seminary archives, p. 4.

222. *TNYT*, May 20, 1940, p. 14.

223. Harry Emerson Fosdick, "When Life Goes to Pieces," sermon for May 26, 1940, manuscript in Union Theological Seminary archives,. p. 11.

224. Harry Emerson Fosdick, "If Foresight Equalled Hindsight," sermon for March 2, 1941, manuscript in Union Theological Seminary archives, p. 8.

225. Harry Emerson Fosdick, "When the Devil Looks Like an Angel," sermon for April 27, 1941, manuscript in Union Theological Seminary archives, p. 9.

226. Fosdick, "When Life Goes to Pieces," sermon for May 26, 1940, manuscript in Union Theological Seminary archives, pp. 11-12.

227. Fosdick, "If Foresight Equalled Hindsight," sermon for March 2, 1941, manuscript in Union Theological Seminary archives, p. 10.

228. Harry Emerson Fosdick, "Christians in Spite of Everything," sermon for January 20, 1935, and April 28, 1940, in *The Power to See It Through*, p. 13.

229. Fosdick, "The Roots of Dependable Character," sermon for October 24, 1937, (radio, May 22, 1938) manuscript in Union Theological Seminary archives, p. 2.

230. Harry Emerson Fosdick, "The Service of Religious Faith to Mental Health," sermon of uncertain date in *The Hope of the World* (1933), p. 50.

231. Ibid., pp. 51ff, 58.

232. A decade earlier, Fosdick had written that "to get out of sin, once you are in it, is a terrific process." He referred to the parable of the Prodigal Son and said that it is far better to be obedient all along than to have to face "the bitter struggle of coming back" (Fosdick, *Twelve Tests of Character* [New York: Association Press, 1923], p. 121).

233. Fosdick, "Does the Present World Situation Refute or Confirm the Christian Faith?", sermon for October 22, 1939, (radio, October 29, 1939) manuscript in Union Theological Seminary archives, pp. 7, 10.

234. Harry Emerson Fosdick, "A Clean Life in a Soiled World," sermon for October 27, 1940, manuscript in Union Theological Seminary archives, pp. 1-2.

235. Ibid., p. 2.

236. Ibid., p. 4.

237. Harry Emerson Fosdick, "The Most Disturbing Factor in the Christian Faith," sermon for March 17, 1940, manuscript in Union Theological Seminary archives, p. 4.

238. Ibid., pp. 4, 10.

239. Harry Emerson Fosdick, "Contemporary Meanings in an Old Word—Salvation," sermon for December 5, 1937, manuscript in Union Theological Seminary archives, p. 5. Cf. TNYT, December 6, 1937, p. 28.

240. Fosdick, "This Is a Miraculous World," sermon for December 12, 1937, (radio, January 16, 1938) manuscript in Union Theological Seminary archives, p. 6.

241. Leininger, pp. 142-43. Leininger finds in the twenties and early thirties a manifest sensitivity to sin in modern life "when it was not fashionable among liberal preachers to do so" (pp. 142-43).

242. Bonney, pp. 66-69.

243. Harry Emerson Fosdick, "A Strange World in Which to Be Christian," sermon for September 25, 1938, manuscript in Union Theological Seminary archives, pp. 7, 9.

244. Fosdick, "The Modern World's Rediscovery of Sin," in Living Under Tension, p. 115. Cf. TNYT, December 19, 1938, p. 20, and August 14, 1939, p. 16.

245. *TNYT*, October 30, 1933, p. 13.

246. Fosdick, "The Modern World's Rediscovery of Sin," in *Living Under Tension*, p. 120.

247. Ibid., pp. 112-13, 115.

248. *TNYT*, July 29, 1940, p. 11.

249. Harry Emerson Fosdick, "When Man Grows Tired of Freedom," sermon for April 23, 1939, manuscript in Union Theological Seminary archives, p. 1.

250. *TNYT*, April 7, 1941, p. 20.

251. Fosdick, "Achieving Personal Integrity," sermon for November 2, 1941 (radio, November 23, 1941), manuscript in Union Theological Seminary archives, p. 1.

252. Harry Emerson Fosdick, "Mastering depression," sermon for October 12, 1941, manuscript in Union Theological Seminary archives, p. 11-12.

253. Harry Emerson Fosdick, "Making the Best of a Bad Mess," sermon for March 2, 1930, and July 13, 1941, in *The Hope of the World*, p. 119.

254. Fosdick, "The Principle of Released Power," sermon for November 20, 1938 (radio, January 15, 1939), manuscript in Union Theological Seminary archives, p. 8.

255. Harry Emerson Fosdick, "Life's Central Demand: Be a Real Person," sermon for October 16, 1938, manuscript in Union Theological Seminary archives, pp. 1ff. Cf. *TNYT*, October 17, 1938, p. 11.

256. *TNYT*, May 6, 1940, p. 11.

257. George A. Buttrick, "Escape from Responsibility," sermon for April 14, 1940, in the *Madison Avenue Presbyterian Church News*, May 31, 1940, p. 5.

CHAPTER VII

1. George A. Buttrick, "Being a Christian," sermon for March 4, 1934, manuscript at Harvard University, number MA 547, p. 1.

2. George A. Buttrick, "Doubt Diversified with Love," sermon for January 28, 1934, in the *Madison Avenue Presbyterian Church Weekly* (October 5, 1934), p. 5 (hereafter cited as *Weekly*). The same point, in essentially the same words is made in *The Christian Fact and Modern Doubt* (New York: C. Scribner, 1935), p. 12.

3. Jeremiah 3:16.

4. George A. Buttrick, "Living Temples: The New Ark of God," sermon for November 23, 1930, manuscript at Harvard University, number MA 321, pp. 4-5, 7, 10.

5. Willis Stanley Gertner, "Paul Scherer: Preacher and Homiletician," unpub. Ph.D. dissertation, Wayne State University (1967), p. 4.

6. Ibid., pp. 6-7.

7. Ibid., p. 7.

8. Buttrick, *The Christian Fact and Modern Doubt*, p. 122. Cf. George A. Buttrick, "On Earth the Broken Arc," sermon for May 22, 1938, in *The Hyphen* (interim newsletter published for two months by the Madison Avenue Presbyterian Church) September 16, 1938, p. 3: "The grandeur of a creed is that it is a banner to rally our inborn faith—not an excursion into theology. The danger of a creed is that it should pretend to know too much about God and His ways." There is also the sermon for April 3, 1932, "At the End of Emmaus Road" (manuscript at Harvard University, number, MA 420, p. 8) which says God "can never be held within the walls of a church or a creed."

9. George A. Buttrick, "With Us, Yet Unknown," sermon for February 1, 1931, *Weekly*, March 6, 1931, p. 6.

10. George A. Buttrick, "Our Church—Today and Tomorrow," sermon for March 13, 1932, manuscript at Harvard University, number MA 414,

pp. 5-6. He resented the way Christians wasted time in petty doctrinal bickering when the time and energy could have been put to better use working in the slums. (George A. Buttrick, "Jesus and the Home," sermon for May 8, 1932, manuscript at Harvard University, number MA 427, p. 7.)

11. George A. Buttrick, "Our Church Today and Tomorrow," sermon for March 13, 1932, manuscript at Harvard University, number MA 414, p. 6. "It is Presbyterian indeed, and strives to fulfill its obligation to its own communion . . . but this church lays no undue stress on the denominational label."

12. George A. Buttrick, "The Function of the Church," sermon for March 11, 1934, manuscript at Harvard University, number MA 549, p. 13.

13. Buttrick, *The Christian Fact and Modern Doubt*, p. 121.

14. George A. Buttrick, "In the Hour of Trial," sermon for the evening of October 11, 1931, manuscript at Harvard University, number MA 382, p. 5.

15. George A. Buttrick, "The Courage of Faith," sermon delivered in Pittsburgh, June 29, 1929, in the *Weekly*, July 5, 1929, p. 4.

16. Ibid., p. 6.

17. George A. Buttrick, "Keeping the Faith," sermon for the evening of June 12, 1927, in the *Weekly*, August 5, 1927, pp. 4-5.

18. George A. Buttrick, "The Beloved Leader," sermon for November 29, 1931, in the *Weekly*, February 5, 1932, p. 4.

19. George A. Buttrick, "Prayer—the Way," sermon for January 31, 1932, in the *Weekly*, May 6, 1932, p. 7. Two months earlier he said that the essence of the Christian faith resides in the dictum that "what is highest in man is deepest in nature." (George A. Buttrick, "The Loneliness of Christ," sermon for November 22, 1931, in the *Weekly*, June 10, 1932, p. 5.)

20. George A. Buttrick, "There Were Shepherds," sermon for December 21, 1930, manuscript at Harvard University, number MA 329, pp. 8-9.

21. George A. Buttrick, "The Word Became Flesh," sermon for December 28, 1930, manuscript at Harvard University, number MA 330, pp. 6-7.

22. Ibid., p. 8.

23. George A. Buttrick, *Jesus Came Preaching: Christian Preaching in a New Age* (New York: Scribner's Sons, 1931), pp. 131-39.

24. Ibid., p. 141.

25. George A. Buttrick, "The Word Became Flesh," sermon for December 28, 1930, manuscript at Harvard University, number MA 330, p. 9.

26. George A. Buttrick, "What I Would Like This Church to Teach My Children," sermon for October 25, 1931, manuscript at Harvard University, number MA 384, p. 2. Cf. "Christ and Children," sermon for October 29, 1933 in the *Weekly*, December 1, 1933, where Buttrick speaks of "fundamental reverences wrought into our nature." And cf. also "Religion and the Home," sermon for February 4, 1940, in the Madison Avenue Presbyterian Church News, February 9, 1940, p. 5 (hereafter cited as *MAPC News*), where he says that we do not choose religion but rather it chooses us "from our inmost nature."

27. George A. Buttrick, "Blind Bartimaeus," sermon for June 19, 1932, manuscript at Harvard University, number MA 438, p. 7.

28. *TNYT*, June 20, 1932, p. 13.

29. George A. Buttrick, "Signs of These Times," sermon for November 11, 1934, manuscript at Harvard University, number MA 583, p. 9.

30. George A. Buttrick, "The Church and the Present Crisis," sermon for March 12, 1933, in the *Weekly*, April 7, 1933, p. 5.

31. George A. Buttrick, "The Rich Young Ruler," sermon for September 11, 1932, manuscript at Harvard University, number MA 440, p. 3. The *New York Times* published an account of the same sermon the following day, and quoted Buttrick's statistics as referring to ten percent of the world's wealth. (*TNYT*, September 12, 1932, p. 22.)

32. Buttrick, *Jesus Came Preaching*, p. 52.

33. George A. Buttrick, "The Finality of Christ," sermon for March 18, 1934, manuscript at Harvard University, number MA 550, p. 11.

34. Buttrick, *The Christian Fact and Modern Doubt*, p. 152.

35. Buttrick, "Can We Believe in Life Everlasting?" sermon for April 1, 1934, manuscript at Harvard University, number MA 555, p. 9.

36. George A. Buttrick, "They Died in Faith," sermon for September 25, 1932, manuscript at Harvard University, number MA 445, p. 9.

37. Ibid., p. 6.

38. One of Buttrick's principles involved a commitment to marriage as an institution which should not be terminated by divorce without sufficient cause. When one of his parishioners, Henry Robinson Luce, arranged to divorce his wife to marry Claire Booth, Buttrick refused the bride-groom's request that he perform the ceremony. Buttrick's grounds for refusal were that no legitimate reason existed for the divorce. The *Weekly* (on April 10, 1936) published a note that Luce had resigned from the Board of Trustees, to which he had been elected just two years earlier (*Weekly*, April 27, 1934). He and Claire Booth were married in a Congregational Church in Connecticut. But a far more celebrated case, also involving a wedding, occurred during his years at Harvard, when he refused to remove or disguise the Christian symbols at Harvard's Memorial Church to accommodate the wishes of a Harvard couple for a non-Christian wedding. Nathan Pusey, the president of the University, supported Buttrick's position. Faculty members including Arthur M. Schlesinger, Jr., John Kenneth Galbraith, and Perry Miller opposed Buttrick. (*TNYT*, November 24, 1935, Section II, p. 5, reports on the Luce wedding; see *TNYT*, April 19, 1958, p. 23, for a report on the Harvard Memorial Church controversy.)

39. *TNYT*, December 5, 1932, p. 15. The sermon text, "The Christian and the World," was published in the *Weekly*, September 1, 1933, pp. 4ff.

40. *TNYT*, May 14, 1934, p. 14. Cf. "Pilgrims," in *Summer Monthly*, a newsletter published by the Madison Avenue Presbyterian Church in lieu of the *Weekly*, August 3, 1934, p. 3.

41. George A. Buttrick, "More Than Conquerors," sermon for January 21, 1934, in the *Weekly*, February 2, 1934, p. 3.

42. George A. Buttrick, "The Alabaster Box: Anointed Unto Death," sermon for April 9, 1933, manuscript at Harvard University, number MA 497, pp. 3-4.

43. Buttrick, "Pilgrims," in *Summer Monthly*, August 3, 1934, p. 4.

44. George A. Buttrick, "Christ Gives Repentence [sic]," sermon for November 6, 1932, manuscript at Harvard University, number MA 453, p. 6.

45. George A. Buttrick, "The Return to God," sermon for April 2, 1933, manuscript at Harvard University, number MA 495, p. 7.

46. George A. Buttrick, "The Untroubled Heart," sermon for May 22, 1932, in the *Summer Monthly*, August 5, 1932, p. 6.

47. In "Pilgrims," *Summer Monthly*, August 3, 1934, p. 3, Buttrick discusses the point that we shall always be strangers in the world and adds: "I would not have spoken to you thus ten or fifteen years ago; it is one of the kindly illusions of youth to assume that the brimming zest of physical powers is ever undrained."

48. George A. Buttrick, "Seeing and Believing," sermon for April 28, 1935, manuscript at Harvard University, number MA 626, p. 7. Cf. the *Summer Monthly*, June 7, 1935, p. 5.

49. George A. Buttrick, "The Means of Grace," sermon for November 21, 1937, manuscript at Harvard University, number MA 784, p. 2.

50. Buttrick, *Jesus Came Preaching*, p. 45.

51. George A. Buttrick, "The Nameless of a Thousand Names," sermon for May 19, 1937, in *Summer Monthly*, August 6, 1937, p. 3.

52. George A. Buttrick, "Saved by Grace," sermon for October 6, 1935, manuscript at Harvard University, number MA 641, p. 1-2.

53. Ibid., p. 7.

54. George A. Buttrick, "The Focus of Religion," sermon for May 24, 1936, in the *Summer Monthly*, July 3, 1936, p. 5.

55. George A. Buttrick, "Why We Are Christians," sermon for October 25, 1936, manuscript at Harvard University, number MA 705, p. 9.

56. George A. Buttrick, "Time, the Interpreter," sermon for December 29, 1935, in the *Weekly*, February 1, 1936, p. 5.

57. George A. Buttrick, "But We See Jesus," sermon for December 29, 1935, in the *Weekly*, February 7, 1936, p. 4.

58. George A. Buttrick, "The Cure of Care," sermon for May 23, 1937, in the *Weekly*, September 3, 1937, pp. 4-6.

59. George A. Buttrick, "The Yoke of Jesus," sermon for September 19, 1937, in the *Weekly*, October 1, 1937, pp. 3-4.

60. George A. Buttrick, "Christ and the Conscience," sermon for March 27, 1932, manuscript at Harvard University, number MA 416, p. 7.

61. George A. Buttrick, "The Cross and Discipleship," sermon for March 6, 1938, manuscript at Harvard University, number MA 810, p. 3.

62. George A. Buttrick, "The Cross and Our Doubts," sermon for March 27, 1938, manuscript at Harvard University, number MA 816, p. 7.

63. Ibid., p. 9.

64. George A. Buttrick, "The Tower of Babel," sermon for February 12, 1939, manuscript at Harvard University, number MA 871, p. 2.

65. Ibid., p. 8.

66. George A. Buttrick, "Prayer and Faith," sermon for March 10, 1940, manuscript at Harvard Universlty, number MA 953, p. 9.

67. George A. Buttrick, "Prayer, Hope, and Immortality," sermon for March 24, 1940, manuscript at Harvard University, number MA 958, p. 5.

68. George A. Buttrick, "Benediction," sermon for November 2, 1941, manuscript at Harvard Univeristy number 1039, p. 2.

69. George A. Buttrick, "Quest, Clue, and Conviction," sermon for July 16, 1939, manuscript at Harvard University, number MA 906, p. 5.

70. George A. Buttrick, "Interpretations," sermon for January 21, 1940, manuscript at Harvard University, number MA 939, p. 7.

71. George A. Buttrick, "The Transforming Cause," sermon for December 4, 1938, in *MAPC News*, January 9, 1939, p. 6.

72. George A. Buttrick, *The Parables of Jesus* (Garden City, N.Y.: Doubleday, 1928), p. 163.

73. George A. Buttrick, "The Transforming Cause," sermon for December 4, 1938, in *MAPC News*, January 6, 1937, p. 6.

74. George A. Buttrick, "Horizons," sermon for September 18, 1938, in the *Hyphen*, October 7, 1938, p. 3.

75. *TNYT*, October 23, 1939, p. 16.

76. George A. Buttrick, *The Christian Fact and Modern Doubt* (New York: C. Scribner, 1935), p. 62.

77. George A. Buttrick, "The God of Jacob," sermon for February 19, 1939, in *MAPC News*, April 7, 1939, pp. 6-7.

78. George A. Buttrick, "A Watchtower and a Watchword," sermon for November 19, 1939, in *MAPC News*, December 29, 1939, p. 5.

79. George A. Buttrick, "The Divine Intensity," sermon for March 2, 1940, in *MAPC News*, March 7, 1941, p. 6.

80. George A. Buttrick, "The Elusiveness of God," sermon for April 27, 1941, in *MAPC News*, May 9, 1941, pp. 5-6.

81. George A. Buttrick, "A Watchtower and a Watchword," sermon for November 19, 1939, in *MAPC News*, December 29, 1939, p. 5.

82. George A. Buttrick, "Spectators or Gladiators," sermon for January 28, 1940, in *MAPC News*, February 2, 1940, p. 4.

83. George A. Buttrick, "The Pride of God," sermon for June 1, 1941, in *MAPC News*, July 3, 1941, pp. 5-6.

84. George A. Buttrick, "The Uses of Mystery," sermon for November 12, 1939, in *MAPC News*, October 31, 1941, p. 4.

85. *TNYT*, March 14, 1938, p. l0.

86. George A. Buttrick, "To Good and Bad Alike?" sermon for October 19, 1941, in *MAPC News*, December 16, 1941, p. 4.

87. Buttrick, *Christian Fact and Modern Doubt*, p. 76.

88. Ibid., p. 71.

89. Ibid., p. 76.

90. Ibid., pp. 76-77. Cf. p. 91, "The truth is an axiom in every human soul, and it is graven on the pillars of the world. But we shall not be sure of certitudes until we live in them."

91. Ibid., p. 71.

92. Ibid., p. 146.

93. Ibid., p. 91.

94. George A. Buttrick, "Unknown Road," sermon for January 2, 1938, manuscript at Harvard University, number MA 796, p. 4.

95. Buttrick, *The Christian Fact and Modern Doubt*, pp. 170-71.

96. Ibid., p. 160.

97. Ibid., p. 163.

98. Ibid., p. 184.

99. George A. Buttrick, "The Winning of the Soul," sermon for January 11, 1931, manuscript at Harvard University, number MA 334, p. 6. Also, George A. Buttrick, "Does Experience Yield Hope?" sermon for July 9, 1939, manuscript number MA 904, p. l.

100. Buttrick, *The Christian Fact and Modern Doubt*, p. 185.

101. George A. Buttrick, "The Sign of a Savior," sermon for December 23, 1928, in the *Weekly*, January 4, 1929, p. 3.

102. George A. Buttrick, "The Creation," sermon for January 15, 1939, in *MAPC News*, February 3, 1939, p. 4.

103. George A. Buttrick, "The Port of Wishing Folk," sermon for February 11, 1934, in the *Weekly*, March 2, 1934, p. 5.

104. George A. Buttrick, "The Creation," sermon for January 15, 1939, in *MAPC News*, February 3, 1939, p. 4.

105. George A. Buttrick, "But We See Jesus . . .," sermon for December 29, 1935, in the *Weekly*, February 7, 1936, p. 4.

106. George A. Buttrick, "Vocation," sermon for January 26, 1930, in the *Weekly*, March 7, 1930, p. 3.

107. George A. Buttrick, "Foreign Missions Today," sermon for January 27, 1929, in the *Weekly*, March 1, 1929, p. 6.

108. George A. Buttrick, "The Courage of Faith," in the *Weekly*, July 5, 1929, p. 3.

109. George A. Buttrick, "The Bible and Today," sermon for December 10, 1933, manuscript at Harvard University, number MA 530, p. 3.

110. George A. Buttrick, "Living Temples: The New Ark of God," sermon for November 23, 1930, manuscript at Harvard University, number MA 321, p. 5. Also, George A. Buttrick, "Wind in the Trees," sermon for December 6, 1931, in the *Weekly*, January 1, 1932, p. 3; and George A. Buttrick, "Jesus and the Home," sermon for May 8, 1932, manuscript at Harvard University number MA 427, p. 1.

111. Buttrick, *The Christian Fact and Modern Doubt*, pp. 166-67.

112. George A. Buttrick, "The Creation," sermon for January 15, 1939, in *MAPC News*, Feburary 3, 1939, p. 4.

113. Ibid.

114. Buttrick, *Jesus Came Preaching*, p. 147.

115. George A. Buttrick, "Perfection Through Suffering," sermon for April 4, 1937, manuscript at Harvard University, number MA 748, p. 1.

116. George A. Buttrick, "He That Hath Seen Me," sermon for December 27, 1931, manuscript at Harvard University, number MA 399, p. 1.

117. Buttrick, *Jesus Came Preaching*, p. 147.

118. George A. Buttrick, "The Bible and Today," sermon for December 10, 1933, manuscript at Harvard University, number MA 530, p. 9.

119. George A. Buttrick, "The Authority of Jesus," sermon for June 25, 1933, in the *Weekly*, July 7, 1933, p. 3.

120. The diagram is one used by Buttrick in his courses on sermon outlines. It was reproduced in Stevens, pp. 120ff.

121. Ibid.

122. George A. Buttrick, "Altar Fire," sermon for November 9, 1941, manuscript at Harvard University, number MA 1041, p. 4.

123. Ibid., pp. 4-5.

124. Buttrick, *Jesus Came Preaching*, p. 67.

125. Buttrick, *The Christian Fact and Modern Doubt*, p. 101.

126. Buttrick, *The Parables of Jesus*, p. 190.

127. Ibid., pp. 190-91.

128. Ibid., p. 69.

129. George A. Buttrick, "Christ and the Will," sermon for February 28, 1932, manuscript at Harvard University, number MA 412, p. 2.

130. Ibid., pp. 3-4.

131. George A. Buttrick, "The Incarnation," sermon for December 20, 1931, manuscript at Harvard University, number 397, p. 9.

132. George A. Buttrick, "God's Workmanship," sermon for January 23, 1938, in the *Weekly*, March 4, 1938, p. 5.

133. Buttrick, *Jesus Came Preaching*, p. 37.

134. Buttrick, *The Christian Fact and Modern Doubt*, pp. 205-6.

135. George A. Buttrick, "The Disciplines of Liberty," sermon for October 30, 1938, in *MAPC News*, March 3, l939, p. 5.

136. Buttrick, *The Parables of Jesus*, p. 77.

137. George A. Buttrick, "The Unfolding of Truth," sermon for May 27, 1934, manuscript at Harvard University, number MA 567, p. 3.

138. George A. Buttrick, untitled sermon for February 17, 1929, in the *Weekly*, April 5, 1929, p. 3.

139. George A. Buttrick, "The Potter and the Clay," sermon for May 17, 1931, manuscript at Harvard University, numher MA 365, p. 5. Cf. *TNYT*, May 18, 1931, p. 15.

140. George A. Buttrick, "Why Does God Hide Himself?" sermon for September 28, 1930, manuscript at Harvard University, number MA 305, p. 6.

141. Ibid., p. 7.

142. George A. Buttrick, "The Untroubled Heart," sermon for May 22, 1932, in the *Weekly*, August 5, 1932, p. 6.

143. Buttrick, *The Christian Fact and Modern Doubt*, p. 282.

144. George A. Buttrick, "He that Hath Seen Me," sermon for December 27, 1931, manuscript at Harvard University, number MA 399, p. l.

145. *TNYT*, November 20, 1933, v. 13.

146. *TNYT*, June 4, 1934, p. 13.

147. "If we are to become good, there must be evil in such a universe (at least potential evil), for no goodness is real which does not choose between good and evil." (George A. Buttrick, "The Challenge of Pain," sermon for November 24, 1929, in the *Weekly*, November 29, 1929, p. 6).

148. George A. Buttrick, "The Mystery of Outward Disaster," sermon for February 21, 1937, manuscript at Harvard University, number MA 734, p. 8.

149. George A. Buttrick, "The Problem of Suffering: Some Elements in the Christian Answer," sermon for March 14, 1937, manuscript at Harvard University, number MA 740, pp. 2-3.

150. George A. Buttrick, "The Sacramental Value of Life," sermon for January 6, 1935, manuscript at Harvard University, number MA 598, p. 5.

151. George A. Buttrick, "Christ's Appeal to Human Judgment," sermon for February 22, 1931, in the *Weekly*, September 18, 1931, p. 5.

152.   George A. Buttrick, "Life's Business Being Just the Terrible Choice," sermon for June 3, 1934, manuscript at Harvard University, number MA 569, pp. l, 10.

153. George A. Buttrick, "Christ and the Will," sermon for February 28, 1932, manuscript at Harvard University, number MA 412, pp. 7-10.

154. Ibid., pp. 10-ll.

155. George A. Buttrick, "Aeroplane Thoughts on Religion," sermon for October 16, 1932, manuscript at Harvard University, number MA 448, pp. 4-5.

156. George A. Buttrick, "Saved by Grace," sermon for October 6, 1935, manuscript at Harvard University, number MA 641, p. 5.

157.   George A. Buttrick, "Nearer than Hands and Feet," sermon for September 22, 1935, in the *Weekly*, October 4, 1935, p. 6.

158. George A. Buttrick, "God's Workmanship," sermon for January 23, 1938, in the *Weekly*, March 4, 1938, p. 5.

159. George A. Buttrick, "Windows in Heaven," sermon for December 11, 1938, in *MAPC News*, December 16, 1938, p. 4. For instance, if we prayed for God to kill Hitler, we are asking God to become a Hitler (George A. Buttrick, "Is it Any Way to Pray for Peace?" sermon for September 24, 1939, manuscript at Harvard University, number MA 915).

160. George A. Buttrick, "The Creation," sermon for January 15, 1939, in *MAPC News*, February 3, 1939, p. 4.

161. George A. Buttrick, "The Interpretation of the Cross," sermon for March 20, 1938, manuscript at Harvard University, number MA 810, p. 4.

162. *TNYT*, December 30, 1940, p. 15.

163. George A. Buttrick, "What Shall an American Do Now?" sermon for September 17, 1939, in *MAPC News*, November 10, 1939, p. 7.

164. George A. Buttrick, "Altar Fire," sermon for November 9, 1941, manuscript at Harvard University, number MA 1041, p. 4.

165. *TNYT*, May 18, 1931, p. 15.

166. George A. Buttrick, "Does God Care?" sermon for June 2, 1940, in *MAPC News*, July 5, 1940, p. 5.

167. George A. Buttrick, "Basic Confidence," sermon for September 25, 1938, manuscript at Harvard University, number MA 839, p. 3.

168. George A. Buttrick, "Dusty Answer," sermon for October 2, 1938, in the *Weekly*, November 4, 1938, n.p.

169. Four million copies of *Gone with the Wind* were sold making it the best-selling book of the century. A 1938 Gallup poll said it was "running neck and neck with the Bible in popularity," (Dixon Wecter, *The Age of The Great Depression: 1929-1941* [Chicago: Quadrangle Books, 1971], p. 158.)

INTERLUDE

1. Harry Emerson Fosdick, "A Plea for Fellowship," sermon for March 22, 1936, manuscript at Union Theological Seminary Archives, p. 8.

2. Ibid., p. 12.

3. George A. Buttrick, "Time, the Interpreter," sermon for January 20, 1935, in the *Weekly*, February 1, 1935, p. 5.

4. Margaret Mitchell, *Gone with the Wind* (New York: Macmillan Co., 1936), p. 1037.

CHAPTER VIII

1. Paul E. Scherer, "Why Put On?" sermon for November 30, 1941, manuscript at Union Theological Seminary, vol. IV, series II, pp. 81b.

2. Paul E. Scherer, "God Is His Own Interpreter," sermon for December 7, 1941, manuscript at Union Theological Seminary, vol. IV, series II, p. 82a.

3. Ibid., p. 82b.

4. Ibid., p. 84b. He did say a year later, however, that "the fundamental principles upon which democracy was built have been rooted from Christian soil" (*TNYT*, November 9, 1942, p. 18).

5. Harry Emerson Fosdick, "Loyalty, the Basic Condition of Liberty," sermon for December 7, 1941, in *A Great Time to Be Alive: Sermons on Christianity in War Time* (London: SCM Press, 1945), p. 140. [Hereafter, *Great Time*]

6. Ibid., p. 143.

7. George A. Buttrick, "Our Homelessness," sermon for December 7, 1941, in *MAPC News*, January 23, 1942, p. 2.

8. Ibid., p. 2.

9. Ibid., p. 4.

10. Ralph W. Sockman, "Where Enemies Enter Not," sermon for December 7, 1941, manuscript in the Syracuse University archives Box 15, p. 13.

11. Fosdick, *The Living of These Days*, p. 295.

12. Paul E. Scherer, "Prison Moods," sermon for December 14, 1941, manuscript at Union Theological Seminary, Miscellaneous Sermons volume, p. 93b.

13. Sockman, "Forty Years of Fosdick," p. 293.

14. Paul E. Scherer, "The Peril and Promise of the Unusual," sermon for May 5, 1935, manuscript at Union Theological Seminary, vol. IV, series II, p. 169a.

15. Fosdick, *The Living of These Days*, p. 195. Fosdick had considered leaving Riverside to become a Quaker.

16. Paul E. Scherer, "The Faithfulness of God," sermon for October 24, 1943, manuscript at Union Theological Seminary, vol. V, series II, pp. 493b-494a.

17. Scherer, "Prison Moods," p. 32. (The pages here are numbered out of sequence; this one follows p. 93.)

18. Scherer "The Faithfulness of God," sermon for October 24, 1943, manuscript at Union Theological Seminary archives, vol. V, series II, p. 494a.

19. Paul E. Scherer, "Some Strange Thing," sermon for January 4, 1942, manuscript at Union Theological Seminary, vol. V, series II, p. 106b.

20. Interview with Geneva Helm. In his Beecher lectures, *The Highway of God*, Sockman said that "the grim conclusion" has been reached by "the pulpit majority that war is still the lesser evil in more than one situation" (p. 20). Hibbard wrote that Sockman was a pacifist before the war, but after December 7, 1941, he sought "to bring the conflict to a peaceful conclusion as soon as possible. Therefore, he cannot be called a thorough-going pacifist" (Hibbard, p. 153).

21. *TNYT*, December 15, 1941, p. 28.

22. Harry Emerson Fosdick, "The Church of Christ in a Warring World," sermon for December 14, 1941, manuscript at Union Theological Seminary, p. 8. This was broadcast twice on radio: at the special time of 8:00 p.m. on December 14 and again at the usual time of 4:00 p.m. on the following Sunday.

23. Ibid., p. 7.

24. *TNYT*, December 15, 1941, p. 28.

25. George A. Buttrick, "God With Us," sermon for December 14, 1941, manuscript at Harvard University, number MA 1051, p. 4.

26. Ibid., p. 1.

27. Ibid., p. 4.

28. Ibid., p. 7. A dozen or so from the Madison Avenue Presbyterian Church were listed as conscientious objectors. (About 750 members of the Church were in uniform during the war. Charles N. Davidson, "George Arthur Buttrick; Christocentric Preacher and Pacifist," *Journal of Presbyterian History* 53 [Summer 1975]: 148-49.)

29. George A. Buttrick, "God with Us," sermon for December 14, 1941, manuscript at Harvard University, number MA 1051, p. 6.

30. Harry Emerson Fosdick, "Maintaining the Spiritual Front," sermon for January 10, 1943, manuscript at Union Theological Seminary.

31. Ralph W. Sockman, "The Contagion of Courage," sermon for May 2, 1943, manuscript at Syracuse University.

32. A dentist named Dr. Charles Hattauer, who was a member of Madison Avenue Presbyterian, had among his patients his own pastor, George Buttrick, and other prominent New Yorkers including Ralph Sockman and Gov. Thomas E. Dewey. When the black-out provisions were announced, the dentist reminded the governor by letter that Sunday evening services would have to be abandoned at great cost to public morale. Soon afterward, the black-out regulations for Sunday evening were waived.

33. Paul E. Scherer, *Event in Eternity* (New York: Harper and Bros., 1945), p. 126.

34. The persistent anxiety about German U-boats in the vicinity of New York harbor remained, of course.

35. Ralph W. Sockman, "The Tie That Binds," sermon for October 4, 1942, manuscript at Syracuse University, Box 25, p. 3.

36. *MAPC News*, May 17, 1946, p. 1. Shortly after VE day, a memorial service was held at Madison Avenue Presbyterian, with Buttrick preaching "The Heroic Past—and Tomorrow," on May 27, 1945, in *MAPC News*, June 29, 1945, pp. 3ff.

37. *MAPC News*, July 31, 1942, p. 6.

38. *MAPC News*, November 19, 1943, p. 8.

39. *MAPC News*, December 10, 1943. Other information came in an interview with Ethel King of Madison Avenue Presbyterian Church. For a sketch of Riverside's wartime ministries, see Fosdick, *The Living of These Days*, p. 300; and Robert Moats Miller, *Harry Emerson Fosdick*, pp. 535ff.

40. Paul E. Scherer, "There They Crucified Him," sermon for April 3, 1942, manuscript at Union Theological Seminary, vol. IV, series II, p. 168a.

41. *TNYT*, March 6, 1944, p. 22.

42. Paul E. Scherer, "The Steep Ascent," sermon for February 18, 1945, manuscript at Union Theological Seminary, vol. IV, series II, p. 211a.

43. Sockman, *The Highway of God*, p. 21.

44. Harry Emerson Fosdick, "One Kingdom that Cannot be Shaken," sermon for March 1, 1942, manuscript at Union Theological Seminary, p. 4.

45. Paul E. Scherer, "Behind the Scenes," sermon for December 21, 1941, manuscript at Union theological Seminary, vol. VI, series II, p. 102a. "The central fact in this world is God," he said ("On Getting the Better of Evil," sermon for January 24, 1943, manuscript at Union Theological Seminary, vol. V, series II, p. 334a).

46. Paul E. Scherer, "The Day of the Lord is Darkness," sermon for September 20, 1942, manuscript at Union Theological Seminary, vol. V, series II, p. 259a.

47. Ibid., p. 259a.

48. George A. Buttrick, "The Exile Test," sermon for February 14, 1943, manuscript at Harvard University, number MA 1136, p. 1.

49. *TNYT*, February 14, 1944, p. 20.

50. Paul E. Scherer, "Does Christianity Have a Ghost of a Chance?" sermon for March 11, 1945, manuscript at Union Theological Seminary, vol. V, series II, p. 226a.

51. Paul E. Scherer, "Through Defeat to Victory," sermon for March 14, 1943, manuscript at Union Theological Seminary, vol. IV, series II, p. 363a.

52. Paul E. Scherer, "Now Is Christ Risen," sermon for April 5, 1942, manuscript at Union Theological Seminary, vol. IV, series II, p. 171b.

53. Paul E. Scherer, "Take That Thine Is," sermon for January 28, 1945, manuscript at Union Theological Seminary, vol. IV, series II, p. 194a.

54. Paul E. Scherer, "Pride and Prejudice," sermon for March 22, 1942, manuscript at Union Theological Seminary, vol. V, series II, pp. 157a-157b.

55. *TNYT*, May 11, 1942, p. 9.

56. Harry Emerson Fosdick, "A Kind of Penitence that Does Some Good," sermon for October 11, 1942, in *Great Time*, p. 84; "A Time to Stress Unity," sermon for February 13, 1944, in *Great Time*, p. 153;

"What Do Ye More Than Others?" sermon for May 10, 1942, manuscript at Union Theological Seminary, p. 7. Ralph W. Sockman, "Running Away from Life," sermon for January 18, 1942, manuscript at Syracuse University, Box 24, p. 23.

57. Paul E. Scherer, "The Alert," sermon for December 28, 1941, manuscript at Union Theological Seminary, vol. V, series II, pp. 109a-109b.

58. Ralph W. Sockman, "Strength for the Day," sermon for January 4, 1942, manuscript at Syracuse University, Box 25, p. 6.

59. *TNYT*, May 10, 1943, p. 13; February 21, 1944, p. 13; March 6, 1944, p. 22; April 24, 1944, p. 15; May 15, 1944, p. 24. It is worth noting that Fosdick's daughter Dorothy worked for the State Department and, beginning with Dumbarton Oaks, she was active in every conference leading up to the establishment of the United Nations. Fosdick's brother Raymond had been active in the preliminary stages of organization for the League of Nations a generation earlier (Fosdick, *The Living of These Days*, pp. 308-9).

60. Harry Emerson Fosdick, "Worshipping the Gods of a Beaten Enemy," sermon for November 21, 1943, in *Great Time*, p. 159. Cf. *TNYT*, November 22, 1943, p. 19.

61. *TNYT*, November 20, 1944, p. 16.

62. George A. Buttrick, "Goal and Power," sermon for November 5, 1944, manuscript at Harvard University, number MA 1261, pp. 1-2.

63. Ibid., p. 2.

64. Ibid., pp. 4-5.

65. Paul E. Scherer, "The Necessity of Religion," sermon for April 4, 1943, manuscript at Union Theological Seminary, vol. V, series II, pp. 375-76.

66. Ibid., p. 378b.

67. Harry Emerson Fosdick, "Fresh Light on an Old Beatitude," sermon for October 22, 1944, radio manuscript at Union Theological Seminary, p. 4. Cf. *TNYT*, October 23, 1944, p. 14.

68. Harry Emerson Fosdick, "Christmas This Year Means Something Special," sermon for December 20, 1942, manuscript at Union Theological Seminary, p. 9.

69. Harry Emerson Fosdick, "A Religion That Really Gets Us," sermon for March 14, 1943, in *What Is Vital in Religion: Sermons on Contemporary Christianity* (New York: Harper, 1955), p. 56. Cf. *TNYT*, March 15, 1943, p. 9.

70. Harry Emerson Fosdick, "After Forty Years in the Ministry," sermon for November 14, 1943, in *Great Time*, pp. 201-2.

71. Ibid., p. 202. Cf. *TNYT*, November 15, 1943, p. 16.

72. George A. Buttrick, "The Sign at Bethlehem," sermon for December 20, 1942, in *MAPC News*, December 17, 1943, p. 4.

73. Paul E. Scherer, "Measure for Measure," sermon for June 24, 1945, manuscript at Union Theological Seminary, Miscellaneous Sermons, vol. B, p. 297a.

74. Ibid., p. 297a.

CHAPTER IX

1. Ralph W. Sockman, "Christ and Him Crucified," sermon for April 19, 1942, manuscript at Syracuse University, p. 1. A few early manuscripts did escape the flames, however. In July, 1945, Sockman reported having stumbled across a sermon from 1923, which contained a paragraph that "I am rather glad I wrote somehow or other." (Ralph W. Sockman, "The Magic of Mutual Trust," sermon for July 1, 1945, manuscript at Syracuse University, p. 6.) Fosdick, too, destroyed his sermons from the Montclair days. (Douglas M. Lawson, "The Idea of Progress in the Theology of Harry Emerson Fosdick," Ph.D. dissertation, Duke University, 1968, p. viii.) On Scherer, see p. 334, n. 50 below.

2. Hibbard, p. 95.

3. Sockman, "Christ and Him Crucified," sermon for April 19, 1942, pp. 3, 11.

4. Quoted by *TNYT*, July 10, 1944, p. 8.

5. Sockman, *The Highway of God*, pp. 77f.

6. Ralph W. Sockman, "The Cost of Conviction," sermon for February 27, 1944, manuscript at Syracuse University, p. 2.

7. Ralph W. Sockman, "Sharing Our Spiritual Wealth," sermon for July 15, 1945, manuscript at Syracuse University, pp. 5-6.

8. Ralph W. Sockman, *Date with Destiny: A Preamble to Christian Culture* (New York, Nashville: Abingdon-Cokesbury, 1944) p. 49.

9. Ibid., pp. 49-51.

10. Ibid., p. 54.

11. Ralph W. Sockman, "Religion's Third Front," sermon for October 11, 1942, manuscript at Syracuse University, p. 5.

12. Ibid., pp. 8-10.

13. Sockman, *The Highway of God*, pp. 5-6.

14. Ralph W. Sockman, "Determiners of Destiny," sermon for November 15, 1942, manuscript at Syracuse University, p. 3.

15. Ralph W. Sockman, "The Investment of Influence," sermon for January 28, 1945, manuscript at Syracuse University, p. 3. (Alternate title, "Men and Their Shadows.")

16. Ralph W. Sockman, "The Vital Spark," sermon for February 22, 1942, manuscript at Syracuse University, p. 3.

17. Sockman, *Date with Destiny*, p. 73.

18. Sockman, *Highway of God*, p. 79.

19. Sockman, *Date with Destiny*, p. 156.

20. Ibid., p. 33.

21. Sockman, *Highway of God*, p. 16.

22. Quoted by *TNYT*, April 20, 1942, p. 12.

23. Sockman, "Determiners of Destiny," sermon for November 15, 1942, pp. 12-15.

24. Hibbard, p. 30.

25. Ibid., p. 78.

26. Ibid., pp. 150ff.

27. Ibid., pp. 113-14.

28. Ralph W. Sockman, *The Fine Art of Using* (New York: Joint Division of Education and Cultivation, Board of Missions and Church Extension, the Methodist Church, 1946), p. 102.

29. Ralph W. Sockman, "Foretastes of the Future," sermon for April 12, 1942, manuscript at Syracuse University, p. 4.

30. Ibid., p. 2.

31. Ralph W. Sockman, "Christmas: The Hinge of History," sermon for December 19, 1943, manuscript at Syracuse University, p. 20.

32. Ralph W. Sockman, "A Savior Is Born," sermon for December 24, 1944, manuscript at Syracuse University, p. 10.

33. Ralph W. Sockman, "On God's Terms," sermon for June 11, 1944, manuscript at Syracuse University, p. 7.

34. Sockman, *Date with Destiny*, p. 148.

35. Sockman, "A Savior Is Born," sermon for December 24, 1944, p. 8.

36. Ralph W. Sockman, "Unify Your Command," sermon for November 8, 1942, manuscript at Syracuse University, p. 4.

37. Ibid., p. 6.

38. Ibid.

39. Sockman, *Date with Destiny*, p. 70.

40. *TNYT*, December 21, 1942, p. 30.

41. Ralph W. Sockman, "The Price of Power," sermon for March 8, 1942, manuscript at Syracuse University, p. 8.

42. Ibid., p. 10. Cf. *TNYT*, March 9, 1942, p. 16.

43. Ralph W. Sockman, "Living Below Par," sermon for October 18, 1942, manuscript at Syracuse University, p. 3.

44. Ralph W. Sockman, "A Fifth Freedom," sermon for November 22, 1942, manuscript at Syracuse University, p. 7. Cf. *TNYT*, November 23, 1942, p. 17.

45. Ralph W. Sockman, "Life's Deepest Law," sermon for April 11, 1943, manuscript at Syracuse University, p. 2.

46. *TNYT*, February 8, 1943, p. 11.

47. Ralph W. Sockman, "You and Your Call," sermon for May 7, 1943, manuscript at Syracuse University, p. 6.

48. Ralph W. Sockman, "Anchors to Windward," sermon for October 24, 1943, manuscript at Syracuse University, pp. 3, 20.

49. Ralph W. Sockman, "The Last Stand," sermon for December 31, 1944, manuscript at Syracuse University, p. 7. (Emphasis his.)   Cf. Sockman, *The Highway of God*, p. 77.

50. Ralph W. Sockman, "Heirs of Promise," (alternate title, "On God's Terms") sermon for June 18,.1944, manuscript at Syracuse University, p. 4.

51. Ibid., p. 5.

52.   Ralph W. Sockman, "God Gives the Answers," sermon for November 26, 1944, manuscript at Syracuse University, p. 7.

53. Her child-like scribbles, sketches, and notes to her father decorate a number of the sermon manuscripts.

54. Sockman, "God Gives the Answers," sermon for November 26, 1944, pp. 6-7.

55. Kyle Haselden, "An Honor Roll of American Preachers," actually calls Sockman's style a "composite" of theology, evangelism, and life situation preaching (p. 18).

56. Sockman, *Highway of God*, pp. 122-23.

57. Ibid., pp. 88-89.

58. Hibbard, p. 81.

59. Ralph W. Sockman, "Our Unused Gains," sermon for February 11, 1945, manuscript at Syracuse University, p. 3.

60. Ralph W. Sockman, "Living at Random," sermon for February 4, 1945, manuscript at Syracuse University, p. 5

61. Sockman, "Lives Adrift," sermon for December 9, 1934, pp. 10-11.

62. Sockman, *Highway of God*, p. 69.

63. Ibid., p. 90.

64. Ibid., p. 69.

65. Ralph W. Sockman, "We are Saved by Hope," sermon for March 19, 1944, manuscript at Syracuse University, p. 10.

66. Ralph W. Sockman, "The Endless Chain," sermon for May 3, 1942, manuscript at Syracuse University, p. 3.

67. Sockman, *Highway of God*, p. 70.

68. Ibid., p. 69.

69. *TNYT*, September 21, 1942, p. 12. By this phrase he means, presumably, the dignity and freedom of the individual.

70. Sockman, *Highway of God*, p. 78.

71. Sockman, "Heirs of Promise," sermon for June 18, 1944, manuscript at Syracuse University, p. 3.

72. Sockman, *Date with Destiny*, p. 15.

73. Sockman, "Determiners of Destiny," sermon for November 15, 1942, manuscript at Syracuse University, p. 9.

74. Sockman, *Date with Destiny*, p. 36.

75. Ralph W. Sockman, "Creators of Courage," sermon for October 15, 1944, manuscript at Syracuse University, p. 8.

76. Ralph W. Sockman, "Life's Invisible Lines," sermon for January 7, 1945, manuscript at Syracuse University, p. 7.

77. Sockman, *Date with Destiny*, p. 13.

78. Ibid., p. 16.

79. Sockman, "The Price of Power," sermon for March 8, 1942, manuscript at Syracuse University, p. 14.

80. *TNYT*, April 19, 1943, p. 13.

81. Ralph W. Sockman, "The Keys of Knowledge," sermon for March 25, 1944, manuscript at Syracuse University, p. 5.

82. Sockman, *Date with Destiny*, p. 67.

83. Ralph W. Sockman, "When Are We Free to Choose?" sermon for October 29, 1944, manuscript at Syracuse University, pp. 10-13.

84. Sockman, *Highway of God*, p. 161.

85. Ralph W. Sockman, "Search for Security," sermon for July 30, 1944, manuscript at Syracuse University, p. 8.

86. *TNYT*, March 26, 1945, p. 15.

87. Ralph W. Sockman, "Lead On, O King Eternal," sermon for March 25, 1945, manuscript at Syracuse University, p. 6.

88. Ralph W. Sockman, "Building the Bethlehem Road" (alternate title, "God's Road Builders"), sermon for December 10, 1944, manuscript at Syracuse University, p. 2.

89. Sockman, *Highway of God*, pp. 56-57. (Italics his.)

90. Quoted by *TNYT*, April 3, 1944, p. 26.

91. Sockman, "Building the Bethlehem Road," sermon for December 10, 1944, manuscript at Syracuse University, p. 2.

92. Sockman, "Determiners of Destiny," sermon for November 15, 1942, manuscript at Syracuse University, p. 15.

93. Quoted by *TNYT*, January 17, 1944, p. 13.

94. *TNYT*, December 20, 1943, p. 19.

95. *TNYT*, May 11, 1942, p. 9.

CHAPTER X

1. Scherer, *For We Have This Treasure*, p. 11.

2. Scherer, *Event in Eternity* (New York: Harper and Bros., 1945), p. 83.

3. Scherer, *For We Have This Treasure*, p. 72.

4. Scherer, "Does Christianity Have a Ghost of a Chance?", sermon for March 11, 1945, vol. V., series II, p. 226b.

5. In "Measure for Measure," sermon for June 24, 1945, miscellaneous sermons B, p. 297a, Scherer points out the ways in which, at war's end, Reformation doctrine has been forsaken.

6. Paul E. Scherer, "Do We Want a Protestant Church?" sermon for October 31, 1943, manuscript at Union Theological Seminary, vol. V, series II, p. 500b.

7. Paul E. Scherer, "You Shall Also Bear Witness," sermon for June 6, 1943, manuscript at Union Theological Seminary, vol. V, series II, p. 433b.

8. Paul E. Scherer, "One World at a Time?" sermon for November 12, 1944, manuscript at Union Theological Seminary, vol. IV, series II, p. 154b. Scherer's sermon notebooks list the other times and places when a sermon was preached. This one appears to have the longest list: it was used sixteen times!

9. Paul E. Scherer, "Tighten the Tensions," *Christian Century*, April 15, 1942, p. 490.

10. Ibid., p. 491.

11. Ibid., p. 492.

12. Ibid.

13. Ibid.

14. Scherer, *For We Have This Treasure*, p. 71.

15. Ibid., pp. 70-71.

16. Ibid., pp. 82-93.

17. Ibid., p. 165.

18. Ibid., p. 109.

19. Paul E. Scherer, "Does God Make Sense?" in *The Place Where Thou Standest*, pp. 53-54.

20. Scherer, "Tighten the Tensions," *The Christian Century*, April 15, 1942, pp. 490-91.

21. Ibid., p. 491.

22. Paul E. Scherer, "How Much Is Enough?" sermon for September 12, 1943, manuscript at Union Theological Seminary, vol. V, series II, pp. 454b-455a.

23. Paul E. Scherer, "Until the Day Dawn," in *The Place Where Thou Standest*, p. 173.

24. Scherer, "Tighten the Tensions," *The Christian Century*, April 15, 1942, p. 492.

25. Paul E. Scherer, "The Risen Christ," sermon for April 1, 1945 (Easter), manuscript at Union Theological Seminary, vol. IV, series II, p. 244b.

26. Ibid., p. 246b.

27. Ibid., p. 247b.

28. Scherer, *For We Have This Treasure*, p. 76.

29. Paul E. Scherer, "Christians in an Unchristian World," sermon for April 26, 1942, manuscript at Union Theological Seminary, vol. IV, series II, p. 193a.

30. Paul E. Scherer, "Yet Many Things—But Not Now," sermon for April 29, 1945, manuscript at Union Theological Seminary, vol. IV, series II, p. 260a.

31. Paul E. Scherer, "If They Hear Not Moses and the Prophets," sermon for June 3, 1945, manuscript at Union Theological Seminary, vol. IV, series II, p. 274a.

32. Ibid., p. 274b.

33. Paul E. Scherer, "This Troublesome Christmas," sermon for December 17, 1944, manuscript at Union Theological Seminary, vol. IV, series II, p. 166b.

34. Paul E. Scherer, "New Lives for Old," sermon for October 11, 1942, manuscript at Union Theological Seminary, vol. V, series II, p. 275a.

35. Scherer, "Is Christianity Childish?", sermon for February 19, 1939, and June 28, 1942, vol. V, series II, p. 245b.

36. Paul E. Scherer, "When God Breaks Through," in *The Place Where Thou Standest*, p. 97.

37. Paul E. Scherer, "On Setting Limits to Faith," sermon for April 12, 1942, manuscript at Union Theological Seminary, vol. V, series II, pp. 186a-186b.

38. Paul E. Scherer, "The Glory and Majesty of God," in *Event in Eternity*, p. 40. (Cf. "The Final Goal of Ill," in *The Place Where Thou Standest*, p. 102: "Don't build on man your faith in God!")

39. Ibid., p. 33.

40. Ibid., p. 40.

41. Paul E. Scherer, "God in History," in *Event in Eternity*, p. 77.

42. Scherer, "The Glory and Majesty of God," in *Event in Eternity*, p. 33.

43. Ibid., p. 51.

44. Scherer, "Protestantism: Its Assets and Liabilities," sermon for November 1, 1942, vol. V, series II, p. 282a.

45. Ibid., p. 285b.

46. Paul E. Scherer, "On Setting Christianity Right Side Up," sermon for September 19, 1943, manuscript at Union Theological Seminary, vol. V, series II, p. 460a.

47. Paul E. Scherer, "The Inevitableness of Our Religion," sermon for September 12, 1943, manuscript at Union Theological Seminary, vol. V, series II, pp. 252a-252b, 254a-254b.

48. Paul E. Scherer, "The God Who Would Be Man," in *Event in Eternity*, p. 190.

49. Paul E. Scherer, "The Road to Power," sermon for September 28, 1941, manuscript at Union Theological Seminary, vol. V, series II, p. 26a.

50. Paul E. Scherer, "Art Thou He That Should Come?" sermon for December 17, 1944, manuscript at Union Theological Seminary, vol. IV, series II, p. 172b. From the perspective of systematic theology, of course, it would be possible to infer that Scherer shifted from a substitutionary or satisfaction view of the atonement, with Christ making up our "deficits," to a "classic" view with Christ as the "victor" whose triumph is manifest on the other side of death. The evidence is not sufficiently available here to draw that conclusion. But the main point remains that, for Scherer, the cross is the center of human hope and faith.

51. Paul E. Scherer, "As Good Stewards," sermon for May 21, 1944, manuscript at Union Theological Seminary, Miscellaneous Sermons vol., p. 85a.

52. Paul E. Scherer, "You Know What This Crisis Means," sermon for November 28, 1943, manuscript at Union Theological Seminary, vol. V, series II, p. 519b.

53. Paul E. Scherer, "On Being Proud," sermon for March 28, 1943, manuscript at Union Theological Seminary, vol. VI, series II, pp. 356a-356b.

54. Paul E. Scherer, "What Are You Making of Life?" sermon for February 22, 1942, manuscript at Union Theological Seminary, vol. VI, series II, pp. 142a-142b.

55. Paul E. Scherer, "On Putting Yourself at God's Disposal," sermon for January 18, 1942, manuscript at Union Theological Seminary, vol. V, series II, p. 119a.

56. Paul E. Scherer, "The Pilgrimage of Conscience," sermon for October 1, 1944, manuscript at Union Theological Seminary, vol. V, series II, pp. 1, 5.

57. Paul E. Scherer, "The Perfect Law," sermon for May 10, 1942, manuscript at Union Theological Seminary, vol. VI, series II, p. 205b.

58. Scherer, "How to Keep Religion from Becoming a Burden," *The Place where Thou Standest*, p. 68. The sermon, and its quoted line originally were delivered at Holy Trinity on October 31, 1937. The theme remained persistent in his preaching.

59. Scherer, "Tighten the Tensions," *The Christian Century*, p. 490.

60. Scherer "Such a Man as I," sermon for March 5, 1939, vol. III, series II (cf. *The Place Where Thou Standest*), p. 131.

61. Paul E. Scherer, "The Eternal Purpose," in *The Place Where Thou Standest*, pp. 144-45.

62. Creighton, "Reconciliation in American Protestant Preaching," p. 238.

63. Scherer, *For We Have This Treasure*, p. 85.

64. Scherer, "The Glory and the Majesty of God," in *Event in Eternity*, pp. 53, 38; *For We Have This Treasure*, p. 108.

65. Paul E. Scherer, "Summons and Response," sermon for December 19, 1943, manuscript at Union Theological Seminary, vol. B, p. 177a.

66. Scherer, "Do We Want a Protestant Church?", sermon for October 31, 1943, vol. V, series II, p. 497b.

67. Scherer, "If They Hear Not Moses and the Prophets," sermon for June 3, 1945, vol. IV, series II, p. 274a.

68. Scherer, "Summons and Response," sermon for December 19, 1943, miscellaneous sermons B, p. 174b.

69. Scherer, "If They Hear Not Moses and the Prophets," sermon for June 3, 1945, vol. IV, series II, pp. 273a-273b.

70. Paul E. Scherer, "God in Human Life," sermon for April 11, 1943, manuscript at Union Theological Seminary, vol. VI, series II, p. 394a.

71. Paul E. Scherer, "On Facing Yourself," in *The Place Where Thou Standest*, pp. 110-14.

72. Ibid., p. 114.

73. *TNYT*, March 15, 1943, p. 9.

74. Scherer, "The Glory and Majesty of God," in *Event in Eternity*, p. 50.

75. Paul E. Scherer, "Rescue and Requirement," sermon for November 7, 1943, manuscript at Union Theological Seminary, vol. V, series II, p. 503b.

76. Paul E. Scherer, "On Embracing the Future," sermon for December 31, 1944, manuscript at Union Theological Seminary, vol. IV, series II, pp. 531a-531b.

77. Paul E. Scherer, "God's Indicatives Are Life's Imperatives," sermon for May 9, 1943, manuscript at Union Theological Seminary, vol. V, series II, p. 412b.

78. Scherer, "The Alert," sermon for December 28, 1941, vol. V, series II, p. 11a.

79. Ibid., p. 111.

80. Paul E. Scherer, "Man—Paradox of Dust and Divinity," sermon for February 8, 1942, manuscript at Union Theological Seminary, vol. V, series II, p. 130b.

81. Paul E. Scherer, "When the Zest Goes Out of Life," sermon for October 22, 1944, manuscript at Union Theological Seminary, Miscellaneous Sermons vol. B, p. 131b.

82. Scherer, "The Inevitableness of Our Religion," sermon for September 13, 1942, (radio, 1943, n.d.) vol. V, series II, p. 252a.

83. Paul E. Scherer, "Do You Find Things Hard?" in *The Place Where Thou Standest*, p. 77.

84. Scherer, "Some Fleeting Good," sermon for October 23, 1938, vol. IV, series II, p. 90.

85. Ibid., p. 87.

86. Paul E. Scherer, "The Roots of Freedom," sermon for May 16, 1943, manuscript at Union Theological Seminary, vol. VI, series II, p. 421a.

87. Scherer, "Rescue and Requirement," sermon for November 7, 1943, vol. V, series II, p. 503b, and "Except a Man Be Born Again," sermon for May 27, 1945, manuscript at Union Theological Seminary, vol. V, series II, p. 267a.

88. Paul E. Scherer, "The God Who Would Be Man," sermon for Christmas but of uncertain date; manuscript at Union Seminary, vol. IV, series II. A lecture under the same title was published in *Event in Eternity* (1945). The illustrations used in the manuscript sermon—e.g., our

"dismal" world has "famine, concentration camps, fields of battle, great ships floundering on the sea"—clearly suggest that it is a war-time sermon.

89. Scherer, "On Getting the Better of Evil," sermon for January 24, 1943, vol. V, series II, p. 334a.

90. Ibid., p. 335a.

91. Scherer, "Measure for Measure," sermon for June 24, 1945, vol. V, series II, p. 253a.

92. Paul E. Scherer, "Each His Own and One Another's," sermon for September 17, 1944, manuscript at Union Theological Seminary, Miscellaneous Sermons vol., p. 114b.

93. Paul E. Scherer, "A World, Some Men, and God," sermon for February 15, 1942, manuscript at Union Theological Seminary, vol. V, series II, p. 137b.

94. Ibid., p. 136b.

95. Paul E. Scherer, "Is Life Good, Bad, or Indifferent?" sermon for June 14, 1942, manuscript at Union Theological Seminary, vol. V, series II, n.p. (this sermon was originally delivered in 1934).

96. Scherer, "The Eternal Purpose," *The Place Where Thou Standest*, p. 126.

97. Ibid., p. 137.

98. Ibid., pp. 134-35.

99. Paul E. Scherer, "Freedom for What?" sermon for November 14, 1943, manuscript at Union Theological Seminary, vol. VI, series II, p. 510b (alternate title, "The Four Freedoms of Religion").

100. Paul E. Scherer, "Does Truth Hold Things Together?" sermon for October 29, 1944, manuscript at Union Theological Seminary, vol. V, series II, p. 139a.

101. Scherer, "The Day of the Lord Is Darkness," sermon for September 20, 1942, vol. V, series II, p. 259a.

102. Scherer, "Except a Man Be Born Again," sermon for May 27, 1945, vol. V, series II, p. 268a.

103. Scherer, "God in Human Life," sermon for April 11, 1943, vol. VI, series II, pp. 391b-392a.

CHAPTER XI

1. Fosdick, *The Living of These Days*, p. 295. It would truly have been astonishing for the nation's foremost preacher to enter a Christian community where so little emphasis is placed on preaching!

2. Sockman, "Forty Years of Fosdick," *Religion in Life,* vol. 26 (1956-1957), p. 293.

3. *Newsweek*, vol. 27, April 9, 1946, pp. 76-77.

4. Harry Emerson Fosdick, "The New Demand for Personal Religion," sermon for March 22, 1942, manuscript at Union Theological Seminary, p. 11.

5. "Harry Emerson Fosdick," editorial in *The Christian Century*, vol. 75, May 21, 1958, p. 611. For his work as an apologist, see Leininger, passim.

6. Hardy Clemons, "Key Theological Ideas of Harry Emerson Fosdick" (Th.D. dissertation, Southwestern Baptist Theological Seminary, Fort Worth, TX, 1966), p. 187. Samuel Robert Weaver, "The Theology and Times of Harry Emerson Fosdick" (Th.D. dissertation, Princeton, 1961), pp. 22f, says Fosdick did not quite place all religions on the same level, but that he did see in all religions the revelation of God.

7. "Honor to Dr. Fosdick," editorial in *The Christian Century*, vol. 70, May 20, 1953, p. 595. Cf. "Liberal," in *Time*, vol. 61, May 25, 1953, pp. 62f. Interestingly enough, one of the first occupants of the chair was George Buttrick.

8. Loral W. Pancake, "Theological Liberalism in the Life and Ministry of Harry Emerson Fosdick" (M.A. Thesis, Drew University, 1946), p. 55n.

9. Eugene Exman, "Fosdick as Author," in *The Christian Century*, vol. 75, May 21, 1958, p. 617.

10. Fabaus Landry, "The Preaching of Harry Emerson Fosdick: An Analysis of Its Intent, Style, and Language" (D.Div. dissertation, Vanderbilt University, 1972), p. 2.

11. Virtually all commentators on Fosdick's work make this point: H. Gordon Clinard, "An Evangelical Critique of the use of The Classic Biblical Solutions to the Problem of Suffering. . . ." (Th.D. dissertation, Southwestern Baptist Theological Seminary, Fort Worth, TX, 1958), p. 146; Clemons, pp. 118, 456; Creighton, pp. 128ff; Elmer Edwin Burtner, "The Use of biblical Materials of Harry Emerson Fosdick" (Th.D. dissertation, Boston University, 1959), p. 156. Cf. Deane W. Ferm, "Living of These Days: A Tribute to Harry Emerson Fosdick," *Christian Century*, vol. 95, May 3, 1978, p. 474.

12. Harry Emerson Fosdick, "The Christmas Message Girds Us for the New Year," sermon for December 2 8, 1941, manuscript at Union Theological Seminary, p. 12.

13. Ibid., p. 7.

14. Clemons, p. 118.

15. Douglas Miller Lawson, "The Idea of Progress in the Theology of Harry Emerson Fosdick" (Ph.D. dissertation, Duke University, 1963), pp. 128f.

16. Fosdick, "The Christmas Message Girds Us for the New Year," sermon for December 28, 1941, manuscript at Union Theological Seminary, p. 6.

17. Harry Emerson Fosdick, "The Deepest Experience in Christian Living," sermon for June 3, 1945, manuscript at Union Theological Seminary, p. 2.

18. Joseph Calvin Hall, "Basic Theological and Ethical Concepts of Harry Emerson Fosdick," pp. 13, 38.

19. Robert M. Shelton, "The Relationship Between Reason and Revelation in the Preaching of Harry Emerson Fosdick" (Th.D. dissertation, Princeton University, 1965), p. 181.

20. W.S. Skinner, in a review of the sermon volume *What Is Vital in Religion* (New York: Harper and Bros., 1955), found a "mystical" element which he sensed not to have been present in Fosdick's earlier books of sermons. While it does seem to be the case that Fosdick's pulpit theology became more "experiential" and perhaps "mystical" in his later career, there is some doubt that this volume could be cited as evidence for the trend. It was Fosdick's final book of sermons and it included samples of his preaching that spanned his career: one of the messages originally dated from 1920; a few are of uncertain date; only two come from the war years; only five are post-war sermons.

21. Deane W. Ferm, "Living of These Days. . ." (*Christian Century*, May 3, 1978), p. 474.

22. Shelton, p. 3.

23. Ibid., p. 285. Reason, for example, was the remedy for such intellectually correctible matters as the "stupidity" or the human "folly" that helped cause World War II. Perhaps that was why Fosdick saw himself as an educator rather than an evangelist. (Harry Emerson Fosdick, "The New Demand for Personal Religion," sermon for March 22, 1942, manuscript at Union Theological Seminary, p. 11. Cf. Clinard, p. 169.)

24. Clemons, p. 386.

25. *TNYT*, April 10, 1944, p. 24.

26. Harry Emerson Fosdick, "This Year We Need Easter," sermon for April 9, 1944, manuscript at Union Theological Seminary, p. 2.

27. Ibid., p. 8.

28. Harry Emerson Fosdick, "On Being Only a Drop in the Bucket," sermon for February 4, 1945, in *On Being Fit to Live with: Sermons on Post-War Christianity* (New York: Harper and Bros., 1946), p. 183.

29. Harry Emerson Fosdick, *On Being a Real Person* (New York: Harper and Bros., 1943), p. xii.

30. Quoted by *TNYT*, April 26, 1943, p. 11.

31. Harry Emerson Fosdick, "That Strange Realist from Bethlehem," sermon for December 21, 1941, manuscript at Union Theological Seminary, p. 6.

32. Bonney, p. 48.

33. Edmund Holt Linn, *Preaching as Counseling: The Unique Method of Harry Emerson Fosdick* (Valley Forge: Judson Press, 1966), pp. 32-33.

34. Douglas Miller Lawson, p. 120.

35. *TNYT*, November 30, 1942, p. 15.

36. Harry Emerson Fosdick, "Taking God Seriously," sermon for February 15, 1942, manuscript at Union Theological Seminary, pp. 9-10. (However, in this same sermon, Fosdick lauded Calvin's personal concern for his friend Farel at the time of the death of Farel's wife.)

37. Shelton, p. 149.

38. Fosdick, "A Religion that Really Gets Us," *What Is Vital in Religion*, p. 55.

39. Ibid., p. 58.

40. Fosdick, "The Christmas Message Girds Us for the New Year," sermon for December 28, 1941, manuscript at Union Theological Seminary, p. 9.

41. Harry Emerson Fosdick, "On Getting Christianity Out of Its Pigeonholes," sermon for October 22, 1944, in *On Being Fit to Live With*, pp. 31-32.

42. Bonney, p. 89.

43. "Fosdick constructed his sermons on the assumption that God could work through the sermon only if the sermon got next to the person." Jerald Huntsinger, "Sermons Designed for Listening," *Christian Advocate*, May 10, 1962, p. 14.

44. Harry Emerson Fosdick, "On Feeling That God Is Real," sermon for February 14, 1943, manuscript at Union Theological Seminary, pp. 2-3.

45. Harry Emerson Fosdick, "A Man Is What He Proves to be in an Emergency," sermon for January 14, 1945, in *On Being Fit to Live With*, p. 158.

46. Harry Emerson Fosdick, "The Impossibility of Being Irreligious," sermon for October 1, 1944, and "What Does It Really Mean to be Great?" sermon for October 29, 1944, both in *On Being Fit to Live With*, pp. 87 and 52 respectively; they are examples of the genre. A more fully developed discussion will appear below.

47. "Open Shop Parson," *Time*, vol. 41, March 15, 1943, p. 54. Cf. Robert D. Clark, "Harry Emerson Fosdick: The Growth of a Great Preacher," in Crocker, ed., *Harry Emerson Fosdick's Art of Preaching: An Anthology* (Springfield, Illinois: Thomas, 1971), p. 179.

48. Fosdick, "After Forty Years in the Ministry," in *A Great Time to Be Alive*, p. 207. Cf. *TNYT*, November 15, 1943, p. 16.

49. Bonney, p. 80.

50. *TNYT*, January 11, 1943, p. 10.

51. *TNYT*, January 10, 1944, p. 10.

52. Harry Emerson Fosdick, "This is the Time to Believe in the Church," sermon for January 9, 1944, manuscript at Union Theological Seminary, p. 1. (This was his budget sermon for the year.)

53. Harry Emerson Fosdick, "Works without Faith Are Dead," sermon for November 19, 1944, manuscript at Union Theological Seminary, p. 1.

54. Harry Emerson Fosdick, "Being Rich without Knowing It," sermon for February 1, 1942, manuscript at Union Theological Seminary, p. 11.

55. Fosdick, "What Do Ye More Than Others?", sermon for May 10, 1942 (radio, May 24, 1942), and April 22, 1928, p. 12.

56. Bonney, p. 60.

57. Robert D. Clark, "Harry Emerson Fosdick: The Growth of a Great Preacher," in Crocker, p. 159.

58. Harry Emerson Fosdick, "The Power to Turn Evil into Good," sermon for October 3, 1943, manuscript at Union Theological Seminary, p. 2.

59. Fosdick, *On Being a Real Person*, p. 240.

60. Fosdick, "The Impossibility of Being Irreligious," sermon on October 1, 1944, manuscript at Union Theological Seminary, p. 17.

61. Raymond Blaine Fosdick, *John D. Rockefeller, Jr.: A Portrait* (New York: Harper and Bros., 1956), p. 226.

62. Fosdick, *On Being a Real Person*, p. 264.

63. Fosdick, "The Power to Turn Evil into Good," sermon for October 3, 1943, Union Theological Seminary, p. 2.

64. Fosdick, "The Impossibility of Being Irreligious," sermon for October 1, 1944, p. 81.

65. Leininger, p. 91.

66. Fosdick, "Works Without Faith Are Dead," sermon for November 19, 1944, p. 6. (Cf. *TNYT*, November 20, 1944, p. 16.)

67. Ibid., p. 8.

68. Ibid., p. 11.

69. Harry Emerson Fosdick, "Spiritual Priorities," sermon for January 11, 1942, manuscript at Union Theological Seminary, p. 2.

70. Clemons, p. 200.

71. Harry Emerson Fosdick, "Not for Sale," sermon for November 26, 1944, manuscript at Union Theological Seminary, p. 10.

72. *TNYT*, February 28, 1944, p. 15.

73. Harry Emerson Fosdick, "A Religion that Really Works," sermon for November 5, 1944, manuscript at Union Theological Seminary, pp. 2-3.

74. *TNYT*, January 18, 1943, p. 12.

75. Ibid.

76. Harry Emerson Fosdick, "The Revolt Against Paganism, sermon for December 3, 1944, manuscript at Union Theological Seminary, p. 9. Cf. *TNYT*, December 4, 1944, p. 26.

77. Harry Emerson Fosdick, "Christianity Not a Form but a Force," sermon for October 31, 1943, in *Great Time*, p. 92.

78. Ibid., pp. 92-96.

79. Harry Emerson Fosdick, "Wartime's Effect on Our Personal Religion," sermon for December 17, 1944, manuscript at Union Theological Seminary, p. 7.

80.   Harry Emerson Fosdick, "Will the New Year Really Be New?" sermon for January 7, 1945, manuscript at Union Theological Seminary, p. 5.

81. Harry Emerson Fosdick, "A New Year When Almost Anything May Happen," sermon for December 27, 1942, manuscript at Union Theological Seminary, p. 9.

82.   Harry Emerson Fosdick, "Having a Faith that Really Works," Sermon for April 19, 1942, in *What Is Vital in Religion*, p. 20.

83. Ibid., pp. 22-23.

84. Clemons, p. 221.

85. "Harry Emerson Fosdick," editorial in *Christian Century*, vol. 75, May 21, 1958, p. 611.

86. Burtner, p. 23.

87.   Burtner, pp. 153, 162, 234; Clemons, p. 456; Hall, pp. 13, 38; Leininger, p. 33; Ferm, p. 474; Clinard, p. 146.

88.   Harry Emerson Fosdick, "Don't Be Discouraged about Human Nature," sermon for March 15, 1942 and June 26, 1942, plus a radio broadcast on May 10, 1942, manuscript at Union Theological Seminary, p. 9.

89. Harry Emerson Fosdick, "Decisive Battles Behind Closed Doors," sermon for October 18, 1942, and August 6, 1944, in *Great Time*, p. 11.

90. Harry Emerson Fosdick, "The Strange Mystery of Trouble in God's World," sermon for April 15, 1945, manuscript at Union Theological Seminary, pp. 3, l0.

91.   Cf. May, "How Dr. Fosdick Used the Bible in Preaching," in Crocker, ed., *Harry Emerson Fosdick's Art of Preaching*, p. 81.

92. Fosdick, "On Feeling that God Is Real," sermon on February 14, 1943, p. 4.

93. Burtner, p. 234.

94. Ibid., p. 153.

95. Hall, p. 38.

96. Harry Emerson Fosdick, "Faith in Life Confronts Cynicism," sermon for January 4, 1942, manuscript at Union Theological Seminary, p. 6.

97. Fosdick, *On Being a Real Person*, pp. 164-65.

98. *TNYT*, August 3, 1942, p. 13.

99. Fosdick, "Being Rich Without Knowing It," sermon for February 1, 1942, manuscript at Union Theological Seminary, p. 11.

100. *TNYT*, February 2, 1942, p. 20.

101. Quoted in *TNYT*, February 2, 1942, p. 20.

102. Creighton, p. 138.

103. Weaver, p. 78.

104. *TNYT*, October 19, 1942, p. 26.

105. Ibid.

106. Fosdick, *On Being a Real Person*, pp. 213f, 237f.

107. Lawson, p. 145.

108. Ibid., pp. 14-16.

109. Cauthen, p. 79.

110. Harry Emerson Fosdick, "Why Is God Silent While Evil Rages?" sermon for October 10, 19~3, in *Great Time*, p. 170.

111. Creighton, pp. 152-53.

112. Fosdick, "A Kind of Penitence That Does Some Good," in *Great Time*, p. 88.

113. Harry Emerson Fosdick, "When We Are at Our Wit's End," sermon for April 4, 1943, manuscript at Union Theological Seminary, p. 7. Cf. *TNYT*, April 5, 1943, p. 24.

114. Harry Emerson Fosdick, "Getting the Best Out of the Worst," sermon for April 30, 1944, in *Great Time*, p. 55.

115. Bonney, pp. 76-77.

116. Harry Emerson Fosdick, "Reenforcement for a Time of Sacrifice," sermon for November 15, 1942, manuscript at Union Theological Seminary, pp. 1, 5.

117. *TNYT*, November 9, 1942, p. 18.

118. Fosdick, "Reenforcement for a Time of Sacrifice," sermon for November 15, 1942, p. 10.

119. Based on figures reported by CBS News, February 26, 1982.

120. Harry Emerson Fosdick, "On Being Realistic," sermon for April 26, 1942, manuscript at Union Theological Seminary, p. 1.

121. Fosdick, "Christmas This Year Means Something Special," sermon for December 20, 1942, manuscript at Union Theological Seminary, p. 6.

122. Harry Emerson Fosdick, "The Most Thrilling Rescue Story in the World," sermon for March 25, 1945, in *On Being Fit to Live With*, pp. 196-97. Cf. *TNYT*, March 26, 1945, p. 15.

123. Harry Emerson Fosdick, "Our Difficulties in Forgiving Our Enemies," sermon for May 27, 1945, in *On Being Fit to Live With*, p. 76.

124. Harry Emerson Fosdick, "The Cross Is a Fact," sermon for November 7, 1943, manuscript at Union Theological Seminary, pp. 1-2. Cf. *TNYT*, November 8, 1943, p. 16.

125. Fosdick, "Don't Be Discouraged about Human Nature," sermon for March 15, 1942 and June 26, 1942, manuscript at Union Theological Seminary, p. 12.

126. Harry Emerson Fosdick, "Getting Ready to Keep Christmas," sermon for December 12, 1943, manuscript at Union Theological Seminary, p. 3.

127. *TNYT*, March 16, 1942, p. 22.

128. Harry Emerson Fosdick, "On Worshipping Things We Manufacture," sermon for October 8, 1943, in *On Being Fit to Live With*, p. 119.

129. Harry Emerson Fosdick, "When Faith in God Costs a Struggle," sermon for November 28, 1943, manuscript at Union Theological Seminary, p. 8.

130. Harry Emerson Fosdick, "The Light That No Darkness Can Put Out," sermon for December 19, 1943, in *Great Time*, p. 212.

131. Fosdick, "The Impossibility of Being Irreligious," sermon for October 1, 1944, in *On Being Fit to Live With*, p. 87.

132. Harry Emerson Fosdick, "What Does It Really Mean to be Great?" sermon for October 29, 1944, in *On Being Fit to Live With*, p. 52.

133. Harry Emerson Fosdick, "Fresh Light on an Old Beatitude," sermon for October 29, 1944 (radio) manuscript at Union Theological Seminary, p. 5.

134. Harry Emerson Fosdick, "On Catching the Wrong Bus," sermon for February 25, 1945, in *On Being Fit to Live With*, p. 142.

135. Clemons, p. 285.

136. Hall, pp. 216ff.

137. Harry Emerson Fosdick, "What It Means to Grow Up," sermon for November 6, 1938 and May 16, 1943, manuscript at Union Theological Seminary, p. 9.

CHAPTER XII

1. Buttrick, "Our Homelessness," sermon for December 7, 1941, published in the *MAPC News* (January 23, 1942), pp. 2-3.

2. George A. Buttrick, *Prayer* (New York: Abingdon-Cokesbury, 1942), pp. 9-10.

3. George A. Buttrick, "Books to Fill the World," sermon for June 14, 1942, in *MAPC News*, October 16, 1942, p. 5.

4. George A. Buttrick, "To Him No High, No Low, No Great, No Small," sermon for April 19, 1942, in *MAPC News*, November 6, 1942, p. 3.

5. Ibid., p. 4.

6. Ibid.

7. George A. Buttrick, "The Steadfast Heart," sermon for November 1, 1942, in *MAPC News*, January 15, 1943, p. 3.

8. George A. Buttrick, "All That Matters," sermon for January 3, 1943, in *MAPC News*, January 15, 1943, p. 5.

9. George A. Buttrick, "The Stars and a Broken Heart," sermon for February 1, 1942, in *MAPC News*, March 13, 1942, p. 3.

10. Buttrick, "The Sign at Bethlehem," sermon for December 20, 1942, in *MAPC News*, (December 17, 1943), p. 4.

11. George A. Buttrick, "Distraction and Peace," sermon for February 11, 1945, in *MAPC News*, August 3, 1945, p. 3.

12. George A. Buttrick, "Basis of Brotherhood," sermon for March 18, 1945, manuscript at Harvard, no. MA 1292, p. 4.

13. George A. Buttrick, "The Beginning of a Better World," sermon for September 17, 1944, manuscript at Harvard University, number MA 1249, p. 3.

14. George A. Buttrick, "New Day," sermon for May 13, 1945, manuscript at Harvard University, number MA 1305, p. 8.

15. *TNYT*, November 10, 1943, pp. 1, 17.

16. George A. Buttrick, "Mission," sermon for November 14, 1943, manuscript at Harvard University, number MA 1181, p. 8.

17. Ibid., p. 2.

18. George A. Buttrick, "Seeking or Sought," sermon for October 8, 1944, manuscript at Harvard University, number MA 1255, p. 4.

19. Buttrick, "Goal and Power," sermon for November 5, 1944, manuscript at Harvard University, number MA 1261, pp. 2-3.

20. George A. Buttrick, "When War Ends: Misgivings and Hopes," sermon for February 25, 1945, manuscript at Harvard University, number MA 1286, p. 8.

21. George A. Buttrick, "The Interpreter," sermon for December 26, 1943, manuscript at Harvard University, number MA 1193, p. 7.

22. Buttrick, *Prayer*, p. 143.

23. Fribley, p. 233.

24. George A. Buttrick, "Worse or Better than We Think," sermon for January 10, 1943, manuscript at Harvard University, number MA 1128, pp. 5-6.

25. Buttrick, *Prayer*, pp. 131-32.

26. Buttrick, "Worse or Better Than We Think," sermon for January 10, 1943, manuscript at Harvard University, number MA 1128, p. 7.

27. George A. Buttrick, "Advent Hope," sermon for December 5, 1943, manuscript at Harvard University, number MA 1187, p. 6.

28. Buttrick, "Changing with the Years," sermon of uncertain date in *MAPC News*, January 26, 1945, pp. 3-4.

29. Blankenship, p. 59.

30. George A. Buttrick, The sixth sermon in a series on the Lord's Prayer, delivered April 2, 1944, manuscript at Harvard University, number MA 1227, p. 7.

31. George A. Buttrick, "The Triumphant Church," sermon for March 22, 1943, in *MAPC News*, July 31, 1942, p. 4. It is interesting to note that this phrase "invincible surmise" may have been borrowed from Buttrick by Paul Scherer. It appears here in this sermon and then in one by Scherer the following month: faith begins "with a kind of invincible surmise. . . . A man starts to live as though God were" (Scherer, "On Setting Limits to Faith," pp. 186a-186b). There are frequent notations in Scherer's sermon manuscripts that simply say "Buttrick." One might conclude that Scherer found a few of his friend's ideas useful in his own pulpit.

32. George A. Buttrick, "The Grace of Christ," sermon for June 11, 1944, manuscript at Harvard University, number MA 1245, p. 6.

33. Buttrick, *Prayer*, p. 144.

34. Ibid., p. 153.

35. George A. Buttrick, "In Your Stead," sermon for September 19, 1943, in *MAPC News*, November 12, 1943, p. 3.

36. George A. Buttrick, "Somebody's Knocking at Your Door," sermon for January 24, 1943, manuscript at Harvard University, number MA 1130, p. 3.

37. Buttrick, "In Your Stead," p. 3.

38. George A. Buttrick, "A New Start," sermon for April 18, 1943, manuscript at Harvard University, number MA 1153, p. 7.

39. George A. Buttrick, "On Being a Christian," sermon for March 4, 1945, manuscript at Harvard University, number MA 1288, pp. 2-3.

40. George A. Buttrick, "Faith on the Earth," sermon for November 15, 1942, in *MAPC News*, July 9, 1943, p. 3.

41. Ibid., p. 5.

42. Blankenship, p. 157.

43. George A. Buttrick, "Affliction and a Presence," sermon for June 7, 1942, manuscript at Harvard University, number MA 1092, p. 7.

44. Buttrick, *Prayer*, p. 38.

45. George A. Buttrick, "The Atoning Cross," sermon for March 29, 1942, manuscript at Harvard University, number MA 1076, p. 5.

46. Blankenship, p. 60.

47. Buttrick, *Prayer*, p. 150. The same language and imagery appeared in a sermon on February 20, 1944, titled "The Dynamics of Faith," manuscript at Harvard University, number MA 1206, p. 2.

48. Buttrick, *Prayer*, p. 143.

49. Ibid., p. 232.

50. Ibid., p. 236.

51. Stevens, p. 59.

52. Fribley, p. 242.

53. Letter dated July 15, 1970, to Wayne A. Blankenship and quoted by the recipient, p. 21.

54. Buttrick, "Worse or Better Than We Think," sermon for January 10, 1943, manuscript at Harvard, number MA 1128, p. 6.

55. Buttrick, "The Stars and a Broken Heart," sermon for February 1, 1942, in *MAPC News*, March 13, 1942, p. 3.

56. George A. Buttrick, "Consolation," sermon for April 29, 1945, in *MAPC News*, June 1, 1945, p. 4.

57. Stevens, pp. 3-4.

58. Letter dated July 15, 1970, to Blankenship and quoted by the recipient, p. 19.

59. George A. Buttrick, "Voice in the Silence," sermon for December 19, 1943, manuscript at Harvard University, number MA 1190, p. 6.

60. Clemons, p. 455.

61. Blankenship, p. 60.

62. Ibid., p. 184.

63. Buttrick, *Prayer*, p. 282.

64. George A. Buttrick, "Power and the Man," *Review and Expositor*, July 1943, pp. 286-87.

65. George A. Buttrick, "Choosing and Chosen," sermon for January 18, 1942, manuscript at Harvard University, number MA 1062, p. 6.

66. George A. Buttrick, "Home Religion," sermon for May 10, 1942, in *MAPC News*, June 5, 1942, p. 4.

67. Blankenship, p. 133.

68. Buttrick, "Changing with the Years," sermon of uncertain date, published in *MAPC News*, January 26, 1945, p. 4.

69. George A. Buttrick, "Wish or Will," sermon for May 21, 1944, manuscript at Harvard University, number MA 1240, p. 6.

70. George A. Buttrick, "Self Fulfillment," sermon for May 31, 1942, in *MAPC News*, February 15, 1943, p. 3.

71. Buttrick, "All that Matters," sermon for January 1, 1943, in *MAPC News*, January 15, 1943, p. 5.

72. Buttrick, *Prayer*, p. 55.

73. George A. Buttrick, "Advent Power," sermon for December 10, 1944, manuscript at Harvard University, number MA 1270, p. 4.

74. George A. Buttrick, "Prevailing Prayer," sermon for March 15, 1942, manuscript at Harvard University, number MA 1072, p. 2.

75. George A. Buttrick, "The Sacramental Life," sermon for November 7, 1943, in *MAPC News*, November 12, 1943, p. 5.

76. Buttrick, "The Atoning Cross," sermon for March 29, 1942, manuscript at Harvard, number MA 1076, p. 3.

77. Buttrick, "Changing with the Years," sermon of uncertain date, in *MAPC News*, January 26, 1945, p. 4.

78. Buttrick, "Advent Power," sermon for December 10, 1944, manuscript at Harvard, number MA 1270, p. 4. "No Room?" sermon for December 24, 1944, manuscript at Harvard University, number MA 1273, p. 3.

79. Buttrick, The sixth sermon in a series on the Lord's Prayer, April 2, 1944, manuscript at Harvard, number MA 1227, p. 4.

80. Ibid., pp. 3-4.

81. George A. Buttrick, "Debts," sermon for May 20, 1945, manuscript at Harvard University, number MA 1306, p. 7.

82. George A. Buttrick, "Christ and Education," sermon for October 31, 1943, manuscript at Harvard University, no. MA 1178, p. 4.

83. George A. Buttrick, "What Can We Believe," sermon for March 21, 1943, manuscript at Harvard University, no. MA 1143, p. 9.

84. Ibid., p. 1.

85. Buttrick, "A New Start," sermon for April 18, 1943, manuscript at Harvard, number MA 1153, p. 2.

86. Buttrick, *Prayer*, pp. 206ff.

87. George A. Buttrick, "Deliverance and Venture," sermon for January 31, 1943, manuscript at Harvard University, no. MA 1132, p. 5.

88. Buttrick, "The Triumphant Church," sermon for March 22, 1942, *MAPC News*, July 31, 1942, p. 6.

89. George A. Buttrick, "God and Power," sermon for November 5, 1944, manuscript at Harvard University, no. MA 1261, pp. 4-5.

90. Buttrick, *Prayer*, p. 125.

INTERLUDE

1.   Charles N. Davidson, "George Arthur Buttrick: Christocentric Preacher and Pacifist," *Journal of Presbyterian History* 53 (summer 1975): 148-49.

2. Manchester, p. 420; Dixon Wecter, *The Age of the Great depression: 1924-1941* (Chicago: Quadrangle Books, 1971) p. 315.

3.   Buttrick, "New Day," sermon for May 13, 1945, manuscript at Harvard, number MA 1305, p. 8.

CHAPTER XIII

1. *TNYT*, August 6, 1945, p. 11.

2. Ellis, *The Epic of New York City*, p. 561.

3. John Lukacs, *1945: Year Zero* (Garden City, N.Y.: Doubleday and Co. 1978), p. 12.

4. *TNYT*, April 22, 1946, p. 17.

5. Ralph W. Sockman, "The Lord of All Being," sermon for March 30, 1947, manuscript at Syracuse University, p. 1.

6. Sockman, *The Fine Art of Using*, p. 38.

7. Ralph W. Sockman, "The Lord's Lend Lease," sermon for September 23, 1945, manuscript at Syracuse University, p. 5.

8. *TNYT*, September 17, 1945, p. 23.

9. Ralph W. Sockman, "A Gospel for Victors," sermon for September 16, 1945, manuscript at Syracuse University, pp. 20-21.

10. *TNYT*, September 17, 1945, p. 23; September 24, 1945, p. 22.

11. Ralph W. Sockman, "How Easy Is Evil?" sermon for October 14, 1945, manuscript at Syracuse University, p. 10.

12. George A. Buttrick, *Christ and Man's Dilemma* (Nashville: Abingdon-Cokesbury Press, 1946), p. 8. The issues with which the book was concerned had simmered in the author for three years. But the entrance into the atomic age produced the occasion and the creative rage to get the book written. It was completed between August 6 and September 7, 1945.

13. George A. Buttrick, "Living at the End of an Age," sermon for May 12, 1946, manuscript at Harvard University, no. MA 1366, pp. 1-2.

14. George A. Buttrick, "Fellow Soldiers," sermon for January 20, 1946, manuscript at Harvard University, no. MA 1342, p. 1.

15. George A. Buttrick, "New Road," sermon for January 5, 1947, in *MAPC News*, January 10, 1947, p. 3.

16. George A. Buttrick, "Strength—False and True," sermon for November 30, 1947, manuscript at Harvard University, no. MA 1456, p. 3.

17. *TNYT*, March 24, 1947, p. 23.

18. Henry Steele Commager, *The American Mind: An Interpretation of American Thought and Character Since the 1880's* (New Haven: Yale University Press, 1950), p. 167.

19. Manchester, p. 242.

20. Eric F. Goldman, *The Crucial Decade—And After: America, 1945-1960* (New York: Alfred A. Knopf, 1973), p. 235.

21. Manchester, p. 777.

22. Ibid., pp. 777-78.

23. Frederick A. Shippey, "Changing Fortunes of Urban Protestantism," *Religion in Life*, vol. 18, no. 4, 1949, pp. 526-27.

24. Ibid., pp. 530, 532.

25. Fant and Pinson, *Twenty Centuries of Great Preaching*, vol. 10, pp. 297f.

26. *TNYT*, September 19, 1949, p. 20.

27. Ralph W. Sockman, "God's Advance Guard," sermon for November 20, 1950, manuscript at Syracuse University, Box 17, p. 9.

28. Harry Emerson Fosdick, "How Much Do We Really Care for the Church?" sermon for November 17, 1946, manuscript at Union Theological Seminary, p. 9. *TNYT*, January 23, 1950, p. 15.

29. George A. Buttrick, "The Church and Our Church," sermon for November 24, 1946, manuscript at Harvard University, no. MA 1391, p. 5.

30. *MAPC News*, January 3, 1947, p. 1.

31. Ibid.

32. George A. Buttrick, "Record of a Conversation," sermon for November 21, 1948, manuscript at Harvard University, no. MA 1528, p. 2.

33. George A. Buttrick, "The Angel of Prayer and Praise," sermon for October 23, 1949, manuscript at Harvard University, no. MA 1583, p. 2.

34. *TNYT*, March 31, 1952, p. 14.

35. George A. Buttrick, "The Essential Gift," sermon for November 16, 1952, manuscript at Harvard University, no. MA 1758, p. 3.

36. *TNYT*, September 10, 1951, p. 19.

37. George A. Buttrick, "A New Day for Our Church," sermon for March 30, 1952, manuscript at Harvard University, no. MA 1724, pp. 5-6.

38. Ibid., p. 1. In general, Buttrick loved the urban environment. He cherished it as a place of learning, a center for the arts, and a milieu of ethnic ferment. He "practically rhapsodizes about the contributions of the city as a place for richer variety of friendships, new sights and sounds, religious teachers and shrines, as well as workshops, cloisters, and schools." (Fribley, pp. 383-84.)

39. Apparently it happened without much fanfare. There was no major discussion of it in the *MAPC News* to be found, and Ethel King (who was

Buttrick's secretary at the time) could not recall anything significant about the circumstances of the discontinuance.

40. Goldman, p. 53.

41. *MAPC News*, January 11, 1946.

42. Goldman, p. 49.

43. Manchester, p. 291.

44. Samuel Eliot Morison, Henry Steele Commager, and William E. Leuchtenburg, *The Growth of the American Republic* (New York: Oxford University Press, 1969), vol. II, p. 728.

45. Karl Marx and Fredrich Engels, *The Communist Manifesto* (New York: Appleton-Century-Crofts, 1955), p. 8.

46. George A. Buttrick, "Glad Tidings," sermon for December 28, 1947, manuscript at Harvard University, no. MA 1463, p. 8.

47. George A. Buttrick, "Bane of the Self-Righteous," sermon for March 12, 1950, manuscript at Harvard University, no. MA 1615, pp. 5-6.

48. *TNYT*, September 16, 1946, p. 6.

49. Ralph W. Sockman, "Make Up Your Mind," *Vital Speeches*, vol. 16, October 1, 1950, p. 763. Cf. Ralph W. Sockman, "Worth of One," *Vital Speeches*, vol. 15, August 15, 1949, p. 655.

50. Ralph W. Sockman, "The End of the Easy Way," sermon for April 30, 1950, manuscript at Syracuse University, p. 6.

51. *TNYT*, September 16, 1946, p. 6.

52. Quoted by *TNYT*, September 25, 1950, p. 24.

53. Ralph W. Sockman, "Has America Come of Age?" sermon for July 2, 1950, manuscript at Syracuse University, p. 3.

54. *TNYT*, July 3, 1950, p. 16.

55. Sockman, "Has America Come of Age?" sermon for July 2, 1950, manuscript at Syracuse University, p. 5.

56. Hibbard, pp. 160-63.

57. *TNYT*, January 1, 1951, p. 15.

58. *TNYT*, October 1, 1951, p. 16.

59. *TNYT*, July 13, 1953, p. 23.

60. *TNYT*, July 27, 1953, p. 16.

61. *TNYT*, September 28, 1953, p. 20.

62. *TNYT*, November 16, 1953, p. 20.

63. Harry Emerson Fosdick, "Don't Let This Grim Generation Get You Down," sermon for April 24, 1949, manuscript at Union Theological Seminary, p. 5. *TNYT*, April 25, 1949, p. 16.

64. *TNYT*, January 21, 1952, p. 18. Harry Emerson Fosdick, "Are We First Hand or Second Hand Christians?" sermon for January 20, 1952, manuscript at Union Theological Seminary, p. 5.

65. Harry Emerson Fosdick, "The Nation Needs a Rebirth of Honorable Character," sermon for November 11, 1951, manuscript at Union Theological Seminary, p. 10.

66. Harry Emerson Fosdick, "Courage for Tough Times," sermon for November 19, 1950, manuscript at Union Theological Seminary, pp. 8-9.

67. *TNYT*, May 27, 1946, p. 20.

68. Harry Black Beverly, *Harry Emerson Fosdick's Predightweise: Its Significance for America, Its Limits, Its Overcoming* (Winterthur, Switzerland: P. G. Keller, 1965), p. 5. Sydney Ahlstrom, *A Religious History of the American People* (New Haven: Yale University Press,

1972), p. 911, calls Fosdick America's "most influential preacher" from the founding of Riverside until his retirement.

69. Harry Emerson Fosdick, "The Urgency of Ethical as Well as Economic Reconversion," sermon for September 30, 1945, in *On Being Fit to Live With: Sermons on Post-War Christianity*, p. 64. *TNYT*, October 1, 1945, p. 22. Harry Emerson Fosdick, "A Prophet's Summons to Modern America," sermon for February 10, 1946, manuscript at Union Theological Seminary, p. 3.

70. *TNYT*, April 5, 1948, p. 19.

71. *TNYT*, November 14, 1949, p. 17.

72. Ralph W. Sockman, "The Power Behind the Polls," sermon for October 29, 1950, manuscript at Syracuse University, p. 5. Ralph W. Sockman, "A Free Church in a Free World," sermon for October 23, 1949, manuscript at Syracuse University, pp. 3-4.

73. Ralph W. Sockman, "Life's Extra Dividends," sermon for April 23, 1950, manuscript at Syracuse University, p. 3.

74. Ralph W. Sockman, "Our Mother Country," sermon for May 14, 1950, manuscript at Syracuse University, p. 4.

75. Scherer, *The Plight of Freedom*, pp. 20-22.

76. Ibid., p. 20.

77. Ibid., p. 21.

78. Scherer, *The Word God Sent*, pp. 10-11.

79. Ibid., p. 11.

80. Scherer, *The Plight of Freedom*, p. 19.

81. Ibid., p. 16.

82. Ibid., p. 17.

83. Ibid., pp. 100-101.

84. Ibid., p. 101.

85. Ibid., p. 157.

86. Fosdick, "Are We First Hand or Second Hand Christians?" sermon for January 20, 1952, manuscript at Union Theological Seminary, p. 1.

87. *TNYT*, November 23, 1953, p. 21. The peak did not occur until about 1960.

88. Ahlstrom, p. 952.

89. Will Herberg, *Protestant-Catholic-Jew: An Essay in American Religious Sociology*, p. 60.

90. Ibid., p. 78n.

91. Manchester, p. 733.

92. Ahlstrom, p. 954. It had been on United States coins since 1865.

93. "Great Preachers," *Life*, vol. 34, April 6, 1953, p. 127.

94. Manchester, p. 772.

95. Edward McNall Burns, *The American Idea of Mission: Concepts of National Purpose and Destiny* (New Brunswick: Rutgers University Press, 1957), pp. 220-21.

96. Charles W. Gilkey, "Preaching," in A. S. Nash, ed., *Protestant Thought in the Twentieth Century* (New York: Macmillan, 1951), p. 208. If Gilkey had a bias toward the Madison Avenue Presbyterian Church, it would have been understandable. He had been a student assistant minister there, as were his son Langdon, his brother James, and his nephew James G. Gilkey, Jr. (*MAPC News*, October 25, 1946, p. 4.)

97. Daniel J. Boorstin, *The Image: Or What Happened to the American Dream* (New York: Atheneum, 1962), pp. 230-31.

98. Quoted by Herberg, p. 67.

99.   Ralph W. Sockman, "Our Door of Opportunity," sermon for November 6, 1949, manuscript at Syracuse University, pp. 2-3.

100. Fosdick, "Are We First or Second Hand Christians?" sermon for January 20, 1952, manuscript at Union Theological Seminary, p. 1.

101. Published in Fosdick, *What Is Vital in Religion*, pp. 133-42.

102. George A. Buttrick, "Penitence and Pardon," *Sermons Preached in a University Church* (New York: Abingdon Press, 1959), p. 176.

103. Edward L. R. Elson, "Evaluating Our Religious Revival," *Journal of Religious Thought* 14 (Autumn-Winter 1956-1957): 56-57.

104.   Ralph W. Sockman, "Mapping Our Tomorrows," sermon for January 4, 1948, manuscript at Syracuse University, pp. 8-9.

105. *TNYT*, January 5, 1948, p. 16.

106. Ralph W. Sockman, "The Unpardonable Sin," sermon for January 13, 1952, manuscript at Syracuse University, p. 7.

107. *TNYT*, February 9, 1953, p. 30.

108. Herberg, p. 52.

109. Ibid., p. 15.

110. Ibid., p. 90.

111. Ibid., pp. 92-95.

112. Ibid., pp. 102-103.

113. Ibid., pp. 94-95, 102.

114. Joshua Loth Liebman, *Peace of Mind* (New York: Simon and Schuster, 1946).

115. Ralph W. Sockman, "How to Be Free from Guilty Feelings," sermon for February 26, 1950, manuscript at Syracuse University, p. 6.

116. Ralph W. Sockman, *Whom Christ Commended* (New York: Abingdon, 1963), p. 81.

117. Ralph W. Sockman, "A Creed that Counts," sermon for October 27, 1946, manuscript at Syracuse University, Box 15, p. 1.

118. Ibid., pp. 1-8.

119. *TNYT*, June 24, 1946, p. 21.

120. Gertner, pp. 33-34.

121. Scherer, *The Word God Sent*, pp. x-xi.

122. Scherer, *The Plight of Freedom*, p. 3.

123. Ibid., p. 27.

124. Ibid., p. 166.

125. Scherer, *The Word God Sent*, p. 209.

126. Ibid., p. 166.

127. Ibid., p. 36.

128. Ibid., p. 42.

129. Ibid., p. 70.

130. Ibid., pp. 71-72.

131. Ibid., p. 84.

132. Scherer, *The Plight of Freedom*, p. 207.

133. Paul E. Scherer, "The Credibility and Relevance of the Gospel," *Review and Expositor* 54 (July 1957): 361-62.

134. Paul E. Scherer, "Gauntlet with a Gift in It," *Interpretation* 20 (October 1966): 387-99.

135. Quoted by Robert Moats Miller, "Harry Emerson Fosdick and John D. Rockefeller, Jr.: The Origins of an Enduring Association," p. 293, and in *Harry Emerson Fosdick: Preacher, Pastor, Prophet*, p. 335. King's remarks are contained in his *Stride Toward Freedom*.

136. Harry Emerson Fosdick, "The Great Christ and the Little Churches," sermon for September 29, 1946, in *What Is Vital in Religion*, p. 32. Cf. *TNYT*, September 30, 1946, p. 33.

137. Beverly, p. 10.

138. Harry Emerson Fosdick, *Dear Mr. Brown: Letters to a Person Perplexed about Religion* (New York: Harper, 1961), p. 31 (hereafter cited as *Dear Mr. Brown*).

139. Fosdick, "The Great Christ and the Little Churches," in *What Is Vital in Religion*, p. 32.

140. Fosdick, *Dear Mr. Brown*, pp. 174ff.

141. Ephesians 2:4-5 (KJV): "But God, who is rich in mercy, for his great love wherewith he loved us, even when we were dead in sins, hath quickened us together with Christ (by grace ye are saved)."

142. Harry Emerson Fosdick, "Having a Good Excuse and Not Using It," sermon for June 8, 1947, manuscript at Union Theological Seminary, p. 9.

143. Fosdick, *Dear Mr. Brown*, p. 126.

144. Harry Emerson Fosdick, *On Being Fit to Live With*, p. vii.

145. Harry Emerson Fosdick,"Are We Part of the Problem or the Answer?" sermon for February 24, 1946 in *On Being Fit to Live With*, p. 18.

146. Harry Emerson Fosdick, "God's Call to Christian Laymen," sermon for October 21, 1945, manuscript at Union Theological Seminary, p. 3. *TNYT*, January 20, 1947, p. 35.

147. Harry Emerson Fosdick, *Great Voices of the Reformation: An Anthology* (New York: Random House, 1952), p. xxv.

148. Ibid., p. 69.

149. Ibid., p. 494.

150. Ibid., p. 542.

151. Harry Emerson Fosdick, *A Faith for Tough Times* (London: SCM Press, 1953), p. 100.

152. Ibid., pp. 60-62.

153. Ibid., pp. 109-110.

154. Harry Emerson Fosdick, "That Fascinating Man on the Cross," sermon for March 3, 1946, manuscript at Union Theological Seminary, p. 3.

155. Harry Emerson Fosdick, "When Christ Is Born in Us," sermon for December 23, 1945, manuscript at Union Theological Seminary, p. 2.

156. Ibid., pp. 2-3.

157. Ibid., p. 7.

158. Harry Emerson Fosdick, "A Confused Generation Wants Religious Certainty," sermon for May 11, 1947, manuscript at Union Theological Seminary, p. 9.

159. Harry Emerson Fosdick, "Science Demands Religion," sermon for October 14, 1945, in *On Being Fit to Live With*, p. 27.

160. Fosdick, *Dear Mr. Brown*, p. 135.

161. Ibid., p. 60.

162. *TNYT*, April 13, 1953, p. 23.

163. Fosdick, *Great Voices of the Reformation*, p. 126.

164. Ibid., p. 540.

165. Ibid., p. 541.

166. Ibid., p. xiii.

167. Harry Emerson Fosdick, *The Man from Nazareth as His Contemporaries Saw Him* (New York: Harper, 1949), pp. 96, 246-47 (hereafter cited as *The Man from Nazareth*).

168. Weaver, p. 113.

169. Fosdick, *The Man from Nazareth*, p. 96.

170. McDiarmid, p. 91.

171. Harry Emerson Fosdick, "What an Armistice Day!" sermon for November 11, 1945, manuscript at Union Theological Seminary, p. 10.

172. Harry Emerson Fosdick, "People Who Suppose They Have No Personal Relationships with God," sermon for May 12, 1946, in *On Being Fit to Live With*, p. 173.

173. Harry Emerson Fosdick, "Who Do You Think You Are?" sermon for April 25, 1954, in *What Is Vital in Religion*, p. 183.

174. Ibid., p. 178.

175. Harry Emerson Fosdick, "After All, It's Character that Counts," sermon for September 21, 1947, manuscript at Union Theological Seminary, pp. 6-7.

176. Fosdick, "Who Do You Think You Are?" sermon for April 25, 1954, in *What Is Vital in Religion*, p. 179.

177. Fosdick, *Dear Mr. Brown*, p. 71.

178. Fosdick, "Science Demands Religion," in *On Being Fit to Live With*, p. 27.

179. Harry Emerson Fosdick, "The Kind of Prayer These Times call For," sermon for November 18, 1945, manuscript at Union Theological Seminary, p. 9.

180. Leininger, p. 137.

181. Weaver, p. 316.

182. Goldman, p. 182.

183. *TNYT*, October 3, 1955, p. 52.

184. Quoted by *TNYT*, December 26, 1955, p. 20.

CHAPTER XIV

1. Sockman, *Whom Christ Commended*, pp. 128-29.

2. Ralph W. Sockman, "God's Move Now," sermon for June 22, 1947, manuscript at Syracuse University, p. 7.

3. Ralph W. Sockman, "Our Saving Common Sense," sermon for June 18, 1950, manuscript at Syracuse University, p. 7.

4. *TNYT*, January 2, 1950, p. 21.

5. Ralph W. Sockman, "How to Keep from Feeling Cheap," sermon for March 5, 1950, manuscript at Syracuse University, p. 7.

6. Sockman, *The Fine Art of Using*, p. 16.

7.   Ralph W. Sockman, "Who Meet at the Manger?" sermon for December 23, 1945, manuscript at Syracuse University, p. 9.

8. Ralph W. Sockman, "Living Your Whole Life," sermon for January 8, 1940, manuscript at Syracuse University, p. 1.

9. Sockman, "Down to Earth," sermon for May 6, 1951, manuscript at Syracuse University, p. 2.

10. Ralph W. Sockman, "The Preacher," *Religion in Life* (Spring 1949), p. 198.

11. Sockman, *The Fine Art of Using*, p. 15.

12.   Ralph W. Sockman, *The Higher Happiness* (New York: Abingdon-Cokesbury, 1950), pp. 56-57. Ralph W. Sockman, *The Meaning of Suffering* (New York: Abingdon, 1961), p. 93.

13. Sockman, *The Meaning of Suffering*, p. xi.

14. Ralph W. Sockman, "God's Gentlemen," sermon for March 23, 1952, manuscript at Syracuse University, p. 10.

15. Ralph W. Sockman, "You and Your World," sermon for May 11, 1947, manuscript at Syracuse University, p. 7.

16. Ralph W. Sockman, *Now to Live* (New York: Abingdon-Cokesbury, 1946), p. 160.

17. Ralph W. Sockman, "How God Helps in Temptation," sermon for March 2, 1947, manuscript at Syracuse University, p. 11.

18. Ralph W. Sockman, "The Whole Man and the Whole Gospel," sermon for January 30, 1955, manuscript at Syracuse University, p. 9.

19. Ralph W. Sockman, "To Save Our Lives," sermon for uncertain date in September, 1950, manuscript at Syracuse University, pp. 19-20.

20. Ralph W. Sockman, *How to Believe: The Questions that Challenge Man's Faith Answered in the Light of the Apostles' Creed* (Garden City, New York: Doubleday, 1953), p. 29.

21. Sockman, *Whom Christ Commended*, p. 19.

22. Ralph W. Sockman, "What Is Faith?" sermon for October 8, 1950, manuscript at Syracuse University, p. 1.

23. Ibid., p. 5.

24. Ralph W. Sockman, "The Use of Faith," sermon for June 15, 1952, manuscript at Syracuse University, p. 1.

25. Sockman, *How to Believe*, p. 127.

26. Ibid., pp. 128-29.

27. Ralph W. Sockman, "When Each Walks Alone," sermon for March 3, 1946, manuscript at Syracuse University, pp. 13-14.

28. Ralph W. Sockman, "God at the Gateways," sermon for April 16, 1950, manuscript at Syracuse University, p. 6.

29. Sockman, "Search for Security," sermon for July 30, 1944, and June 30, 1946, manuscript at Syracuse University, p. 8.

30. Sockman, "The Eternal Contemporary," also titled "The Undying Ally," sermon for September 15, 1935, and May 1954, manuscript at Syracuse University, pp. 5-7.

31. Ralph W. Sockman, "The Company We Keep," sermon for November 18, 1951, manuscript at Syracuse University, p. 6.

32. Ralph W. Sockman, "His Only Son Our Lord," sermon for December 16, 1951, manuscript at Syracuse University, p. 2.

33. Ibid., p. 5.

34. Sockman, *How to Believe*, p. 200.

35. Sockman, *The Higher Happiness*, p. 37.

36. Ralph W. Sockman, "The Center of the Century," sermon for December 31, 1950, manuscript at Syracuse University, p. 18.

37. Ralph W. Sockman, "Bonds that Do Not Break," sermon for October 1, 1950, manuscript at Syracuse University, p. 6.

38. Ibid., p. 1.

39. Ralph W. Sockman, "A Voice above Ours," sermon for June 12, 1949, manuscript at Syracuse University, p. 9.

40. Ralph W. Sockman, "The Gift of Growth," sermon for February 2, 1952, manuscript at Syracuse University, p. 5.

41. Sockman, *Now to Live*, p. 49.

42. Ibid., p. 47.

43. Ralph W. Sockman, "How God Helps in Trouble," sermon for March 9, 1947, manuscript at Syracuse University, p. 8.

44. Sockman, "A Free Church in a Free World," sermon for October 23, 1949, manuscript at Syracuse University, pp. 5-6.

45. Sockman, "A Voice Not Our Own," sermon for March 27, 1955 and December 31, 1939, manuscript at Syracuse University, p. 6. Cf. *Now to Live*, p. 59. Joseph Stalin, on February 9, 1946, said "that communism and capitalism were incompatible and that another war was inevitable." A month later Winston Churchill spoke in Missouri, declaring that "an iron curtain had descended across the continent [of Europe]." (David McCullough, *Truman* [New York: Simon and Schuster, 1992], pp. 486-490.)

46. Ralph W. Sockman, *A Lift for Living* (New York: Abingdon, 1956), p. 80.

47. Sockman, *Now to Live*, p. 184.

48. Sockman, "God at the Gateways," sermon for April 16, 1950, manuscript at Syracuse University, p. 1.

49. Ralph W. Sockman, "Faith in God and Trust in Man," sermon for January 14, 1951, manuscript at Syracuse University, p. 7.

50. Ibid., pp. 5-6.

51. *TNYT*, September 29, 1952, p. 14. Cf. Ralph W. Sockman, *Man's First Love: The Great Commandment* (Garden City, New York: Doubleday, 1958), p. 91.

52. Sockman, *Man's First Love*, p. 92.

53. Sockman, "The Preacher," *Religion in Life*, spring 1949, pp. 193-94.

54. Ralph W. Sockman, "Who Knows When God Speaks?" sermon for July 9, 1950, manuscript at Syracuse University, p. 1.

55. Ralph W. Sockman, "How Secure Can We Be?" sermon for September 18, 1949, manuscript at Syracuse University, pp. 3-4.

56. Ralph W. Sockman, *The Whole Armor of God* (New York: Abingdon, 1955), p. 12. Cf. *The Higher Happiness*, pp. 46-47.

57. Sockman, "A Creed that Counts," sermon for October 27, 1946, manuscript at Syracuse University, p. 7.

58. Sockman, *Now to Live*, p. 62.

59. Ralph W. Sockman, "Give God a Chance," sermon for October 21, 1951, manuscript at Syracuse University, p. 3. "A Preface to Peace," sermon for July 4, 1954, manuscript at Syracuse University, p. 8.

60. Ralph W. Sockman, "Creative Christians," sermon for January 13, 1946, manuscript at Syracuse University, p. 2.

61. Ralph W. Sockman, "Coming into God's Kingdom," sermon for April 3, 1955, manuscript at Syracuse University, p. 4.

62. Ralph W. Sockman, "The Ruler Who Redeems," sermon for March 21, 1948, manuscript at Syracuse University, p. 7.

63. Ralph W. Sockman, "Comfort or Cure," sermon for April 7, 1946, manuscript at Syracuse University, p. 6.

64. Ralph W. Sockman, *The Lord's Prayer: An Interpretation* (Boston: Pilgrim Press, 1947), p. 18.

65. Ralph W. Sockman, "How God Helps in Forgiveness," sermon for March 23, 1947, manuscript at Syracuse University, p. 6.

66. Ralph W. Sockman, "Being Good in Bad Places," sermon for September 29, 1946, manuscript at Syracuse University, p. 3.

67. Sockman, "Faith in God and Trust in Man," sermon for January 14, 1951, manuscript at Syracuse University, p. 6.

68. *TNYT*, January 15, 1951, p. 20.

69. Sockman, *How to Believe*, p. 201.

70. Sockman, *The Fine Art of Using*, p. 52.

71. Ralph W. Sockman, "Fingerprints and Footprints," sermon for May 22, 1955, manuscript at Syracuse University, p. 2.

72. *TNYT*, November 8, 1954, p. 18.

73. Ralph W. Sockman, "The Faith that Heals," sermon for May 25, 1947, manuscript at Syracuse University, p. 5.

74. Ralph W. Sockman, "Our Surprising Selves," sermon for April 17, 1955, manuscript at Syracuse University, p. 4.

75. Sockman "A Preface to Peace," sermon for July 4, 1954, manuscript at Syracuse University, p. 8.

76. Ralph W. Sockman, "How Can We Love Our Enemies," sermon for January 29, 1950, manuscript at Syracuse University, p. 10.

77. Sockman, "Make Up Your Mind," sermon for May 28, 1950, manuscript at Syracuse University, p. 5.

78. Sockman, *Now to Live*, pp. 13-14.

79. Sockman, *The Fine Art of Using*, p. 92.

80. Sockman, *Lift for Living*, p. 13.

81. Sockman, *Now to Live*, p. 22.

82. Sockman, *How to Believe*, p. 54.

83. Ralph W. Sockman, "You and Your World," sermon for May 11, 1947, manuscript at Syracuse University, p. 7.

84. Hibbard, p. 141.

CHAPTER XV

1. *MAPC News*, April 11, 1947, p. 6.

2. He took the leave soon after the manuscripts were completed, but not before he had—hurriedly and unexpectedly—to write the exposition of Philemon. Its commissioned author died, and Buttrick confronted the emergency by writing the material himself. He had already written the expositions of Matthew and of portions of Luke.

3. "Great Preachers," *Life*, April 6, 1953, p. 127.

4. *TNYT*, April 4, 1949, p. 21.

5. George A. Buttrick, *Faith and Education* (New York: Abingdon-Cokesbury Press, 1952), p. 54.

6. George A. Buttrick, *God, Pain, and Evil* (Nashville: Abingdon Press, 1966), p. 191.

7. George A. Buttrick, *Prayer in Life: Life in Prayer* (Nashville: Upper Room, 1976), pp. 6-7.

8. George A. Buttrick, *So We Believe, So We Pray* (New York: Abingdon-Cokesbury, 1951), p. 126.

9. *TNYT*, February 19, 1951, p. 17.

10. George A. Buttrick, *Sermons Preached in a University Church* (New York: Abingdon Press, 1959), p. 176.

11. Buttrick, *God, Pain, and Evil*, p. 150.

12. George A. Buttrick, "Victory Over Dejection," sermon for September 14, 1952, in *MAPC News*, n.d., n.p.

13. George A. Buttrick, "The Lonely Prayers of Jesus," sermon for May 20, 1951, in *MAPC News*, n.d., n.p.

14. George A. Buttrick, "Our Home—And God," sermon for May 8, 1949, in *MAPC News*, May 1950, p. 1.

15. George A. Buttrick, "Unprofitable Servants," sermon for March 5, 1950, manuscript at Harvard University, number MA 1612, p. 1.

16. George A. Buttrick, "The City and Christ," sermon for April 29, 1951, manuscript at Harvard University, number MA 1700, p. 5. Cf. George A. Buttrick, *The Beatitudes: A Contemporary Meditation* (Nashville: Abingdon Press, 1968), p. 55.

17. Buttrick, *So We Believe, So We Pray*, pp. 230-31.

18. George A. Buttrick, "Deep Will," sermon for February 20, 1949, manuscript at Harvard University, number MA 1548, p. 7.

19. George A. Buttrick, *Biblical Thought and the Secular University* (Baton Rouge: Louisiana State University Press, 1960), p. 47.

20. Buttrick, *Faith and Education*, pp. 7-8, 87.

21. Buttrick, *God, Pain, and Evil*, p. 23.

22. Buttrick, *Christ and Man's Dilemma*, pp. 184, 187.

23. Buttrick, *Sermons Preached in a University Church*, p. 41.

24. Buttrick, *Christ and Man's Dilemma*, p. 184.

25. Blankenship, p. 59.

26. Buttrick, *Biblical Thought and the Secular University*, p. 47.

27. *TNYT*, December 10, 1945, p. 17.

28. Buttrick, *So We Believe, So We Pray*, p. 31.

29. George A. Buttrick, "Faith and Salvation," sermon for October 31, 1948, manuscript at Harvard University, number MA 1522, p. 8.

30. George A. Buttrick, "I Believe in Jesus Christ," sermon for March 9, 1947, in *MAPC News*, March 14, 1947, p. 3.

31. George A. Buttrick, "The Home of the Soul," sermon for June 13, 1948, manuscript at Harvard University, number MA 1511, pp. 6-7.

32. Buttrick, *God, Pain, and Evil*, pp. 108-9.

33. Buttrick, "Faith and Salvation," sermon for October 31, 1943, manuscript at Harvard University, number MA 1522, p. 2.

34. George A. Buttrick, "Thanksgiving, 1949," sermon for November 24, 1949, in *MAPC News*, n.p.

35. Ibid.

36. George A. Buttrick, "Through Faith to Peace," sermon for October 30, 1949, manuscript at Harvard University, number MA 1585, p. 8.

37. George A. Buttrick, "The Coming Kingdom," sermon for October 29, 1950, manuscript at Harvard University, number MA 1650, p. 5.

38. Buttrick, "The Word Became Flesh," sermon for December 14, 1947, manuscript at Harvard University, number MA 1459, p. 6.

39. George A. Buttrick, "The Yoke of Christ," sermon for September 2, 1951, in *MAPC News*, n.d., n.p.

40. *TNYT*, September 29, 1947, p. 14.

41. George A. Buttrick, "Bread and Brotherhood," sermon for March 23, 1952, manuscript at Harvard University, number MA 1722, p. 7.

42. George A. Buttrick, "Gambling, Higher Style," sermon for October 17, 1948, in *MAPC News*, June 1949, p. 8.

43. Buttrick, *So We Believe, So We Pray*, p. 18.

44. George A. Buttrick, "God's Perfecting," sermon for February 1, 1948, in *MAPC News*, May 1948, p. 1.

45. Buttrick, *Sermons Preached in a University Church*, p. 29.

46. George A. Buttrick, "Unpardonable Sins or Invincible Grace," sermon for October 19, 1947, manuscript at Harvard University, number MA 1445, p. 5.

47. George A. Buttrick, "Indwelling Light," sermon for November 25, 1945, manuscript at Harvard University, number MA 1327, p. 1.

48. George A. Buttrick, "Power and Gentleness," sermon for December 23, 1945, manuscript at Harvard University, number MA 1333, pp. 3-5.

49. George A. Buttrick, *Christ and History* (New York: Abingdon Press, 1963), pp. 16-17.

50. Ibid., p. 17.

51. Buttrick, *God, Pain, and Evil*, p. 59.

52. Ibid., p. 92.

53. Ibid., pp. 85-92.

54. George A. Buttrick, "Strange Paths," sermon for January 2, 1949, manuscript at Harvard University, number MA 1539, p. 4.

55. George A. Buttrick, "How to Study the Bible," sermon for September 28, 1952, manuscript at Harvard University, number MA 1747, pp. 4-5. (This sermon came two days in advance of the publication of the Revised Standard Version.)

56. George A. Buttrick, "Eternal Life: Longing and Fulfillment," sermon for April 13, 1952, in *MAPC News*, n.d., n.p.

57. Buttrick, *biblical Thought and the Secular University*, p. 59.

58. George A. Buttrick, "Pilgrims—and Giant Despair," sermon for November 10, 1946, manuscript at Harvard University, number MA 1388, p. 2.

59. Buttrick, *God, Pain, and Evil*, p. 36.

60. Buttrick, *Sermons Preached in a University Church*, p. 124.

61. George A. Buttrick, "The Bible and Our Crisis," sermon for March 14, 1954, manuscript at Harvard University, number MA 1842, p. 8.

62. Ibid., p. 5.

63. Ibid., p. 2.

64. Buttrick, *Christ and Man's Dilemma*, pp. 26-27.

65. George A. Buttrick, "The Longing for Life," sermon for November 23, 1952, manuscript at Harvard University, number MA 1759, p. 2.

66. Buttrick, *God, Pain, and Evil*, p. 76.

67. Buttrick, *Sermons Preached in a University Church*, p. 174.

68. George A. Buttrick, "Christ and the World Problem," sermon for March 16, 1952, manuscript at Harvard University, number MA 1719, p. 6.

69. George A. Buttrick, "God and Goodness," sermon for May 25, 1952, manuscript at Harvard University, number MA 1739, n.p.

70. George A. Buttrick, "Improved People or New People," sermon for October 28, 1945, manuscript at Harvard University, number MA 1320, p. 8.

71. George A. Buttrick, "Well Guarded," sermon for September 26, 1948, manuscript at Harvard University, number MA 1514, p. 6.

72. George A. Buttrick, "Hopeless Yet Hoping Folk," sermon for December 14, 1952, manuscript at Harvard University, number MA 1765, p. 1.

73. Buttrick, "Well Guarded," sermon for September 26, 1948, manuscript at Harvard University, number 1514, p. 6.

74. George A. Buttrick, "The Paradox of Human Nature," sermon for November 13, 1949, manuscript at Harvard University, number MA 1588, p. 4.

75. Buttrick, *Sermons Preached in a University Church*, p. 182.

76. George A. Buttrick, "The Betrayal," sermon for March 17, l946, manuscript at Harvard University, number MA 1352, p. 5.

77. George A. Buttrick, "I Believe in the Forgiveness of Sins," sermon for March 30, 1947, in *MAPC News*, April 4, 1947, p. 4.

78. George A. Buttrick, "New Advent," sermon for December 7, 1947, in *MAPC News*, March 1948, p. 1.

79. Buttrick, *God, Pain, and Evil*, pp. 60-61.

80. Buttrick, "The Betrayal," sermon for March 17, 1946, manuscript at Harvard University, number MA 1352, p. 7. Cf. George A. Buttrick, "Christ the King," sermon for June 6, 1948, in *MAPC News*, n.d., n.p.

81. George A. Buttrick, "God's Will and Man's Will," sermon for November 12, 1950, manuscript at Harvard University, number MA 1654, pp. 2-4.

82. George A. Buttrick, "Harvest of Light," sermon for April 25, 1948, manuscript at Harvard University, number MA 1498, p. 3.

83. Buttrick, "New Advent," sermon for December 7, 1947, in *MAPC News*, March 1948, p. 1.

84. George A. Buttrick, "Gethsemane," sermon for March 10, 1946, manuscript at Harvard University, number MA 1351, p. 5.

85. Buttrick, "New Advent," sermon for December 7, 1947, in *MAPC News* March 1948, p. 3.

86. Buttrick, *Christ and Man's Dilemma*, p. 8.

87. Ibid., pp. 45-46.

88. Buttrick, *God, Pain, and Evil*, p. 124.

89. Buttrick, *So We Believe, So We Pray*, pp. 169-75.

90. Buttrick, *Christ and Man's Dilemma*, p. 57.

91. Buttrick, *God, Pain, and Evil*, p. 72.

92. Buttrick, "Our Home—and God," sermon for May 8, 1949, in *MAPC News* May 1950, p. 4.

93. George A. Buttrick, "Good News of a Great Joy," sermon for December 24, 1950, manuscript at Harvard University, number MA 1664, p. 2.

94. Buttrick, *Christ and History,* p. 120.

95. Buttrick, *Sermons Preached in a University Church*, p. 60.

96. Ibid., p. 59.

97. Buttrick, *Sermons Preached in a University Church*, p. 151.

98. George A. Buttrick, "The Star and the Manger," sermon for December 16, 1945, manuscript at Harvard University, number MA 1332, p. 8.

99. George A. Buttrick, "Deliverance from Evil," sermon for December 10, 1950, manuscript at Harvard University, number MA 1660, p. 2.

100. George A. Buttrick, "The Power of the Gospel," sermon for June 29, 1947, manuscript at Harvard University, number MA 1436, p. 3.

101. Buttrick, *Faith and Education*, p. 8.

102. Buttrick, *biblical Thought and the Secular University*, pp. 9-10.

103. George A. Buttrick, "The Heart of the Matter," sermon for February 27, 1949, manuscript at Harvard University, number MA 1550, pp. 2-3.

EPILOGUE

1. Herberg, p. 61.

2. Ibid., p. 78n.

3. DeWitte T. Holland, *The Preaching Tradition: A Brief History* (Nashville: Abingdon, 1980), p. 86.

CHAPTER XVI

1.   Joseph Sittler, "George Buttrick: A Tribute and a Reflection," *Christian Century*, vol. 97, April 16, 1980, p. 430.

2.   Commager, *The American Mind*, p. 166. Charles Clayton Morrison put Fosdick in a class with Henry Ward Beecher and Brooks ("About Preachers and a Preacher," *Christian Century*, vol. 76, August 5, 1959, p. 903).

3.   "The New York City Pulpit," *The Pulpit*, May 1964, p. 10. (An index identified the author as William L. Miller. The issue of the journal, however, referred to the "anonymous" writer as a person with thirty years of ministerial experience in Manhattan.)

4.   Manchester, p. 81.

5.   Heiko Oberman, "Preaching and the Word in the Reformation," *Theology Today*, April 1961, vol. xviii, no. 1, p. 28.

6.   Reinhold Niebuhr, "The Significance of Dr. Fosdick in American Religious Thought," *Union Seminary Quarterly Review*, vol. 8, May 1953, pp. 3-4.

7.   Ronald E. Osborn, "The Effect of Preaching on American Life—and Vice Versa," *Encounter*, vol. 36, no. 3, Summer 1975, p. 255.

8.   Gertner, p. 33.

9.   Quoted in Schroeder, p. 45.

10.   Ray C. Petry, *Preaching in the Great Tradition: Neglected Chapters in the History of Preaching* (Philadelphia: Westminster Press, 1950), p. 40.

11.   Ibid., p. 46.

12.   Osborn, p. 268.

13.   Landry, pp. 3-4.

14. Hall, p. 217.

15. Gertner, p. 50

16. Creighton, p. 131.

17. Carl Braaten, "The Interdependence of Theology and Preaching," *Dialog, A Journal of Theology* 3 (Winter, 1964) :14.

18. Ibid, p. 16.

19. Dillenberger and Welch, p. 305.

20. Ibid., p. 323.

21. Ibid., p. 305.

22. Ibid., p. 25.

23. Osborn, p. 268.

24. Ban, p. 169.

25. Buttrick, *Christ and Man's Dilemma*, p. 184.

26. George A. Buttrick, "I Believe in Life Everlasting," sermon for April 6, 1947, in *MAPC News*, April 11, 1947, p. 3.

27. Buttrick, "Unpardonable Sin or Invincible Grace," sermon for October 19, 1947, manuscript at Harvard University, number MA 1443, p. 5.

28. George A. Buttrick, "The Wonderment of Jesus," sermon for April 3, 1949, manuscript at Harvard University, number MA 1559, pp. 4, 6-7.

29. Leininger, p. 212.

30. Sockman, "How God Helps in Forgiveness," sermon for March 23, 1947, manuscript at Syracuse University, p. 10.

31. Dillenberger and Welch, p. x.

32. Manchester, p. 1259.

BIBLIOGRAPHY

A. Primary Sources

Among the most important sources for this research were the manuscripts of unpublished sermons by Buttrick, Fosdick, Scherer, and Sockman. Many of these specific sermons are cited in footnotes by title and date(s) of delivery, with information about the location of each manuscript in the archival collections at Union Theological Seminary, Harvard, or Syracuse. In some cases, where a sermon was printed for limited distribution through a church newsletter, that source is cited as well. Though these unpublished sermons are not listed individually in the bibliography, their importance (and the author's gratitude, already acknowledged, to the curators of the collections) is incalculable.

1. George A. Buttrick

a. Books

The Beatitudes: A Contemporary Meditation. Nashville: Abingdon Press, 1968.

Biblical Thought and the Secular University. Baton Rouge: Louisiana State University Press, 1960.

Christ and History. New York: Abingdon Press, 1963.

Christ and Man's Dilemma. Nashville: Abingdon-Cokesbury Press, 1946.

The Christian Fact and Modern Doubt. New York: C. Scribner, 1935.

Faith and Education. New York: Abingdon-Cokesbury Press, 1952.

God, Pain, and Evil. Nashville: Abingdon Press, 1966.

Is Prayer Intelligent? Nashville: The Upper Room, 1976.

Jesus Came Preaching: Christian Preaching in the New Age. New York: C. Scribner's Sons, 1931.

The Parables of Jesus. Garden City, New York: Doubleday, 1928.

The Power of Prayer Today. Waco: Word Books, 1970.

Prayer. New York: Abingdon-Cokesbury, 1942.

Prayer in Life: Life in Prayer. Nashville: Upper Room, 1976

Preaching in These Times. New York: C. Scribner's Sons, 1940.

Sermons Preached in a University Church. New York: Abingdon
     Press, 1959.

So We Believe, So We Pray. New York: Abingdon-Cokesbury,
     1951.

b. Published Articles and Sermons

"Anniversary Address." *Southern Workman (Hampton Institute)*
     65 (June 1936): 163-71.

"Crisis and the Hereafter." *Rice Institute Pamphlet* 32 (April 1945):
     37-89.

"Disharmony about TM." *Christian Century*, 17 March 1976,
     259-62.

"Fire Bringer." *Rice Institute Pamphlet* 19 (October 1932): 343-
     51.

"Genuine Faith is Real Lack in Modern Education." *Vital
     Speeches*, 15 March 1947, 339-41.

"Lenten Reading List." *Publishers Weekly*, 8 May 1943, 1188-
     90.

"Lenten Reading List—1944." *Publishers Weekly,* 19 February 1944,
     868-69.

"List of Books for Lenten Reading." *Publishers Weekly,* 17 February 1940, 796-97.

"Our Shaken World and the Unshaken Kingdom." *Theology Today* 7 (October 1950): 301-7.

"Power and the Man." *Expositor* 40 (July 1943): 280-95.

"Prayer and the Return of Faith." *Christian Century*, 3 June 1942, 722-24.

"Slave of Christ." *Pulpit Digest* 34 (January 1954).

"The Study of the Bible." In *The Interpreter's Bible*, vol. 1, 165-71. New York: Abingdon, 1952.

"What is Truth?" *Union Seminary Quarterly Review* 16 (December 1960): 106-114.

2. Harry Emerson Fosdick

a. Books

Adventurous Religion and Other Essays. New York: Harper and Bros., 1926.

The American Hymnal. New York: Century and Co., 1913.

As I See Religion. New York: Harper and Bros., 1932.

The Assurance of Immortality. New York: Macmillan, 1916.

A Book of Public Prayers. New York: Harper, 1959.

The Challenge of the Present Crisis. New York: Association Press, 1917.

A Christian Conscience about War. Geneva: League of Nations, 1925.

Christianity and Progress. New York: Fleming H. Revell, 1922.

Dear Mr. Brown: Letters to a Person Perplexed about Religion.
        New York: Harper, 1961.

A Faith for Tough Times. London: SCM Press, 1953.

First Sermon as Pastor of Park Avenue Baptist Church. New York:
        Park Avenue Baptist Church, 1925.

A Great Time to Be Alive: Sermons on Christianity in Wartime.
        London: SCM Press, 1945.

Great Voices of the Reformation: An Anthology. New York: Random
        House, 1952.

*A Guide to Understanding the Bible: The Development of Ideas
        within the Old and New Testaments*. New York: Harper and
        Bros., 1938.

*The Hope of the World: Twenty-Five Sermons on Christianity
        Today*. New York: Harper and Bros., 1933.

Hymns of the Living Church. New York: Century and Co., 1970.

Jesus of Nazareth. New York: Random House, 1959.

The Life of St. Paul. New York: Random House, 1962.

The Living of These Days: An Autobiography. New York: Harper,
        1956.

Living under Tension: Sermons on Christianity Today. New York:
        Harper and Bros., 1941.

The Man from Nazareth as His Contemporaries Saw Him. New
        York: Harper, 1949.

The Manhood of the Master. New York: Association Press, 1913.

Martin Luther. New York: Random House, 1956.

The Meaning of Being a Christian. New York: Association Press, 1964.

The Meaning of Faith. New York: Abingdon, 1921.

The Meaning of Prayer. New York: Association Press, 1920.

The Meaning of Service. New York: Association Press, 1920.

A Modern Preacher's Problem in His Use of the Scriptures. New York: Union Theological Seminary, 1915.

The Modern Use of the Bible. New York: Macmillan, 1924.

On Being Fit to Live With: Sermons on Post-War Christianity. New York: Harper and Bros., 1946.

On Being a Real Person. New York: Harper and Bros., 1943.

A Pilgrimage to Palestine. New York: Macmillan, 1949.

The Power to See It Through. New York: Harper and Bros., 1935.

Riverside Sermons. New York: Harper, 1958.

The Second Mile. New York: Association Press, 1922.

The Secret of Victorious Living: Sermons on Christianity Today. New York: Harper and Bros., 1934.

Shall We End War? A Sermon Preached at First Presbyterian Church, New York. New York: Clearing House for Limitation of Armament, n.d.

Spiritual Values and Eternal Life. Cambridge, Mass.: Harvard, 1927.

Successful Christian Living: Sermons on Christianity Today. New
    York: Harper and Bros., 1937.

Twelve Tests of Character. New York: Association Press, 1923.

*What Is Vital in Religion? Sermons on Contemporary Christian
    Problems*. New York: Harper, 1955.

b. Published Articles and Sermons

"America's Biggest Problem." *American Magazine*, May 1929, 11-13.

"Animated Conversation." In *Harry Emerson Fosdick's Art of
    Preaching: An Anthology*, edited by Lionel George Crocker.
    Springfield, Ill.: Charles C. Thoman, 1971.

"Are Religious People Fooling Themselves?" *Harper's Monthly
    Magazine*, June 1930, 59-70.

"Are We Fit for Democracy?" *Scribner's Commentator* 9 (January
    1941): 89-92.

"The Best Advice I Ever Had." *Reader's Digest*, April 1954, 63f.

"The Best Years of Our Lives." *Reader's Digest*, January 1947, 117-
    18.

"Beyond Modernism." *The Christian Century*, December 4, 1935,
    1549-52.

"Beyond Reason." *Religious Education* 23 (May 1928): 471-78.

"Building a Personality." *Reader's Digest*, May 1937, 79-81.

"Can the Church Stop War?" *World Tomorrow* 14 (June 1931): 187-
    88.

"Capitalizing Discontent." *Homiletic Review* 107 (March 1934):
    211-16.

"The Christian Ministry." In *Harry Emerson Fosdick's Art of Preaching: An Anthology,* edited by Lionel G. Crocker. Springfield, Ill.: Charles C. Thomas, 1971.

"The Christian Ministry." *Atlantic.* January 1929, 24-30.

"Christianity's Supreme Rival." *Christian Century*, 19 January 1928, 74-77.

"Christmas and the Family." *Pictorial Review*, January 1931, 1.

"Civilized to Death." *Vital Speeches*, 1 July 1937, 567-69.

"Crisis Confronting the Nation." *Vital Speeches*, 1 September 1940, 686-87.

"Democracy Begins at Home." *Scholastic*, 25 April 1951, 3.

"Ethical Problems of Neutrality." *Reference Shelf* 14 (1940): 427-37.

"Faith for Tough Times." *Reader's Digest,* December 1952, 86-88.

"Family Religion." *Journal of Social Hygiene* 21 (May 1935): 243-45.

"First Things First." *Library Journal*, 15 October 1939, 780.

"God: An Idea That Never Stops Growing." *Good Housekeeping*, May 1929, 59.

"Have We Lost Our Moral Heritage?" *Vital Speeches,* 1 August 1952, 628-31.

"Hope of the World in Its Minorities." *World Tomorrow*, October 1931, 320.

"How I Prepare My Sermons." *The Quarterly Journal of Speech* 40 (February 1954): 50-54. Also in *Harry Emerson Fosdick's Art of Preaching: An Anthology,* edited by Lionel G. Crocker. Springfield, Ill.: Charles C. Thomas, 1971.

"How to Keep Out of the Psychiatrists' Hands." *Reader's Digest*, July
        1947, 9-13.

"If America Is Drawn into the War." *Christian Century*, 22 January
        1941, 115-18.

"If You Have a Good Excuse, Don't Use It." *Reader's Digest*,
        June 1948, 19-21.

"International Prayer Meeting." *Christian Century*, 11 March 1942,
        319.

"Introduction." In *Preaching in Theory and Practice,* by Samuel
        McComb. New York: Oxford University Press, 1926.

"Jesus' Ethical Message Confronts the World." *Reference Shelf* 13
        (1939): 223-33.

"Living for the Fun of It." *American Magazine*, April 1930, 57.

"Living for the Fun of It." *Ladies Home Journal*, November 1949,
        192.

"Minister and Psychotherapy." *Pastoral Psychology* 11 (February
        1960): 11-13.

"Modern Child Should Guide Himself." *World's Work*, January
        1929, 54-58.

"The Modern World's Rediscovery of Sin." *The Pulpit*, March
        1939, 49-52.

"Morals Secede from the Union." *Harper's Monthly Magazine*, May
        1932, 682-92.

"My Account with the Unknown Soldier." *Christian Century*, 6 June
        1934, 754-56.

"On Being a Real Person." *Reader's Digest*, March 1943, 121-37.

"One Unfailing Resource." *Reader's Digest*, June 1946, 51-54.

"One World for Religion, Too." *Reader's Digest*, May 1946, 72-74.

"Our Religious Illiterates." *Reader's Digest*, February 1949, 97-100.

"Pacifism Means Peace." *Review of Reviews* 95 (May 1937): 54-55.

"Personal Counseling and Preaching." *Pastoral Psychology*, March 1952, 11-15.

"The Personality that Christmas Celebrates." *Life*, 24 December 1945, 74-85. Also in *Reader's Digest*, October 1954, 292f.

"Positive Protestantism." *The Pulpit*, October 1954, 292f.

"Protestant Lenten Reading List, 1947." *Publishers Weekly*, 22 February 1947, 1242-44.

"Putting Christ into Uniform." *Christian Century*, 13 December 1939, 1539-42.

"Religion and Birth Control." *Outlook*, 19 June 1929, 301.

"Religion without God? The Limits of Humanism." *Harper's Monthly Magazine*, December 1929, 50-60.

"Revolt against Paganism." *Ladies Home Journal*, February 1946, 6f.

"Second Mile." *Reader's Digest*, March 1944, 63-64.

"Shall American School Children Be Religiously Illiterate?" *School and Society*, 29 November 1947, 401-406.

"Should Legal Barriers Against Birth Control Be Removed?" *Congressional Digest* 10 (April 1931): 110-12.

"Should Your Child Be Allowed to Choose His Own Religion?" *Reader's Digest*, May 1947, 59-62.

"Step Toward Fascism." *Parents Magazine*, November 1944, 17. Also
     in *Congressional Digest* 24 (January 1945): 23.

"Teaching Your Child Religion." *World Today*, July 1929, 148-57.
     Also in *World's Work*, February 1929, 52-56.

"To Those Interested in the Profession of the Ministry." In *Harry
     Emerson Fosdick's Art of Preaching: An Anthology,* edited by
     Lionel G. Crocker. Springfield, Ill.: Charles C. Thomas, 1971.

"Time for Great Faiths." *Ladies Home Journal*, October 1947, 42f.

"The Trenches and the Church at Home." *Atlantic Monthly*, January
     1919.

"Tomorrow's Religion." *UN World*, December 1951, 40-43.

"Union and Liberty in the Churches." *Outlook*, 13 November 1929,
     423.

"The Unshaken Christ." *Homiletic Review* 78 (September 1919).

"The Value of a Great Heritage." Address before Washington
     Association of New Jersey, 22 February 1921.

"Vitality Is Mightier Than Size." *Ladies Home Journal*, December
     1950, 11.

"War against Unemployment." *American City*, December 1930, 153.

"We Were Unmercifully Gypped." *Vital Speeches*, 15 April 1937, 415-
     16.

"What Can the Minister Do?" *Review of Reviews* 86 (December
     1932): 44-46.

"What Do You Say to Yourself?" *American Magazine*, October 1929,
     35.

"What Force Is Stronger Than the Atomic Bomb?" *Ladies Home Journal*, April 1946, 48f.

"What Is Christianity?" *Harper's Monthly Magazine*, April 1929, 551-61.

"What Is Happening to the American Family?" *Journal of Social Hygiene* 15 (March 1929): 139-51.

"What Is the Matter with Preaching?" *Harper's Monthly Magazine*, June 1928, 133-41. Also in *College of the Bible Quarterly*, October 1952, 5-18.

"What Is Religion?" *Harper's Monthly Magazine*, March 1929, 424-34.

"What the War Did to My Mind." *Christian Century*, January 5, 1928, 10-11.

"Why Religion Helps Mess Up the World." *Ladies Home Journal,* April 1947, 40f.

"Yes, But Religion Is an Art." *Harper's Monthly Magazine*, January 1931, 129-40.

"You're More Important Than You Think." *Ladies Home Journal*, March 1946, 45f.

3. Paul E. Scherer

a. Books

Event in Eternity. New York: Harper and Bros., 1945.

Facts That Undergird Life. New York: Harper and Bros., 1938.

For We Have This Treasure: The Yale Lectures on Preaching, 1943. New York: Harper and Bros., 1944.

The Place Where Thou Standest. New York: Harper and Bros., 1942.

The Plight of Freedom. New York: Harper, 1948.

When God Hides. New York: Harper and Bros., 1934.

The Word God Sent. New York: Harper and Bros., 1965.

b. Published Articles and Sermons

"After All, What Is Left?" *The Lutheran*, 30 April 1947, 14-16.

"Bibliography for Ministers: Homiletics." *Union Seminary Quarterly Review* 15 (November 1959): 39-44.

"Christian Faith and Personal Relationships." *Union Theological Seminary Monday Morning Lectures*, January 1959.

"Creative Insecurity." *Princeton Seminary Bulletin* 56 (February 1963): 44-49.

"Credibility and Relevance of the Gospel." *Review and Expositor* 54 (July 1957): 355-76.

"Cripples with Queer Remedies." *Homiletic Review* 108 (November 1934): 363-71.

"The Difference Easter Makes." *Advance*, 19 April 1954, 5-6.

"Exodus at Jerusalem." *Union Seminary Quarterly Review* 13 (May 1958): 37-42.

"The Fellowship of His Son." *Princeton Seminary Bulletin* 55 (January 1962): 40-43.

"From Curse to Prayer." In *Best Sermons*, edited by G. P. Butler, 163-68. Chicago: Ziff-Davis Publishing Co., 1949-1950.

"Gauntlet with a Gift in It: From Text to Sermon on Matthew 15:21-28 and Mark 7:24-30." *Interpretation* 20 (October 1966): 387-99.

"God's Insistent 'Yes' to Man's Peevish 'No.'" *Messenger*, 6 April 1954, 8-10.

"God's Weakness and Man's Insight." *In Sermons from an Ecumenical Pulpit*, edited by Max F. Daskam. Boston: Starr King Press, 1956.

"History That Becomes History: Preaching from the Old Testament." *Union Seminary Quarterly Review* 15 (May 1960): 273-80.

"It's Christmas Again." *Christianity and Crisis*, vol. 14, no. 21 (1954): 164-65.

"Jesus Stands in the Midst." In *Notable Sermons from Protestant Pulpits*, edited by Charles Langworth Wallis, 196-203. New York: Abingdon, 1958.

"Let's Keep the Best of Our Heritage." *Advance*, November 10, 1952, 16-17.

"Love That God Defines." *Theology Today* 21 (July 1964): 159-60.

"Near East Kaleidoscope." *Christianity and Crisis,* vol. 13, no. 15 (1953): 114-19.

"One World with Another to Attend to It." *Union Seminary Quarterly Review* 12 (November 1956): 3-8.

"Preaching as a Radical Transaction." *Review and Expositor* 54 (October 1957): 560-73.

"Then Came Jesus and Stood in the Midst." *Interpretation* 12 (January 1958): 52-58. Also in *Christian Century*, 15 April 1942, 490-92.

"The Unreached Goal of the Protestant Reformation." *Messenger*, vol. 10, no. 22, 8-11.

"Ye Seek Jesus of Nazareth." *Lutheran Church Quarterly* 1 (April 1928): 129-36.

4. Ralph W. Sockman

a. Books

Date with Destiny: A Preamble to Christian Culture. New York: Abingdon-Cokesbury, 1944.

The Easter Story for Children. New York: Abingdon Press, 1966.

The Fine Art of Using. New York: Joint Division of Education and Cultivation, Board of Missions and Church Extension, Methodist Church, 1946.

The Higher Happiness. New York: Abingdon-Cokesbury, 1950.

The Highway of God. New York: Macmillan, 1942.

How to Believe: The Questions That Challenge Man's Faith Answered in the Light of the Apostles' Creed. Garden City, N.Y.: Doubleday, 1953.

A Lift for Living. New York: Abingdon, 1956.

Live for Tomorrow. New York: Macmillan, 1939.

The Lord's Prayer: An Interpretation. Boston: Pilgrim Press, 1947.

Man's First Love: The Great Commandment. Garden City, N.Y.: Doubleday, 1958.

The Meaning of Suffering. New York: Abingdon, 1961.

Men of the Mysteries. New York: Abingdon, 1927.

Morals of Tomorrow. New York: Harper, 1931.

Now to Live. New York: Abingdon-Cokesbury, 1946.

The Paradoxes of Jesus. New York: Abingdon Press, 1936.

Recoveries in Religion. Nashville: Cokesbury, 1938.

Suburbs of Christianity. New York: Abingdon, 1924.

The Unemployed Carpenter. New York: Harper, 1933.

The Whole Armor of God. New York: Abingdon, 1955.

Whom Christ Commended. New York: Abingdon, 1963.

b. Published Articles and Sermons

"Case for Immortality." *Coronet* 39 (December 1955): 57-61.

"Catholics and Protestants." *Christian Century*, 2 May 1945, 545-47.

"Challenge of Change." *Rice Institute Pamphlet* 23 (July 1936):
        195-202.

"A Christmas Message to Parents." *Parents Magazine*, December
        1948, 21f.

"Citizens of Tomorrow." *National Education Association Journal*
        30 (April 1941): 97-98.

"The Future of Parish Preaching." *Pulpit Digest* 44 (May 1964):
        13-18.

"Golden Spurs." *Vital Speeches*, 15 August 1948, 657-58.

"Higher Religion for Higher Education." *Vital Speeches*, 1 March
        1948, 304-8.

"How Things Contribute to Life Values." *Playground and Recreation*
    22 (January 1929): 555-60.

"Juts on the Social Skyline." *Rotarian* 48 (May 1936): 6-10.

"Letter to the Editor Withdrawing Support for Goodwin Plan."
    Christian Century, 17 January 1934, 91-92.

"List of Books for Lenten Reading." *Publishers Weekly*, 1 March 1941,
    1012-14.

"Make Up Your Mind." *Vital Speeches*, 1 October 1950, 762-63.

"Meet the Challenge of Wartime." *Woman's Home Companion* 70
    (January 1943): 23.

"Methodists." *Homiletic Review* 108 (August 1934): 83-85.

"Minister in Moscow." *Christian Century*, 11 September 1946, 1089-
    91.

"Mistakes of Moralists." *Harper's Monthly Magazine* 162 (December
    1930): 72-80.

"Morals in a Machine Age." *Harper's Monthly Magazine* 162
    (February 1931): 365-374.

"Nothing Can Stop Christmas." *Parents Magazine,* December 1952,
    35.

"Parson Looks at the Press." *Christian Century*, 28 June 1928, 821-23.

"Perils of the Middle Road." *Homiletic Review* 95 (January 1928):
    66-69.

"Pioneering in Human Achievement." *National Education
    Association Journal* 25 (September 1936): 175-76.

"The Preacher." *Religion in Life* (Spring 1949): 190-98.

"Preface to Peace: Barriers to Be Removed; Mind of the
        Peacemakers; Some Dynamics of Advance." *Rice Institute
        Pamphlet* 31 (July 1944): 87-157.

"The Quick and the Dead." *Homiletic Review* 101 (June 1931):
        489-94.

"Reclaiming Our Wasted Powers." *Recreation* 36 (March 1943):
        685-86.

"Redeeming Our Regrets." *Reference Shelf*, vol. 20, no. 1 (1947):
        271-78, 285.

"Roots of the Reconciling Message." *Union Seminary Quarterly
        Review* 19 (January 1964): 145-52.

"Rx Creative Cures for the Ills of Modern Life." *Recreation* 47
        (April 1954): 205-7.

"Traitors to Ourselves." *Homiletic Review* 107 (June 1934): 478-
        83.

"Twelve Ways to Make January a Better Month." *Good
        Housekeeping* 136 (January 1953): 38f.

"Vanishing Sinner." *Harper's Monthly Magazine* 161 (November
        1930): 676-84.

"What Is a Methodist?" *Look*, October 6, 1953, pp. 116-18.

"What Is the Minister's Real Task?" *Religion in Life* (Summer
        1955): 323-60.

"Worth of One." *Vital Speeches*, 15 August 1949, 654-55.

B. Secondary Sources

1. Books

Ahlstrom, Sydney. *A Religious History of the American People.*
     New Haven: Yale University Press, 1972.

Beverly, Harry Black. *Harry Emerson Fosdick's* Predigtweise: *Its
     Significance for America, Its Limits, Its Overcoming.*
     Winterthur, Switzerland: P. G. Keller, 1965.

Bethge, Eberhard. *Dietrich Bonhoeffer: Man of Vision, Man of
     Courage.* New York: Harper and Row, 1970.

Blackwood, Andrew. *The Protestant Pulpit.* Nashville: Abingdon-
     Cokesbury Press, 1947.

Boorstin, Daniel J. *The Image: or, What Happened to the
     American Dream.* New York: Atheneum, 1962.

Burns, Edward McNall. *The American Idea of Mission: Concepts
     of National Purpose and Destiny.* New Brunswick: Rutgers
     University Press, 1957.

Calkins, Harold L. *Master Preachers: Their Study and Devotional
     Habits.* Washington D.C.: Review and Herald Publishing
     Assn., 1960.

Cauthen, Kenneth. *The Impact of American Religious Liberalism.*
     New York: Harper and Row, 1962.

Chiles, Robert E. *Theological Transition in American Methodism:
     1790-1935.* Nashville: Abingdon Press, 1965.

Cleary, James W., and Frederick W. Haberman. *Rhetoric and Public
     Address: A Bibliography, 1947-1961.* Madison,
     Wisconsin: University of Wisconsin Press, 1964.

Commager, Henry Steele. *The American Mind: An Interpretation of
     American Thought and Character Since the 1880's.* New
     Haven: Yale University Press, 1950.

Crocker, Lionel G. *Harry Emerson Fosdick's Art of Preaching: An
     Anthology.* Springfield, Ill.: Charles C. Thomas, 1971.

Dillenberger, John, and Claude Welch. *Protestant Christianity: Interpreted through Its Development.* New York: Charles Scribner's Sons, 1954.

Ellis, Edward Robb. *The Epic of New York City.* New York: Coward-McCann, Inc. 1966.

Erasmus, Desiderius. *Freedom of the Will.* The Library of Christian Classics, Philadelphia: Westminster Press, 1969.

Fant, Clyde E., and William M. Pinson, Jr., eds. *Twenty Centuries of Great Preaching.* Waco, Texas: Word Books, 1971.

Finklestein, Louis. *American Spiritual Autobiographies.* New York: Harper and Bros., 1948.

Fosdick, Raymond B. *John D. Rockefeller, Jr.: A Portrait.* New York: Harper and Bros., 1956.

_____. *A Philosophy for a Foundation.* New York: Rockefeller Foundation, 1963.

Furniss, Norman F. *The Fundamentalist Controversy, 1918-1931.* New Haven: Yale University Press, 1954.

Gabriel, Ralph Henry. *The Course of American Democratic Thought: An Intellectual History Since 1815.* New York: The Ronald Press Co., 1940.

Gill, Theodore A., ed. *To God Be the Glory: Sermons in Honor of George Arthur Buttrick.* Nashville: Abingdon, 1973.

Goldman, Eric F. *The Crucial Decade—And After: America, 1945-1960.* New York: Alfred A. Knopf, 1973.

Handy, Robert T. *A Christian America: Protestant Hopes and Historical Realities.* New York: Oxford University Press, 1971.

Herberg, Will. *Protestant, Catholic, Jew: An Essay in American Religious Sociology*. Garden City, New York: Doubleday and Co., 1956.

Hochmuth, Marie and W. N. Brigance. eds. *A History and Criticism of American Public Address*. New York: Longmans, Green, 1955.

Holland, DeWitte T. *The Preaching Tradition: A Brief History*. Nashville: Abingdon, 1980.

Hudson, Winthrop S. *Religion in America*. New York: Charles Scribner's Sons, 1965.

Jones, Edgar De Witt. *The Royalty of the Pulpit*. New York: Harper and Bros., 1951.

Linn, Edmund Holt. *Preaching as Counseling: The Unique Method of Harry Emerson Fosdick*. Valley Forge: Judson Press, 1966.

Lukacs, John. *1945: Year Zero*. Garden City, N.Y.: Doubleday and Co., 1978.

Luther, Martin. *The Bondage of the Will*. Vol. 33 in *Luther's Works*. Philadelphia: Fortress Press, 1972.

Macleod, Donald, ed. *Here Is My Method*. Westwood, N.J.: Fleming H. Revell Co., 1952.

Manchester, William. *The Glory and the Dream: A Narrative History of America, 1932-1972*. Boston: Little, Borwn and Co., 1973.

Marty, Martin E. *Righteous Empire: The Protestant Experience in America*. New York: Dial Press, 1970.

Miller, Robert Moats. *Harry Emerson Fosdick: Preacher, Pastor, Prophet*. New York: Oxford University Press, 1985.

Morison, Samuel Eliot, Henry Steele Commager, and William E.
        Leuchtenburg. *The Growth of the American Republic*. New
        York: Oxford University Press, 1969.

Oberman, Heiko. *The Harvest of Medieval Theology*. Grand Rapids:
        Eerdmans, 1967.

Oliver, Robert T. *History of Public Speaking in America*. Boston:
        Allyn and Bacon, 1965.

Petry, Ray C. *Preaching in the Great Tradition: Neglected
        Chapters in the History of Preaching*. Philadelphia:
        Westminster Press, 1950.

Robinson, John A. T. *Honest to God*. Philadelphia: Westminster
        Press, 1963.

Rosenwaike, Ira. *Population History of New York City*. Syracuse
        University Press, nd.

Schlesinger, Arthur M., Sr. *A Critical Period in American
        Religion: 1875-1900*. Philadelphia: Fortress, 1967.

Schroeder, Frederick W. *Preaching the Word with Authority*.
        Philadelphia: Westminster Press, 1954.

Scruggs, Julius R. *Baptist Preachers with Social Consciousness: A
        Comparative Study of Martin Luther King, Jr., and Harry
        Emerson Fosdick*. Philadelphia: Dorrance and Co., 1978.

Simon, Rita James, ed. *As We Saw the Thirties: Essays on Social
        and Political Movements of a Decade*. Urbana, Ill.: University
        of Illinois Press, 1967.

Sleeth, Ronald. *Proclaiming the Word*. New York: Abingdon Press,
        1964.

Talese, Gay. *The Kingdom and the Power*. New York: World
        Publishing Company, 1969.

Toohey, William and William D. Thompson. *Recent Homiletic Thought: A Bibliography, 1935-1965.* Nashville: Abingdon Press, 1967.

U.S. Works Progress Administration, Division of Professional and Service Projects. *Inventory of the Church Archives of New York City.* New York: Historical Records Survey, 1940.

Van Dusen, Henry Pitney. *The Vindication of Liberal Theology: A Tract for the Times.* New York: Charles Scribner's Sons, 1963.

Van Dusen, Henry Pitney, and Samuel M. Cavert. eds. *The Church through a Half Century.* New York: Scribners, 1936.

Wecter, Dixon. *The Age of the Great Depression: 1929-1941.* Chicago: Quadrangle Books, 1971.

2. Articles

Abbott, Ernest Hamlin. "Dr. Fosdick's Religion." *Outlook*, 11 March 1925, 364f.

"The Air's Oldest Pulpit." *Newsweek*, 13 October 1947, 74.

"Ave Atque Vale." *Time*, 8 April 1946, 66.

Ban, Joseph D. "Two Views of One Age: Fosdick and Straton." *Foundations* (Baptist) 14 (April/June 1971): 153-71.

Barton, Fred Jackson. "Ralph Washington Sockman: Twentieth-Century Circuit Rider." *American Public Address.* Columbia, Mo.: University of Missouri Press, 1961.

"Biography of Paul E. Scherer." *Trinity Tidings* (Newsletter of the Evangelical Lutheran Church of the Holy Trinity), September 1920, 5-6.

Bliven, B. "Mr. Rockefeller's Pastor." *New Republic*, 31 December 1956, 20.

Braaten, Carl E. "The Interdependence of Theology and Preaching." *Dialog, A Journal of Theology* 3 (Winter 1964): 12ff.

Carnegie, Andrew. "Wealth." *North American Review.* June 1889, 653-64.

Chiles, Robert E. "Methodist Apostasy: From Free Grace to Free Will." *Religion in Life* 27 (Summer 1958).

Davidson, Charles N. "George Arthur Buttrick: Christocentric Preacher and Pacifist." *Journal of Presbyterian History* 53 (Summer 1975): 143-67.

"Dr. Fosdick Accepts the Challenge." *Christian Century*, 15 October 1930, 1239-41.

"Dr. Fosdick Shifts the Emphasis: Modernism Not Enough." *Christian Century.* 20 November 1935, 1480-82.

"Dr. Fosdick Will Retire Next May." *Christian Century*, 20 June 1945, 725.

Elson, Edward L. R. "Evaluating Our Religious Revival." *Journal of Religious Thought* 14 (Autumn/Winter 1956-57): 55-62.

Exman, Eugene. "Fosdick as Author." *Christian Century*, 21 May 1958, 617.

Ferm, Deane W. "Living of These Days: A Tribute to Harry Emerson Fosdick." *Christian Century,* 3 May 1978, 472-74.

"Fosdick's Last Year." *Time*, 18 June 1945, 56f.

Gager, C. S. "We Should Be Constructive: Reply to H. H. Smith." *Outlook*, 30 October 1929, 321.

Gilkey, Charles W. "Preaching." In *Protestant Thought in the Twentieth-Century,* edited by A. S. Nash. New York: Macmillan, 1951.

_____. "Protestant Preaching." In *The Church Through a Half-Century: Essays in Honor of William Adams Brown*, edited by Samuel McCrea Cavert and Henry Pitney Van Dusen. New York: Charles Scribner's Sons, 1936.

Goodbar, Octavia W. "Dr. Sockman at Christ Church." *Church Management*, June 1942, 16.

Gray, James M. "The Static and the Dynamic: An Examination of Dr. Harry Emerson Fosdick's Now Famous Sermon on Progressive Christianity." *Moody Bible Monthly,* May 1922.

"Great Preachers: George A. Buttrick." *Life*, 6 April 1953, 129.

"Great Preachers: Ralph A. Sockman." *Life*, 6 April 1953, 128.

Handy, Robert T. "Dr. Fosdick's Use of History." *Union Seminary Quarterly Review* 8 (May 1953): 6.

Harris, Erdman. "Harry Emerson Fosdick and Reinhold Niebuhr: A Contrast in the Methods of the Teaching Preacher." *Religion in Life* (Summer 1943): 389-400.

"Harry Emerson Fosdick." *Christian Century*, 21 May 1958, 611.

Haselden, Kyle. "An Honor Roll of American Preachers." *The Pulpit* 35 (October 1964): 3f.

Hodges, Graham R. "Fosdick at 90: Tribute to a Man for All Seasons." *Christian Century*, 22 May 1968, 684.

"Honor to Dr. Fosdick." *Christian Century*, 20 May 1953, 595.

Hudnut, William H., Jr. "Fosdick as Teacher." *Christian Century*, 21 May 1958, 615-16.

Huntsinger, Jerald. "Sermons Designed for Listening." *Christian Advocate*, 10 May 1962, 14-15.

Lantz, John Edward. "A Survey of Modern Preaching." *Quarterly Journal of Speech* (April 1943): 167-72.

"Liberal." *Time*, 25 May 1953, 62f.

Macnab, John B. "Fosdick at First Church [New York, 1918-1925]." *Journal of Presbyterian History* 52 (Spring 1974): 59-77.

McBrien, Richard P. "The Reformation: A Catholic Reflection." *Theology Today*, (October 1981): 298-304.

McCall, Roy C. "Harry Emerson Fosdick: Paragon and Paradox." *The Quarterly Journal of Speech* 39 (October 1953): 283-90.

"Memorial: Paul Ehrman Scherer." *Princeton Seminary Bulletin* 62 (Autumn 1969): 82-84.

Miller, Robert M. "Harry Emerson Fosdick and John D. Rockefeller, Jr.: The Origins of an Enduring Association." *Foundations* (Baptist) 21 (October/December 1978): 292-304.

Morrison, Charles Clayton. "About Preachers and a Preacher." *Christian Century*, 5 August 1959, 903.

"Most Lavish Church Is Most Democratic." *Literary Digest*, 17 March 1934, 20.

"The New York City Pulpit." *The Pulpit* (May 1964): 10.

Niebuhr, Reinhold. "Fosdick: Theologian and Preacher." *Christian Century*, 3 June 1953, 657-58.

_____. "The Significance of Dr. Fosdick in American Religious Thought." *Union Seminary Quarterly Review* 8 (May 1953): 3ff.

Oberman, Heiko A. "Preaching and the Word in the Reformation."
    Theology Today 18 (April 1961): 16-29.

"Open Shop Parson." *Time*, 15 March 1943, 54.

Osborn, Ronald E. "The Effect of Preaching on American Life—and
    Vice Versa." *Encounter* 36 (Summer 1975): 254ff.

_____. "In the Fight to Set Men Free: Harry Emerson Fosdick,
    1878-1969." *Encounter* 31 (Spring 1970): 177-81.

Pannenberg, Wolfhart. "Freedom and the Lutheran Reformation."
    Theology Today (October 1981): 287-297.

Phillips, Robert A. "Fosdick and the People's Concerns."
    Foundations (Baptist) 13 (July/September 1970): 262-76.

"Practical Pastor." *Time*, 23 January 1950, 53.

Preston, John Hyde. "Dr. Fosdick's New Church." *World's Work*
    58 (July 1929): 56-58.

"Radio Religion." *Time*, 21 January 1946, 74f.

"Russians in Church." *Time*, 23 September 1946, 72.

Samuels, Gertrude. "Fosdick at Seventy-Five: Still a Rebel." *The
    New York Times Magazine*, 24 May 1953, 14f.

Shippey, Frederick A. "Changing Fortunes of Urban Protestantism."
    Religion in Life 18 (1949): 523-32.

Simpson, James B. "The Man and the Ministers." *Look*, 21 November
    1961, 137f.

Sittler, Joseph. "George Buttrick: A Tribute and a Reflection."
    Christian Century, 16 April 1980, 429-30.

Skinner, W. S. "Master Preacher." *Christian Century*, June 1956, 695.

Sleeth, Ronald. "What Is the Matter with Preaching: A Fosdick
          Retrospective." *Perkins School of Theology Journal* 32
          (Summer 1979): 28-30.

Smith, Helena Huntington. "Respectable Heretic: A Portrait of Dr.
          Fosdick." *Outlook*, 9 October 1929, 238.

Sockman, Ralph W. "Forty Years of Fosdick." *Religion in Life* 26
          (1956-1957): 289-94.

"This Liberal Christian." *Newsweek*, 8 October 1956, 60.

"Two Men and Two Churches." *Newsweek*, 8 April 1946, 76-77.

Van Dusen, Henry Pitney, "The Liberal Theological Movement in
          Theology." In *The Church Through a Half-Century,* edited by
          Henry Pitney Van Dusen and Samuel Cavert. New York:
          Scribners, 1936.

Villard, O. G. "Dr. Fosdick Renounces War." *The Nation*, 23 May
          1934, 581.

"What Price the Baptist Cathedral?" *Literary Digest*, 1 November
          1930, 20-21.

                    3. Theses and Dissertations

Adams, Henry Babcock. "Selected Sermons of Fulton J. Sheen and
          Harry Emerson Fosdick." Master's thesis, Stanford, 1956.

Atzert, Edward P. "Subject Matter in the New York Pulpit." Master's
          thesis, University of Michigan, 1954.

Blankenship, Wayne Alton. "The Approach of George A. Buttrick to
          Representative Problems in Christian Philosophy." Th.D.
          diss., Southwestern Baptist Theological Seminary, Fort Worth,
          Texas, 1970.

Boecler, Paul A. O. "The Preaching of Law in the Sermons of
          Geisemann, Fosdick, Spurgeon, and Macartney and the

Application of Psychological Principles." S.T.M. thesis, Concordia Theological Seminary, St. Louis, 1957.

Bonney, Katherine A. "Harry Emerson Fosdick's Doctrine of Man." Ph.D. diss., Boston University, 1958.

Brees, Paul Rexford. "A Comparative Study of Devices of Persuasion Used in Ten Sermons by Harry Emerson Fosdick and Eight Sermons by William Ashley Sunday." Ph.D. diss., University of Southern California, 1948.

Burtner, Elmer Edwin. "The Use of Biblical Materials in the sermons of Harry Emerson Fosdick." Th.D. diss., Boston University School of Theology, 1959.

Casteel, John L. "Conceptions of Preaching in the Lyman Beecher Lectures, 1872-1941." Ph.D. diss., Northwestern University, 1943.

Clemons, Hardy. "The Key Theological Ideas of Harry Emerson Fosdick." Th.D. diss., Southwestern Baptist Theological Seminary, Fort Worth, Texas, 1966.

Clinard, H. Gordon. "An Evangelical Critique of the Use of the Classic Biblical Solutions to the Problem of Suffering by Representative Contemporary Preachers." Th.D. diss., Southwestern Baptist Theological Seminary, Fort Worth, Texas, 1958.

Creighton, Linn James. "Reconciliation in American Protestant Preaching." Th.D. diss., Princeton Theological Seminary, 1972.

Drafahl, Elnora M. "An Analysis of the Figures of Speech as Aids to Clearness in the War Sermons of Dr. Harry Emerson Fosdick." Master's thesis, University of South Dakota, 1946.

Duncan, William Walter. "A Study of the Clergyman, Ralph W. Sockman, as a Radio Speaker." Master's thesis, University of Michigan, 1949.

Fribley, Peter Craven. "The Pulpit Ministry to Alienation: A Dialectical Study of Alienation and the Preaching Ministries of Gerald Kennedy and George Arthur Buttrick Using Sociological Criteria from Robert A. Nisbet and Theological Criteria from Paul Tillich and H. Richard Niebuhr, with Particular Emphasis upon 'Redemptive Alienation' as a Positive Heuristic for the Understanding of Sermonic Discourse." Ph.D. diss., Princeton, 1974.

Gertner, Willis Stanley. "Paul Scherer: Preacher and Homiletician." Ph.D. diss., Wayne State University, 1967.

Hall, Joseph Calvin. "Basic Theological and Ethical Concepts of Harry Emerson Fosdick." Th.D. diss., Southern Baptist Theological Seminary, Louisville, 1958.

Hibbard, Robert Bruce. "The Life and Ministry of Ralph Washington Sockman." Ph.D. diss., Boston University School of Theology, 1957.

Huntsinger, Jerald. "The Sermons of Harry Emerson Fosdick: A Study." S.T.M. thesis, Temple University School of Theology, 1959.

Landry, Fabaus. "The Preaching of Harry Emerson Fosdick: An Analysis of Its Intent, Style, and Language." D.Div. diss., Vanderbilt University Divinity School, 1972.

Lawson, Douglas Miller. "The Idea of Progress in the Theology of Harry Emerson Fosdick." Ph.D. diss., Duke University, 1963.

Leininger, Charles Earl. "The Christian Apologetic of Harry Emerson Fosdick." Th.D. diss., Southern Baptist Theological Seminary, Louisville, 1967.

Le Vander, Theodor. "A Critical Evaluation of Dr. Fosdick's Radio Address in 'National Vespers' for the Season 1939-1940." Master's thesis, Iowa State, 1940.

Lindsay, John Philip. "Harry Emerson Fosdick's Views on Religion."
Ph.D. diss., Boston University, 1941.

Linn, Edmund H. "The Rhetorical Theory and Practice of Harry
Emerson Fosdick." Ph.D. diss., Iowa State, 1952.

Mason, Paul H. "The Value of Preaching for Protestant Worship: An
Evaluation of the Controversy Since 1928." Th.D. diss.,
Southwestern Baptist Theological Seminary, Fort Worth,
Texas, 1974.

McDiarmid, A.B. "A Critique of Harry Emerson Fosdick's
Conception of Preaching as Personal Counseling on a Group
Scale." Th.D. diss., Pacific School of Religion, 1961.

McLeister, William. "The Use of the Bible in the Sermons of Selected
Protestant Preachers in the United States from 1925-1950."
Ph.D. diss., University of Pittsburgh, 1957.

Miller, George William. "A Study of Motivation in the Preaching of
Harry Emerson Fosdick." Th.M. thesis, Southern Baptist
Theological Seminary, Louisville, 1955.

Page, Gladys W. "The Comparison of Oral and Written Style of
Harry Emerson Fosdick." Master's thesis, University of
Wisconsin, 1938.

Pancake, Loral W. "Liberal Theology in the Yale Lectures: An
Inquiry into the Extent and Influence of Liberal Theology
upon Christian Preaching as Set Forth in the Lyman Beecher
Lectures on Preaching, 1872-1948." Ph.D. diss., Drew
University, 1951.

_____. "Theological Liberalism in the Life and Ministry of Harry
Emerson Fosdick." Master's thesis, Drew University, 1946.

Parrott, John Henry. "The Preaching of Social Christianity in the
United States in the Twentieth Century." Th.D. diss.,
Southern Baptist Theological Seminary, Louisville, 1950.

Pexton, Thomas C. "The Effect on Religious Thinking of Harry
      Emerson Fosdick's Speaking." Master's thesis, Kent State
      University, 1960.

Shelton, Robert McElroy. "The Relationship between Reason and
      Revelation in the Preaching of Harry Emerson Fosdick."
      Th.D. diss., Princeton Theological Seminary, 1965.

Snell, Jack Alton. "The Use of the Bible in the Preaching of George
      A. Buttrick." Th.M. thesis, Southern Baptist Theological
      Seminary, 1968.

Stevens, Paul W. "A Critical Examination of the Preaching of George
      Arthur Buttrick." Th.D. diss., New Orleans Baptist
      Theological Seminary, 1972.

Stewart, C. S. "A Critical Study of the Homiletical Method of Drs.
      Fosdick, Jefferson, Chappel, and Morgan." Th.D. diss.,
      Iliff School of Theology, 1938.

Walters, Edith Irene. "The Aesthetic Elements in Several Speeches by
      Dr. Ralph W. Sockman." Master's thesis, Ohio University,
      1962.

Weaver, Samuel Robert. "The Theology and Times of Harry Emerson
      Fosdick." Th.D. diss., Princeton Theological
      Seminary, 1961.

Wessell, Grant H. "A Critical Analysis of the Methods of Persuasion
      Employed by Dr. Harry Emerson Fosdick as Experienced in
      Selected Sermons." Master's thesis, University of Michigan,
      1953.

Yohe, Gladys Parsons. "A Rhetorical Analysis of the Speeches of
      Ralph W. Sockman Given in the 1947-1948 National Radio
      Pulpit Program." Master's thesis, University of Colorado,
      1949.

INDEX

ABOUT THE AUTHOR

William B. Lawrence is professor of the practice of Christian ministry and associate director of the J.M. Ormond Center for Research, Planning, and Development at Duke Divinity School in Durham, North Carolina. He teaches courses in homiletics, Methodist studies, and pastoral ministry. He also serves as a consultant to local churches and denominational bodies. A graduate of Duke University, Union Theological Seminary in New York, and Drew University, he has served as a United Methodist pastor and district superintendent in New York and Pennsylvania. He and his wife Naomi are the parents of two sons. He has published articles about preaching as well as his own sermons and poetry. This is his first book.